Planet & People

Second Edition

Leaving Certificate

Geography

Sue Honan & Sue Mulholland

**MENTOR
BOOKS**

MENTOR BOOKS
43 Furze Road
Sandyford Industrial Estate
Dublin 18
Tel: 01-2952112
Fax: 01-2952114
Website: www.mentorbooks.ie
email: admin@mentorbooks.ie

Edited by:	Treasa O'Mahony
	Una Whelan
Subject Editor:	Dr Tom Hunt
Book Design:	Nicola Sedgwick/Mary Byrne
Typesetting:	Nicola Sedgwick
	Kathryn O'Sullivan
Cover photograph:	Thinkstock Photos
Cover Design:	Mary Byrne
Illustrations:	Michael Phillips
	Christine Warner

ISBN: 978-1-906623-64-7
© Sue Honan, Sue Mulholland 2011

1 3 5 7 9 10 8 6 4 2

Printed in Ireland by Colourbooks Ltd.

Contents

CORE UNIT: Patterns and Processes in the Physical Environment

Chapter 1   Plate Tectonics 1
Chapter 2   Earthquakes. 19
Chapter 3   Volcanoes 37
Chapter 4   Folding and Faulting in the Earth's Crust 54
Chapter 5   Rock Types and their Formation 63
Chapter 6   Weathering and Erosion. 81
Chapter 7   Rock Types and Landscapes 91

Landform development

Chapter 8   Fluvial Processes, Patterns and Landforms. 102
Chapter 9   Glacial Processes, Patterns and Landforms 141
Chapter 10   Coastal Procesess, Patterns and Landforms 163
Chapter 11   Mass Movement Processes, Patterns and Landforms 194

CORE UNIT: Geographical Skills

Chapter 12   OS Maps and Aerial Photos 210
Chapter 13   Weather Maps, Satellite Images
and Graphical Skills 243

CORE UNIT: Regional Geography

Chapter 14   The Concept of a Region –
Physical, administative and cultural regions 262
Chapter 15   The Concept of a Region –
Socio-economic regions. 291
Chapter 16   The Dynamics of Regions (1) –
An Irish Peripheral Region 309
Chapter 17   The Dynamics of Regions (2) –
An Irish core region and an Irish city/nodal/urban region . . 333
Chapter 18   The Dynamics of Regions (3) –
A European Peripheral Region 362
Chapter 19   The Dynamics of Regions (4) –
A European core and city region 381
Chapter 20   Brazil – A Non-European Region. 396
Chapter 21   The Complexity of Regions 429
(a) The growth and impact of the European Union
(b) The interaction between the Republic of Ireland and Northern
Ireland

Dedication

This book is dedicated to:

Chris, Eleanor and Maedhbh Honan and
Gerard, Patricia and Eoghan Mulholland

Acknowledgements

The authors wish to thank Danny McCarthy, Nicola Sedgwick, Una Whelan, Mary Byrne and Treasa O'Mahony of Mentor Books.

Arctic Refuge; Arigna Mining Experience; Ballymun Regeneration Project; Bear Mountaineering, Canada; Olga Beegan; Boliden Tara Mines; Bord Gáis; Bord Iascaigh Mhara; Brazilian Embassy, London; Bull Island Nature Reserve; John Carter; Central Statistics Office; Chuck de Mets; Karl Cikste; Clare County Council and Library; Ann Cleary; Clonmel Corporation; Coillte; Tony Collinson; Joanne Connolly; Cork City Council; Matt Corbett; Crag Caves; Daniel Deery; Department of Agriculture; Department of Community, Rural and Gaeltacht Affairs; John Donnelly of Largo Foods; Mike Doukas, USGS; Dave Drew; Dublin Port Tunnel / Siobhan Maher; Dublin Regional Authority; Dublin Transportation Office; Jean Duffy; Dundalk County Council; Tony Dunne; EC/ECHO/Olivier Brouant; EC/ECHO/Nick Bridger; EC/ECHO South Asia Office; John and Maureen Enright; eriding.net; ESB; European Photo Services; European Commission; examvillage.com; Fáilte Ireland; Fingal County Council; German Embassy; Geokem.com; Guggenheim Museum, Bilbao; Greenpeace; Pat Hayes; Chris Honan; Heritage Council; IDA; *Irish Examiner*; JPL-Caltech; Junglephotos.com; Karst Working Group; Landau Forte College, UK; Peter W Lipman, USGS; Vincent McAlinden; Dermot McCarthy; Con McGinley; Billy and Mimi McNabb; Kevin, Paul and Will McNabb; Tom Marmion; mayang.com; Met Éireann; Mid-East Regional Authority; Chris Miley; Frank Milling; Bruce F Molnia, USGS; Anne Marie Morgan; Gerry Morgan; Rory Mulholland; Anne Mulligan; Brigid Murray; NASA; NOAA; Graham Neilan of the Department of Agriculture, Fisheries and Food; Olive O'Brien, Fáilte Ireland; Fiona O'Connor; Páraic Ó Náraigh; Office of the NDP; Ó Ingólfsson, www.hi.is/~oi/index.htm; Ordnance Survey Ireland; Joe O'Shaughnessy; Lisa O'Shaughnessy; Photos.com; Kevin Poe; Polishroots.org; Port of Bilbao; Gearoid Quinn, Merit Medical Ireland Ltd.; Red Bull Storm Chase; Readers Digest; Michael Redmond; Val Redmond; Brother Fred Reich; rpg.ie; Ian Sanders; Mike Simms; ski-dondiego.com; Oliver and Conor Seery; Staff and students at St Laurence College, Loughlinstown; Staff and students at St Mary's College, Dundalk; States Examination Commission; Gregory Takats, AusAID; *The Irish Times*; Teagasc; Trócaire; United States Geological Survey (USGS); UpTheDeise.com; USGS Cascades Volcano Observatory/Lyn Topinka; Oisín Van Gelderen; Sooz Wallace; Wexford County Council; Anita White; wicklowtoday.com

Introduction

In this second edition of the *Planet & People* **Core Book** we have:

(1) Kept the language clear and concise.

(2) Fully addressed the syllabus and exam requirements of the Leaving Certificate Geography course.

(3) Updated significant amounts of material in all three Core Units.

(4) Provided clear **Significant Relevant Points (SRPs)** – as required in the Leaving Certificate exam – throughout the book.

(5) Reorganised content in the Regional Geography section to reflect preferred teaching methods rather than syllabus order.

Geography is a dynamic subject. The global physical, social and economic landscape is constantly changing. **Natural disasters** and **changes to the economic and social environment** impact on each aspect of the course. The material in this Second Edition has been carefully updated to reflect the enormous changes that have occurred – particularly in Ireland's economy and society – since publication of the first edition.

We have provided helpful and relevant **website links** in each chapter so that teachers can easily source information when and where necessary.

A useful list of **skills** and **knowledge objectives** is presented at the beginning of each chapter. **Higher Level material** is clearly shown where relevant. Important key terms and concepts are highlighted in blue throughout the book.

In the section on landform development, the syllabus requires students to choose one topic (rivers, ice, sea or mass movement) to study in detail. The extra material they need to cover is clearly marked in boxes labelled **In Depth**.

Important diagrams that students may be expected to draw in the Leaving Cert exam have helpful **Exam Diagram** captions. They are designed to be easily reproduced by students. Geographical skills exercises appear throughout the book.

Reorganisation of material in the **Regional Geography** unit improves linkages across topics in different sections of the syllabus and removes the need to cross reference within the book itself.

We have provided **updated** and new exam-oriented **case studies** throughout the book. They provide important **SRP** material required in the Leaving Cert exam.

A wide variety of questions are provided at the end of each chapter. Higher and Ordinary Level questions are clearly marked. **Chapter revision questions** test students' knowledge of the text. Official State Exams Commission **(SEC) questions** provide students with experience in completing Leaving Cert exam questions.

This core book is carefully designed to **link closely** with the two Electives and the Optional Units. As a result, students will see the interaction between physical and human processes which will reinforce their knowledge of any topic they study.

Chapter 1
Plate Tectonics

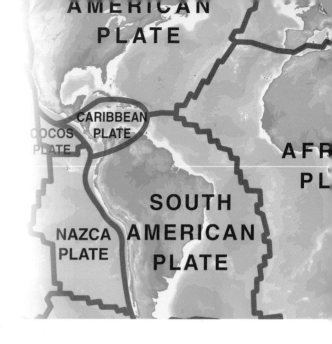

At the end of this chapter you should be able to:

- Describe and draw the internal workings of the earth.
- Explain the structure of the earth's crust.
- Describe and explain the tectonic cycle.
- Explain the theory of plate tectonics.
- Understand the formation of landforms associated with plate margins.

Contents

1.1   Introduction: The world beneath our feet

1.2   The internal structure of the earth

1.3   The theory of plate tectonics

1.4   Plate boundaries and their associated landforms
      Case Study: Sea-floor spreading in Iceland

1.5   Tectonic activity in the middle of plates – hotspots
      Case Study: The Hawaiian hotspot and its associated islands

Questions

KEY THEME

Forces within the earth create, alter and destroy landforms on the earth's surface.

1.1 Introduction: The world beneath our feet

The surface of planet Earth is constantly changing. These changes may be due to **surface (exogenic)** forces such as weathering and erosion or **internal (endogenic)** forces such as moving magma.

Internal and external forces combine constantly to produce the world we live in. They are responsible for the amazing landscapes we see and the terrifying forces that can kill. These forces have created oceans, landmasses and the atmosphere and they have determined where humans, plants and animals live and survive.

Fig. 1 Lava, a product of the earth's internal heat

Fig. 2 Mount Eyjafjallajokull eruption, Iceland

1.2 The internal structure of the earth

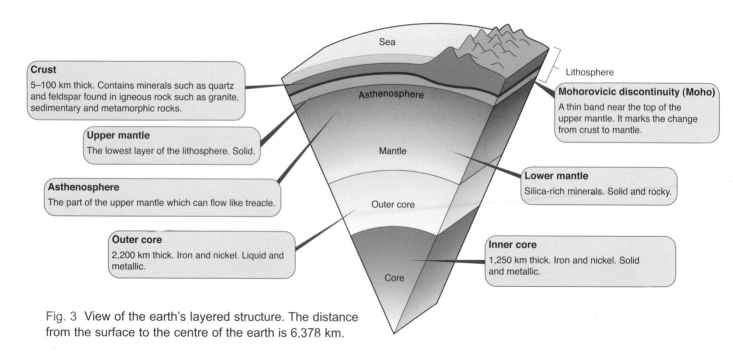

Crust
5–100 km thick. Contains minerals such as quartz and feldspar found in igneous rock such as granite, sedimentary and metamorphic rocks.

Upper mantle
The lowest layer of the lithosphere. Solid.

Asthenosphere
The part of the upper mantle which can flow like treacle.

Outer core
2,200 km thick. Iron and nickel. Liquid and metallic.

Mohorovicic discontinuity (Moho)
A thin band near the top of the upper mantle. It marks the change from crust to mantle.

Lower mantle
Silica-rich minerals. Solid and rocky.

Inner core
1,250 km thick. Iron and nickel. Solid and metallic.

Sea

Lithosphere

Asthenosphere

Mantle

Outer core

Core

Fig. 3 View of the earth's layered structure. The distance from the surface to the centre of the earth is 6,378 km.

The earth's crust

The earth's crust is home to over six billion people and other living things. The crust is not stable; it moves, breaks, is destroyed and recycled **(the tectonic cycle)**. These movements are usually very slow but may be sudden and catastrophic as in the case of earthquakes and volcanoes.

The solid crust is made of **continental crust** and **oceanic crust**, both of which 'float' on the mantle below. These two types of crust are carried about by huge convection currents which occur in a region of the upper part of the mantle called the **asthenosphere**, a hot zone where molten rock flows. Within the asthenosphere, heat is transferred upwards from the core by convection currents. These currents create the tectonic cycle where the crust moves and is split into slabs of rock called **plates**.

These plates have oceans and continents on them, but some plates have both, e.g. North American and Eurasian plates. The zone where continental crust changes to oceanic crust on the same plate is called a **passive plate margin.** No earthquake or volcanic activity occurs at passive margins (see Fig. 4).

> In 2000 scientists in Japan began a mission to drill to a depth of more than 5 km and recover samples of the mantle by 2012.

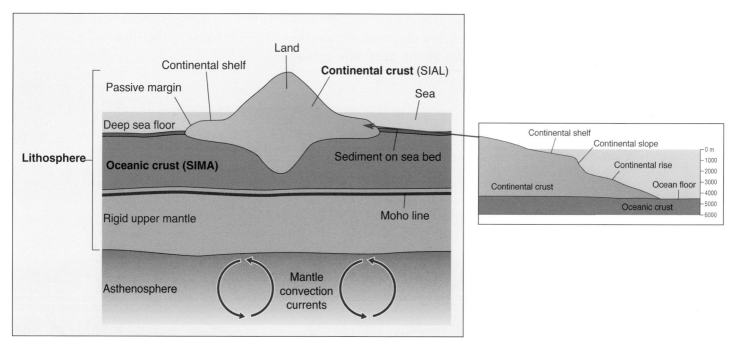

Fig. 4 Exam Diagram: The earth's crust

Oceanic crust

6–12 km thick. Dense, heavy rock, e.g. basalt. Younger than continental crust. Made of silicon- and magnesium-rich rocks. Short name: SIMA

Continental crust

40–60 km thick. Less dense, light rocks, e.g. granite. Older than oceanic crust. Made of silicon- and aluminium-rich rocks. Short name: SIAL

How do we know what is inside the earth?

Our knowledge of the interior of the earth is gained in part from the study of earthquake waves. Rock density can affect the speed at which earthquake waves travel. Some rocks allow these waves to pass quickly, for example granite, others such as shale let the waves pass more slowly. Earthquake waves cannot pass through liquids.

Analysis of travel paths and travel times for earthquake waves enables geologists to develop models of the earth's interior.

1.3 The theory of plate tectonics

Plate tectonics is the study of the processes that cause the movement of the earth's plates and the landforms that result. The theory of plate tectonics states that the earth's crust is broken into a dozen or more larger and smaller sections of rock called plates that carry the oceans and continents. The plates are in continual slow motion around the globe. The massive convection currents within the asthenosphere drive this motion. They drag the plates along as they circulate causing them to collide and separate. This is known as the **tectonic cycle.**

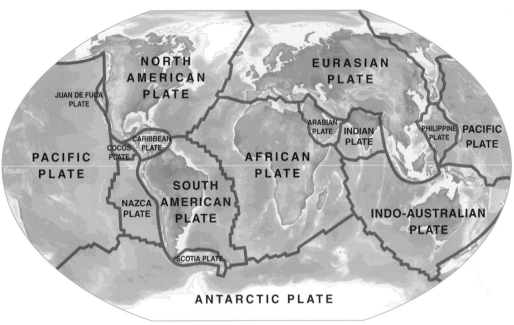

Fig. 5 The major crustal plates of the world

The theory of plate tectonics explains why earthquakes, volcanoes, fault lines and fold mountains occur in specific places in the world.

The plates collide, separate and slide past each other, all the while destroying, creating and modifying the crust. This is all part of the tectonic cycle.

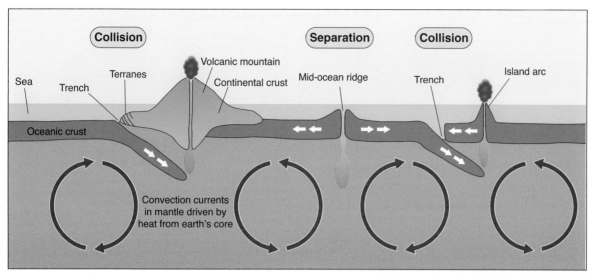

Fig. 6 Exam Diagram: **The tectonic cycle: the continuous destruction and formation of the earth's crust at plate boundaries.**

Development of the theory of plate tectonics

Continental drift – Wegener 1912

The basis for modern plate tectonic theory was proposed by Alfred Wegener in 1912. Wegener believed the earth was once one large landmass which he called **Pangaea** (all land). He stated that Pangaea split into two large continents called **Gondwanaland** and **Laurasia.** With time these then split into the landmasses and oceans we see today. He called this **continental drift.**

Wegener based his theory on the evidence listed below:

1. The distribution of identical fossils around the world.

2. Matching mountain trends and rock types on continents separated by thousands of miles of sea (Scandinavia and the Appalachians in the USA).

3. Matching coastline shape (Africa and South America).

At first most scientists did not accept Wegener's theory because he could not explain how the continents moved. He was convinced, however, and continued to collect data in support of his ideas. He died while on expedition in Greenland trying to prove his theory. Today the idea of continents moving around is widely accepted.

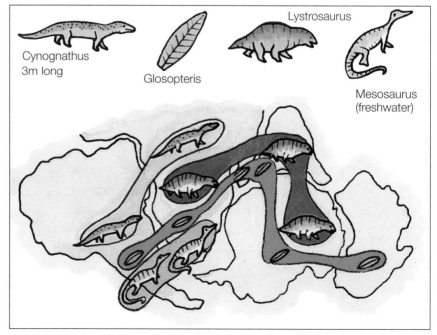

Fig. 7 Distribution of fossils across the southern continents of Pangaea

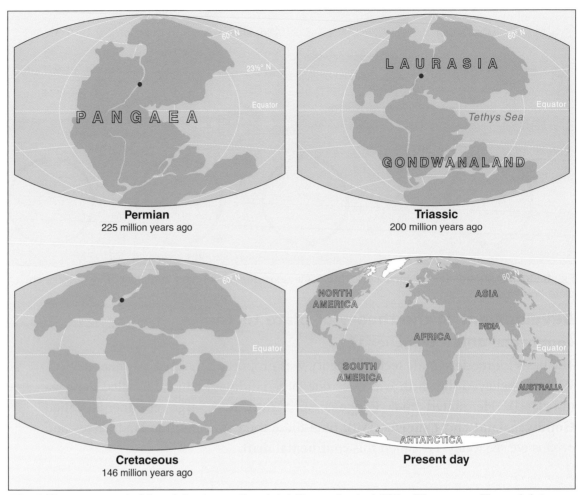

Permian
225 million years ago

Triassic
200 million years ago

Cretaceous
146 million years ago

Present day

Fig. 8 The movement of the plates by continental drift over the last 225 million years. The red dot indicates the position of Ireland.

Fig. 9 shows how Ireland has moved over the planet during the last 500 million years. This is because the continents have been moved around by mantle convection currents beneath the crust. In later chapters you will learn more about how these movements helped to create the rocks and landscapes we see today.

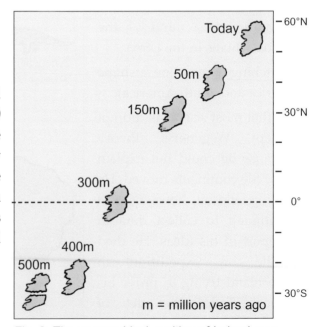

Fig. 9 The geographical position of Ireland over the last 500 million years

Sea-floor spreading - Hess, 1960s

In the mid-twentieth century American geologist Harry Hess mapped and viewed the sea floor while on naval patrol. He saw volcanoes erupting from the sea floor, making long mountain ridges. He realised that new crust was being created here and he called this process **sea-floor spreading**. This is the mechanism by which plates could move.

Proof that sea-floor spreading occurs

1. The different magnetisms locked into the rocks either side of the mid-ocean ridge match up.
2. The age of the sea floor is youngest at the mid-ocean ridges and older further away from it.
3. Young volcanic islands are found near the ridge; older volcanic islands are found further away from it.

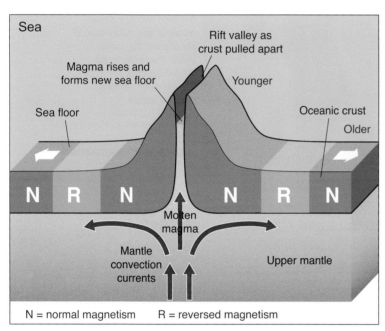

Fig. 10 Magnetism locked into rocks as they cool is a proof of sea-floor spreading. Lava contains grains of iron that point toward the magnetic pole as the lava solidifies. The grains are a permanent record of the earth's magnetic field. The earth's magnetic poles have reversed many times in the past. Scientists have matched the magnetic bands in the rock either side of the Mid-Atlantic Ridge and used them as proof that sea-floor spreading occurs.

The Atlantic Ocean is getting wider at the same speed that your fingernails grow.

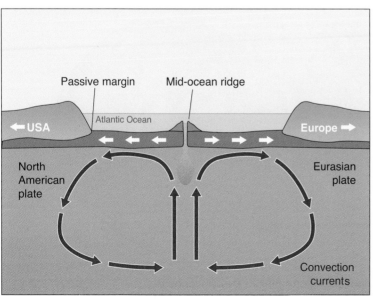

Fig. 11 Exam Diagram: How sea-floor spreading is making the Atlantic Ocean wider. Note the passive margin. This is where continental crust and oceanic crust share the same plate. The junction of the two types of crust is not an active plate margin.

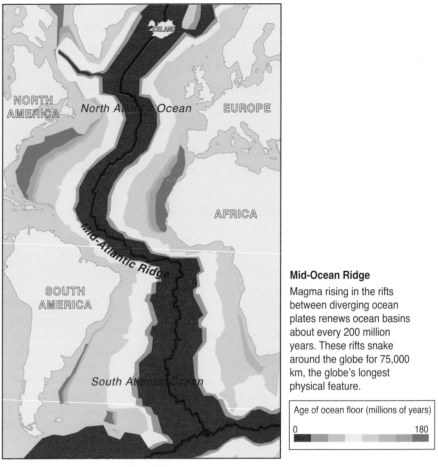

Mid-Ocean Ridge

Magma rising in the rifts between diverging ocean plates renews ocean basins about every 200 million years. These rifts snake around the globe for 75,000 km, the globe's longest physical feature.

Age of ocean floor (millions of years)

0   180

Fig. 12 The location of the Mid-Atlantic Ridge

Plate Tectonic Theory - Vine and Matthews (late 1960s)

Vine and Matthews mapped the distribution of earthquakes and volcanoes across the world. These maps revealed how the crust is broken up into large and small plates. Hess's sea-floor spreading and Wegener's theory of continental drift were now combined and formed the basis of the plate tectonic theory we know today.

Note the relationship between plate boundaries and the location of earthquakes and volcanoes. See Fig. 13.

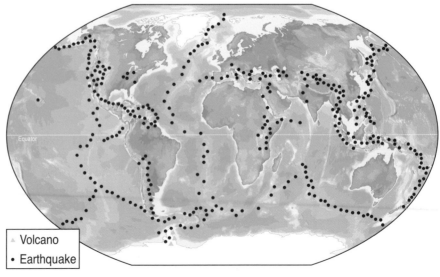

▲ Volcano

• Earthquake

Fig. 13 Map to show the distribution of earthquakes and volcanoes

1.4 Plate boundaries and their associated landforms

Geologists now recognise three types of plate boundary.

1. Destructive (**convergent**)
2. Constructive (**divergent**)
3. Conservative (**transform** or **transverse**)

1. Destructive (convergent) plate boundaries

Here plates move together and collide, destroying the crust. There are three situations where this happens.

(a) Collision between oceanic and continental plates.
(b) Collision between two oceanic plates.
(c) Collision between two continental plates.

(a) Oceanic–continental plate collision – subduction zones

In this case heavier oceanic crust collides with and slides beneath the lighter continental crust. As it slides into the mantle it melts and is recycled. This process is called **subduction** and it is an important part of the tectonic cycle.

The melted crust turns to magma and moves up through the continental crust above to create some of the most explosive volcanoes in the world, e.g. Mount St Helens in the United States. Deep earthquakes are also common in these areas.

At the junction of the two colliding plates a massively deep **trench** is created. Such trenches mark all subduction zones. Many are thousands of kilometres long and 8–11 km deep (see Fig. 14).

Sediments that are carried on the sea bed of the sinking oceanic plate are scraped off and pile up against the edge of the continent, forming fold mountains. These sediments form unique geological areas known as **terranes**.

The Pacific Ring of Fire is so named because many active volcanoes created at subduction zones mark the edge of the Pacific plate. Mount Pinatubo and Mount Fuji are classic examples.

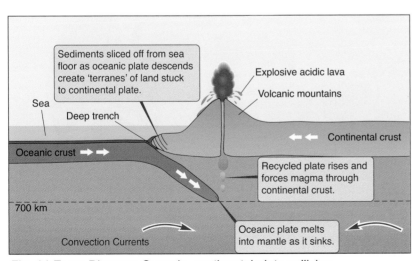

Fig. 14 Exam Diagram: Oceanic–continental plate collision

(b) Oceanic–oceanic plate collision – trenches and island arcs

When two oceanic plates collide, one is usually subducted beneath the other. Where one plate bends beneath the other, deep trenches form. These are the deepest parts of the ocean. The Mariana Trench marks the place where the fast-moving Pacific plate collides with and subducts under the slower-moving Philippines plate. Trenches are also marked by strong deep earthquakes due to the stresses that are released as the plates slide into the asthenosphere, e.g. Kobe 1995.

Oceanic-oceanic plate collision zones are also marked by curved lines of volcanic islands known as **island arcs**. These volcanoes form when the subducted plate descends and melts, creating rising bubbles (**plumes**) of magma that break through the crust above. These active volcanoes have built up on the sea floor over millions of years until they appear above the surface of the water. The Aleutian Islands, the Philippine Islands and Japanese islands have all been formed in this way.

> The Mariana Trench is the deepest part of the ocean. It is over 11 km deep. The highest mountain on land (Mount Everest) at over 8 km high would fit easily into it.

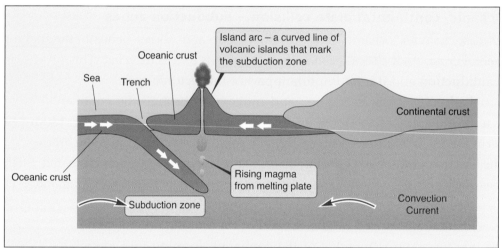

Fig. 15 Exam Diagram: Oceanic–Oceanic plate collision

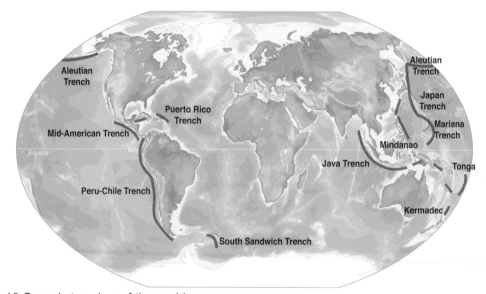

Fig. 16 Oceanic trenches of the world

(c) Continental–continental plate collision – fold mountains

When two continental plates collide **fold mountains** are created. Mountain ranges such as the Himalayas and Alps have been folded up by the massive power of plate collision. Fifty million years ago the Indian plate began its slow collision with the Eurasian plate. This caused the Eurasian plate to crumple and rise creating the Tibetan Plateua and the Himalayas.

Fold mountains are often composed of sedimentary rocks such as limestone that formed beneath the sea. Climbers and trekkers in Nepal frequently see marine fossils thousands of kilometres inland and several thousand metres above sea level in the Himalayas. This situation arises because when two continental plates collide, neither of them tends to sink into the mantle. They resist sinking much like two icebergs colliding at sea. Colliding continental plates tend to move upwards or sideways, sometimes causing devastating shallow earthquakes such as the one that occurred in Pakistan in 2005 when over 89,000 people died.

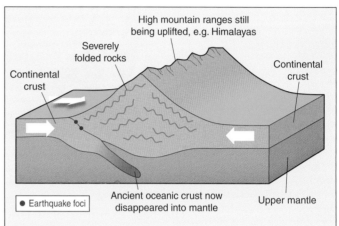

Fig. 17 Exam Diagram: Two continents collide to form fold mountains.

2. Constructive (divergent) plate boundaries – mid-ocean ridges

These boundaries occur where plates are pulled apart by the convection currents below. As the crust splits, a **rift valley** is formed allowing magma to rise and fill the gap making new crust. Shallow earthquakes and volcanoes also occur, e.g. Iceland 2010. As magma solidifies, it forces the plates apart even further, allowing more magma to rise. Over millions of years repeated separations and eruptions have formed the ocean floors. This process is known as sea-floor spreading.

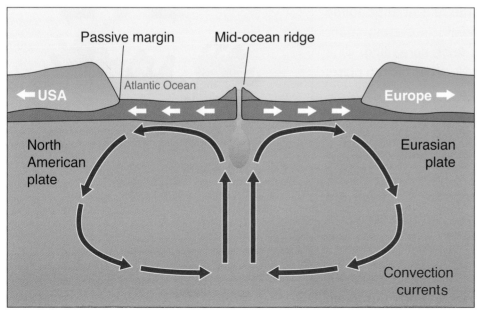

Fig. 18 Exam Diagram: The formation of new crust at a constructive/divergent plate boundary

11

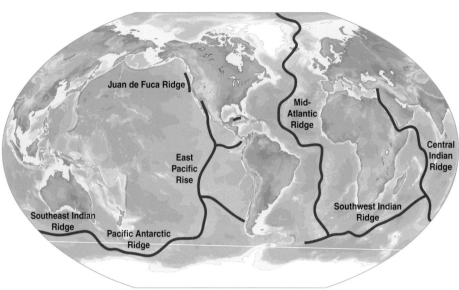

Fig. 19 Mid-ocean ridges of the world

The best example of a landform resulting from sea-floor spreading is the Mid-Atlantic Ridge. This submerged mountain chain stretches over 40,000 km from the North Pole to the South Pole.

The crust is moving apart at a rate of about five cm per year. This works out at about 25 km per million years. This may seem slow to us, but the Atlantic Ocean was created in 200 million years.

case study

Sea-floor spreading in Iceland

- Iceland has formed where the Mid-Atlantic Ridge appears above the sea. Iceland is getting wider due to the process of sea-floor spreading. One side of the country is on the North American plate, the other on the Eurasian plate.

- Iceland has over 200 active and dormant volcanoes. There are also many long cracks, or fissures, which form as the crust is split. Magma erupts through these. Submarine eruptions are common in the south-west. Earthquakes are frequent but rarely dangerous.

- The Eyjafjallajokull volcano erupted throughout 2010, disrupting transatlantic and European flights.

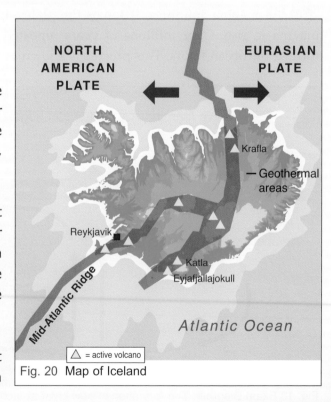

Fig. 20 Map of Iceland

3. Conservative (transverse or transform) plate boundaries – fault lines

A conservative plate boundary is where two plates slide past each other. Land is neither created nor destroyed at these boundaries. These boundaries are marked by **fault lines**; they are thousands of kilometres long and up to eight km deep. They are associated with shallow earthquakes. Most occur under the sea.

A few conservative boundaries occur on land. The best known is the San Andreas Fault in California. This fault is 1,300 km long and tens of kilometres wide in places.

At this fault the Pacific plate and the North American plate are both moving in a northwesterly direction. The Pacific plate, however, is moving faster at a rate of about five cm per year. The slippage is not smooth and the plates may stick for many decades. This leads to the build-up of enormous pressure between the two plates until they suddenly lurch past each other causing an earthquake. In the 1906 San Francisco earthquake the Pacific plate moved over six metres in one minute.

Los Angeles will eventually arrive beside San Francisco if the Pacific plate keeps moving northwards, but it will take 16 million years! The Haiti 2010 earthquake also occurred on a transform boundary between the Caribbean and North American plates.

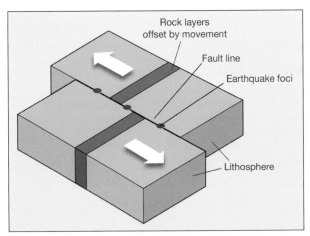

Fig. 21 Exam Diagram: A conservative plate boundary

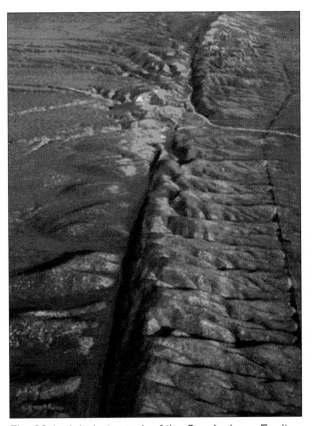

Fig. 22 Aerial photograph of the San Andreas Fault

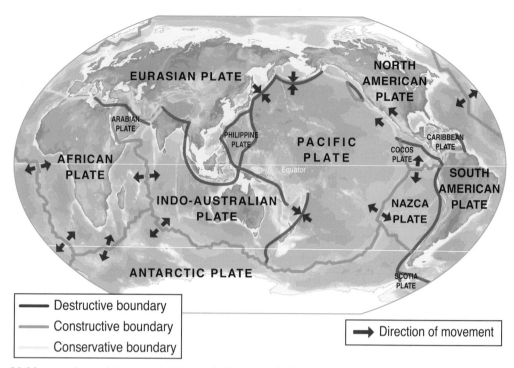

Fig. 23 Map to show plate boundaries and direction of plate movement

SUMMARY OF PLATE BOUNDARIES

Type of boundary	Processes involved (cause)	Resulting landforms	Examples
Destructive (Convergent) (a) Oceanic–continental crust (b) Oceanic–oceanic crust	Collision Subduction Melting Rising magma	Volcanic mountains Deep earthquakes Trenches Island arcs	Andes Mariana Trench Japan
(c) Continental–continental crust	Folding of ocean sediments Uplift	Fold mountains Shallow earthquakes	Himalayas, Alps
Constructive (Divergent)	Separation Rift valley formation Upwelling of magma	Mid-ocean ridges New ocean floor Shallow earthquakes Volcanic islands	Iceland East Pacific Rise Tristan da Cunha
Conservative (Transverse or Transform)	Plates slide horizontally past each other	Transform faults Shallow earthquakes	San Andreas Fault

1.5 Tectonic activity in the middle of plates – hotspots

Sometimes volcanoes are found thousands of miles from the edges of plates. They occur in areas where high temperatures in the mantle produce a rising fountain (**plume**) of molten rock known as a **hotspot**. Hotspots are extremely hot areas deep in the upper mantle (asthenosphere). A column of magma rises from the hotspot and pushes to the surface erupting through the plate above. It is thought that these fountains are stationary inside the asthenosphere and the plates move over them. As this happens magma erupts through fissures or other weaknesses in the crust, creating volcanoes. The Hawaiian Islands were formed over one such hotspot. Some hotspots stretch and split the crust causing rift valleys, e.g. the East African Rift Valley.

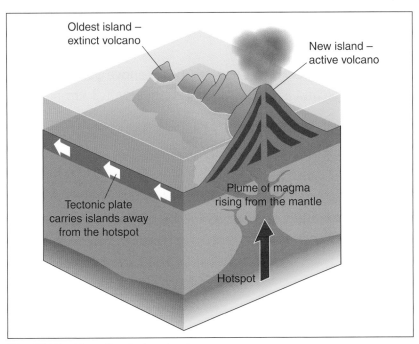

Fig. 24 The Hawaiian hotspot volcanoes

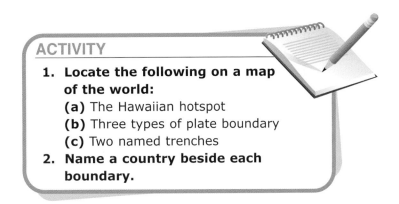

ACTIVITY

1. **Locate the following on a map of the world:**
   (a) The Hawaiian hotspot
   (b) Three types of plate boundary
   (c) Two named trenches
2. **Name a country beside each boundary.**

The Hawaiian hotspot and its associated islands

- The Hawaiian hotspot is responsible for the formation of the Hawaiian Islands. The Hawaiian Islands are a chain of volcanic islands in the middle of the Pacific plate located over 3,200 km from the nearest plate boundary. As the Pacific plate passes over the hotspot, volcanoes burst through in succession, producing the islands.

- As the Pacific plate moves over the hotspot, volcanoes grow, become dormant and eventually become extinct over a period of 500,000 years. The Pacific plate moves northwest over the hotspot at a rate of about 10 cm per year.

- The Hawaiian hotspot is about 500 – 600 km wide and lies about 100 km below the surface. The hotspot is approximately 86 million years old. The Hawaiian Islands are the most recent volcanoes to grow over it.

- The tallest volcanic mountain in Hawaii is Mauna Kea (4,205 m above sea level). If measured from the seabed, this volcano is 10,203 m high – nearly 1.3 km higher than Mount Everest.

- Since the hotspot was formed the frequency of volcanic eruptions has increased. At the time of its formation the hotspot produced widely spaced volcanoes about 100 km apart. In more recent times (the last 700,000 years) it has produced a large island – Hawaii – which is composed of 5 active volcanoes joined together.

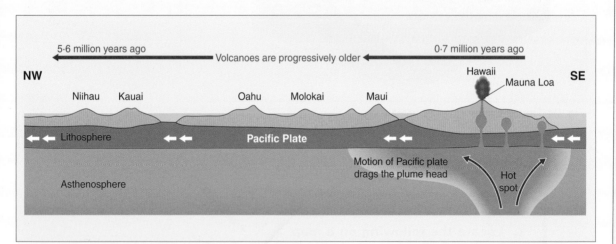

Fig. 25 The Hawaiian hotspot

Chapter Revision Questions

1. Explain the following terms: (a) surface (exogenic) forces and (b) internal (endogenic) forces.

2. Draw a labelled diagram showing the internal structure of the earth.

3. What is the lithosphere? Draw a well-labelled diagram of it.

4. What are convection currents? What is their importance to plate tectonic theory?

5. What is the tectonic cycle?

6. Explain the terms sea-floor spreading, subduction zone and hotspots.

7. Explain what plate tectonic theory is and how it was developed.

8. Briefly explain why earthquakes and volcanoes only occur in certain areas of the world.

9. What are island arcs and ocean trenches? How do they form?

10. Explain with the aid of a diagram how the Himalayas were formed.

11. Describe with the aid of diagrams three ways in which plates can collide.

12. 'Mid-ocean ridges form at constructive plate boundaries.' Explain this statement.

13. Look at the diagram below of the tectonic cycle. Label the parts A–G shown.

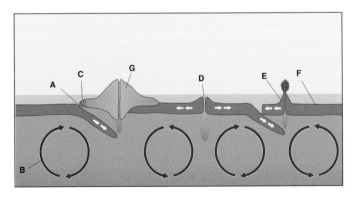

14. Link each of the features 1–7 with its matching process (a)–(g).

Feature	Process
(1) Iceland	(a) Subduction zone
(2) Himalayas	(b) Continental-continental collision
(3) Hawaii	(c) Conservative plate boundary
(4) Philippine Islands	(d) Sea-floor spreading
(5) Terranes	(e) Hotspot
(6) Mariana Trench	(f) Island Arc
(7) San Andreas Fault	(g) Oceanic-continental collision

OL Short Questions

15. Match the letters A to E with the following features: Ocean, Core, Crust, Mantle, Continent. *LC Sample Paper*

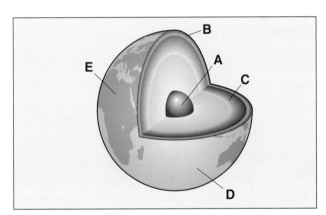

A: _____

B: _____

C: _____

D: _____

E: _____

16. With reference to the labels V, W, X, Y and Z on the map below, state which points to:
    (a) A constructive margin
    (b) A destructive margin
    (c) A transverse/transform margin
    (d) A ridge of fold mountains
    (e) A hotspot

    LC Exam Paper

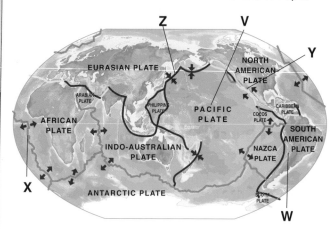

HL Long Questions

17. Examine the map of global crustal plates.

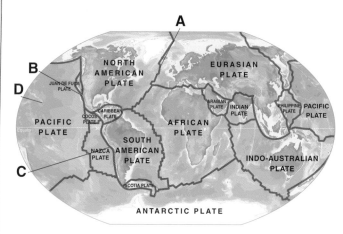

(a) With reference to the labels A-D on the map, identify:

    (i)   A convergent plate margin
    (ii) A divergent plate margin
    (iii) A transverse plate margin
    (iv) A mid-plate volcanic island arc

(b) Explain with the aid of a labelled diagram or diagrams, the process of global crustal plate movement as it is currently understood.

(c) Explain how the theory of plate tectonics has aided our understanding of the occurrence of volcanic activity.

    LC Sample Paper

18. Examine the map below relating to the earthquake in Haiti in January 2010 and answer the following questions.

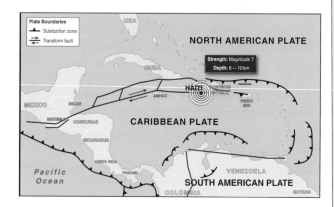

(i)   Activity along which **two** plates resulted in the earthquake in Haiti?
(ii) What type of fault caused the earthquake?
(iii) Describe the fault responsible for the earthquake.
(iv) What tectonic activity along the subduction zone created the island arc on the map?

19. "Plate boundaries are zones where crust is both created and destroyed". Examine the above statement, with reference to examples you have studied.

Chapter 2
Earthquakes

At the end of this chapter you should be able to:

- Explain the terms focus, tremor, epicentre.
- Name and explain the methods used to measure earthquakes.
- Briefly describe the different types of earthquake waves.
- Describe the effects of earthquakes using the case studies provided.
- Outline methods used to predict and prevent earthquake damage.

Contents

2.1. Earthquakes

2.2. Location and depth of earthquakes

2.3. Earthquake waves

2.4. The effects of earthquakes

   Case Studies: The Southeast Asian Earthquake and Tsunami December 2004
                   Earthquake in Haiti, January 2010

2.5. Predicting earthquakes and preventing earthquake damage
     Questions

KEY THEME

Earthquakes are created by forces within the earth.

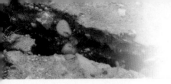

2.1 Earthquakes

Earthquakes occur at all plate boundaries (see Chapter 1). They are vibrations or tremors in the earth's crust, and are caused by the movement of plates over the mantle which makes the crust stretch and tear. This increase in stress and pressure is greater than the strength of the rocks which suddenly give way along a fault line in the crust.

Shock waves or **tremors** travel out from the origin or **focus** of the earthquake just as ripples travel across the surface of water when a stone is thrown. The site directly above the focus on the surface of the earth is known as the **epicentre**. Most damage is done here. There are thousands of earthquakes that are strong enough to be felt by people each year but there are over one million other earthquakes that are detected only by instruments.

As the plates settle back to their normal positions after the earthquake (**elastic rebound**) more earthquakes, or **aftershocks**, can occur. These can do more damage to already weakened buildings and send panic through affected populations.

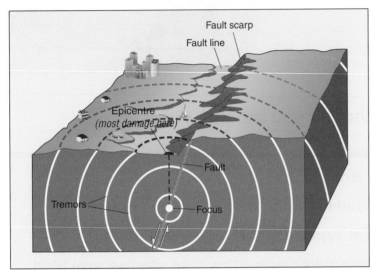

Fig. 1 Exam Diagram: Focus and epicentre of an earthquake

2.2 Location and depth of earthquakes

Earthquakes occur at all types of plate boundaries and at different depths in the crust.

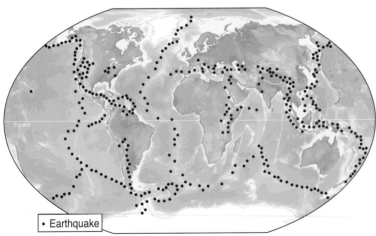

Fig. 2 Map to show the distribution of earthquakes

Shallow earthquakes: Less than 70 km below the surface; associated with mid-ocean ridges, continental–continental plate collision and conservative plate boundaries

Intermediate earthquakes: 70 – 300 km below the surface; associated with oceanic–continental plate collision

Deep earthquakes: Greater than 300 km below the surface; associated with oceanic–oceanic plate collision

2.3 Earthquake waves

Earthquake tremors/waves travel inside the earth and along the surface at great speed. There are three main types:

1. **P waves**, or **compressional waves**, shake the ground back and forth in the same direction as the wave is moving. These are very fast and do little damage; they can pass through a building in less than a second.

2. An **S wave**, or **shear wave**, shakes the ground back and forth perpendicular to the direction in which the wave is moving. They arrive after the P waves as they travel more slowly; they can damage buildings.

3. **Surface waves** travel slowly along the earth's surface. They move the surface of the earth up and down as well as from side to side. They are extremely devastating because they travel slowly. They are also called Love and Rayleigh waves.

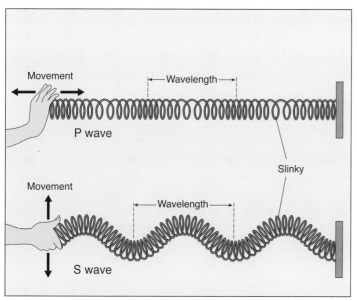

Fig. 3 The different types of earthquake waves

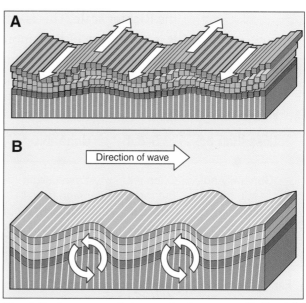

Fig. 4 Surface wave A: Love; Surface wave B: Rayleigh

Recording and measuring earthquakes

1. Seismographs

2. The Richter scale

3. The Modified Mercalli scale

1. Seismographs

Sensitive instruments called **seismographs** record earthquake waves. The Global Seismic Network (GSN) is a web of 128 recording stations across the world. These detect earthquakes and help monitor nuclear tests.

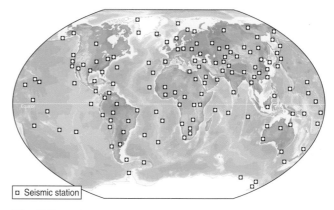

Fig. 5 The global seismic network

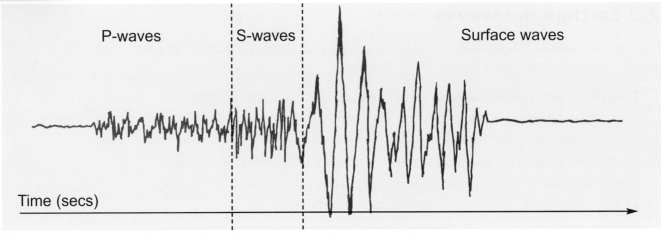

Fig. 6 A seismograph reading is used to calculate the magnitude of an earthquake.

2. The Richter scale

The **energy** released by an earthquake is called its **magnitude** and is measured using the **Richter scale**. This is an open-ended scale which was devised by Charles F. Richter. It is a measure of the amount of energy released by an earthquake. An earthquake of magnitude 6 (M6) is ten times as powerful as one of M5 on the scale. The Richter scale is usually quoted on TV and news bulletins when an earthquake happens.

Typical effects of some earthquake magnitudes are shown in Fig. 7.

Less than 3.5	3.5–5.4	Under 6.0	6.0	6.1–6.9	7.0–7.9	8.0
Generally not felt, but recorded.	Often felt, but rarely causes damage.	At most slight damage to well-designed buildings.	Can cause major damage to poorly constructed buildings over small regions.	Can be destructive in areas up to 100 km across.	Major earthquake. Can cause serious damage over larger areas.	Great earthquake. Can cause serious damage in areas several hundred km across.

Fig. 7 Some Richter magnitudes and their effects

3. The Modified Mercalli scale

Earthquake **intensity** is a measure of the **effects** experienced and observed by people during an earthquake and is recorded using the **Modified Mercalli scale**.

The Modified Mercalli scale is commonly used in the United States by seismologists seeking information from people on the severity of earthquake effects.

The effects of any one earthquake vary greatly from place to place, being severe at the epicentre and less so further away. There may be many intensity values (denoted by the Roman numerals i to xii) measured during an earthquake depending on where people were when the earthquake happened.

Measuring the intensity of an earthquake's effects does not require any instruments. Seismologists can use newspaper accounts, diaries and other historical records to give intensity ratings for past earthquakes. Such research helps promote our understanding of earthquake history in a region and helps estimate future hazards.

Do you want to see how the Mercalli scale is really used? The United States Geological Survey asks people to report what they felt in an earthquake by logging on to: http://earthquake.usgs.gov/eqcenter/dyfi.php

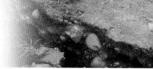

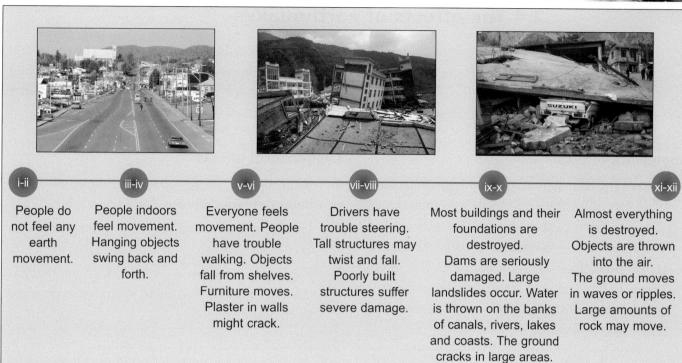

i-ii	iii-iv	v-vi	vii-viii	ix-x	xi-xii
People do not feel any earth movement.	People indoors feel movement. Hanging objects swing back and forth.	Everyone feels movement. People have trouble walking. Objects fall from shelves. Furniture moves. Plaster in walls might crack.	Drivers have trouble steering. Tall structures may twist and fall. Poorly built structures suffer severe damage.	Most buildings and their foundations are destroyed. Dams are seriously damaged. Large landslides occur. Water is thrown on the banks of canals, rivers, lakes and coasts. The ground cracks in large areas.	Almost everything is destroyed. Objects are thrown into the air. The ground moves in waves or ripples. Large amounts of rock may move.

Fig. 8 Modified Mercalli scale

Richter Scale	Modified Mercalli Scale
Measures the energy released (its magnitude) by an earthquake.	Measures the intensity (what people feel/see) of an earthquake.
Uses instruments called seismometers / seismographs.	Uses peoples' accounts and observations of what they see, hear and feel happening during a quake.
Seismographs record the strength of the P, S and Surface waves released during a quake.	No instruments are used.
The readings on a seismograph are converted to a single magnitude on the Richter Scale.	Peoples' accounts are fitted into a scale of damage and effects. A quake can have many intensity readings depending on where people are during the quake.
The Richter Scale is open-ended.	The Modified Mercalli scale goes from I to XII
Each number on the scale represents a quake ten times stronger than the one below it.	Each number on the Modified Mercalli scale is a separate description of the increasing damage observed.
Quakes with a magnitude less than 3.5 are not usually felt. Quakes measuring over 7 may cause major damage.	Quakes measuring I are rarely felt, a quake measuring XII results in complete devastation.
An advantage of using this scale is that each quake has one magnitude that is internationally accepted.	An advantage of this scale is that historical accounts of quakes that occurred centuries ago can be used to assign an intensity reading to the quake.
The Richter Scale was invented by Charles Richter in 1935.	The original Mercalli Scale (I to X) was invented by Guiseppe Mercalli in 1902. It was later expanded (I to XII) and is now called the Modified Mercalli Scale.

Fig. 9 Summary of Richter Scale and Modified Mercalli Scale

2.4 The effects of earthquakes

Earthquakes are traumatic events for the people who experience them. The social and economic effects are devastating. It may take years to rebuild damaged buildings and some people never recover from the psychological distress. Whole economies suffer as industrial capability is reduced and generations of people disappear.

Immediate effects:

1. Death and destruction, tsunamis, gas explosions, fire, loss of fresh water supplies, homelessness.

2. Liquefaction occurs where settlements are built on deep, loosely-consolidated soils or reclaimed land rather than on solid bedrock. The ground turns to liquid due to intense shaking during an earthquake. Buildings sink into the ground, e.g. Mexico City, Los Angeles.

Longer-term effects:

1. Migration – thousands are displaced while damaged buildings are cleared and rebuilt.

2. Disease – water and sewerage pipes burst and take time to repair.

3. Economic slowdown – shops close, industry is destroyed and government spending is diverted from other projects.

Tsunamis

A tsunami is a destructive wave of water. Most tsunamis are generated by earthquakes, but they may also be caused by volcanic eruptions, landslides, undersea slumps or meteor impacts. The most devastating tsunami ever recorded occurred on December 26, 2004, in the Indian Ocean after the Southeast Asian earthquake.

Sometimes when an earthquake occurs under the sea, movement of the sea floor causes ripples on the sea surface, much like carrying a bowl of water makes it slosh around. The ripples travel extremely fast (500–800 km/h). In the open ocean they are barely noticeable but when they reach shallow water these waves slow down and the water piles up to heights of over 30 m. If the seabed is not disturbed by an earthquake, a tsunami will not occur.

One of the first warnings of a tsunami can be a rapid withdrawal of water from the beach. The water goes out suddenly, and between 5 and 30 minutes later it surges back and washes over the land with incredible power.

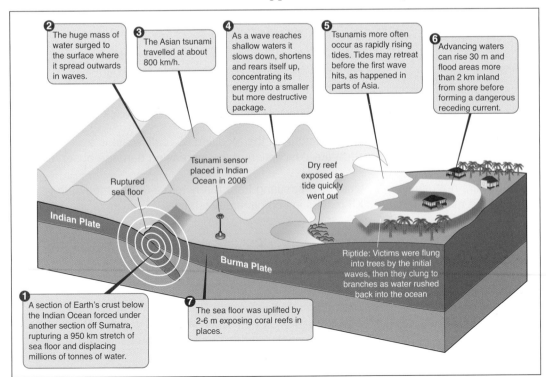

Fig. 10 How the Indian Ocean tsunami was caused

The Southeast Asian Earthquake and Tsunami December 2004

Cause

- This earthquake, lasting 8 minutes and measuring 9.0 on the Richter Scale, was caused by the sudden movement of the Indian plate as it slid beneath the Burma plate. It was a **mega-thrust** earthquake (a name given to quakes that move the crust by large amounts along great distances).

- This region is prone to earthquakes because the Indian plate moves toward the Burma plate at a rate of about six cm/year. A deep trench called the **Sunda Trench** marks the subduction zone at the junction of the two plates.

- This was a very shallow earthquake; the focus was just 24 km below the seabed.

Short-term effects

- During the quake the Burma plate was suddenly pushed up by six m. The uplift occurred along 1,000 km of the Sunda Trench. This sudden movement of the seabed caused the devastating tsunami.

- The tsunami wave affected 11 countries in Southeast Asia, India and East Africa and caused more casualties than any other in recorded history.

- Due to the distances involved, the tsunami took from 15 minutes to 7 hours (for Somalia) to reach the various coastlines. It was over five m high when it reached land. In Sumatra waves surged five km inland. Up to 320,000 people were killed and 1.5 million people were forced to move elsewhere by the earthquake and subsequent tsunami. In addition to the large number of local residents, up to 5,000 foreign tourists enjoying the peak Christmas travel season were killed.

- The earthquake itself caused severe damage and casualties in northern Sumatra, Indonesia and in the Nicobar Islands, India. In Banda Aceh a large ship was carried 1.5 km inland and deposited in the centre of a small town.

Long-term effects

- Afterwards mass graves containing over 60,000 unidentified people had to be dug. In the end more than four times as many women were killed than men because many men were out at sea and survived the tsunami.

- People were badly traumatised and this was made worse by the occurrence of large aftershocks which raised the fear of another tsunami in the weeks following the main quake.

case study

The uplift of land along the fault line has lowered sea levels in the area. This has had a negative effect on the local fishing economy. Economically valuable coral reefs have been lifted from the sea. The local fishing industry that depends on the reefs has been destroyed leaving fishermen and their families in poverty. The quake has altered the geographical map of the region slightly: Some of the smaller islands southwest of Sumatra have moved southwest by up to 20 m. The northern tip of Sumatra moved southwest by up to 36 m. The earthquake was so massive it caused the earth to pause its rotation by a few milliseconds.

Fig. 11 Banda Aceh in Sumatra before the tsunami, and below, after the tsunami. Note the tall white pillar in the top left of the photographs. It will help to give you an idea of how the coastal landscape changed. The tsunami led to the setting up of the Indian Ocean Tsunami Warning system.

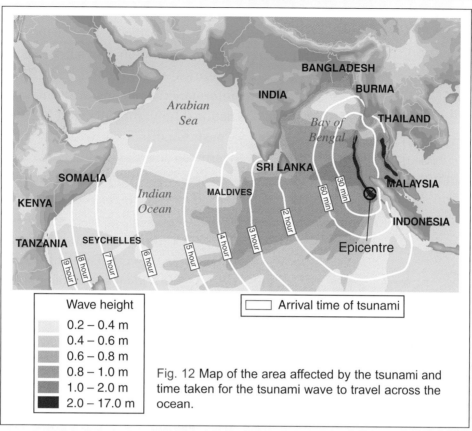

Wave height
- 0.2 – 0.4 m
- 0.4 – 0.6 m
- 0.6 – 0.8 m
- 0.8 – 1.0 m
- 1.0 – 2.0 m
- 2.0 – 17.0 m

Arrival time of tsunami

Fig. 12 Map of the area affected by the tsunami and time taken for the tsunami wave to travel across the ocean.

Asian earthquake recorded in Ireland

● The Asian earthquake had an effect on water levels in three wells monitored by the Geological Survey of Ireland. The three wells in County Kilkenny have been monitored since the early 1980s. Each well is equipped with a recorder. The changes in water level are transmitted via a float suspended on a wire to a pen marking a chart on a rotating drum.

● All three wells recorded sudden water level changes early on December 26, 2004. The maximum change in water level was 280 mm. The fact that such changes can be observed at a distance of over 10,000 km reflects the magnitude of the earthquake.

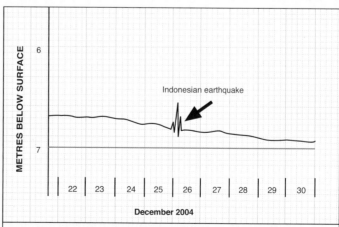

Fig. 13 Chart to show changes to the water level in a borehole in Kilkenny, December 26, 2004

● The Pakistan earthquake of 2005 also had a similar impact on water levels when records were examined.

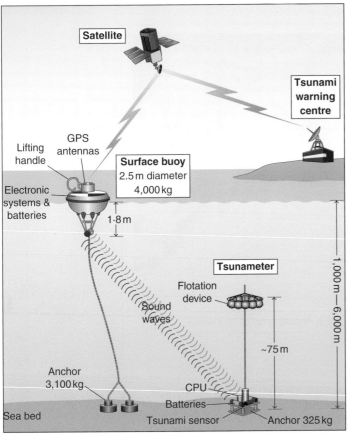

Fig. 14 A tsunami warning system

Tsunami warning systems

Tsunami warning systems were set up in the Pacific Ocean in the 1960s. The Pacific Tsunami Warning Centre located in Hawaii issues warnings to all countries around the Pacific Rim. Warning and information bulletins are sent to local, state and national governments and media organisations. Coast Guards and weather stations broadcast warnings to local populations. The Indian Ocean Tsunami Warning system became active in late June 2006. There are 25 seismographic stations as well as three deep-ocean sensors which send information to 26 national tsunami information centres.

The Indian Ocean Tsunami Warning System was set up to provide warning of approaching tsunamis to people who live close to the Indian Ocean. Its creation was prompted by the 2004 Indian Ocean earthquake and resulting tsunami, which left some 320,000 people dead or missing. If there had been a proper warning system in place, people in some areas would have had more than enough time to seek safety.

Research indicates that Ireland was hit by tsunamis on at least three occasions in the past 250 years. In 1755, waves of 8 to 12 metres reached Kinsale after an earthquake in Lisbon in Portugal.

How are people informed of a tsunami in the Pacific Ocean?

The following system is in place in the 26 countries belonging to the Pacific Tsunami Early Warning System.

1. **Tsunami watch:** Warning and information bulletins are sent to local, state, national and international users as well as to the media. These users in turn spread the tsunami information to the public, generally over commercial radio and television channels.

2. **A weather radio system** provides direct broadcast of tsunami information to the public.

3. **The US Coast Guard** also broadcasts urgent marine warnings and related tsunami information to coastal users.

4. **Local authorities** and emergency managers are responsible for implementing evacuation plans for areas under a tsunami warning. The public should stay tuned to the local media for evacuation orders should a tsunami warning be issued. People should not return to low-lying areas until the tsunami threat has passed and the area declared safe by the local authorities.

Earthquake in Haiti, January 2010

- Haiti is the poorest country in the western hemisphere. It is ranked 149th out of 182 countries on the HDI (Human Development Index). Most people live on less than €1.50 a day. It has a population of 10 million people.

- Haiti is located on a Caribbean island called Hispaniola which lies on the transform/conservative plate boundary between the Caribbean plate and the North American plate. The region is seismically active, suffering many earthquakes and tsunamis over centuries.

- A devastating earthquake measuring 7.0 on the Richter scale occurred on 12 January 2010 killing 230,000 people.

- The quake was also felt in neighbouring countries, including Cuba, Venezuela, Dominican Republic (which shares the island of Hispaniola with Haiti) and Puerto Rico.

Cause

- The quake occurred close to a fault line where the Caribbean plate shifts eastwards by about 20 mm per year in relation to the North American plate. This fault system has two branches in Haiti. It was along one of these branch faults that the earthquake happened. There had been a long period of seismic silence on this fault. It had not moved for 250 years during which time huge pressure built up and was suddenly released during the quake.

- It was a shallow quake. The focus was at a depth of just 13 km. The epicentre was about 25 km from the capital city, Port-au-Prince.

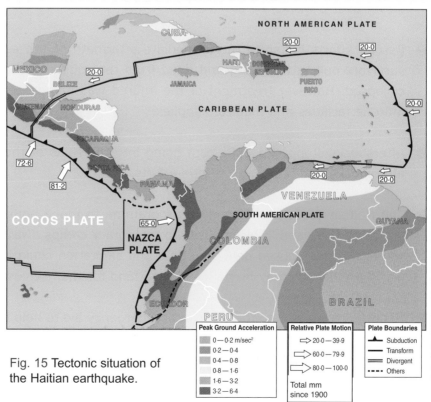

Fig. 15 Tectonic situation of the Haitian earthquake.

Immediate effects

- 222,570 people were killed.

- 300,000 people were injured.

- Over 1.3 million people were left homeless and had to move out of the devastated capital city, Port-au-Prince.

- The Pacific Ocean Tsunami Centre issued a tsunami warning immediately after the initial quake, but quickly cancelled it.

- Widespread devastation and damage occurred throughout Port-au-Prince. Ninety per cent of buildings in the capital city were destroyed or heavily damaged, including the National Palace, Port-au-Prince Cathedral and a prison with 4,000 inmates who escaped. Vital infrastructure necessary to respond to the disaster was severely damaged or destroyed, including all hospitals in the capital, air, sea and land transport facilities and communication systems.

- The quake also seriously damaged the harbour at Port-au-Prince making it unusable for immediate rescue and aid operations. A port many kilometres away in the Dominican Republic was used for relief supplies but the link road between it and Port-au-Prince was blocked for over 10 days. Telecommunications were damaged with radio and TV off the air for over a week.

- Rescue efforts began in the immediate aftermath of the earthquake, with able-bodied survivors pulling the living and dead from the rubble of the many buildings which had collapsed. However treatment of the injured was hampered by the lack of hospital and morgue facilities and medical supplies.

- Aftershocks stopped people from going into the ruins of their homes and shops. These aftershocks also hampered rescue efforts.

- The Haitian government began a programme to move homeless people out of Port-au-Prince by ferry and in hired buses to temporary camps away from the devastation zone, where a more focused delivery of aid and sanitation could be achieved. Others went to areas where they may be better able to fend for themselves or be with relatives.

- Countries from around the world sent emergency aid to help the people. Medical supplies, tents, clothes, blankets and food and water were sent to Haiti. Also teams of doctors, nurses and search-and-rescue teams travelled there to provide assistance.

Long-term effects

- The Trade and Industry Minister estimated that the earthquake's toll on the Haitian economy would be massive, with one in five jobs lost. Hundreds of Haitians were employed to clear roads and to make fuel pellets in a cash-for-work scheme set up by the UN development programme. The president of Senegal even offered Haitians free land in Senegal.

- Brazil announced a €140-million donation for long-term recovery aid. The UK offered £24 million in aid while France promised €10 million. Italy announced it would waive repayment of the €40 million it had loaned to Haiti. The World Bank waived the country's debt repayments for five years.

- Port-au-Prince was ill-equipped even before the disaster to sustain the number of people who had migrated there from the countryside in search of work over the previous ten years. Many of these rural migrants lived in shanty towns around the city. After the earthquake, thousands of Port-au-Prince residents began returning to the rural towns which they had left years earlier in search of a better way of life.

- Haiti's government has estimated the economic damage and loss from the quake at close to €7 billion.

- A rebuilding plan being considered by aid donors foresees the creation of a Multi-Donors Trust Fund and a Reconstruction Agency to be managed by Haiti's government and representatives of donors.

- Haiti's government and donor country partners are insisting on a decentralisation strategy to be at the heart of the reconstruction plan. This will seek to decongest the crowded and wrecked capital and set up economic development poles in the rest of the country in order to create jobs and industries.
The population, capital city and economy will take many years to recover.

- A severe outbreak of cholera in the months following the earthquake led to more deaths.

Fig. 16 A makeshift hospital in Haiti

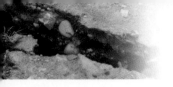

2.5 Predicting earthquakes and preventing earthquake damage

Being able to predict earthquakes reliably and successfully would save thousands of lives and billions of dollars. Also, knowing when and where earthquakes might occur is very useful when making decisions on building structures such as bridges, dams, tall buildings and nuclear and other power stations.

At present we know which **regions** of the earth are most likely to experience earthquakes but we cannot determine when, within a short time frame, a major earthquake will occur. This makes evacuation almost impossible.

Methods used to try to predict earthquakes

1. Looking at patterns of **seismograph activity** to see which areas might be next.
2. Measuring **crustal stress levels** with instruments placed in holes 1.5 km deep to map what is happening in the crust.
3. Measuring **ground tilting** with lasers to see which areas are moving.
4. Measuring **radon gas emissions** from wells and rocks which often increase when rocks are under stress.
5. Observing changes in **levels of oil and water** in wells. Rising levels mean the ground is under pressure.
6. Observing **unusual animal behaviour**. There have been reports of snakes coming out of hibernation early, farm animals refusing to enter buildings and restless pets. However, there are many reasons why animals may be restless so this is not very helpful.

Recently, scientists have measured electromagnetic signals coming from the ground in areas that experience earthquakes and corresponding changes in the atmosphere above. They are hopeful that this will show a pattern, allowing a more accurate prediction of when an earthquake will occur.

Since it is so difficult to successfully predict when an earthquake will occur, most governments invest millions of dollars in protecting their cities from structural damage. They also prepare rescue and recovery plans to deal with the aftermath of an earthquake. Computer models are developed and used to predict the possible locations and times of future earthquakes.

Many towns in earthquake-prone areas have public awareness programmes and 'earthquake drills' for their civil defence teams. Many schools have earthquake drills in the same way that Irish schools practise fire drills.

Most people are killed by falling furniture and other unsecured items in buildings. Imagine all the cupboards in your home suddenly opening and the contents falling on you or the contents of the attic suddenly falling on top of you as you sleep. The simple measures shown in the table on the next page are very effective in reducing death and injury in the home during an earthquake.

> Few wild animals were killed by the Southeast Asian tsunami; they had sensed something and moved away from the coast.

TO MAKE BUILDINGS EARTHQUAKE-PROOF

1. All kitchen items should be secured to the wall, e.g. fridges, cookers, cupboards, washing machines.

2. A bar should be placed across the front of cupboards to stop jars and tins sliding out.

3. Open-fronted shelving should not be used in sitting rooms or bedrooms. They should be fixed to the wall and cupboards locked.

4. In offices filing cabinets, photocopiers, desks and chairs should be fixed so they can't move around in an earthquake.

5. All windows should be shatterproof.

6. Building foundations should have 'seismic isolators' which absorb the force of the quake and reduce movement of the building.

7. Flexible material that can sway with and absorb the movement of the ground should be used.

8. Extra supports are attached to the corners on each floor to support the building as it shakes. These supports are cheap but effective.

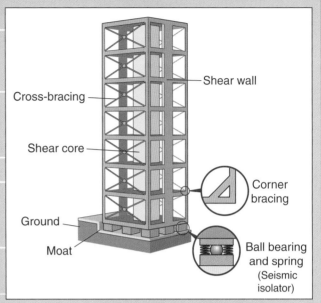

Fig. 17 How to make a building earthquake-proof

ACTIVITY

Study the table and answer the questions:

1. Copy out the table opposite and write the names of the plates involved in causing the earthquakes. Some have been done for you.

2. Locate on a world map each of the places named in the table.

3. Give three reasons why Japan and San Francisco had lower numbers of fatalities than Haiti, despite having stronger earthquakes.

4. Read the case study of the SE Asian earthquake and tsunami and, with reference to the table, account for the high loss of life.

Location	Year	Richter	Deaths	Plates
Chile	2010	8.8	507	South American & Nazca
Haiti	2010	7.0	230,000	Caribbean & North America
Italy	2009	6.8	290	
China	2008	7.8	9,000	
Pakistan	2005	7.6	89,000	
Indonesia (tsunami)	2004	9.0	320,000	
Japan	2001	6.9	1 person	
Turkey	1999	7.2	18,000	
India	1993	6.6	100,000	
San Francisco	1989	6.9	64	

questions

Chapter Revision Question

1. Explain the terms (a) focus, (b) epicentre, (c) aftershock, (d) tremor, (e) earthquake.

2. Name and describe **three** types of earthquake wave.

3. What is a tsunami? Why are they so devastating?

4. How are people warned of a tsunami in the Pacific Ocean region?

5. Describe **four** of the methods used in earthquake prediction.

6. Look at the map below and answer the questions which follow.

(a) What type of plate boundary is shown in this diagram?

(b) Name the two plates involved.

(c) What type of tectonic activity occurs along the plate boundary shown?

7. Describe the cause and effects of the Asian tsunami.

8. Examine the methods used to reduce the destructive effects of earthquakes.

OL Short Questions

9. Using the diagram, answer the questions below.

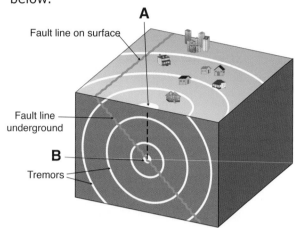

(a) B is the point where the actual earthquake occurred. It is known as the: epicentre / focus / Richter point.

(b) A is the point on the earth's surface directly above where the earthquake occurred. It is known as the: epicentre / focus / hot point.

(c) Earthquakes are measured using an instrument called a: seismograph / thermograph / cardiogram.

(d) Earthquake magnitude is classified according to the: Mercalli scale / Beaufort scale / Richter scale.

LC Sample Paper

10. Examine this diagram showing earthquake activity under the sea floor.

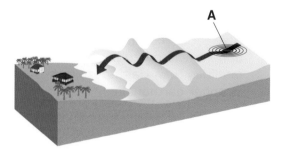

(a) The area marked A on the sketch is: the focus / the epicentre.

(b) The large waves that have formed as a result of this earthquake are known as: tsunami waves / P waves.

11. (a) What instrument is used to record earthquake activity?

(b) What scale is used to measure the magnitude of an earthquake?

(c) What scale is used to measure the intensity of an earthquake?

(d) How do the scales you named in (b) and (c) above differ?

12.

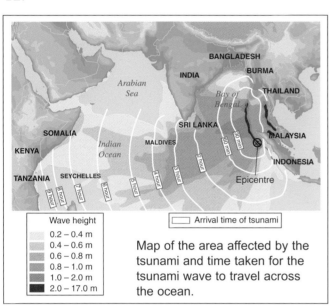

Wave height	
0.2 – 0.4 m	
0.4 – 0.6 m	
0.6 – 0.8 m	
0.8 – 1.0 m	
1.0 – 2.0 m	
2.0 – 17.0 m	

Arrival time of tsunami

Map of the area affected by the tsunami and time taken for the tsunami wave to travel across the ocean.

(a) Using the diagram above, calculate how long it took the tsunami to reach: (i) Sri Lanka, (ii) Southern India, (iii) Somalia.

(b) What was the wave height after (i) 3 minutes, (ii) 2 hours, (iii) 5 hours?

OL Long Questions

13. Using the headings below describe and explain the earthquake in Haiti, or any other earthquake you have studied.

• Plates involved
• What caused the earthquake
• Long and short-term effects
• Recovery

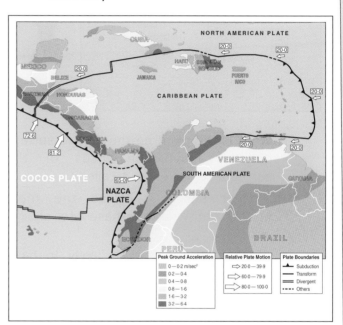

14. Examine briefly how:

(a) Earthquakes are measured

(b) Earthquakes may be predicted one day.

LC Sample Paper

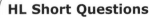

HL Short Questions

15. Examine the map of the Pakistan-India border region and answer the questions that follow.

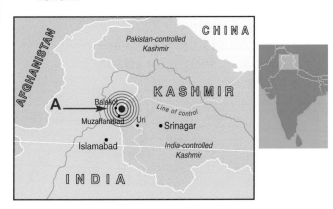

(a) What is the point on the earth's surface directly above the focus of the earthquake shown at A called?

(b) Smaller shocks followed the main earthquake. What are these later shocks called?

(c) Which of these cities is likely to have suffered the greatest damage: Uri, Balakot or Islamabad?

(d) To what scale does the term '7.6 magnitude earthquake' refer?

LC Exam Paper

HL Long Questions

16. Explain how a study of plate tectonics helps us understand the occurrence of earthquakes.

17. Examine, with reference to actual examples, the measurement and effects of earthquakes.

LC Sample Paper

18. Describe the damage caused by earthquakes in two countries you have studied.

Chapter 3
Volcanoes

At the end of this chapter you should be able to:

- Explain why volcanoes occur where they do in the world.

- Name and describe the formation of volcanic landforms.

- Describe the effects of volcanoes on people using the case studies provided.

- Outline methods used to predict volcanoes.

Contents

3.1   The parts of a volcano

3.2   The distribution of volcanic activity

3.3   The life cycle of volcanoes

3.4   Products of eruptions

3.5   External/extrusive landforms (volcanic)

3.6   Internal/intrusive landforms (plutonic)

3.7   Positive and negative effects of volcanoes

3.8   Predicting volcanic eruptions

Case Studies: Mount St Helens, USA

Soufriére Hills Volcano, Montserrat

Questions

KEY THEME

Volcanoes and their associated landforms are created by forces within the earth.

3.1 The parts of a volcano

A volcano occurs when molten magma forces its way up to the earth's surface either through a **vent** or through a **fissure**. As magma rises, gas bubbles expand and help force it up to the earth's surface through the crust. Once the magma reaches the surface the sudden release of pressure causes a volcanic eruption. A vent eruption leads to the formation of the typical **cone**-shaped mountain. Fissure eruptions lead to the formation of a wider and flatter **plateau**. Upon reaching the surface the magma is called **lava**.

Depending on the type of lava being ejected, eruptions may be extremely violent or more quiet.

Fig. 1 Stromboli volcano erupting in Italy

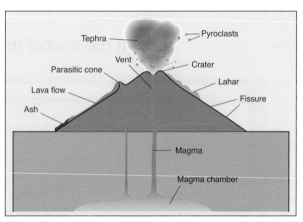

Fig. 2 Exam Diagram: Parts and products of a typical volcano

3.2 The distribution of volcanic activity

Volcanoes occur in three types of locations:

1. Mid-ocean ridges (at constructive plate margins).
2. Subduction zones (at destructive plate margins, i.e. oceanic–oceanic and oceanic–continental plate collision zones).
3. Hotspots in the middle of plates.

The reasons for these locations have been explained in Chapter 1.

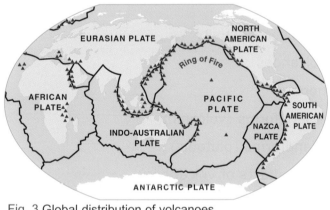

Fig. 3 Global distribution of volcanoes

3.3 The life cycle of volcanoes

A volcano may fall into one of three categories:

Active volcano: Continuously erupting, e.g. Stromboli, Italy.

Dormant volcano: This is a volcano which has not erupted for many hundreds of years. Mount St Helens in the US was dormant for 123 years until its spectacular but predicted eruption in 1980, and Mount Pinatubo in the Philippines had not erupted for 600 years before its 1995 eruption.

Extinct volcano: A volcano that has not erupted in recorded history, for example Slemish in County Antrim.

Over time, the magma beneath the earth's surface may cool down or move away. This can reduce volcanic activity on the surface, leaving areas with hot springs and geysers. Yellowstone National Park in the United States and Bath in England are such areas.

3.4 Products of volcanic eruptions

Volcanic eruptions produce the following substances:

1. Lava
2. Pyroclasts and pyroclastic flows
3. Poisonous gases
4. Ash, pumice and dust (tephra)
5. Water vapour

1. Lava

There are two types of lava. They each have different compositions.

(a) Acidic lava

This type of lava is produced at destructive plate boundaries at subduction zones. Acidic lava has a silica content of 70% or more. It is sticky and moves slowly. Because it is so sticky, gases are trapped and great pressure can build up within the magma chamber. As the magma rises to the surface huge domes are formed within the crater of the volcano. At a critical point the magma can no longer hold its gases and a massive explosion occurs. Acidic lava produces steeply convex volcanic cones called dome volcanoes. Le Puys in France and Mount St Helens in the USA are typical.

Fig. 4 Castle Geyser spews water and steam at Yellowstone National Park, Wyoming, USA.

(b) Basic lava

This type of lava is produced at constructive plate boundaries and at hotspots. Basic lava has a silica content of 55% or less which allows gases to escape easily forming a runny type of lava. When it erupts the lava flows like a fountain into the air forming a wide, gently sloping volcanic cone known as a shield volcano. The Hawaiian island of Mauna Loa is a good example.

Ninety to sixty-five million years ago County Antrim was the site of spectacular fissure eruptions that produced massive amounts of basic lava. This lava ran over the landscape and created the Antrim Plateau.

Fig. 5 Lava at Kilauea in Hawaii

Table to Summarise the Characteristics of Acid and Basic Lava

Properties	Acid lava	Basic lava
Silica content	70% or more	Less than 55%
Trapped gases	Lots of trapped gases due to high silica content which makes lava highly viscous (sticky). Gases cannot escape.	Few trapped gases due to low silica content. Lava is very fluid and runny allowing gases to escape easily.
Type of eruption	Very explosive, violent, destructive e.g. Mount St Helens, USA.	Non-explosive, gentle lava eruptions. Lava fountains, e.g. Mauna Loa, Hawaii.
Typical location	Subduction zones. Destructive plates boundaries involving oceanic crust.	(a) Constructive plate boundaries – mid-ocean ridges. (b) Hotspots
Examples	Destructive boundary between Nazca plate and South American plate.	Mid-Atlantic Ridge (Iceland), Hawaii.

Fig. 6 A pyroclastic flow travels down the side of Mount St Helens.

2. Pyroclasts and pyroclastic flows

Pyroclasts are hot ash, lava and rock fragments that are thrown out of the volcano. These are sometimes called **volcanic bombs**.

Pyroclastic flows are boiling clouds of ash and rock which travel at great speeds (up to 600 km/h) down the sides of the volcano. They smother and destroy everything in their path. These flows are also called **nuée ardentes**. Examples include Mount Pinabuto in the Philippines and Mount Vesuvius in Italy. In AD 69, Mount Vesuvius erupted during which the pyroclastic flow covered the town of Pompeii in southern Italy.

3. Poisonous gases

Volcanoes release several dangerous gases. Carbon dioxide suffocates people and animals when it bubbles from crater lakes as has happened several times in Lake Nyos, Cameroon. Chlorine and sulfur dioxide are also released. The amount of sulfur dioxide gas released increases rapidly close to the time of eruption, e.g. Mount St Helens.

4. Ash, pumice and dust (tephra)

In explosive volcanoes the power of the eruption pulverises rock into a fine ash inside the vent and cone. The ash is thrown many kilometres into the sky and may be carried by winds across the world and can disrupt air travel.

When lava is thrown from the volcano it is whipped up and becomes full of air bubbles. If it cools quickly enough these bubbles are trapped in the rock and it is now called **pumice**. Some pieces contain so much air that they float in water.

5. Water vapour

Many volcanoes along subduction zones release huge amounts of water vapour (from the sea water carried into the mantle by the sinking oceanic plates). As this vapour rises into the air it cools rapidly creating torrential rain during the eruption. The intense rainfall can trigger **lahars**, e.g. Mount St Helens, 1980.

IN DEPTH - Lahars

Lahar is an Indonesian word that describes a mixture of water and rock fragments flowing down the slopes of a volcano. When moving, a lahar looks like a mass of wet concrete that can carry rock debris up to 10 m in diameter. Lahars vary in size and speed. Small lahars less than a few metres wide and several centimetres deep may flow at speeds of a few metres per second. Large lahars hundreds of metres wide and tens of metres deep can flow at over 80 km/h – much too fast for people to outrun, e.g. Nevado del Ruiz, Colombia.

Volcanic eruptions may trigger one or more lahars by quickly melting snow and ice on a volcano. Usually lahars are formed by intense rainfall during or after an eruption – rainwater can easily erode loose volcanic rock and soil on hillsides and in river valleys. Some of the largest lahars begin as landslides of saturated rock on the sides of a volcano.

Fig. 7 A lahar flows from Mount St Helens' crater.

3.5 External/extrusive landforms (volcanic)

Volcanic features found on the earth's surface include:

1. Lava plateaux, e.g. the Antrim Plateau in Northern Ireland and the Deccan Plateaux in India.

2. Volcanic cones, e.g. Mount Etna. These can be of varying shapes, sizes and composition depending upon the type of lava and/or ash ejected. Examples include a dome volcano, shield volcano, ash/cinder cone, composite volcano.

3. Craters and calderas, e.g. Crater Lake, Oregon, USA

4. Volcanic plugs – the remains of magma that solidified in the vent. The volcano has since eroded away. Examples include Le Puy, France and the location of Edinburgh Castle, Scotland.

This section will focus on volcanic cones and lava plateaux.

Volcanic cones

Volcanic cones are **extrusive volcanic landforms**. Volcanic cones form when magma rises from the mantle and forces its way to the surface through a weakness (vent) in the crust. As the magma rises gas bubbles expand within it, helping to force it through cracks in the rock above. Once the magma reaches the surface, a volcanic eruption occurs gradually forming a volcanic cone. There are many types of volcanic cones. We shall focus on two types. Shield volcanoes and volcanic domes.

Fig. 8 Mauna Loa, Hawaii – a shield volcano

(a) Shield volcanoes

Shield volcanoes are volcanic cones with broad, gentle, concave slopes, e.g. Mauna Loa, Hawaii. They are associated with hotspots where large amounts of highly fluid, basic (less than 55% silica) lava erupts to the surface. Basic lava tends to build enormous low angle cones because it flows so easily over the ground for many kilometres before it solidifies into basalt rock.

Over time thousands of lava flows build up and cool, one above the other to form some of the largest volcanoes in the world. Mauna Loa in Hawaii rises over 4,160 m above sea level but when measured from its base on the sea floor it is just over 10,000 m high, almost 2 km taller than Mount Everest.

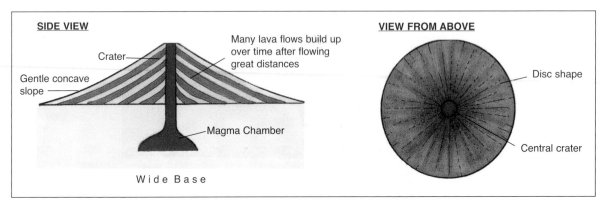

SIDE VIEW

Crater

Many lava flows build up over time after flowing great distances

Gentle concave slope

Magma Chamber

Wide Base

VIEW FROM ABOVE

Disc shape

Central crater

Fig. 9 Exam Diagram: A shield volcano

(b) Volcanic domes

Volcanic domes are mounds that form when viscous acidic (greater than 70% silica) lava is erupted slowly and piles up covering the vent, rather than flowing away down the mountain. Volcanic domes are common at subduction zones where they may grow inside strato volcanoes (volcanic cones made of layers of ash, lava and dust). Volcanic domes have steep-sided convex slopes that are very unstable and may collapse causing massive landslides. This happened at Mount St Helens during the eruption in 1980.

Volcanic domes can grow in two ways: (i) magma from the magma chamber rises into the volcano causing it to bulge, (ii) magma can rise through the vent to the volcanic crater and form a dome structure in the crater. Both of these types of doming can occur in the same volcano, e.g. Mount St Helens, USA.

Fig. 10 Mount St Helens, Washington State, USA

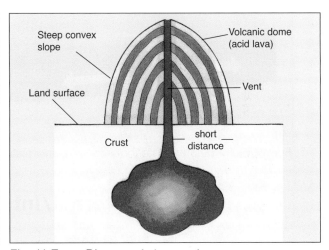

Fig. 11 Exam Diagram: A dome volcano

Lava plateaux

Lava plateaux are steep-sided flat-topped uplands of basalt that cover large areas.

They are formed by the large but less explosive eruptions of highly fluid basic lava that pours from long narrow openings or fissures in the crust. During each eruption, the lava flows out from these openings, solidifies and builds up layer upon layer each time.

The eruptions are less explosive because the basic lava does not contain trapped gases.

Examples include the Antrim Plateau in County Antrim, Northern Ireland and the Deccan Plateau, India.

All lava plateaux have the same characteristics:

- They cover very large areas of land.
- They have a layered structure due to basalt flows solidifying one above the other.
- Each lava flow eruption makes the plateau higher.

In Ireland the Antrim Plateau was formed when a constructive plate boundary formed about 60 million years ago. When the plates started to move apart, the landscape of north-east Ireland would have resembled that of present-day Iceland. The crust of the earth was stretched and huge cracks or fissures were produced out of which poured enormous flows of basic lava that covered the land. These lava flows continued for nearly 2 million years producing a plateau almost 1,800 m high. The lava flows cooled to form basalt, a dark fine-grained rock characteristic of fissure eruptions.

As the thick lava flows cooled and contracted, the basalt formed unique polygonal (many-sided) columns. At the Giant's Causeway in County Antrim the columns are hexagonal and are an important tourist attraction.

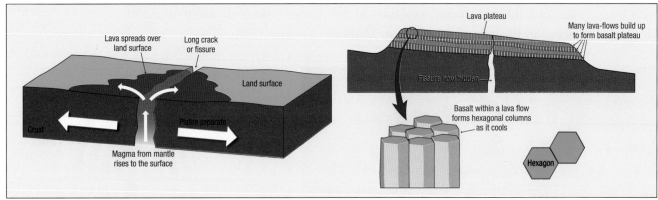

Fig. 12 Exam Diagram: The formation of a lava plateau

3.6 Internal/intrusive landforms (plutonic)

Plutonic landforms occur beneath the earth's surface but are visible today because weathering and erosion have removed the overlying rocks. The size, shape and location of these landforms vary, as did the length of time it took for the magma to cool and harden into rock.

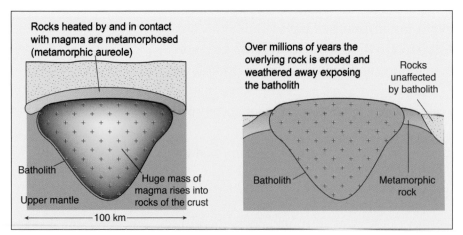

Fig. 13 Exam Diagram: The formation of a batholith

1. Batholiths

A batholith is a large mass of igneous rock (granite) that formed as magma from the mantle pushed (intruded) into the crust above and slowly, over thousands of years, cooled down and solidified.

In Ireland, a granite batholith formed 400 million years ago during the Caledonian fold mountain building period. Magma was injected into and cooled inside the folded rocks. Heat from the magma metamorphosed the overlying rock forming a **metamorphic aureole** around the batholith. Weathering and erosion removed the rocks above so that today we see the exposed batholiths as low, rounded, granite mountains, e.g. the Wicklow mountains range and the Mourne mountains in County Down.

2. Sills

Magma forces its way between layers of rock and solidifies as large flat areas of igneous rock, for example Fair Head, County Antrim.

3. Dykes

Magma slices across rock layers and solidifies forming walls of basalt or granite running perpendicular to the rock layers. They are very common in volcanoes where magma forces its way through fissures in the cone and then cools. They add strength and support to the cone, acting like a ribcage for the volcano.

4. Laccoliths

Magma seeps between rock layers pushing them upwards and cools to form dome-like structures.

5. Lopoliths

These form in a similar way to laccoliths except the weight of magma causes the rock layers to sag downwards.

Fig. 14 Basalt Dyke, County Down

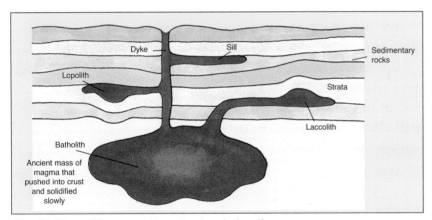
Fig. 15 Exam Diagram: Internal volcanic landforms

Fig. 16 Laccolith in Montana, USA

3.7 Positive and negative effects of volcanoes

Positive effects

1. New land created – Surtsey Island, Iceland and Hawaii – a physical and economic benefit.
2. Geothermal energy – New Zealand and Iceland – an economic benefit.
3. Fertile soil after lava has been weathered and eroded – Terra Rossa soils in the Canary Islands and Brazil – a physical, economic and social benefit.
4. Minerals – sulfur rock outcrops in Malaysia – an economic benefit.
5. Tourism – geysers – Old Faithful Geyser in Yellowstone National Park and Iceland – economic and social benefit.

Negative effects

1. Lava flows: basic lava destroys land as it flows long distances, e.g. Mount Etna.

2. Lahars: hot rivers of mud that flow down the slopes of volcanoes and travel many kilometres often at great speeds. In 1985 the Nevado del Ruiz lahar in Colombia killed 22,000 people in the town of Armero as the eruption melted the snow cap.

3. Pyroclastic flows: hot clouds of ash and rock flow down valleys – Mount Pinatubo in the Philippines in 1991.

4. Poisonous gases: chlorine, sulfur, carbon dioxide. In 1986 carbon dioxide burst out of Lake Nyos in Cameroon killing over 2,000 people.

5. Jokulhlaups: a volcano erupting under an ice sheet can melt it causing massive flooding – Loki volcano, Iceland.

6. Tsunamis: volcanic islands may cause these when they erupt. The Krakatoa tsunami killed 33,000 people in Indonesia in 1883.

7. Volcanic ash blown into the atmosphere can disrupt air travel, e.g. Iceland 2010.

3.8 Predicting volcanic eruptions

The prediction of volcanic eruptions is generally more reliable than that of earthquakes. Most active volcanoes are well known, monitored and mapped by vulcanologists. Twenty per cent of the world's volcanoes are watched 24 hours a day.

Dormant volcanoes are also well known and those likely to erupt near large populations are under surveillance.

Methods of predicting volcanic eruptions

1. Ground deformation

Swelling of a volcano signals that magma is rising within it. Scientists monitoring an active volcano will often measure the tilt of the slope and track changes in the rate of swelling. The Mount St Helens dome swelled by 1.5 m per day in the month before it erupted in May 1980 due to magma rising into the volcanic cone. When the land around a volcano is deformed by magma underground, the water level in nearby wells may rise or fall. If the volcano is near the coast, the shoreline may rise or be submerged. An increased rate of swelling, especially if accompanied by an increase in sulfur dioxide emissions and earthquakes, is almost a sure sign of an impending eruption.

2. History of volcanic eruptions

Checking historic records can identify the pattern of eruptions. For example, Mount Katla in Iceland erupts about every 80 years on average. It last erupted in 1918.

3. Gas emissions

As magma nears the surface, gases escape more easily. This process is much like what happens when you open a bottle of soda and carbon dioxide escapes. Sulfur dioxide is one of the main volcanic gases, and increasing amounts of it usually herald the arrival of more and more magma near the surface. For example, on 13 May 1991, 500 tonnes of sulfur dioxide per day was released from Mount Pinatubo in the Philippines. On 28 May, just two weeks later, sulfur dioxide emissions had increased to 5,000 tonnes per day, ten times the earlier amount. Mount Pinatubo erupted on 12 June 1991. Gas emissions can increase 5 to 10 times during eruptions compared to normal levels.

4. Seismic patterns

Volcanoes trigger earthquakes before they erupt. These quakes have a pattern that can help predict when the volcano will erupt. Volcanic earthquakes have three major forms: short-period earthquakes, long-period earthquakes and harmonic tremor.

- Short wavelength earthquakes: These are related to the fracturing of brittle rock as the magma forces its way upward from the magma chamber. These earthquakes signify the growth of a magma body near the surface.
- Long wavelength quakes: These earthquakes are believed to indicate increased gas pressure in a volcano's 'plumbing system'. They are similar to the clanging sometimes heard in your home/school plumbing system.
- Harmonic tremor quakes occur when there is sustained movement of magma below the surface. The volcano is continuously shaking as if it is humming.

Patterns of seismic activity are complex and often difficult to interpret. However, increasing activity is very serious especially if episodes of harmonic tremor appear.

These methods were combined to help avert major loss of life before the Mount St Helens (USA) eruption in 1980 and the Mount Pinatubo (Philippines) eruption in 1995. They were also used to predict the 2010 eruption of Mount Merapi in Indonesia.

Fig. 17 Geologists measure the shape of the volcanic dome to help predict when it will erupt.

case study

Mount St Helens, USA

[Note: Choose Option 1 OR 2]

Option 1: A predicted volcanic eruption in 1980

● Mount St Helens is an active stratovolcano (volcanic cone is composed of layers of ash and lava) located on the west coast of North America in Washington State.

● It is located along the Pacific Ring of Fire at the destructive plate boundary between the Juan de Fuca plate and the North American plate.

● It lay dormant for 123 years until March 1980. Two months later on 18 May 1980 a devastating eruption and landslide occurred.

Fig. 18 Mount St Helens before and after the eruption. In the 'after' photo note the new dome growing within the crater.

Predicting the eruption

Geologists had set up a network of monitoring equipment on the volcano:
- Laser measurements monitored the shape of the cone.
- Heat sensors took the ground temperature.
- Seismometers measured the vibrations caused by moving magma.
- Gas sensors measured sulfur dioxide, carbon dioxide and radon emissions.

● During March 1980, there were many small earthquakes and steam-venting episodes as magma moved below the volcano.

● Slowly a huge bulge (volcanic dome) and a fracture system formed on the north slope of the volcano. Deep underground, huge volumes of magma were being pushed up into the volcano. The dome in the crater grew by up to 1.8 m per day.

● The earthquake activity continued and caused avalanches of snow and ice. People were evacuated from their homes. The side of the volcano was pushed upwards and outwards by over 135 m.

case study

- Geologists warned that sliding/movement of the bulge could cause a landslide which might trigger volcanic eruptions.

- More than 10,000 earthquakes were recorded prior to 18 May, most occurring 2.6 km under the bulge.

The eruption

- On May 18 a 5.1 earthquake, centred beneath the mountain, triggered the largest landslide in recorded history on the north slope of the volcano. This near supersonic lateral blast swept out of the north side of the mountain, travelled at 483 km/h and devastated everything in its path. A 60 km^2 fan-shaped area was completely destroyed.

- The massive ash cloud rose 24 km into the atmosphere in just 15 minutes and reached the east coast of America in 3 days. Most of the ash fell within 500 km of the mountain; finer ash circled the earth in 15 days.

- The landslide swept down the mountain at speeds of up to 250 km/h into the valley below. Mudflows/lahars of melted snow and ice were created and travelled down the valleys destroying bridges, homes, roadways and railways.

- Pyroclastic flows with temperatures of 70°C rolled out of the crater at 1,080 km/h for hours after the eruption. These flows covered 10 km^2, and they burned and destroyed everything in their path. Fifty-seven people were killed by the pyroclastic flows.

case study

Effects of the eruption

On infrastructure

As a result of the eruption, 27 bridges, 24 km of railway and 300 km of roads were destroyed. The mudflows and flooding affected sewage and water treatment. Flights were cancelled due to the ash. Electricity transformers were shortcircuited by the ash causing major blackouts.

On wildlife

It is estimated that 7,000 big game animals (deer, elk, and bear), 12 million salmon and millions of birds and small mammals perished in the eruption. Twenty-four thousand hectares of forest were damaged/destroyed, crops were ruined and animals and fish were wiped out.

On the economy

The eruption cost €1 billion in terms of timber, civil works and agricultural losses.

On the volcano

The top 400 m of the volcano was blown away by the eruption.

Since 1980

Mount St Helens remains active. It is expected to continue erupting but no one knows for how long. The volcano is being carefully monitored by a volcano observatory 5 km away. Seismic disturbances, gas emissions, temperature, changes in height, water levels, sediment flow rates and even magma movement are all carefully measured and evaluated for risk. A new dome continues to grow slowly in the crater.

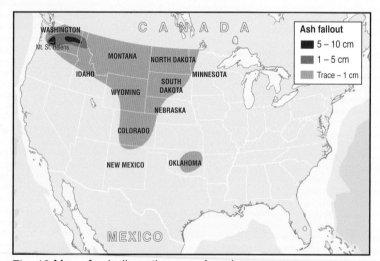

Fig. 19 Map of ash disruption over America

Find out more about volcanoes at www.volcanoes.com

Soufriére Hills Volcano, Montserrat

Option 2

● The volcanoes on the island of Montserrat in the Caribbean formed when two oceanic plates collided, creating an island arc called the Windward Islands which stretches from Puerto Rico to Trinidad.

● European settlers in the seventeenth century farmed its rich volcanic soil. Sugar was, and is, a major product.

● Erupting in the early 1600s, Montserrat's southern volcano in the Soufriére Hills lay dormant for three centuries. In early 1995 increases in gas emissions and seismic activity and changes in the shape of the volcano occurred. This activity prompted evacuations of over 8,000 people from the southern part of the island. The volcano began to erupt violently in July 1995. Ash, pyroclasts and volcanic bombs were thrown over a wide area. The ash cloud was so dense it blocked out the sun downwind of the volcano.

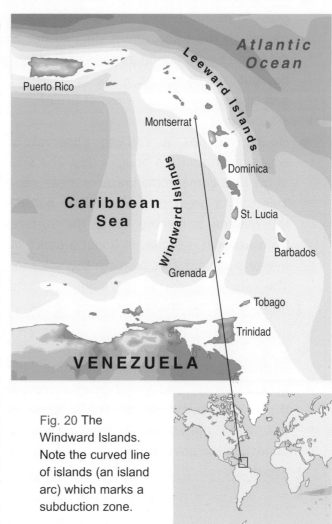

Fig. 20 The Windward Islands. Note the curved line of islands (an island arc) which marks a subduction zone.

● In June 1997 a large pyroclastic flow came down from the Soufriére Hills. In a matter of minutes it covered 4 km², killing 9 people and destroying 100 homes. This pyroclastic flow moved at over 160 km/h. Villages which had been evacuated were destroyed by the volcano. A delta, formed at the mouth of the White River by previous ash flows, grew even larger.

● Some explosions on Montserrat have thrown a rain of pumice pebbles onto villages such as Cork Hill several kilometres northwest of the crater. Closer to the volcano, sizzling rocks the size of rugby balls have landed like bombs, leaving craters in farmers' fields and setting homes ablaze.

● The lava's high silica content makes it so thick that it often squeezes out of the dome in massive pillars called **spines**.

case study

● Ash gets everywhere, even through the tiniest of cracks. It chokes gardens, kills the grass in pastures, and makes roads slippery. The weight of it can collapse roofs. It travels on the trade winds, dusting neighbouring islands and has occasionally shut down the neighbouring airports of Guadeloupe and Antigua. Breathing ash day in and day out could bring on a deadly disease called silicosis, which thickens lung tissue and causes severe shortness of breath.

● Montserrat has a volcano observatory which monitors it 24 hours a day. The size of the lava dome in the crater is measured. This tells a great deal about how quickly the magma is coming up to the surface from where it is stored at about a depth of five or six kilometres beneath the volcano. The rate of ascent of the magma affects how violent the eruption is going to be.

● Over 3,000 people still live on the safer northern part of the island. Ashfall, air quality, rainfall and water quality around the volcano is monitored. This is done to ensure that the volcano isn't having a large impact on the environment and on people's health.

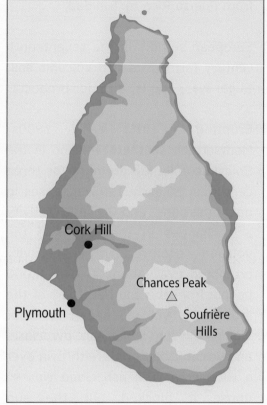

Fig. 21 Montserrat

To find out what is happening at the Montserrat volcano at the moment, log onto http://www.mvo.ms/

Chapter Revision Questions

1. Draw a labelled diagram showing the main parts of a typical volcano.

2. Describe the **three** stages in the life cycle of a volcano.

3. Name and describe **three** products of volcanic eruptions.

4. Explain the differences between acidic and basic lava. How do their eruptions differ?

5. Explain each of the following terms: (a) pyroclastic flow, (b) lahar, (c) magma chamber.

6. Name, describe and give an example of **two** external and two internal volcanic landforms. Draw a diagram to illustrate your answer.

7. Explain **three** methods used to predict volcanic eruptions.

8. Outline the consequences of the eruption of the volcano on Mount St Helens. Describe how the volcano is monitored and the methods used to predict further volcanic activity.

OL Short Questions

9. Examine the diagram of a volcano below. Match the letters A–E with the following features: vent; secondary cone; ash cloud; crater; magma chamber.

LC Exam Paper

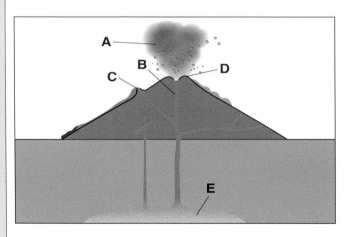

OL Long Questions

10. Explain with the aid of an example which you have studied why volcanic activity happens at plate margins.

LC Exam Paper

11. Volcanoes can have both negative and positive effects on the landscape and on people. Explain one negative and one positive effect of volcanoes.

HL Long Questions

12. Using the diagram below, match each of the intrusive volcanic landforms with the letters A-E in the diagram: still; laccolith; dyke; batholith; lopolith.

LC Exam Paper

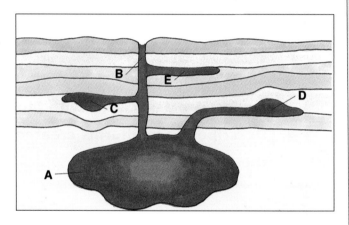

13. Name an example of a volcano which you have studied. State **two** advantages and **one** disadvantage for people living in a volcanic region.

14. Explain how the study of plate tectonics has helped us to understand the global distribution of volcanoes.

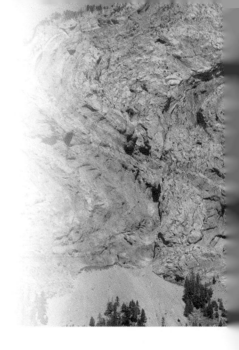

Chapter 4
Folding and Faulting in the Earth's Crust

At the end of this chapter you should be able to:

- Name the parts of a fold and draw the main types of folds.
- Discuss how folding has shaped the landscape of Southern Ireland.
- Explain what a fault is.
- Explain and give Irish and international examples of some of the landscapes associated with faults.
- Describe the landforms created by folding and faulting of the earth's crust.

Contents

4.1   Folding

4.2   *Case Study*: Fold mountains in Ireland

4.3   Faulting

4.4   Landscapes associated with faults

      Case Study: The African Rift Valley

      Questions

KEY THEME

Rocks of the earth's crust are folded and faulted by forces within the earth.

4.1 Folding

The same forces that move plates around the planet also place huge pressure on the rocks of the earth's surface. When rocks are crumpled up by these forces they are said to be **folded.**

Folds can be seen very easily in sedimentary rocks. Loughshinny in North County Dublin has some very well-developed folds. The Rock of Cashel in County Tipperary is another example of folded rock. Rocks can be folded because at depth they are subjected to great heat and pressure which allows the rock to bend without breaking. Different types of fold are created depending on the strength and direction of the pressure put on the rock. These are shown in Figs. 2 and 3.

Fig. 1 Folded limestone rock at Loughshinny, North County Dublin

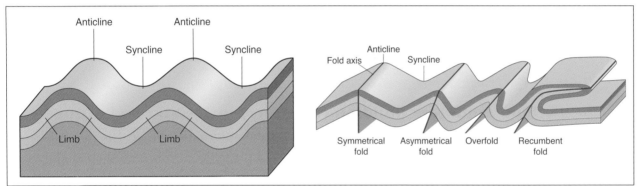

Fig. 2 Exam Diagram: The parts of a fold: anticlines are upfolds, synclines are downfolds.

Fig. 3 Types of fold

Symmetric/simple folds

These folds are formed when pressure is applied gently and equally from either side of the rock layers. They have nearly vertical axial planes and the limbs dip at a similar angle to each other. Symmetrical folds are found near the margins of mountain systems where tectonic activity is relatively quiet.

Asymmetrical folds

These folds are formed when the pressure applied to the rock layer is greater on one side than the other. In asymmetric folds the fold axis is tilted relative to the surface and fold limbs may be of unequal steepness.

Overfold/recumbent fold

When larger amounts of pressure are applied to one side of a rock layer, the rock fold is turned over on itself so that one or both limbs dip in the same direction. If the axial plane is nearly horizontal the fold is called a recumbent fold.

Overthrust fold

When the compression of rock layers is very great, a crack or fracture occurs in the fold. One limb is then pushed over the other limb forming an overthrust fold.

Fig. 4 Recumbent fold in the Swiss Alps

Fold mountain building (orogeny) in Ireland and abroad

1. **Caledonian folding** occurred around 400 million years ago. The mountain ridges trend from northeast to southwest, e.g the Leinster mountains and the mountains of north-west Ireland and Scotland.

2. **Armorican folding** occurred around 300 million years ago. The mountain ridges trend from east to west, e.g. the Munster ridge and valley province, Paris Basin in France.

3. **Alpine folding** occurred 50 million years ago. This is not found in Ireland. Mountain ridges trend from east to west, e.g. Alps and Himalayas.

ACTIVITY

Name the Caledonian mountain ranges 1–6 and the Armorican mountain ranges A–D.

Caledonian mountains

Armorican mountains

Fig. 5 Fold mountains in Ireland

4.2 Fold mountains in Ireland

The Munster ridge and valley province

● Between 350 and 400 million years ago Ireland lay closer to the equator and experienced a dry desert climate. Huge amounts of sand were deposited in the south and south-west of Ireland. Today this is known as **Old Red Sandstone**. Later, a muddy sea covered the area and limestone was laid down.

● About 300 million years ago the rocks of Ireland were squeezed by earth movements, creating **fold mountains**. These foldings are known as Armorican folds. Similar fold mountains occur in southern England and Brittany in France.

● These fold mountains stretch from Waterford to Kerry. The east-west trending anticlines, or ridges, are responsible for mountains such as the Comeraghs, Silvermines and Galtee Mountains. These ridges are made of resistant sandstone rock. During folding, rocks in the anticlines were stretched and cracks formed, weakening the limestone. Over time, weathering and erosion removed the limestone from the anticlines exposing the sandstone beneath.

● Today the fold synclines are still covered with this limestone and form broad valleys. The Golden Vale and the Blackwater Valley are examples.

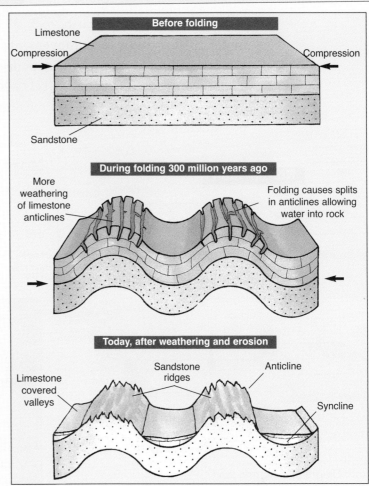

Fig. 6 Exam diagram: The formation of the Munster ridge and valley province.

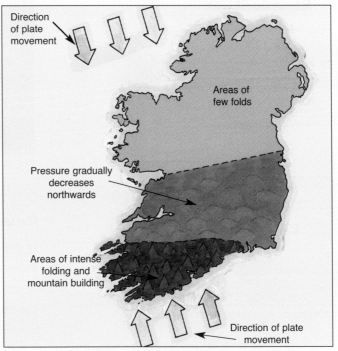

Fig. 7 Location map of Munster ridge and valley province

4.3 Faulting

Near the surface of the earth, rock is brittle and will crack or fracture when placed under great stress by earth movements. Rocks contain many small fractures or joints. When a lot of movement has happened along a fracture it is called a **fault**.

Faults often occur in parallel sets because the stress that produces them operates over a large area. Pressure and tension make the land either side of the fault move up, down or sideways.

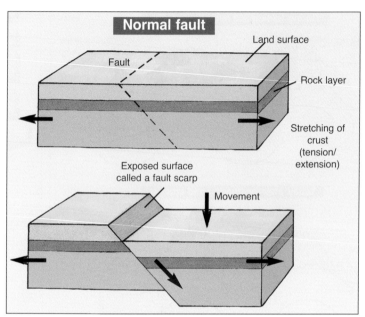

Fig. 8 Exam Diagram: A normal fault

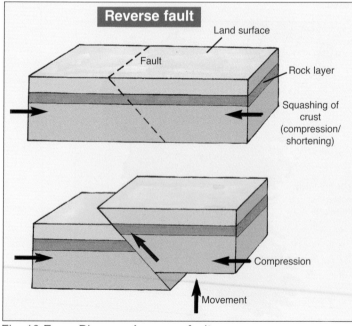

Fig. 10 Exam Diagram: A reverse fault

Normal faults

When a sloping fault is created and land slips down along one side of it, a normal fault is formed. These are caused by the land being pulled apart (**tension**), sometimes making a rift valley. The exposed face of the fault is called the **fault scarp.**

Fig. 9 A normal fault in sedimentary rock in El Salvador

Reverse faults

If pressure from earth movements (**compression**) causes land to move up along a sloping fault line a reverse fault is formed, sometimes making block mountains, for example the Ox Mountains of County Sligo.

Thrust faults

A thrust fault is a type of reverse fault where the angle of the fault plane is very low.

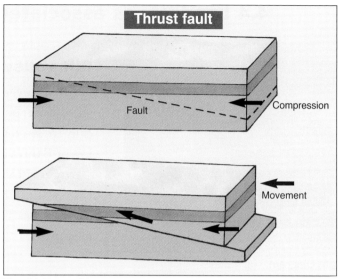

Fig. 11 Exam Diagram: A thrust fault

Tear faults

Tear faults (**transform faults**) occur when there is a vertical fault in the landscape but movement has been horizontal. This is similar to the movement along the San Andreas fault in California.

The long east to west anticlines of Cork and Waterford are crossed by many tear faults, and geological maps show that movement of 2 km occurred along tear faults close to Slieve Gullion in County Armagh.

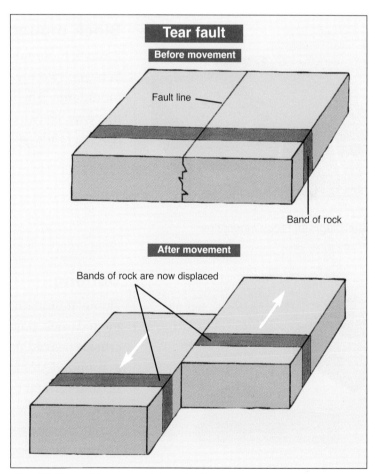

Fig. 12 Exam Diagram: A tear fault

4.4 Landscapes associated with faults

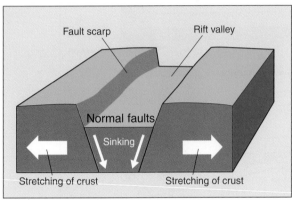

Fig. 13 Exam Diagram: Rift valleys

Rift valleys (graben)

A rift valley, or graben, is formed when a block of land slips down between sets of parallel normal faults. This is due to stretching of the crust. Lough Neagh and the lower Bann valley occupy such a rift valley.

Larger rift valleys occur in Germany, such as the Rhine Rift Valley between the Vosges and Black Forest Mountains. The Midland Valley of Scotland is another example.

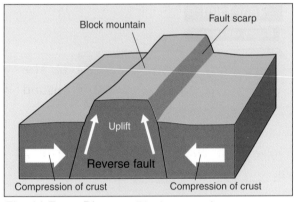

Fig. 14 Exam Diagram: Block mountains

Block mountains (horsts)

A block mountain (horst) is a block of land left standing between two reverse faults e.g. Vosges and Black Forest mountains. The Ox Mountains of Sligo were formed in this way. Here a block of gneiss was pushed up between reverse faults in limestone and conglomerate rocks.

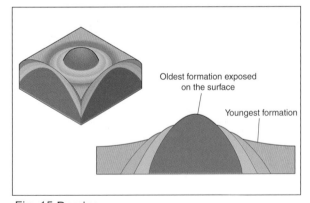

Fig. 15 Doming

Doming

Dome mountains are the result of a great amount of melted rock pushing its way up under the earth. The crust is heaved upward, without folding or faulting, into a rounded dome. Weathering and erosion attack the upland formed by the dome, often exposing the igneous rock at the heart of the dome mountains. Dome mountains are common in North America, e.g. the Black Mountains of South Dakota.

The African Rift Valley – A landscape formed by faulting

- The African Rift Valley is a landform made by faulting. This huge rift valley is visible from space as it is the world's largest surface fracture.

- In the African Rift Valley, a newly-forming constructive plate boundary above a hotspot is in the process of splitting the African plate into two new separate plates. Geologists generally refer to these plates-to-be as the 'Nubian plate' (the current African plate) and the Somali plate.

- The African Rift Valley formed during the last 20 million years due to the presence of a hotspot beneath the crust. The hotspot is causing the African continent to bulge and stretch and split. As the crust is pulled apart, huge parallel cracks called normal faults are formed. In the zone these faults extend over 6,000 km from the Red Sea in the north to Mozambique in the south.

- As the crust in the rift valley is stretched, huge blocks of crust sink between the normal faults forming a large flat-floored rift valley or graben.

- The land has subsided so much in places that it lies more than 153 m below sea level. The fault lines are marked by high fault scarps or escarpments rising steeply several thousand metres from the valley floor.

- At the same time magma is forced up to the surface in places and erupts, forming volcanoes, e.g. Mount Kilimanjaro and Mount Kenya.

- The African Rift Valley varies in width from 40 to 100 km and is widening at a rate of up to 4 mm per year.

- Many lakes have also formed in the floor of the rift valley. The deepest is Lake Tanganyika which is nearly 1,420 m deep.

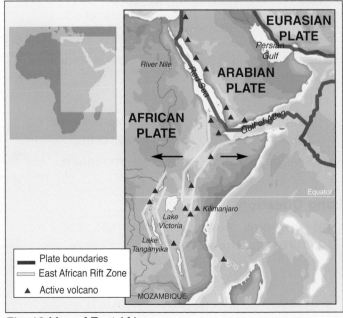

Fig. 16 Map of East Africa

Chapter Revision Questions

1. Draw and label a symmetric fold.

2. Explain the terms (a) compression and (b) tension.

3. Describe the formation of the Munster ridge and valley province.

4. What is a fault? Using examples and diagrams, describe the formation of a block mountain and rift valley.

5. Draw a labelled diagram of normal, reverse and thrust faults.

OL Long Questions

6. Explain with the aid of a diagram or diagrams how fold mountains are formed. In your answer name an example you have studied.

HL Short Questions

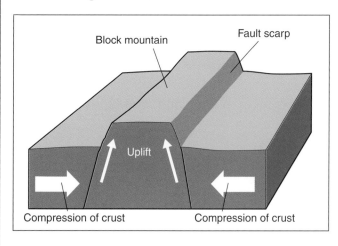

7. Examine the diagram above of a block mountain.

   (a) Explain the term reverse fault.

   (b) Using the diagram, briefly explain how block mountains (horsts) may form.

   (c) Give one example of a block mountain.

HL Long Questions

8. The diagrams above to the right show structures of deformation.

Match each of the structures given with the correct label A–D in the diagrams that follow: normal fault; reverse or thrust fault; doming; transverse or tear fault.

LC Exam Paper

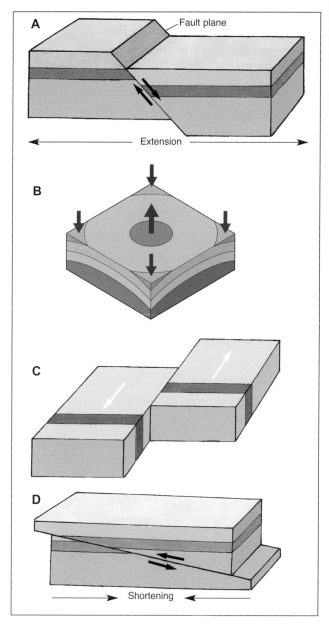

9. Explain how the study of plate tectonics has helped us to understand the global distribution of fold mountains.

LC Exam Paper

10. Examine the impact of folding and faulting on the landscape. In your answer refer to one landform in each case.

LC Exam Paper

Chapter 5
Rock Types and their Formation

At the end of this chapter you should be able to:

- Explain the formation of igneous, sedimentary and metamorphic rocks.
- Name and give examples of three different rock types found in Ireland.
- Explain how the rock cycle works.
- Describe how sediment is turned into rock (lithification).
- Discuss human interaction with the rock cycle.
- Using one of the case studies, describe how people exploit rock resources.

Contents

5.1 Igneous rocks

5.2 Sedimentary rocks

5.3 Metamorphic rocks

5.4 The rock cycle

5.5 Human interaction with the rock cycle

Case Studies: Tara lead and zinc mines

Geothermal energy in Iceland

Questions

KEY THEME

Rocks are continually formed, changed, destroyed and reconstructed as part of the rock cycle. They are formed and changed by forces within the earth. They are destroyed by forces at work on the earth's surface such as weathering and erosion. Rocks are reconstructed by the deposition of sediments.

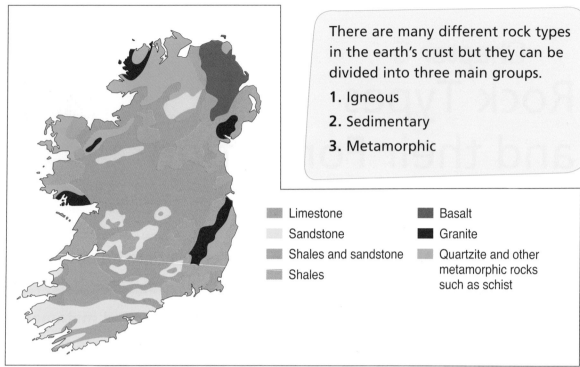

There are many different rock types in the earth's crust but they can be divided into three main groups.

1. Igneous

2. Sedimentary

3. Metamorphic

▣ Limestone	▣ Basalt
▣ Sandstone	▣ Granite
▣ Shales and sandstone	▣ Quartzite and other metamorphic rocks such as schist
▣ Shales	

Fig. 1 Geological map of Ireland

5.1 Igneous rocks

Igneous rocks are formed from magma which cools and solidifies either below ground, forming **intrusive** igneous rock, or on the earth's surface, forming **volcanic** (**extrusive**) igneous rock. These rocks are made of crystals, which may be large or small depending on how fast the magma cools.

Fig. 2 Granite is composed of three minerals: feldspar, quartz and mica. The white crystals are feldspar, the black ones are mica and the grey crystals are quartz.

Intrusive igneous rock

Intrusive igneous rock can be divided into two groups:

1. **Plutonic** rocks form as magma cools very slowly (taking thousands of years) deep inside the earth's crust. They have large crystals of quartz, felspar and mica. **Granite** is a common example. It is often grey in colour.

   When very large masses of magma are injected into the crust they slowly cool to form large granite structures called **batholiths**. Weathering and erosion can remove the rock above these structures so that today we can see the batholiths in places such as the Wicklow Mountains.

2. **Intermediate** (**hypabyssal**) rocks form when magma makes its way closer to the earth's surface and cools more quickly than plutonic rock so that the crystals are smaller. **Dolerite** is a common example. It is a dull grey colour and is found in the Fair Head Sill, County Antrim.

Volcanic/extrusive rock

Volcanic (**extrusive**) igneous rock, e.g. **basalt**, forms when magma reaches the earth's surface, at which point it is called lava. It cools quickly out in the open or under water. It is a dull brown or black colour with **microscopic** crystals. In Ireland basalt formed in the Giant's Causeway 90 to 65 million years ago when the crust split apart and the Atlantic Ocean began to form. This rifting allowed basic magma to reach the surface and pour over the land, forming the Antrim Plateau.

Fig. 3 Exam Diagram: The formation of igneous rocks

5.2 Sedimentary rocks

Sedimentary rocks are made from the build-up (**accumulation**) of layers of inorganic or organic sediments. Each layer (**strata**) is deposited on a lower layer, squashing out water, minerals and air. As the sediment layers are buried they become compacted and eventually cemented together by silica or calcite to form solid rock.

This process of turning sediment into stone is known as **lithification**.

Horizontal joints called **bedding planes** separate the layers.

Sedimentary rocks are classified according to their mode of formation:

1. Organically formed
2. Inorganic or mechanically formed
3. Chemically formed

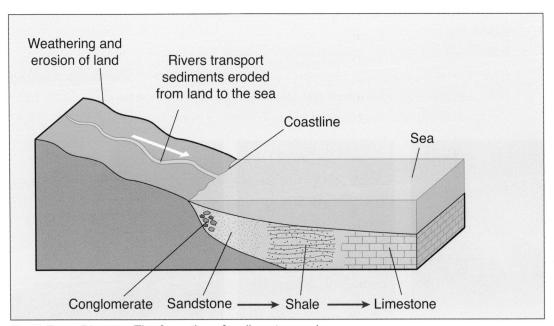

Fig. 4 Exam Diagram: The formation of sedimentary rocks

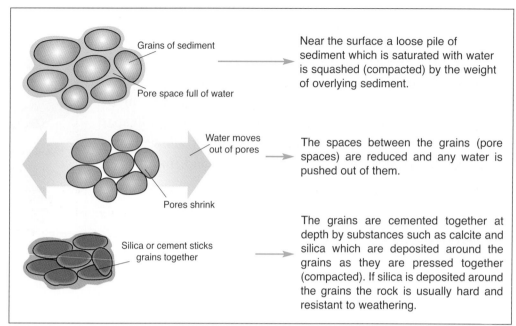

Grains of sediment

Pore space full of water

Near the surface a loose pile of sediment which is saturated with water is squashed (compacted) by the weight of overlying sediment.

Water moves out of pores

Pores shrink

The spaces between the grains (pore spaces) are reduced and any water is pushed out of them.

Silica or cement sticks grains together

The grains are cemented together at depth by substances such as calcite and silica which are deposited around the grains as they are pressed together (compacted). If silica is deposited around the grains the rock is usually hard and resistant to weathering.

Fig. 5 How lithification occurs

1. Organically formed sedimentary rocks

These are rocks made up of layers composed of dead organisms (fish, shells, vegetation). During lithification, calcite cement squeezed from shells in the sediment glues these organic particles together, creating distinctive sedimentary rocks.

Limestone, the most common rock in Ireland, was formed in this way. Most limestone in Ireland formed 350 to 300 million years ago when Ireland lay close to the equator and was covered by a warm shallow sea similar to that found in the Caribbean today. The grains are cemented with calcium carbonate which comes from shells. Sometimes the remains of living things are well preserved as fossils in the rock. Beachcombing will often produce pebbles with fossil shells and corals. Limestone can be seen in the Burren, County Clare.

Chalk is a pure white form of limestone. Much of the chalk deposited in Ireland has been eroded but some is still preserved under the basalt of the Giant's Causeway.

Coal: Decaying vegetation accumulated on poorly drained, waterlogged soil creates peat, e.g. the Bog of Allen in the Midlands. Further compaction squeezes out more water to create coal, e.g. Coalisland in County Tyrone.

Fig. 6 Coal mining at Arigna, County Roscommon

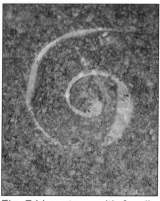

Fig. 7 Limestone with fossil

Fig. 8 Strata and bedding planes of sedimentary rock

2. Inorganic or mechanically formed sedimentary rocks

These rocks form from the lithification of rock fragments.

Sandstone is formed when particles of eroded igneous, metamorphic and other sedimentary rocks are carried by rivers and accumulate on the seabed or in lakes. During lithification silica glues the grains together. Sandstone is a porous, permeable rock. The spaces between sand grains are called pores. These pores may be filled with air, water, oil or gas. Liquids and gases pass easily through the pores, making sandstone a permeable rock. Irish sandstone formed 400 to 350 million years ago when Ireland lay 30° south of the equator. At this time and latitude Ireland experienced very dry desert conditions. Huge rivers flowed across this dry landscape carrying the sediments that eventually formed the Old Red Sandstone which is now found in the Cork and Kerry mountains.

Fig. 9 Sandstone

Fig. 10 Shale cliff – note the fold.

Fig. 11 Conglomerate

Shale or **mudstone**: Layers of fine particles of silt and mud build up in deep water and become dark grey or black rock. Shale is found in south County Clare.

Conglomerates: When a mix of sand grains and pebbles stick together, a conglomerate is formed. The pebbles may be rounded or angular and have many different colours. In some places this rock is known as pudding stone. Conglomerates may be found in Skerries and Rush in north County Dublin.

3. Chemically formed sedimentary rocks

These are rocks formed from the evaporation of sea water from enclosed lakes or seas in hot climates.

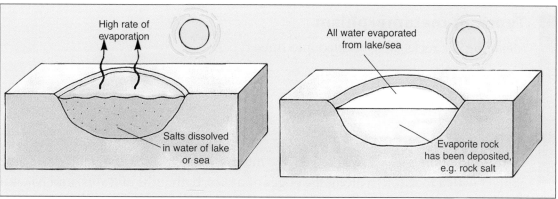

Fig. 12 Exam Diagram: Formation of evaporites

Many times in the geological past, areas of salt water were cut off from the open sea, where they formed vast evaporating basins. This situation has occurred on the eastern side of the Caspian Sea in northern Iran and a thick layer of salt has built up there.

When sea water evaporates, the least soluble salt is deposited first and the most soluble last. Chemically formed rocks are thus deposited in a definite order: gypsum is deposited when 37% of the water has evaporated, rock salt when 93% of the water has gone. Often in the past only one of these rocks would be formed. Gypsum alone is deposited in a thick layer near Kingscourt in County Cavan. Rock salt and gypsum occur in Carrickfergus, County Antrim – 20% of the rock salt from this mine is used in road gritting in the island of Ireland, 60% is exported to Europe and 20% goes to the east coast of America.

5.3 Metamorphic rocks

Metamorphic rocks are igneous or sedimentary rocks which change their form either chemically or physically due to intense heat and/or pressure caused by plate movements. Earthquakes, folding, faulting and vulcanicity can cause metamorphism (changes) in the rock. Some of Ireland's metamorphic rocks were formed around 400 million years ago when the American and European plates collided and formed the Caledonian fold mountains.

The effect of metamorphism on rock

Metamorphism changes the colour, hardness, mineral alignment and chemical composition of rocks.

Hardness: All metamorphic rocks are harder than their original rock type.

Colour: Metamorphism may change the colour of rocks due to the effect of heat, e.g. limestone is grey but when metamorphosed the resulting marble may be green, yellow or white.

Foliation: Mineral crystals may be rearranged to form foliated metamorphic rock such as gneiss. In this case the minerals are flattened into parallel layers. Some rocks have their sediments flattened and hardened into very thin layers, e.g. slate.

Chemical composition: Heat and pressure may cause the rock minerals to recombine to form different minerals in the metamorphic rock.

Types of metamorphism

Metamorphic rocks are classified into three types:
1. Thermal
2. Dynamic
3. Regional

1. Thermal metamorphism

In this situation rocks are changed by intense heat. Molten magma comes into contact with a rock (often along the edges of dykes, batholiths and sills) and bakes it causing recrystallisation of the rock minerals.

Fig. 13 Quartzite

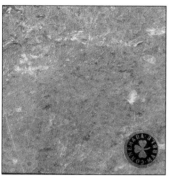

Fig. 14 Marble

Quartzite is a pale-looking rock formed by the thermal metamorphism of sandstone, e.g. Mount Errigal, County Donegal.

Marble is formed from the thermal metamorphism of limestone. Unlike limestone, marble is sparkly and has a variety of colours from green to red according to the mineral content, e.g. Connemara marble is green. The white marble of Rathlin Island, County Antrim is often used by sculptors.

2. Dynamic metamorphism

This happens when plate movement causes great pressure to be placed on rocks. This pressure converts them into much harder rock types.

Plate movement causes intense pressure especially along fault lines within rocks. At these faults the rock is ground into a fine sticky powder called **fault gouge**.

Slate forms from the dynamic metamorphism of shale. Shale forms when fine mud particles on the sea floor are compressed into rock. The great pressure applied during metamorphism compresses the shale, hardening it into a purple-grey foliated rock with very fine layers in it. This is called slate. Slate can be split very easily along the layers, making it a useful building material. Slate from Valentia Island, County Kerry has been used across the world to make roof tiles, fireplaces and tables.

Fig. 15 Fault gouge. The pen is pushed into the soft, ground-up rock in the fault between the two hard rock layers either side of the fault.

3. Regional metamorphism

Large areas of rock covering thousands of square kilometres can be metamorphosed. This widespread change is called regional metamorphism. Much of north-west Scotland, north-west Ireland and Canada were affected in this way during the Caledonian folding 400 million years ago.

Plate movement creates pressure on rocks, deforming them and forcing them deep into the earth's crust where they may be heated to temperatures of up to 1,000 degrees Celsius. This combination of heat and pressure changes the rocks.

Schist and **gneiss (pronounced: nice)** are the most common of metamorphic rocks. Schist is grainier than slate. It has undergone a greater degree of metamorphism than slate. Many schists look glittery and shiny because large crystals of mica form during metamorphism. Identifying the parent rock of schists may be difficult. Some schist was formed deep inside the earth by the thermal and dynamic metamorphism of shale over large areas. This rock may be found at Lugnaquilla, County Wicklow and at Wicklow Head.

Gneiss was originally granite. Many of the original granite minerals are still present but they have become segregated into pale and dark wavy bands. Gneiss is found in the Belmullet peninsula in County Mayo.

Fig. 16 Schist rock

Fig. 17 This gneiss has been polished for use as a kitchen worktop. Notice the bands of black and pink crystals typical of gneiss.

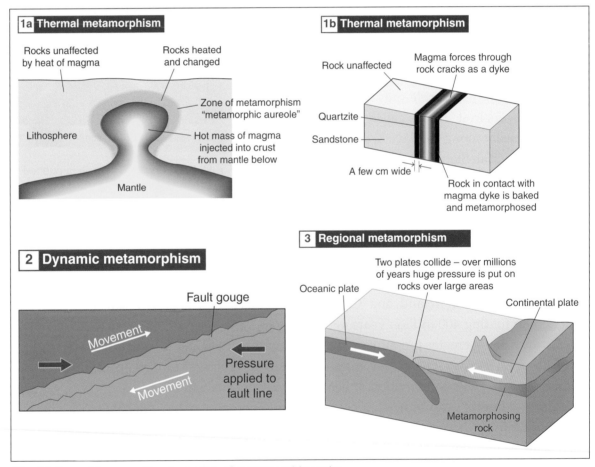

Fig. 18 Exam Diagram: The formation of metamorphic rocks

5.4 The rock cycle

The rock cycle is the process by which each rock type can be changed into another.

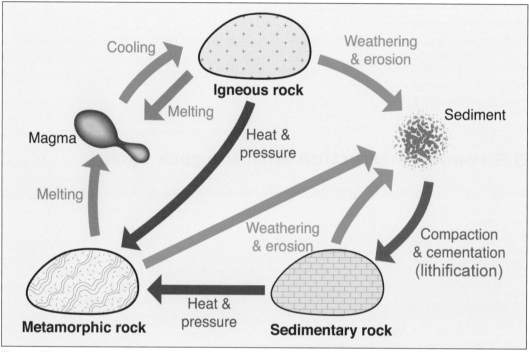

Fig. 19 The rock cycle

ACTIVITY

The rock cycle always begins with the formation of magma. Look carefully at the diagram of the rock cycle and answer the questions which follow.

1   What processes change sedimentary rock to metamorphic rock?
2   What processes change igneous rock to metamorphic rock?
3   How is sediment converted to sedimentary rock?
4   How is metamorphic rock converted to sedimentary rock?
5   How does magma change to igneous rock?
6   How is sedimentary rock changed back into sediment?
7   How is metamorphic rock converted into magma?

The rock cycle is a group of changes that can affect igneous, sedimentary and metamorphic rock. Magma is a hot liquid made from melted minerals that form crystals when they cool. Igneous rock forms when magma cools and mineral crystals grow. Igneous rock can form underground, where the magma cools slowly, or it can form above ground, where the lava cools quickly.

On the earth's surface, the processes of weathering and erosion can break rock into smaller pieces. Wind and water transport these rock pieces to other places. Usually, the rock pieces, called sediments, are deposited under water to make a layer. The layer can be buried under other layers of sediment. After a long time the sediments can be cemented together to make sedimentary rock. In this way, igneous rock has become sedimentary rock.

All rock can be heated. Inside our planet the weight of the earth creates heat at great depths. Heat is also created by friction generated by moving plates and radioactive decay of certain elements. Heat inside the earth bakes the rock. Baked rock does not melt, but it does change. It forms crystals. If it is crystalline already, it forms even larger crystals. Rocks changed by heat and pressure are called metamorphic rock.

5.5 Human interaction with the rock cycle

We get many resources from rocks and use them for a variety of business and leisure activities as shown in Fig. 20.

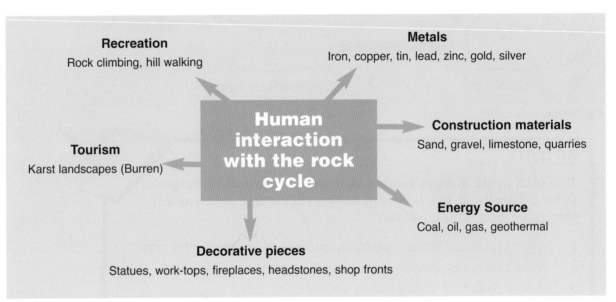

Fig. 20 The value of rocks to people

USE AND LOCATIONS OF ROCK IN IRELAND

Use	Rock/Sediment	National example
Road chippings	Basalt	Antrim Plateau
Glass	Sand	Waterford
Fertiliser	Limestone	Ringaskiddy, Cork
Construction	Sand, gravel, limestone, sandstone, marble, granite	Quarries nationwide
Roofing	Slate	Valentia Island
Chemical industry	Natural gas, limestone	Kinsale
Ornaments	Marble, granite	Connemara marble, Galway granite
Heating	Coal, oil, gas, peat	Bog of Allen
Pottery	China clay	Belleek, County Fermanagh
Minerals	Bauxite, lead and zinc	Tara Mines, County Meath
Precious stones/ metals	Gold, silver	Sperrin Mountains, County Tyrone

One of the ingredients of soap (sodium hydroxide) is processed from rock salt mined from underground. Face packs use a special earth called kaolin clay.

[Note: Choose Option 1 OR 2]

Option 1: Tara Lead and Zinc Mine

● The Tara Lead and Zinc mine in Navan, County Meath is the largest lead and zinc mine in Europe and the fifth largest in the world. It produces over 2.7 million tonnes (Mt) of zinc and lead concentrate each year. This is sent to refineries in Finland, Norway and other EU countries.

Formation of lead and zinc at Tara

● Rock containing metal is referred to as **ore.** At Tara, lead and zinc is found in the sedimentary bedding planes of carboniferous limestone and dolomite rocks. These rocks are known as the Pale Beds and were formed in the shallow tropical seas that covered Ireland over 350 million years ago.

The origin of the lead and zinc ores is linked to the movement of groundwater through the rock. Sea water seeped down many kilometres into the rock under the seabed and was heated up by geothermal energy from deep inside the earth. As the hot sea water (**brine**) moved down through the fault planes, joints and bedding planes in the rock, it dissolved small amounts of lead and zinc out of the rock.

Fig. 21 Aerial photo of Tara Mines at Navan

case study

This brine containing the dissolved lead and zinc then began to rise through the cracks and fissures in the newly-formed limestone. As the brine rose, it cooled causing tiny crystals of lead and zinc sulphide to form. Over millions of years the metal sulphides built up into metal rich layers called **veins** within the rock. These veins are mined for the metal they contain.

Mining operations at Tara

The Tara mine is an underground shaft mine that operates 24 hours a day 52 weeks a year. To extract the metals from the rock, vertical and horizontal mine shafts are cut to a depth of 50-900 m below the surface. A process called **Stope and Pillar** extraction is used.

Stopes are the massive caverns left when huge areas of rock are blasted out and removed. Pillars are the sections of rock that are left behind to act as supports to the mine tunnels.

Fig. 22 Inside a stope in Tara Mines

While underground the huge blasted chunks of ore are crushed. They are then brought to the surface for chemical treatment. On the surface the rock is crushed again and mixed with water and chemicals. The chemicals separate the metal from the rock. This mixture is then filtered and a metal rich powder obtained. This is dried to form a concentrate.

The concentrate is sent by rail to Dublin Port where it is exported to European smelters in Kokkola, Finland and Odda, Norway where lead and zinc metal is produced from the concentrate.

The waste water is re-circulated to reduce water consumption at the mine.

The waste sediment (**tailings**) from the concentration process is deposited in large ponds called Tailings Ponds. The tailings settle and are eventually mixed with concrete and pumped back into the mine to refill the stopes in order to provide support. Each year over one million tonnes of tailings are pumped back into the mine (backfill). Waste water is treated to remove impurities.

Over time the land used for tailings ponds is returned to grassland. This is carefully monitored to reach EU and World Health Organisation (WHO) standards. Eventually it is returned to grazing land suitable for food production.

The Environmental Protection Agency (EPA) also monitors surface and underground operations. It checks air, water, noise and visual pollution levels. The mine is extensively landscaped to reduce its visual impact.

Metal production

Since 1977 the mine has produced over five million tonnes of zinc and over one million tonnes of lead. In 2009 the mine was threatened with closure due to global recession. Car sales worldwide had slumped and the demand for zinc to galvanise car bodies had dropped considerably. However, the mine stayed open due to the continued demand for lead and zinc

in China and India which were still producing vehicles.

Major investment in new equipment and technology continues to be important for the long-term survival of the mine.

Uses of lead and zinc extracted from the mine

Lead and zinc are very useful metals.

Lead: Used in batteries (60% of lead mined is used for batteries), lead solder, plumbing, soundproofing, X-Ray gowns. Lead is added to glass screens in order to block harmful radiation from TV and PC monitors.

Zinc: Used to rustproof (galvanise) steel, cosmetics, food supplements, sun creams, soaps, paint, ink and many other uses.

Spin-off effects of the mine operations

Mine employment has an important multiplier or spin-off effect on the local and national economy. Mining and quarrying in Ireland generates over €1 billion to the Irish economy. It is estimated that for every one job at Tara an additional three indirect jobs are supported. The mine employs over 680 people in a variety of different jobs, e.g. chemists, environmental scientists, miners, geologists. Many indirect jobs are created by the mining operations such as caterers, accountants, truck drivers, safety consultants and metallurgists.

Option 2: Geothermal Energy in Iceland

Iceland is a country of 320,000 people, located on the mid-Atlantic ridge. This is the constructive plate boundary between the North American and Eurasian tectonic plates. The two plates are moving apart at a rate of about 2 cm per year.

In Iceland the active volcanic zone stretches through the country from the south-west to the north-east and contains more than 200 volcanoes. Eruptions in the south of the country in 2010 spread ash across Europe disrupting flights.

The volcanic zone is used to generate geothermal energy.

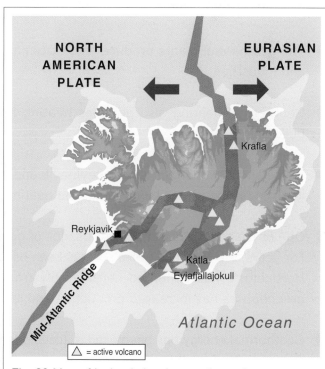

Fig. 23 Map of Iceland showing geothermal zones

case study

How is geothermal energy captured?

● Magma rising from the mantle heats the ground to over 200°C just 1 km below the surface.

● Precipitation falling in the highlands seeps (percolates) down one to three km into the bedrock where it is heated by the hot rocks beneath the surface. In some areas the water is heated to more than 380°C. The hot water then rises towards the surface often forming hot springs and steam vents.

● In order to use the geothermal energy the rocks have to be drilled to capture the hot water. Cold water is passed through the boreholes where it is heated and returned to the surface. In some areas hot water rises naturally to the surface.

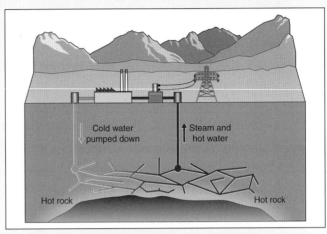

Fig. 24 Capturing geothermal energy in Iceland

Uses of geothermal energy

● Iceland has used geothermal energy since the 1930s. Today five major and many other smaller geothermal power plants exist in Iceland. These produce approximately 29% of the nation's energy (2009).

● The geothermal plants produce electricity and hot water which is piped directly to homes and industries.

● Geothermal heating also provides heating and hot water for approximately 87% of all buildings in Iceland.

● In Iceland's two largest cities, Reykjavík and Akureyri, pavements and car parks are kept ice-free during winter by underground heating systems.

● One of Iceland's most important usages of geothermal energy is for heating greenhouses. For years, the naturally warm soil has been used for growing potatoes and other vegetables. Horticulture has benefited considerably from geothermal resources, as the heating of greenhouses has increased production and lengthened the growing season.

● Geothermal energy has been used in Iceland for drying fish and seaweed for about 25 years. Hot air is blown on the fish and seaweed to dry them out.

Benefits of geothermal energy

- There is potential to generate 40% of Icelandic energy requirements from geothermal sources. This reduces the need to import expensive fossil fuels.

- The cost of geothermal energy is stable over time compared to that of oil. This protects the economy from rapidly changing oil prices.

- The use of geothermal energy has also benefited the environment due to lower CO_2 emissions compared to fossil fuel power plants.

- Besides the economic and environmental benefits, the development of geothermal resources has had a desirable impact on social life in Iceland. The supply of geothermal water for heating and industry led to the formation of several new rural towns and improved the living conditions of a large part of the population.

- Geothermal swimming pools have developed into social meeting places for all generations. They have become culturally important to Icelandic people and are tourist attractions, e.g. the Blue Lagoon.

Fig. 25 A geothermal energy plant in Iceland

questions

Chapter Revision Questions

1. Explain the terms: igneous rock, plutonic rock, intermediate (hypabyssal) rock and volcanic rock.

2. Give an example of the three kinds of igneous rock named in question 1.

3. Explain with the aid of a labelled diagram the process by which sediment is turned to stone (lithification).

4. Contrast organic and inorganic sedimentary rock types. Give an example of each and state where it is found in Ireland.

5. How are chemically formed sedimentary rocks made?

6. Copy out and complete the table below:

	Granite	Limestone	Sandstone	Marble
Formed from:				
Location in Ireland:				
Used for:				

7. (a) Name **one** type of igneous rock.
   (b) Name **one** Irish location for this type of rock.
   (c) Explain in detail how this rock was formed.

8. (a) Name **one** type of sedimentary rock.
   (b) Name **one** Irish location of this type of rock.
   (c) Explain in detail how this rock was formed.

9. (a) Name **one** type of metamorphic rock.
   (b) Give a specific location in Ireland where this metamorphic rock can be found.
   (c) Describe how metamorphic rock is formed.

10. (a) Limestone, basalt, marble, sandstone, slate, granite: place each of these rocks into the category of igneous, sedimentary or metamorphic.
    (b) Select any three rocks from different categories and give an example of their location in Ireland.

11. Draw a sketch map of Ireland to show the location of each of the following rock types: marble, limestone, basalt, sandstone, granite, quartzite.

12. People interact with the rock cycle. Give a brief account of mining at Tara lead and zinc mine in Navan, County Meath.

13. Explain the process of extracting lead and zinc from the rocks mined at Tara.

14. Explain how man interacts with the rock cycle in the production of geothermal energy in Iceland.

questions

OL Short Questions

15. The photograph shows a well-known basalt landscape in Ireland. Select the correct answer from each of the statements below.
    (a) This rock is igneous / sedimentary / metamorphic.
    (b) Basalt cools deep beneath / close to the earth's surface.
    (c) Basalt cools quickly / slowly.
    (d) Basalt is a coarse-grained / fine-grained rock.
    (e) The photograph was taken in Connemara / at the Giant's Causeway / in the Burren.

    LC Exam Paper

16. This is a coarse-grained igneous rock.

    (a) Name this rock.
    (b) Name two locations in Ireland where this rock is found.
    (c) State one common use of this rock.

OL Long Questions

17. With reference to the labels A, B, C and D on the diagram of the rock cycle, state which letter represents each of the following: sedimentary rock; metamorphic rock; magma; igneous rock.

    LC Exam Paper

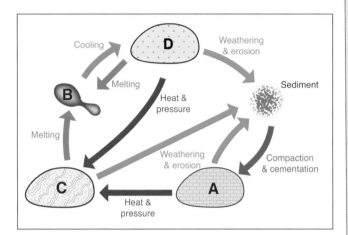

18. The diagram shows the origin of igneous, sedimentary and metamorphic rocks.

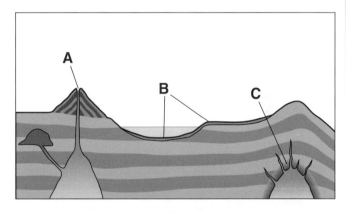

    (a) Identify the rock types that form at A, B and C.
    (b) Name a specific type of rock formed in area C that is widely used across the world.
    (c) Name a specific type of rock formed in area B that is used as a source of energy.

19. What is the chief type of rock found in karst regions such as the Burren in County Clare? Describe fully how this type of rock is formed.

HL Long Questions

20. With reference to Irish examples, explain how igneous rocks form distinct landforms.

21. With reference to Ireland, discuss in detail the formation of batholiths.

22. Discuss, with reference to one of the following, how humans interact with the rock cycle:
    ☐ Mining
    ☐ Extraction of building materials
    ☐ Oil / Gas exploitation
    ☐ Geothermal energy production

23. Examine these images which show landscapes developed on three different rock types. Match each of the rock types listed below with the numbered images.
    (A) Limestone
    (B) Basalt
    (C) Quartzite

Chapter 6
Weathering and Erosion

At the end of this chapter you should be able to:

- Explain the terms **weathering** and **erosion**.
- Explain the difference between these terms.
- Name and describe the processes of chemical and mechanical weathering.
- Name the agents of erosion.

Contents

6.1 Weathering and erosion

6.2 Weathering

6.3 Erosion

Questions

KEY THEME

Rocks are broken down by mechanical and chemical means. The weathered particles are transported elsewhere by the agents of erosion.

6.1 Weathering and erosion

> Weathering is a process that breaks down rocks into smaller pieces.

Weathering and erosion are both exogenic (external) forces responsible for shaping and reshaping the landscape already made by endogenic (internal) forces. This means that weathering and erosion operate on the surface of the earth as opposed to inside it.

Both erosion and weathering are called **agents of denudation** as they wear away the rocks of the landscape and gradually change its surface.

Weathering is the process that breaks down rocks into smaller pieces. The broken rocks are then deposited where they fall. Weathering does not transport material; instead it is transported by the agents of erosion or by the action of gravity (mass movement).

Weathering agents include frost, extreme changes of temperature and chemical reactions with oxygen, carbon dioxide and water.

Erosion is the process by which the earth's rocks are broken down, transported and deposited elsewhere. Erosion agents are rivers, ice, sea and wind.

6.2 Weathering

Types of weathering

Mechanical weathering: This breaks down rocks into smaller pieces. No new substances are formed. It is a physical disintegration (falling apart) of rock.

Chemical weathering: A chemical reaction occurs in the rock causing it to decompose. New substances are formed.

Biological weathering is the disintegration of rocks due to the physical and/or chemical actions of living things. The types of living things that can cause weathering range from bacteria to plants and animals.

Fig. 1 This sandstone rock has been weathered into an unusual shape at the Garden of the Gods, Colorado Springs, USA.

Mechanical (rocks disintegrate)	Chemical (rocks dissolve or rot)	Biological
Freeze-thaw	Carbonation	Plants
Onion weathering	Hydration	Animals
Crystallisation of salts	Oxidation	Humans
	Hydrolysis	

1. Mechanical weathering

There are three processes of mechanical weathering.

(a) Freeze-thaw action

(b) Onion weathering (exfoliation)

(c) Crystallisation of salts

(a) Freeze-thaw action

Water gathers in cracks in rocks. At night (or any time the temperature drops below 0°C) it freezes and expands by about 10%. This expansion places great pressure on a rock face. When daytime comes the ice melts. Repeated freezing and thawing of the water eventually splits the rock fragments off the exposed rock surfaces and they fall as **scree** (**talus**).

The presence of scree is an indicator that freeze-thaw action has occurred. An accumulation of scree can protect the lower slopes of a hill from further weathering.

Freeze-thaw action occurs:

* Where temperatures vary above and below freezing and water is present.
* In arctic as well as temperate zones such as Ireland.
* On mountain tops in equatorial areas such as Kilimanjaro.

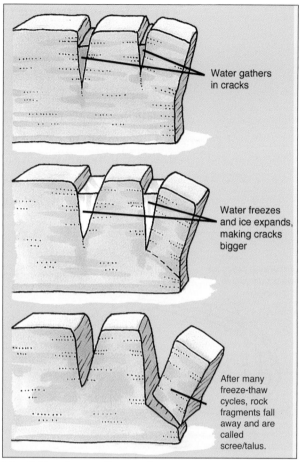

Water gathers in cracks

Water freezes and ice expands, making cracks bigger

After many freeze-thaw cycles, rock fragments fall away and are called scree/talus.

Fig. 2 How freeze-thaw action occurs

Fig. 3 Freeze-thaw action creating scree slopes in the Swiss Alps.

Fig. 4 Scree slope at Glendalough, County Wicklow. Note the angular rocks. Why are they so angular?

(b) Onion weathering (exfoliation)

This is when the surface of the rock peels away layer by layer. The peeled fragments drop to the ground and are themselves weathered.

Extreme heat during the day causes rock to expand. At night as the rock cools it shrinks (contracts) slightly. If this is repeated many times the rock is weakened and surface layers peel away. The presence of even tiny amounts of water can speed up this exfoliation process. Exfoliation is also increased if the rock is composed of many different minerals which can expand and contract at different speeds.

Onion weathering occurs in hot dry climates where the temperature difference between day and night (**diurnal**) is high (40°C), e.g. desert areas such as Arizona.

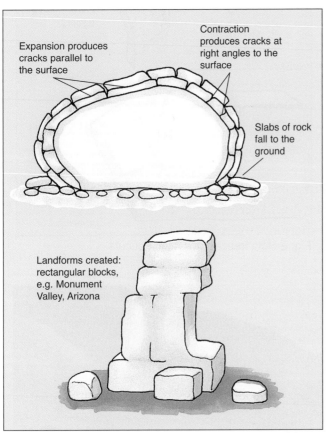

Expansion produces cracks parallel to the surface

Contraction produces cracks at right angles to the surface

Slabs of rock fall to the ground

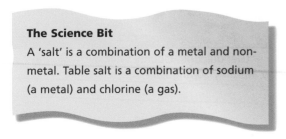

Landforms created: rectangular blocks, e.g. Monument Valley, Arizona

Fig. 5 Onion weathering occurs where there are sudden temperature changes.

Fig. 6 This landform, known as 'The Camel', has been created by onion weathering at the Garden of the Gods, Colorado Springs, USA. Note the layers peeling on the bottom right and bottom left of the rock.

(c) Crystallisation of salts

This type of mechanical weathering is due to pressure caused by the growth of salts in a rock, which then splits it apart.

When water evaporates, any dissolved salts in it are re-crystallised. You may have carried out an experiment in science class to show this. In nature, salts such as calcium sulfate and sodium carbonate are present in water. As water evaporates from rock surfaces, the salt crystals grow inside any cracks that are present. This growth places great pressure on the rock, causing it to crumble or peel away in angular blocks. This has happened in buildings such as Christ Church Cathedral and the National Museum in Dublin.

The Science Bit
A 'salt' is a combination of a metal and non-metal. Table salt is a combination of sodium (a metal) and chlorine (a gas).

2. Chemical weathering

Chemical weathering happens because water contains many dissolved substances, such as carbon dioxide from the air, that can chemically attack rock. Chemical weathering is important for the formation of soils across the world.

Sedimentary rocks have grains bonded together during lithification with cementing agents such as silica and calcite. These cementing agents are easily weathered chemically so that some sedimentary rocks such as limestone and sandstone weather quickly.

Quartz and mica (the glassy and silvery minerals common in granite) are the only minerals resistant to chemical weathering.

There are four processes of chemical weathering.

(a) Carbonation

(b) Hydration

(c) Oxidation

(d) Hydrolysis

(a) Carbonation

Rainwater absorbs carbon dioxide from the air and becomes weak carbonic acid. As the rainwater seeps through the soil it may absorb humic acids created by rotting plant and animal remains. By the time the rainwater has reached the rock below the soil, it is quite acidic and dissolves the rock, especially limestone. This occurs when the acid reacts with the calcium carbonate in the limestone to form soluble calcium bicarbonate.

$$\text{rain} + \text{carbon dioxide} \longrightarrow \text{weak carbonic acid}$$
$$\text{weak carbonic acid} + \text{limestone (insoluble} \longrightarrow \text{calcium bicarbonate (soluble)}$$
$$\text{calcium carbonate)}$$

Limestone regions found in Ireland, Jamaica, Yorkshire and parts of Spain and Italy are weathered by carbonation, producing unusual and beautiful surface and underground landscapes called **karst landscapes.**

Fig. 7 Weathered limestone

ACTIVITY

Class Demonstration
Place a piece of chalk into some dilute hydrochloric acid. The chalk dissolves, and bubbles of carbon dioxide gas are released. This is similar to what happens to limestone in rain, only it happens much faster in acid. Carry out the same experiment with a sample of limestone.

Fig. 8 Bubbles of carbon dioxide gas being released from the reaction of hydrochloric acid on limestone.

(b) Hydration

This is the chemical combination of rock minerals with water. Some minerals in rocks are able to chemically combine with water. As these minerals are hydrated they expand, causing stress and strain within a rock and shattering it.

This may seem similar to the mechanical process of crystallisation of salts; however hydration is a chemical reaction and hydrated minerals are different to their unhydrated parents. Hydration affects shale.

ACTIVITY

Hydration in everyday life
Hydration is used to provide nappies with their water-absorbing properties. The liquid-absorbing substance in nappies undergoes hydration. Water-holding gels for houseplants also work by using hydration. Pour some water onto a nappy or water-holding gel and watch it slowly expand.

(c) Oxidation

When a rock mineral chemically combines with oxygen in water or air, oxidation is said to occur. Rusting iron is a well-known oxidation process. Rocks that contain iron are easily weathered in this way. Iron oxides in rock

Fig. 9 Iron oxide being leached from rock layers in cliffs at Ballybunion, County Kerry

appear as reddish, orange-yellow streaks seeping out of a rock. Oxidised soils may also appear reddish in colour, e.g. latosols and terra rossa soils.

(d) Hydrolysis

Hydrolysis involves the action of acidic water on rock-forming minerals such as feldspars. Feldspar in granite is converted into kaolin (china clay) by hydrolysis. This causes the other minerals in granite, such as quartz (which is resistant to hydrolysis), to fall out of the rock. As a result, hydrolysis causes granite to slowly disintegrate. Hydrolysis is one of the most important weathering agents. It plays a major role in the creation of soils, because hydrolysis leads to the formation of clay.

Fig. 10 This Irish granite rock is being weathered by hydrolysis.

China clay (kaolin) is formed by the hydrolysis of the mineral feldspar in granite rocks. Kaolin deposits in Belleek in County Fermanagh are used to make porcelain objects. Kaolin is also used for many cosmetic skin preparations. As a powder it is used as a pest control in orchards.

Hydrolysis occurs in the top few metres of the earth's crust.

The rate of hydrolysis, like most chemical reactions, is affected by temperature. For every 10°C rise in temperature, the rate of hydrolysis doubles. Thus it is most effective in hot, wet regions of the world such as the tropics, which have deep soils as a result. Brazilian soils are over 20 m deep in places.

3. Biological weathering

The action of plants, animals and man can speed up both mechanical and chemical weathering. Burrowing animals, the growth of plant roots in cracks in rocks, quarrying, road building and deforestation expose rock and soil to all weathering processes.

Fig. 11 Biological weathering in Cambodia. In the photograph plants have grown from seed into a mature tree. Over time the tree roots and trunk are slowly destroying the building.

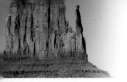

6.3 Erosion

> Erosion is the process by which the earth's surface is broken down, transported from one place to another and deposited.

The main agents of erosion are:

1. Rivers
2. Moving ice
3. The sea
4. Wind

The syllabus requires the study of the agents of river/fluvial, ice/glacial and sea/marine erosion.

SURFACE PROCESSES OF EROSION, TRANSPORTATION AND DEPOSITION

	Rivers	Ice	Sea
Erosion	Hydraulic action Abrasion Solution Attrition	Plucking Abrasion	Hydraulic action Abrasion Air compression Solution Attrition

Transportation	Solution
	Suspension
	Saltation
	Traction
		Sliding (basal flow)
		Plastic flow
		Moraine: debris is
		  transported at sides,
		  in front of, within and
		  under the ice
			Longshore drift

Deposition	Reduced energy
	– slows down
	– load increases
	– reduction in volume
		Melting
		– unsorted (till)
		– sorted (fluvioglacial
		  deposits)
			Change in coastline
			  shape
			Constructive waves
			– sheltered bays
			– calm seas

You will study glacial, river and marine erosional processes and landforms in Chapters 8, 9 and 10.

questions

Chapter Revision Questions

1. Match the photographs A–D with the different weathering processes:
   (i) carbonation   (ii) freeze-thaw action
   (iii) hydrolysis   (iv) oxidation

   A

   B

   C

   D

2. Explain the terms: chemical weathering and mechanical weathering.

3. Give **three** examples of each type of weathering.

4. With the aid of diagrams describe how freeze-thaw action and exfoliation occur.

5. Carbonation, oxidation, hydration, hydrolysis.
   Choose any **three** of these processes and explain how they weather rock.

6. Weathering may be classified into three groups. Name these groups and give an example of **two** types of weathering processes in each group you have named.

7. Explain the term, erosion. List the main agents of erosion.

OL Short Questions

8. Examine this diagram of a weathering process.

   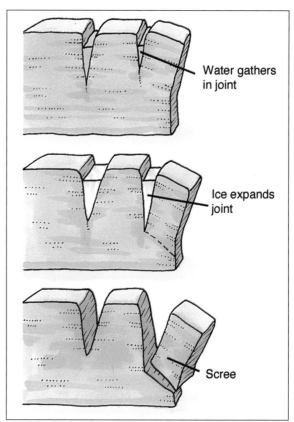

   Water gathers in joint

   Ice expands joint

   Scree

   (a) Name the process shown.
   (b) Name one location in Ireland where this process occurs.
   (c) Name one other type of weathering.

OL Long Questions

9. Choose **one** example of each type of weathering process listed in the table and explain how it occurs.

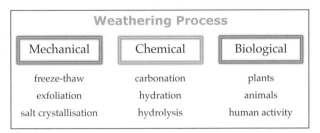

Weathering Process		
Mechanical	Chemical	Biological
freeze-thaw	carbonation	plants
exfoliation	hydration	animals
salt crystallisation	hydrolysis	human activity

HL Short Questions

10. Examine the photograph.

   (a) Identify the type of weathering which shaped this rock.

   (b) Where is this type of weathering most likely to occur?

HL Long Questions

11. Choose **one** example of each type of weathering process listed in the table in Question 9 and explain how each occurs.

12. Examine the impact of mechanical and chemical weathering on the landscape.

Chapter 7
Rock Types and Landscapes

At the end of this chapter you should be able to:

- **Explain that some landscapes are the result of the rock type that lies beneath them.**
- **Give examples of landscapes associated with different rock types.**
- **Explain how limestone landscapes are formed.**

Contents

7.1 Introduction

7.2 Limestone landscapes

7.3 Surface and underground landforms in karst areas

Questions

KEY THEME

The development of a landscape is influenced by the rocks that lie beneath it.

7.1 Introduction

There is a great variety of rock types in Ireland. The landscapes of some parts of the country are unusual because they are associated with certain rock. Look at Fig. 1 below to see how different rock types can form different landscapes.

There are two reasons why rock type influences the landscape:

1. Certain rocks weather or are formed in unique ways producing landforms found in no other rock. The most famous example of this is the Burren in County Clare, which is composed of limestone, and the Giant's Causeway in County Antrim, which is composed of basalt.
2. Earth movements have folded and uplifted the rocks to produce mountains and valleys in certain regions. Munster, which is formed from folded sandstone mountains and limestone-covered valleys, is a good example of this.

The Burren,
County Clare
(limestone)

Giant's Causeway, County Antrim (basalt)

Cliffs of Moher, County
Clare (limestone,
sandstone and shale)

Benbulben, County Sligo
(shale and limestone)

Mount Errigal, County Donegal
(quartzite)

Fig. 1 Famous landscapes around Ireland

Other Irish landscapes associated with particular rocks are the Mourne Mountains and Wicklow Mountains (granite). International examples of unique landscapes are southwest China (limestone tower karst landscape) and the Deccan Plateau in India (basalt plateau area).

7.2 Limestone landscapes

The unusual landscapes formed by the chemical weathering and erosion of limestone are known as **karst** or karstic landscapes. There are many karst areas in the world, since limestone is a common rock covering 15% of the earth's surface. One quarter of the world's population live in these areas. In Ireland, the Burren in County Clare and the Aran Islands in County Galway are karst landscapes.

Fig. 2 Tower karst – China

The word 'karst' comes from the Slovenian word kras meaning bare, stony ground. Some of the best karstic landforms can be seen in Slovenia, Serbia and Croatia.

Fig. 3 Mullaghmore – The Burren, County Clare

General characteristics of karst regions

All karst regions share the same characteristics. These are:

1. A lack of surface water because rainwater and rivers are swallowed up by the cracks and fissures in the rock and flow underground very quickly.
2. The presence of swallow holes.
3. The presence of enclosed hollows called dolines.
4. The presence of underground water.

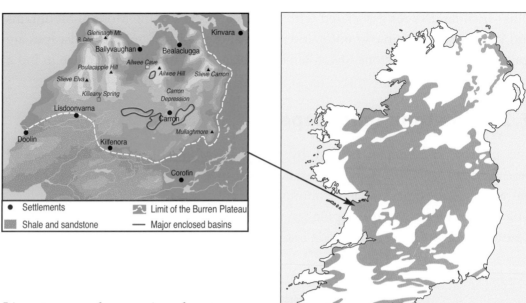

Fig. 4 Limestone deposits in Ireland

Limestone produces unique karst landscapes for the following reasons:

- It is permeable.
- It is jointed.
- It has bedding planes.
- It contains calcium carbonate.

Limestone is **permeable** – it allows water to pass through it. The rainwater passes easily through the many vertical cracks called **fissures** and horizontal cracks called **bedding planes.**

Limestone is chemically weathered by the carbonation process.

Rainwater is slightly acidic because it has absorbed carbon dioxide from the air as it falls. This acid (carbonic acid) reacts with the calcium bicarbonate in limestone forming soluble calcium bicarbonate. This is then carried away in **solution** by the rainwater.

The acidified rainwater trickles down through the cracks and bedding planes enlarging them by the carbonation process so that even more water can pass through the rock. Eventually the fissures are so large that most of the rain that falls goes underground within minutes.

7.3 Surface and underground landforms in karst areas

Surface landforms	Underground landforms
Limestone pavement	Caves
Swallow holes	Stalactites
Dolines	Stalagmites
Turloughs	Pillars

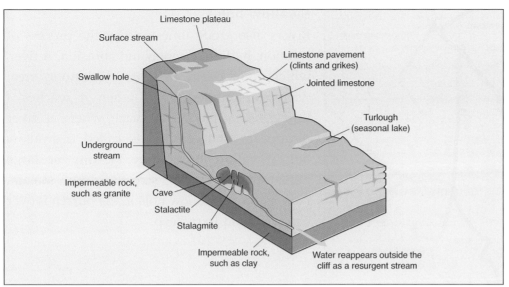

Fig. 5 Surface and underground features in limestone areas

Limestone pavement

This is the name given to the surface of bare limestone rock, e.g. the Burren, County Clare.

The formation of limestone pavements began with the scouring of the limestone by thick glaciers during the last Ice Age. The weight of the ice removed the soil that lay over the limestone, leaving level platforms of limestone. Then a thick layer of boulder clay (glacial till) was deposited as the glaciers retreated.

As rainwater seeped into the soil it became even more acidic as it absorbed organic acids from decaying vegetation. This acidic water easily dissolved vertical lines of weakness (**joints**) in the rock.

The carbonation process widened and deepened the many fissures, which are then termed **grikes**. Flat surfaces of rock a few square metres in area exist between the grikes. These are called **clints**.

Gradually the soil on top of the limestone pavement disappeared down the grikes and was washed deep underground. Today we see this exposed limestone pavement in many areas of Ireland and Europe.

The entire rock surface looks like crazy paving slabs. Grikes provide much-needed shelter for plants and animals in an otherwise barren landscape.

In the Burren area the soil was washed away sometime in the late Bronze Age, roughly 3,000 years ago when the climate deteriorated. The area was cleared of forest and intensely farmed. Without tree roots to bind the soil together it was easily removed by the rain.

Fig. 6 Limestone pavement in the Burren, County Clare

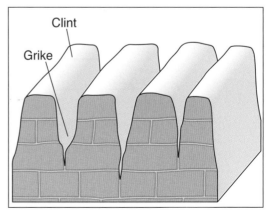

Fig. 7 Exam Diagram: Limestone pavement

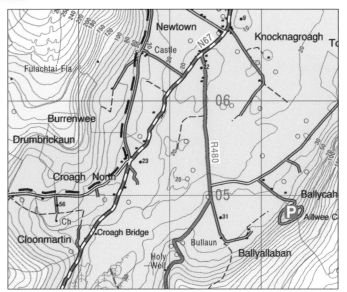

Fig. 8 Map showing a disappearing stream in the Burren. (See the blue line suddenly disappear between Croagh Bridge and the R480.)

Harmless colour dyes are poured into swallow holes to see where the water will reappear. This helps geologists to map underground water reserves.

Swallow holes

Rivers also erode limestone by the process of solution, hydraulic action and abrasion. A river, which may begin in a non-limestone area, disappears underground when it reaches a limestone surface. The place where a river disappears underground is called a swallow hole. Swallow holes may be tiny or large depending on the size of the stream. Pollnagollum swallow hole in the Burren is over 6 m wide and 16 m deep.

Fig. 9 A doline in the Burren, County Clare

Dolines or sinkholes

Another characteristic feature of karst areas is that its surface has many enclosed hollows called dolines. They are also known as sinkholes, e.g. Dunmore Cave, County Kilkenny. Dolines are conical-shaped depressions and it is thought that these hollows form as a result of underground caves collapsing. They may be anything from a few metres up to a kilometre wide and a few metres to 150 m deep.

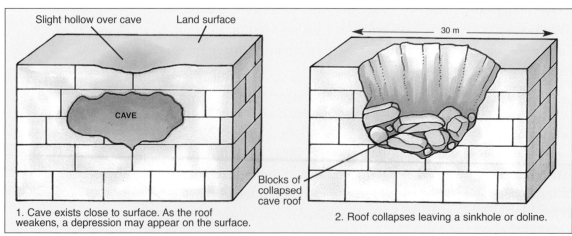

1. Cave exists close to surface. As the roof weakens, a depression may appear on the surface.

2. Roof collapses leaving a sinkhole or doline.

Fig. 10 Exam Diagram: The formation of dolines or sinkholes

Turloughs

In winter and other times of heavy rain all the fissures in limestone fill with water. If this happens, temporary lakes called turloughs form. These are common in the lowland regions of Galway. In summer they dry up as the water sinks underground. Turloughs are often called **seasonal** or **disappearing lakes,** e.g. Gort, County Galway. Filling of the turloughs contributed to the devastating floods in County Galway in the winter of 2009 - 2010.

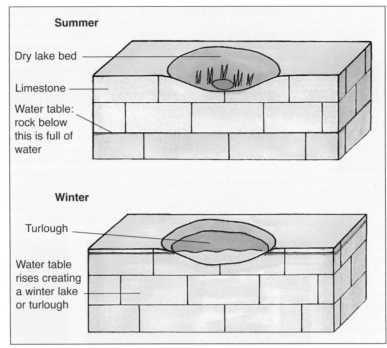

Fig. 11 Exam Diagram: A turlough in summer and winter

Fig. 12 Carron Turlough, County Clare

Underground limestone landforms

Caves/caverns

Once underground, the water from all the swallow holes and **fissures** combine to create streams. By the process of erosion these streams enlarge the passages through which they flow to make caves and caverns. Eventually the underground streams reappear at the surface as **springs** or **resurgences**. Caves can be seen at Dunmore, County Kilkenny and Marble Arch, County Fermanagh. Large caves are called caverns.

Stalactites, stalagmites and pillars

As rainwater flows through the joints and bedding planes of limestone it dissolves the rock by carbonation. The rainwater carries the calcium bicarbonate away in solution deep underground.

When the rainwater reaches the roof of a cave it forms droplets of water which drip constantly from the roof to the floor.

Each droplet evaporates slightly, reversing the carbonation process and leaving a tiny ring-like deposit of **calcite** on the roof. This calcite gradually builds up to form a straw-like tube that hangs from the ceiling. If a tiny fragment of rock blocks the tube, the calcite is deposited on the outside of the straw to form a carrot-shaped formation called a **stalactite** (e.g. Aillwee Cave, County Clare).

Memory Aid
Tites hang on tight to the ceiling, and mites might reach the ceiling!

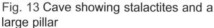

Fig. 13 Cave showing stalactites and a large pillar

Fig. 14 Pillars in a cave in County Clare

If the water drips from a narrow crack in the cave ceiling, a curtain-like formation of calcite is deposited called a curtain stalactite.

At the same time the water droplets splash onto the floor beneath the stalactite and evaporate on the ground, leaving an irregular-shaped mound of calcite known as a **stalagmite.** Sometimes the mounds may cover a large area and are called **flowstone** as they appear to be 'flowing' over the ground but are in fact solid rock.

Eventually a stalactite grows down and meets a stalagmite growing upwards. If this happens a single **column** or **pillar** structure is formed in the cave.

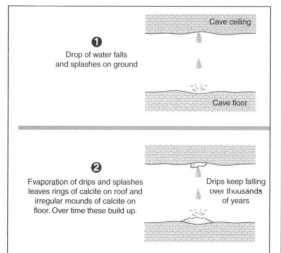

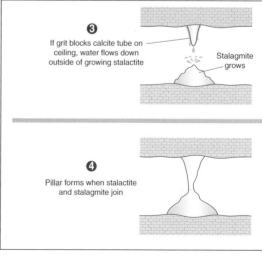

Fig. 15 Exam Diagram: The formation of stalactites, stalagmites and pillars

Chapter Revision Questions

1. Explain two reasons why limestone forms unique landscapes.

2. Explain the term karst.

3. Name three regions of the world apart from Ireland that have karst landscapes.

4. State three characteristics that are common to all karst landscapes.

5. Explain how the process of carbonation weathers limestone.

6. Name and explain the formation of two surface features found in a karst landscape.

7. Name and explain the formation of two underground features found in a karst landscape.

OL Short Questions

8. Select the correct words from the table to complete the paragraph below.

Clints - Pavement - Limestone - Grikes - Carbonation

The sedimentary rock in the photograph is called _____ . It is weathered by the process of _____ . This dissolves calcium carbonate in the rock to form deep grooves called _____ . These grooves are separated from each other by upright blocks called _____ . This forms a landscape which is known as a limestone _____ .

9. Examine the photograph in Question 8.

(i) Which of the following rocks is found in the area in the photograph: **Granite** or **Basalt** or **Limestone**?

(ii) Give the name of a place in Ireland where the rock named in the answer to Part (i) can be found.

(iii) Link the **landform (letter)** with the correct **location (number)** in the box provided. One is completed for you.

Landform	Location	Letter	No
A Clints/Grikes	**1** Underground		
B Cave	**2** Surface		
C Stalactite	**3** Surface		
D Limestone pavement	**4** Underground	**D**	**3**

OL Long Questions

10.

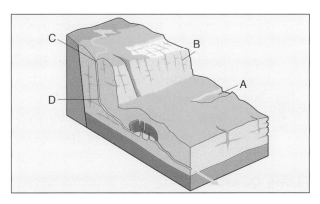

Study the diagram of a karst landscape above and answer the following questions.

(i) Write the correct names for the features labelled A, B, C and D.

(ii) Name the most common type of rock found in areas such as this.

(iii) Name an area in Ireland or in the world where you would find a landscape such as this.

11. Explain with the aid of diagrams how any two underground landforms found in a karst region are formed. Give a named example of each in your answer.

12. Name **one** type of rock which is common in Ireland. Explain (a) how such rocks are formed and (b) how rock structure influences the development of landforms.

    LC Sample Paper

13. Describe how any **two** surface landforms in karst regions are formed.

HL Short Questions

14. (a) Examine this picture of underground karst features. Name **two** features visible in the photograph. Name the type of weathering responsible for the formation of these features.

    (b) Give **one** example in County Clare and **one** example in County Fermanagh of where these features can be found.

HL Long Questions

15. With reference to the Irish landscape, examine the processes which have influenced the development of any landform in a karst region.

16. Examine, with reference to an example you have studied, the formation of one rock type and how it produces a distinctive landscape.

17. With reference to the Irish landscape, examine how the processes of weathering have influenced the development of any **one** limestone feature.

18. Examine the photograph and answer the following questions.

(i) What is the name of the feature marked A?

(ii) What is the name of the feature marked B?

(iii) What is the name of the overall feature in the photograph?

(iv) Name one process which helped to form these features.

(v) Name the type of rock most associated with these features.

Landform Development

Contents

Chapter   8. Fluvial Processes, Patterns and Landforms

Chapter   9. Glacial Processes, Patterns and Landforms

Chapter 10. Coastal Processes, Patterns and Landforms

Chapter 11. Mass Movement Processes, Patterns and Landforms

Note

You are expected to have a general knowledge of *all* surface processes named in chapters 8, 9, 10 and 11. This means that you must be able to *name and describe all the processes and identify the landforms created* on diagrams, maps and photos.

In addition, you must focus on one chapter (8 or 9 or 10 or 11) of your choice and be able to *describe in detail the formation* of the landforms.

You must also study human interaction with river processes OR coastal processes OR mass movement processes. Higher Level students should study how landforms represent a balance between internal and surface forces.

KEY THEME

Surface processes can change in their strength and frequency, influencing the development of landforms. These processes also change over time and place (temporally and spatially). Human activities can impact on the operation of surface processes.

Chapter 8
Fluvial Processes, Patterns and Landforms

At the end of this chapter you should be able to:

- Name and explain the processes of river erosion, transport and deposition.
- Identify river landforms on diagrams, maps and photographs.
- Describe the formation of river landforms.
- Identify the river processes at work on maps and photographs.
- Identify, describe and explain river drainage patterns.
- Describe using case studies how people interact with rivers.
- Explain how changing sea/land levels affect river processes. (HL)
- Discuss the ancient development of Irish rivers. (HL)

Contents

8.1 Rivers
8.2 A river's course
8.3 Fluvial processes
8.4 The life cycle of a river
8.5 Landforms found along a river's course
8.6 Human interaction with river processes

Case Studies:
- The impact of canalisation: *The River Rhine*
- The impact of dam building: *The Three Gorges Dam*
- Flood control on an Irish river

8.7 River rejuvenation **(HL)**
8.8 The ancient development of Irish rivers **(HL)**
Case Study: River capture of the River Suir
Questions

If you are choosing this chapter to study in detail, you must be able to explain river processes, how the landforms are made, and be able to identify them on diagrams, maps and photos. The extra material you need to know is indicated by a green arrow. Higher Level students should study how landforms represent a balance between internal and surface forces. If you are not choosing this chapter, then you should be able to identify the landforms on diagrams, maps and photos and state the processes that made them.

8.1 Rivers

Rivers create a variety of landforms around the world. From immense waterfalls to deep gorges, gentle valleys to vast flood plains, rivers shape our world and provide food, water, energy, recreation, transport and spiritual meaning to millions of people.

Rivers have been used and misused by people across the globe: we dam their flow, confine their course and pollute their waters. They are also a source of conflict: India and Pakistan argue over the Ganges, Egypt and Ethiopia disagree over the Nile, several states in America dispute the best way to manage the Colorado.

In the future, agreement and compromise over river management will be necessary if millions of people are to benefit from the wealth provided by rivers.

Fig. 1 The Seven Falls, Cheyenne Canyon, Colorado, USA

8.2 A river's course

Rivers flow from their source high in the mountains down through their course until they reach their mouth at the sea or lakes. The area drained by one river and its tributaries is called the **drainage basin area**. Hills and mountains, known as **watersheds,** usually separate different drainage basin areas from each other, e.g. the River Slaney and the River Barrow are separated by the watershed of the Blackstairs Mountains. Different river patterns may be seen in each drainage basin area. The point where rivers meet each other is called a **confluence.**

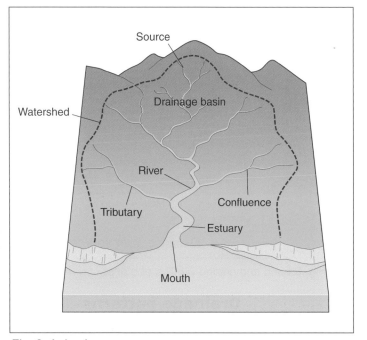
Fig. 2 A river's course

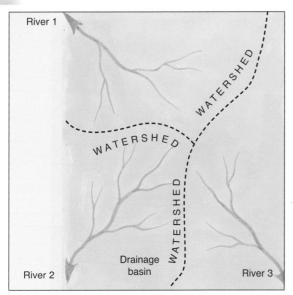

Fig. 3 Watershed and drainage basin

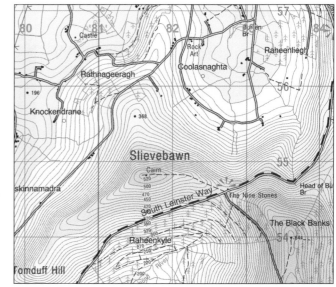

Fig. 4 Draw a line along the watershed on this map.

As the river moves along its course it tries to reach a balance between erosion and deposition. This balance creates a **graded profile.** Because of the varied rock types over which rivers flow, they rarely achieve a graded profile so the slope of a river's course is instead called its **long profile.**

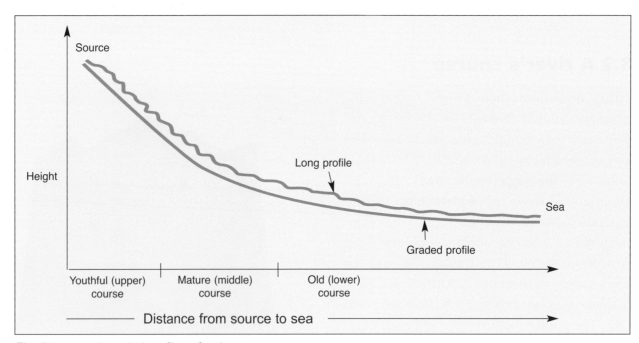

Fig. 5 Long and graded profiles of a river

Drainage patterns

Drainage patterns are the shapes made by a river and its **tributaries** as they flow over the landscape. There are three main patterns visible in the Irish landscape.

1. Dendritic drainage pattern
2. Trellis drainage pattern
3. Radial drainage pattern

1. Dendritic pattern

This pattern is like the branching shape of a tree. Each river consists of a main 'trunk' which is fed by its tributaries (the branches). These patterns form where the slope of the land is fairly even and the rock type is similar (uniform) across the drainage basin.

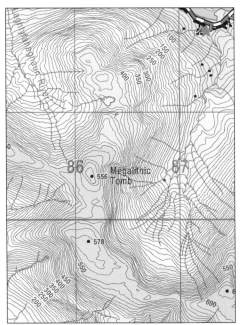

Fig. 6 Close-up of a dendritic drainage pattern

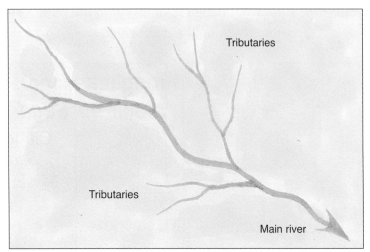

Fig. 7 Dendritic drainage patterns resemble the branching shape of a tree.

Fig. 8 Dendritic drainage pattern in Yemen (space shuttle photograph). In the photograph there is no water in the river channels shown. Yemen is a desert country today. This dendritic river pattern was created thousands of years ago when the climate in this region was much wetter and could support a large river such as the one whose fossil drainage is seen today.

2. Trellis pattern

In this pattern, tributaries join the main river at right angles, forming a pattern similar to a garden-wall trellis.

These patterns form when the main stream flows across landscapes with bands of hard and soft rock. Smaller tributaries cut their valleys in the bands of soft rock. They then join the main river at right angles.

Many glaciated valleys also have this pattern. Streams flow down steep valley sides from hanging valleys into the main valley with little space to meander across before reaching the main river.

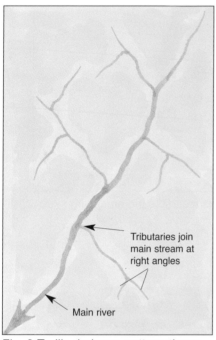

Fig. 9 Trellis drainage pattern shows tributaries joining the main river at right angles.

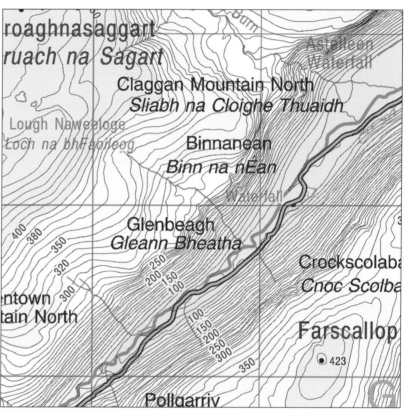

Fig. 10 Trellis drainage pattern

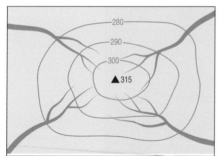

Fig. 11 Radial drainage pattern: rivers flow from a central upland area.

3. Radial pattern

This pattern forms when rivers flow in many directions away from an upland area, much like water flowing off an umbrella. The rivers radiate out from a central upland area. Round or oval-shaped hills show this best, for example Brandon Hill in County Kilkenny.

Find out more about rivers. Log on to:
www.geography.learnontheinternet.co.uk/topics/river.html

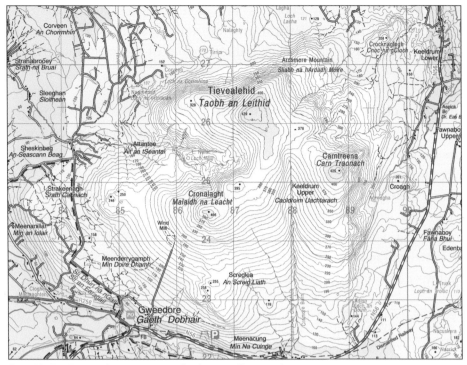

Fig. 12 Radial drainage pattern in County Donegal

8.3 Fluvial processes

Rivers shape the landscape by the processes of erosion, transport and deposition. Erosion breaks down the landscape, transport moves it and deposition drops the eroded river material. The sediment carried by a river is called its **load**. The load is created by erosion and the addition of sediment by mass movement (soil moved downhill by rain and gravity) from the valley sides. Much of the river's **energy** is used in transporting the load. These processes of erosion, transport and deposition continually reshape the landscape over which the river flows. River processes are also known as **fluvial processes**.

Factors affecting fluvial processes

The ability of a river to shape and reshape the landscape depends upon the following factors:
- River volume
- River speed/velocity
- Slope/gradient
- Channel width and depth
- Load

Each of these factors influence the river's energy (its ability to do its work). The more energy a river has, the more erosion it is capable of doing.

River volume and velocity/speed

The energy of a river depends on the volume of water and speed of flow (velocity). Large fast-flowing rivers are very powerful. Rivers in flood do so much damage

because they are faster and larger than normal and have immense energy. They can cut deeply into the river channel (**vertical erosion**) and carry huge quantities of sediment. The Mississippi River carries one million tonnes of sediment into the sea each day.

River gradient and channel width and depth

The speed of a river is affected by the steepness of the slope (**gradient**) down which it flows, by the depth of the water and by the width of the river channel. It is also affected by the roughness of the river bed. Youthful rivers with large boulders in their channel flow more slowly than older rivers with smoother channel beds.

Deep rivers flowing down sloping land are very powerful with lots of energy. Shallow rivers flowing over flatter ground are less powerful. This is because of the drag (**friction**) between the river with its bed and banks. Wide and deep rivers flow faster than shallower and narrower river channels.

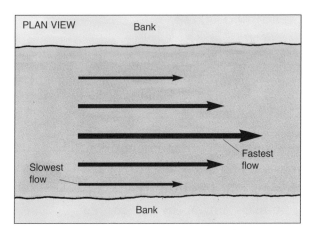
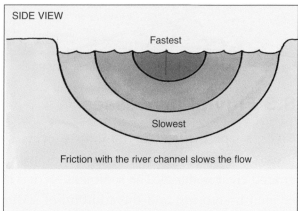

Fig. 13 The effect of friction on a river's flow: the speed of a river changes as you cross from one bank to another.

Fig. 14 The River Dee in Llangollen, Wales, in flood

Processes of river erosion

The processes of river erosion are very important. Erosion can occur at the river banks (**lateral erosion**) and at the riverbed (vertical erosion), causing a widening and deepening of the river channel. River erosion processes are **(a) hydraulic action, (b) abrasion, (c) solution** and **(d) attrition.**

(a) Hydraulic action (the force of moving water)

The force of moving water erodes the river channel. Fast-moving water forces out loose rock and earth from the riverbed and banks. Banks collapse as the turbulent water undercuts the river bank, a process known as **bank caving**. Bubbles of air in the turbulent water burst (**cavitation**) and the tiny shockwaves loosen the rocks and soil on the bed and banks making it easier to wash away.

(b) Abrasion (corrasion)

This is the wearing away of the riverbed and banks by its load. The load scrapes and smoothes the channel as it whirls and rolls along in the moving water.

(c) Attrition

This is when rock particles of the load hit off each other. This process gradually wears away the stones to make them smooth and round.

Fig. 15 Erosion processes are active on the Owenreagh River, County Kerry.

(d) Solution

This is the chemical process whereby river water dissolves the soft rock over which it flows. This process is very effective in limestone regions where soluble minerals are dissolved and transported away in solution. Discoloured river water is evidence of solution.

Processes of river transport

The load created by river erosion is **transported** by the river to a new location. Any material carried along the riverbed is called its **bedload**.

River transport processes are: **(1) solution, (2) suspension, (3) saltation** and **(4) traction.**

(1) Solution

The load is carried dissolved in the water. This load is invisible but may discolour the river water.

(2) Suspension

Fine sediment is carried within the flowing water. Most of the river's load is carried this way. This process gives the water a muddy brown appearance, especially seen during floods when turbulence keeps the sediment mixed up in the water.

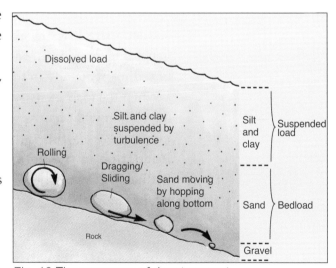

Fig. 16 The processes of river transport

(3) Saltation

The load bounces and hops along the riverbed. This process helps to make the pebbles and stones smooth and more rounded.

(4) Traction

During times of flood the larger bedload (rocks and boulders) is rolled and dragged along the riverbed by the fast-flowing river.

Processes of river deposition

Eventually the load is **deposited**. Deposition processes can shape the land by leaving sediment in new places, making new land or adding to existing land.

There are several reasons why a river deposits its load.

Fig. 17 River deposition in the Glendasan River, County Wicklow

Reduction in the river's velocity

If a river slows down, deposition will occur. Rivers slow down when they enter a lake or the sea. Rivers also slow down when they shrink in times of low rainfall or high temperatures. They slow down when their slope/gradient decreases and when they meet an obstruction to their flow. For example, man-made dams blocking a river's flow cause huge amounts of sediment to be deposited behind them.

The size of the load increases

Many situations cause the load to increase. Mass movements, e.g. a landslide into the river, adds a sudden extra load. Heavy rainfall increases the river's energy and erosive power, generating more load. Fast-flowing tributaries can also add their load to the amount of sediment already in the river.

When the load increases, the river may not have enough energy to carry it and so deposition will occur.

Reduction in the volume of the river

Reducing the volume of water in the river reduces its energy, causing deposition. Evaporation as the river flows through a hot area, the ending of the rainy season, taking water for cities and irrigation schemes, as well as drought can all reduce the amount of water in a river.

For some animations of river processes, log on to:
http://serc.carleton.edu/NAGTWorkshops/geomorph/visualizations/erosion_deposition.htm

8.4 The life cycle of a river

Depending on the river's energy, different processes will occur in different parts of the river along its course. These different processes (erosion, transport and deposition) create distinct landforms along the river valley which enable us to divide the river's long profile into **youthful, mature** and **old age** stages. These can also be called the upper course, middle course and lower course.

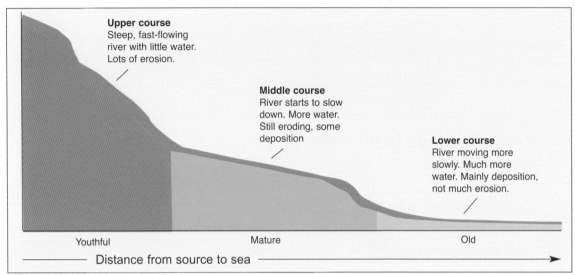

Fig. 18 The processes that occur along the course of a river

8.5 Landforms found along a river's course

> **REMEMBER!**
>
> **You need to name, explain and apply the river processes involved in your explanation of landform formation.**

The table below lists river landforms organised according to the river stage with which they are associated.

RIVER LANDFORMS		
Stage	**Landforms**	**Example**
Youthful stage (vertical erosion is dominant)	V-shaped valleys	Upper course of River Barrow; most Irish rivers
	Interlocking spurs	Upper River Lee
	Waterfalls	Powerscourt, County Wicklow; Sheen Falls, County Mayo; Angel Falls, Paraguay
	Gorges	Upper Glencullen River, County Wicklow; Yangtze Gorge, China
Mature stage (lateral erosion and deposition are dominant)	Meanders	River Boyne
	Oxbow lakes	River Shannon near Roosky, County Roscommon
	Flood plains	River Barrow

RIVER LANDFORMS

Stage	Landforms	Example
Old stage (lateral erosion and deposition are dominant)	Wider flood plains	River Shannon
	Levees	The Rivers Moy, Shannon and Barrow
	Wider, flatter valleys	River Liffey
	Larger meanders	The River Shannon at Carrick-on-Shannon; River Barrow, County Kilkenny
	Oxbow lakes and meander scars	Mississippi River, USA
	Deltas	Estuarine delta in River Shannon; lacustrine delta at the Upper Lake, Glendalough, County Wicklow

Youthful stage landforms

1. V-shaped valleys
2. Interlocking spurs
3. Waterfalls and gorges

The processes of hydraulic action and abrasion are most effective in the youthful stage because the river is flowing fastest here.

1. V-shaped valleys

Main processes: hydraulic action, abrasion, mass movement, weathering, vertical erosion. **Example:** River Moy, County Mayo.

A V-shaped valley is a narrow valley that has a **cross section** suggesting the shape of the letter V. These valleys are landforms of river erosion found in the youthful stage of a river's course.

V-shaped valleys form in mountains or other highland areas where streams are flowing down steep slopes. Such valleys are formed by the river cutting downwards into its bed. This is known as vertical erosion.

The floor of a V-shaped valley is very narrow and there is little or no flat land beside the stream. The stream channel is often very narrow and shallow.

IN DEPTH – V-shaped valley

> **All In Depth sections contain material you need to know if you are studying this chapter in detail.**

The volume and speed of flow of a young river is often low due to the lack of tributaries feeding the river in its upper stages and due to the friction between the water and the rough, stony bed. Where the gradient is steeper and the channel bed is less rough, the river velocity can increase. Vertical erosion will then occur, especially following heavy rainfall or melting of winter snow. Hydraulic action, an erosion process caused by the physical force of flowing water, loosens and carries away the bedrock and soil of the river channel. Abrasion – erosion caused by the river's load – will wear down bedrock as the load hits the sides and bed of the river channel. This will deepen the level of the riverbed and form steeper sides to the channel.

The valley sides will also be exposed to weathering and mass movement. Mechanical and chemical weathering weaken the rock and soil on the valley sides. Rainfall and snowmelt may trigger landslides of material into the river making the valley even deeper.

The depth of the V is controlled by a combination of several factors:

- The speed of vertical erosion: in general fast rates of erosion lead to deeper valleys.
- The type of bedrock: hard rocks such as granite resist erosion, making more shallow valleys.
- Weathering and mass movement on the sides of the valley: These processes weaken and loosen the stones and soil on the sides of the valley. Scree and soil move downhill under the force of gravity and add to the river's load, increasing its ability to erode and deepen its channel by abrasion.

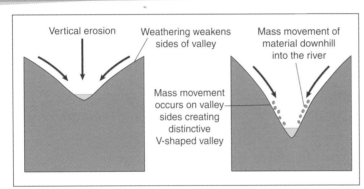

Fig. 19 Exam Diagram: Formation of a V-shaped valley

Fig. 20 A V-shaped valley in a Scottish river

113

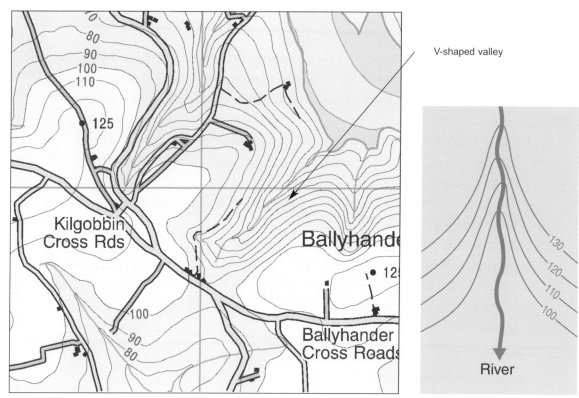

Fig. 21 A V-shaped valley near Kinsale, County Cork and contour pattern of a V-shaped valley

2. Interlocking spurs

Main processes: Hydraulic action, abrasion, solution, vertical erosion, winding streams.

Example: Upper stage of the River Glen, County Down

Interlocking spurs are landforms of river erosion. They are hills or ridges of land (**spurs**) around which the river winds. If you look up a river valley, these spurs or hills seem to overlap across each other **(interlock)** blocking the view of the river. Viewed from above you can clearly see the river winding around these hills/spurs.

IN DEPTH – Interlocking spurs

Interlocking spurs are found in the young stage of the river's lifecycle. As youthful rivers are small they do not have the energy to remove large obstacles in their path. Young rivers do not carry a large load so abrasion is limited. Hydraulic action is the dominant erosion process. As the river flows, it winds around the hard patches of rock found along its course. These irregularities in the channel further deflect the river from side to side, so that it changes from a relatively straight to a winding course.

The current is stronger on the outside of a bend as hydraulic action and abrasion are concentrated here and the bends become more developed. This erosion of the river valley leaves parts of the valley sides projecting as small hills or spurs into the bends in the river channel.

Eventually in the middle and lower stages the river becomes larger and more powerful by the addition of water from tributaries and removes the interlocking spurs completely.

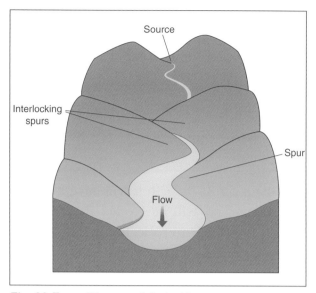

Fig. 22 Exam Diagram: Interlocking spurs

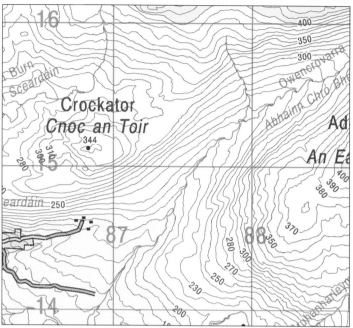

Fig. 23 Map showing interlocking spurs

Fig. 24 Interlocking spurs in Switzerland

3. Waterfalls

Main processes: abrasion, hydraulic action, solution, vertical erosion
Example: Powerscourt, County Wicklow; Torc, County Kerry

A waterfall is a vertical fall of water found in the young stage of a river and is one of the most spectacular erosional features formed by rivers.

IN DEPTH – Waterfalls

The world's highest waterfall is Angel Falls in Venezuela at 979 m in height, over 780 m of which is a free fall.

When a river meets a band of hard rock lying across its path it will have difficulty eroding it. Any soft rock on the downstream end will be eroded more quickly (**differential erosion**), making the river fall over the hard rock. The hydraulic force of the falling water rushing into cracks in the soft rock causes it to break up. This broken rock then uses abrasion to widen and deepen the foot of the waterfall, making a **plunge pool**. The plunge pool under the Niagara Falls is 35 m deep.

The falling water splashes against the back wall of the waterfall, dissolving some of it away by solution. This **splash back** soon creates a cave behind the waterfall leaving an overhang of hard rock at the top of the waterfall. This eventually collapses making the waterfall retreat upstream. This process of retreat is called **headward** erosion.

As the waterfall moves back upstream, a steep-sided valley called a **gorge** is formed downstream from the waterfall. The gorge from the Niagara Falls is 11 km long and up to 91 m deep. In the past, the waterfall retreated between 0.6 to 3 m per year before modern flow-control measures and HEP stations slowed the retreat.

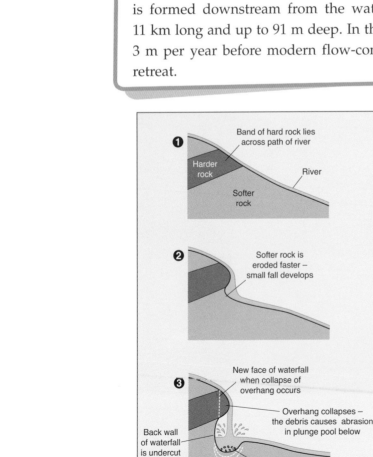

Fig. 26 Exam Diagram: The development of a waterfall

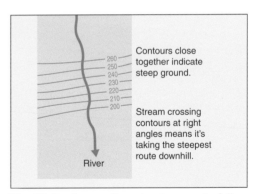

Fig. 25 Contour pattern to show waterfalls

Fig. 27 Waterfall on the Vartry River, County Wicklow

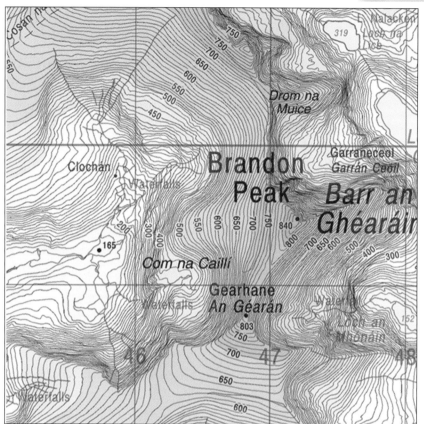

Fig. 28 Waterfalls and possible sites of waterfalls in County Kerry. Look for mountain rivers crossing contour lines at right angles.

Mature stage landforms

1. Meanders
2. Oxbow lakes and meander scars/mortlakes
3. Flood plains

1. Meanders

Main processes: lateral erosion, hydraulic action, abrasion, cavitation, deposition

Example: River Boyne, County Meath

Rivers naturally flow in a winding manner. This makes the water swing from side to side, eroding an S-shaped channel into the landscape. These S-shaped bends are called meanders. They are found in the mature stage of a river and enlarged in the old stage.

IN DEPTH – Meanders

The water flows fastest on the outside bend of the meander, causing erosion by hydraulic action and abrasion. (It is similar to being thrown to one side of a bus as it goes around a corner.) Because the flow is faster and has more energy at this point, it erodes the outer bend with more force. Hydraulic action and abrasion can cause undercutting, creating a steep **river cliff** which is cut into the bank. Hydraulic action also forces bubbles of air into the river bank, creating shock waves inside the bank. This is called **cavitation**. This further loosens the bank and some falls away. The continued undercutting of the bank leads to its collapse (**bank caving**) and a widening of the river channel (lateral erosion).

The speed of flow is much slower on the inside bend causing deposition. A small beach called a **point bar** is deposited on the inside bend. This point bar further deflects the fast-moving water to the outer bend, increasing lateral erosion there.

Gradually, the river wanders over its flood plain in a series of sweeping meanders. The continuous erosion and deposition makes the meanders move across the landscape a bit like a snake. These are called **migrating meanders.**

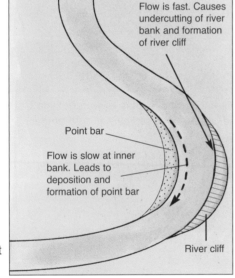

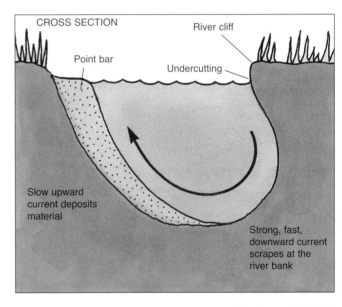

Fig. 29 Exam Diagram: The development of meanders

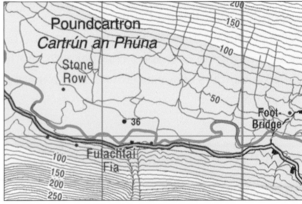

Fig. 30 Map to show meanders on a river near Poundcarton, County Donegal

Fig. 31 Meanders on a river in County Galway

ACTIVITY
Look at the photograph. Identify a point bar and a river cliff.

118

2. Oxbow lakes

Main processes: flooding, erosion, deposition

Example: River Moy, County Mayo

Oxbow lakes are the remains of meanders that have been cut off from the river's course. They are often called **cut-offs** for this reason. They are found in the mature stage of a river.

IN DEPTH – Oxbow lakes

Oxbow lakes form when meanders become so developed that the bend is very tight and there is only a narrow neck of land separating the two sides of the meander bend. In times of flood the water flows across the neck of land rather than going around the bend. By doing this, hydraulic action and abrasion erode a new path for the river, straightening it in the process.

Because the river is not confined between its banks as it flows across the meander loop, it slows down and loses energy. This leads to deposition which, over time, seals off the old meander bend. The old meander loop is now cut off from the new course. Slowly it dries out because of evaporation and seepage through the ground and becomes a dead lake or a **mortlake**. Mortlakes are also known as **meander scars**.

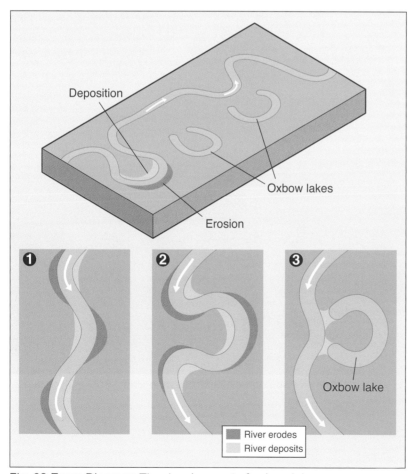

Fig. 32 Exam Diagram: The development of oxbow lakes

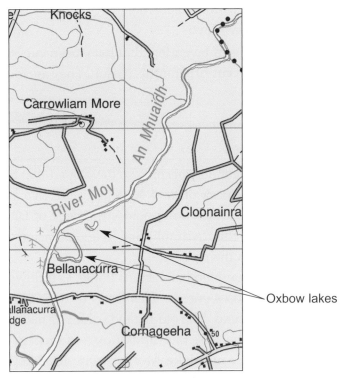

Fig. 33 Oxbow lakes on the River Moy, County Mayo

ACTIVITY

Identify the mature stage river landforms A-D.

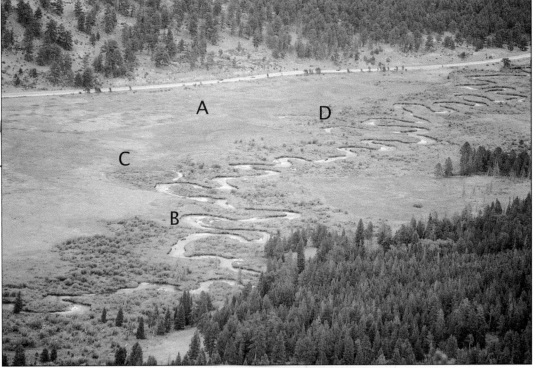

Fig. 34 Meanders, oxbow lakes and flood plain, Horseshoe Park, Rocky Mountain National Park, USA

3. Flood plains

Main processes: flooding, deposition

Example: River Suir, County Waterford

A flood plain is a flat area of land either side of the river. Flood plains are created by river deposition. They may be found in the mature and old stages of a river.

IN DEPTH – Flood plains

Meanders swinging across the valley floor remove interlocking spurs as they migrate downstream. Doing this, they create a flat area in the centre of the valley. This is the flood plain. During a flood the river overspills its banks and the flood water flows across the flood plain. As the river spreads out across the flood plain it loses some of its energy. This causes the river to slow down. The flood water gradually soaks (**percolates**) into the ground, depositing a thin layer of sediment known as **alluvium** onto the flood plain. This is very fertile. These sediments may be many metres deep representing centuries of repeated flooding. Because of their flat and fertile nature, flood plains are heavily populated. The edges of flood plains are known as **bluffs**. One of the flattest flood plains in Ireland is that found on the River Suir near Clonmel.

Flood plains are a river's safety valve. In times of heavy rain the river has to overflow its banks onto its flood plain. The flat ground slows the river down and encourages deposition. This reduces the damage caused by erosion.

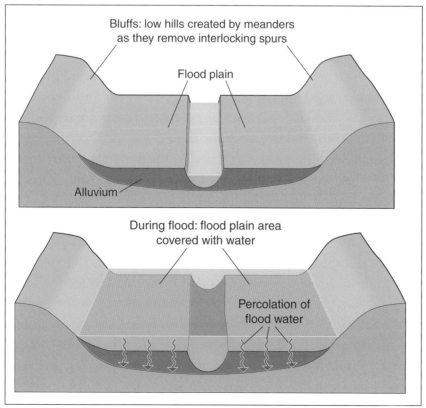

Fig. 35 Exam Diagram: An uncovered and covered flood plain

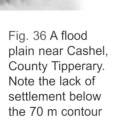

Fig. 36 A flood plain near Cashel, County Tipperary. Note the lack of settlement below the 70 m contour line in some grid squares.

Fig. 37 A flood plain on the River Barrow

Old stage landforms

The landforms made in the old stage are similar to those of the mature stage but are larger. More pronounced meanders swing in wide sweeps across the very wide, flat flood plain of the river valley. There may also be many oxbow lakes and meander scars.

Other characteristic landforms found in the old stage are levees and deltas, both depositional features.

1. Levees

Main processes: flooding, deposition

Example: River Moy, south of Ballina in County Mayo.

A levee is a wide low ridge of sediment deposited on riverbanks. They are landforms of river deposition found in the old stage of a river's course.

IN DEPTH – Levees

On its flood plain an old river flows over very flat land (low gradient). It is carrying a large load of sand and silt.

During a flood, the river spills over its banks and across its flood plain. As the river floods over its banks, the water spreads out, slows down and deposits its load of sediment. The largest/coarsest particles of gravel and sand are deposited closest to the banks due to the sudden decrease in the river's energy. These deposits are called levees. Finer sediments (alluvium) are carried by the flood water further out over the flood plain. The alluvium is then deposited over the flood plain as the water seeps (percolates) into the ground after the flood has finished.

After many flood events the levee is enlarged. At the same time, during normal flow the river will deposit material on the riverbed. This will raise the level of the riverbed and the river itself.

The combination of levee growth and deposition leads to a situation where the entire river is confined between the levees in a channel that is higher than its flood plain. This would cause flooding unless the levees are strong enough to prevent flood water reaching the flood plain. Levees are often built and strengthened by humans to protect valuable farm land and urban settlements built on the flood plain, e.g. along the Mississippi River in the USA. Levees may be built up using sediment dredged from the riverbed, e.g. along the banks of the River Barrow, north of New Ross in County Wexford.

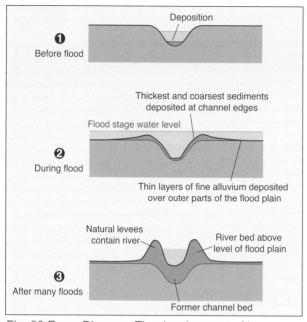

Deposition

① Before flood

② During flood

Thickest and coarsest sediments deposited at channel edges

Flood stage water level

Thin layers of fine alluvium deposited over outer parts of the flood plain

Natural levees contain river

River bed above level of flood plain

③ After many floods

Former channel bed

Fig. 38 Exam Diagram: The development of levees

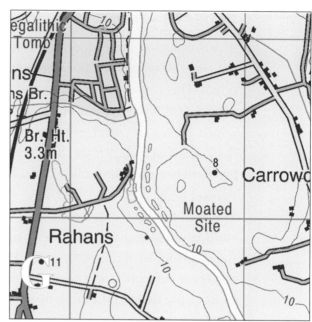

Fig. 39 Map showing levees on the River Moy, County Mayo

Fig. 40 The photographs show both sides of a levee on the banks of the River Barrow, County Kilkenny. The water level is higher than the flood plain in the photo on the right.

2. Deltas

Main processes: deposition

Example: Lough Tay, County Wicklow – a lacustrine delta; Shannon Estuary, County Limerick – an estuarine delta.

Deltas are landforms of river deposition found in the old stage of a river. Deltas are areas of land at the mouth of a river made from deposits of alluvium, sand and gravel. Deltas occur where tidal currents and longshore drift (see Chapter 10) are not powerful enough to remove the river deposits. Deltas can form in a lake and are called **lacustrine** deltas; those that occur at the coast are called **marine deltas.** For marine deltas to form, a river has to flow out into a low energy coastline. As the Irish coastline is so indented (jagged) this does not occur. However delta deposits have built up along some Irish estuaries, e.g. the Shannon Estuary.

IN DEPTH – Deltas

Rivers transport huge amounts of sediment (load) from their source to the sea. When the river enters a sea, lake or reservoir, the river speed is suddenly forced to slow down. This causes a rapid loss of energy so deposition occurs.

As the fresh river water meets the salty sea water, a small electric charge is created which makes the sand, silt and clay particles clump together and sink to the sea floor. Gradually layers of deposited sediment build up at the river mouth. These layers of sediment are called beds. Deltas contain different types of bed.

Foreset beds

The heaviest and coarser silt and sand sediments are deposited first due to the sudden decrease in river velocity upon meeting the sea. These sediments settle on the sea floor at the river mouth. They are called foreset beds. The river is like a conveyor belt constantly adding foreset beds to the sea. The sediment rolls down the front of the delta and builds up in sloping layers covering the sea bed. This makes the delta grow out to sea. Foreset beds make up the majority of the delta.

Bottomset beds

Meanwhile the finest clay sediments are carried in suspension a little further out to sea and slowly settle in front of this main delta. They are laid down in horizontal layers which are called bottomset beds.

The bottomset beds will eventually be covered over by the foreset bed sediments as they roll down the front of the delta face.

Topset beds

Lastly the topset beds are deposited by the river in horizontal layers on the foreset beds of the advancing delta. These are generally smaller gravelly sediments deposited after the larger foreset material.

As the delta sediments build up close to the surface of the water, they are exposed at low tide. The river sometimes splits into smaller streams called **distributaries** as it flows over the exposed sediments. Distributaries occur in larger rivers. Sometimes after floods the main channel of the river shifts elsewhere forming a new delta elsewhere in the river mouth.

Over many years the delta deposits are stabilised by plants and people can live on them, e.g. the Nile delta and Bangladesh on the delta of the River Ganges.

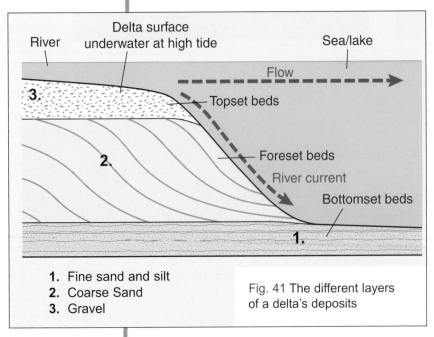

1. Fine sand and silt
2. Coarse Sand
3. Gravel

Fig. 41 The different layers of a delta's deposits

IN DEPTH – Deltas

Delta shapes

Deltas have many shapes and sizes. They are named delta after the letter D in the Greek alphabet.

1. Arcuate delta (arc-shaped)

This delta has a triangular shape and the apex of the triangle points upstream. It is named after the shape of the Nile delta in Egypt.

These deltas are made of coarse sand and gravel which are very porous so there are many distributaries which rarely meet.

Examples: The Po in Italy, which extends at a rate of 12 m per year. The Nile delta in Egypt. The River Flesk has a small arcuate delta where it enters Lough Leane in County Kerry (See Fig. 42).

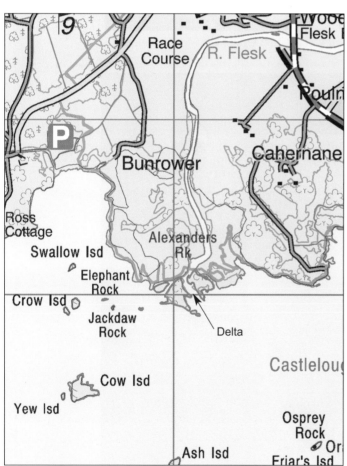

Fig. 42 The lacustrine delta of the River Flesk, near Killarney, County Kerry

2. Bird's foot delta

These deltas form when rivers carry large amounts of fine sediment and there are very few distributaries. Levees are deposited along any distributaries that form, and so long finger-like projections extend into the sea forming a delta with a shape similar to that of a bird's foot.

Example: The Mississippi River, which extends at a rate of 75 m per year.

3. Estuarine delta

This type of delta forms when deposits are dropped in long, narrow lines, like strips, on both sides of the estuary.

Example: The Shannon Estuary.

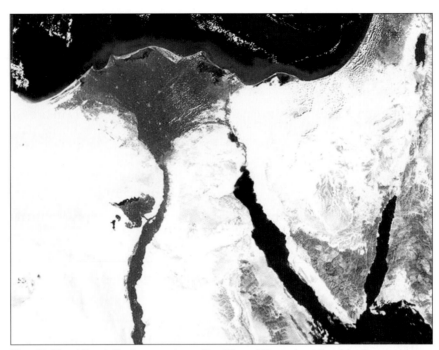

Fig. 43 The Nile delta forms where the River Nile enters the Mediterranean Sea.

Fig. 44 The Mississippi delta from space. River water spills out into the Gulf of Mexico where its suspended load is deposited to form the Mississippi River delta. Marshes and mudflats grow between the shipping channels that have been cut into the delta.

8.6 Human interaction with river processes

> You must study human interaction with river processes OR coastal processes OR mass movement processes

Human activities (processes) can impact on the operation of surface processes. This is seen in the management of rivers. Rivers are important resources for humanity. They have been used and misused by people for centuries. Most major towns and cities in the world were built beside rivers because they provided:

- Water supply and fish
- A fertile flood plain
- Transport and trade artery

- Defence
- Bridging points

Controlling rivers

Many people see rivers as wild things to be tamed and controlled. We do this by:

1. Building **dams** and **reservoirs** to hold back floods and generate power, e.g. the Three Gorges Dam, China.
2. Changing the course of rivers. We straighten and bypass their meanders to allow ships travel more quickly. This is called **canalisation,** e.g. River Rhine, Germany.
3. Strengthening and **raising levees** so that we can settle on once uninhabitable flood plains, e.g. River Rhine, Germany.

But rivers are not always predictable. Changes in the global climate cause more frequent extreme weather events. These create massive floods that quickly wash away man's attempts to restrain our wild rivers. Humanity is beginning to realise that we must work with river processes and not against them. In Ireland controlling floods is an important issue for rural and urban areas, e.g. Clonmel, County Tipperary.

1. The impact of canalisation: the River Rhine

- The River Rhine is a major artery for transporting goods and people through Europe. Its mouth in Rotterdam, Holland is regarded as the 'Gateway to Europe'. The Rhine flows through or links by canals nine European countries, passing through some of the most highly-industrialised and densely-populated urban areas of Europe.

- The need to reduce costs and save time has led to the development of this river. For example, constructing canals and bypassing meander bends has shortened the river by 50 km. This has affected all of the river processes. The river velocity is increased because the river is now flowing higher inside the confined canals and levees.

- Canalisation also increases the erosive power of the river. Because flooding is controlled, deposition cannot occur on the surrounding flood plain. Some deposition occurs on the riverbed, also raising the level of the river within the levees.

case study

case study

● Continued urban sprawl and reduction in farmland has meant run-off from rain reaches streams and rivers more quickly than in the past. Instead of rainwater seeping through the ground and taking many days to reach the river, it now reaches it quickly in a matter of hours through pipes and drains. It used to take up to five days for a flood surge to pass downstream but today, due to man's control of the river's natural processes, it takes three days. This has led to increased flooding during heavy rains. The flood water put great pressure on the polders/reclaimed land and levees along the river. Floods in 1995 and 2002 saw the Rhine return to much of its natural course. Holland spent €1.3 billion on flood control measures in the 1980s. Its polderlands are protected by levees of 10 m high.

● During floods in Strasbourg, the authorities pump water into retention basins outside the levees. These basins reduce the floodwater height by 60 cm for 10–12 hours. When the flood has receded the water is pumped back into the river. These retention basins are then left as nature reserves or grazing land.

Find out more about the Rhine floods.
Log on to:
http://www.geographyfieldwork.com/RhineCauses.htm and
www.rivernet.org/rhin/welcome.htm

Fig. 45 The River Rhine

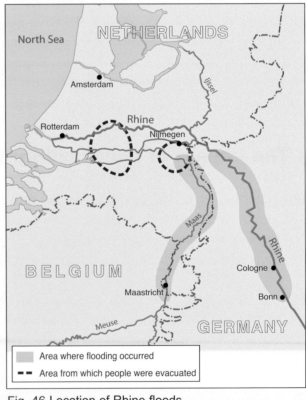

Fig. 46 Location of Rhine floods

2. The impact of dam building: The Three Gorges Dam, China

One of the world's largest schemes to control a river and manage its flow is at the Three Gorges Dam in China – the biggest and most powerful dam ever built in the world. Devastating floods in 1931 killed 250,000 people living along the Yangtze and Whang Ho rivers. Annual floods on these rivers would still kill thousands but for the dam.

The flooding of the land behind the Yangtze dam for the reservoir led to the displacement of over two million people as their land, homes, cities and industries were flooded.

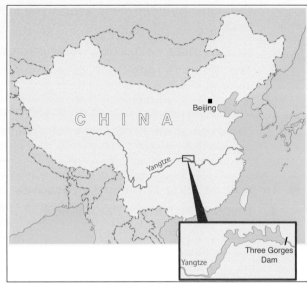

Fig. 47 Location of the Three Gorges Dam project

Hydro Electric Power Station at the Three Gorges Dam, China

The dam was constructed to control floods in the Yangtze River, to provide reliable, clean energy and as a source of water for irrigation and domestic/industrial use. The Three Gorges dam is 185 m high and 2.3 km wide. The reservoir is 560 km long and 160 m deep. From Malin Head to Mizen Head, Ireland would fit into the reservoir's length.

Impact on river erosion processes

1. Dams usually reduce the size and frequency of the high flow/flood events that reshape and **rejuvenate** (make young again) the channel through erosion and the deposition of sediment.
2. As water is trapped and then released to generate electricity, the flow of the water downstream is interrupted, creating surges in velocity and thereby increasing hydraulic action and increasing vertical erosion.
3. Downstream of the dam, the controlled river is often smaller and carries less load; this can increase hydraulic action which can further deepen and widen the river channel resulting in entrenched channels that are much lower than the flood plain.
4. On occasions when heavy rains occur, it may be necessary to release excess water from the reservoir due to dangerous water pressure on the dam wall. This can lead to flooding and erosion downstream, similar to what happened in Ireland at the Inniscarra dam in Cork city in the winter of 2009.

Impact on river deposition processes

1. Dams are built across river valleys to trap river water, creating reservoirs behind the dam wall.
2. Dam walls cause deposition to build up behind them. This sediment would, prior to the dam's construction, have been transported downstream and deposited as alluvium during floods onto floodplains. Because of dams, the middle and lower stages of the river's lifecycle are deprived of fertile alluvium. Soil fertility is lost as flood plain sediments are not replaced.

case study

3. The Yangtze carries 37.6 kg of silt per cubed metre of river water which builds up behind the dam. In older dams across the world, such accumulation of silt would put increasing pressure on the dam wall, but at the Three Gorges engineers have built the dam system so that muddy silt-laden water passes through.

4. The Three Gorges Dam, like many other dams, reduces the level of water in the river channel, affecting the lower stages of the river, especially the delta area; salt water could then seep back into the delta lands and poison freshwater ecosystems and fertile land could be turned into waterlogged salt marsh. The Shanghai Delta is being carefully monitored to ensure this does not happen.

Impact on river transport processes

1. Dams interrupt the natural flow of a river and reduce its ability to carry sediment from source to sea.

2. Some sediments carried by the river are trapped in the reservoir behind the dam. Its impact on the river downstream of the dam is marked by a dramatic change in the quality of the sediments. Deltas at river mouths are deprived of their coarse foreset bed material and are now more easily eroded by the sea. Deltas downstream of dams often shrink as a result of dam building. The Yangtse delta at Shanghai is at risk.

3. Changes in size of load being carried means that the type of transport process occurring such as solution, suspension, saltation and traction also change.

4. River flooding is controlled by the dam so the people and their livelihoods are protected downstream, thereby stopping a repeat of the loss of life.

Fig. 48 The Three Gorges Dam showing the power of the flow of water through the dam.

3. Flood control on an Irish river

The Clonmel experience

Clonmel has become famous for its floods. The flooding process is a result of the interaction between the natural and man-made environment.

Man-made factors contributing to flooding in Clonmel

1. The Old Bridge is too narrow for flood water to pass through easily.

2. A weir prevents flood water moving downstream quickly.

3. Construction of the New Quay restricts the river flow.

In times of normal flow, the Suir passes under the Old Bridge. In times of flood, water cannot get through it quickly enough, leading to a back-up of water upstream. This causes flooding (much like too many people trying to get through a narrow doorway). The weir causes a back-up of flow and flooding occurs. Disturbance of the riverbed by the construction of the New Quay area could have led to an increase in the river's load, leading to deposition and flooding.

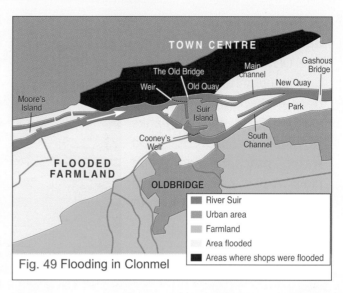

Fig. 49 Flooding in Clonmel

Natural factors leading to flooding in Clonmel

1. The Suir valley is very flat. The gradient falls only 15 m in a 23 km stretch between Clonmel and Carrick-on-Suir. The gradient over this reach is 1:1,500 which is extremely flat for a river flood plain.

2. Climate change has led to increased rainfall which triggers more floods.

3. The volume of water is increased due to the meeting (**confluence**) of the south channel and the main river channel at the town.

Fig. 50 Extent of flooding in Clonmel town centre

The combined flow of water from the two channels is funnelled through the Gashouse Bridge. The increased volume leads to flooding of the town centre, Suir Island and South Channel as the water squeezes under the bridge. When the soil and bedrock are saturated, heavy rainfall has nowhere to go except over the land and into rivers.

How can the human impact on the river be reduced?

1. Remove blockage points on the river

The Office of Public Works (OPW) recommended that the Old Bridge, Cooney's Weir and the Old Mill be removed. However, the Old Bridge is of historical importance and has not been removed. The weir has been modified to allow more water to flow over it. Removing it would damage salmon fishing in the river.

② IMPROVE FLOOD DEFENCES.

case study

higher level

2. Improve flood defences

The OPW proposed to widen and deepen the river, build flood defence walls and build earthen flood defence banks (levees) to prevent flood water reaching the flood plain. A plan has been put in place and is being developed.

Fig. 51 **Old Bridge weir covered during flood**

8.7 River rejuvenation

> **Landforms represent a balance between the action of internal and surface processes. The balance may change over time.**

Rejuvenation means 'to make young again'. For a river this means it will begin to flow faster with renewed energy to reach sea level (known as a river's **base level**), even though it has flowed through its entire course. Rejuvenation happens when the base level either rises or falls. This can happen in two ways.

1. Sea levels may drop during ice ages when water is locked away as ice, causing a lowering of the sea level across large areas. When ice melts, sea levels rise over large areas (called **eustatic** sea level changes).

2. The land may rise out of the sea due to tectonic activity raising the crust (called **isostatic uplift**). Isostatic uplift also occurs when a great weight is removed from the land (e.g. melting of an ice cap). The land gradually rises in response to the removal of the weight, much like a block of wood rises out of water when a weight holding it down is removed. This happens because the crust floats on the mantle below.

In both cases there is a drop in the sea level and the river's mouth is now high above it. This steeper gradient to the new base level gives the river extra energy and allows the river to renew the process of vertical erosion. Erosional processes start to reshape the landscape in an attempt to form a new long profile.

The following distinctive landforms show rejuvenation has occurred:

1. Knickpoints
2. River terraces
3. Incised/Entrenched meanders.

1. Knickpoints

Vertical erosion recommences when the river tries to erode down to a new base level. Erosion starts at the river mouth and works its way back upstream by **headward erosion**, cutting a new long profile. The point at which this newly eroded profile meets the old profile is marked by a waterfall or rapids, and is called a knickpoint.

If rejuvenation has occurred many times, the river may have several knickpoints, each one marking the renewed energy of the river as it starts to cut a new long profile into its old profile. Eventually all evidence of the former long profile is removed.

Some Irish rivers have many knickpoints, indicating several changes in sea level, e.g. the Shannon, Barrow, Nore and Suir rivers. Most knickpoints in Ireland can be found at 150–200 m above sea level showing that the sea once reached this level in the past.

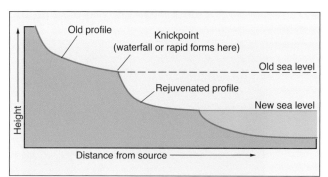

Fig. 52 Exam Diagram: Profile of a rejuvenated river

2. River terraces

As a result of rejuvenation, vertical erosion by the river is renewed and the river cuts a new and narrower channel for itself. This leaves the former valley floor well above the present river level. Over time the river develops a new flood plain at a lower level within the older flood plain.

The new valley is gradually widened by lateral erosion. The remnants of the former flood plain are left as steps (**terraces**) high above either side of the rejuvenated river. These are called **paired river terraces**. If rejuvenation were to happen again, another set of terraces would be left, giving the river valley a stepped appearance. Each set of terraces is often matched with corresponding knickpoints in the long profile.

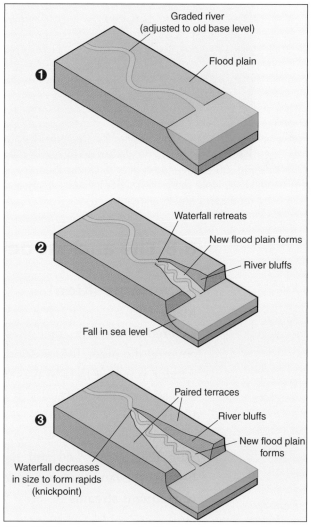

Fig. 54 The development of knickpoints and paired terraces

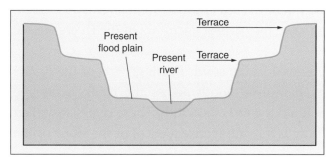

Fig. 53 Exam Diagram: Paired terraces

3. Incised/Entrenched Meanders

As the rejuvenated river has renewed energy it erodes vertically deep into the existing river valley. It engraves its meandering pattern into the rocks below. The meander sides are steep and narrow and are called incised meanders.

This feature is well developed along the River Nore south of Thomastown in County Kilkenny and along the River Barrow north of New Ross, County Wexford.

Fig. 55 Rejuvenated river in Colorado, USA. Note paired terraces, incised meanders and knickpoint.

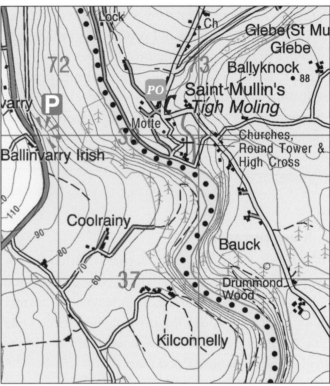

Fig. 56 Incised meanders on the River Barrow. Note the contour lines showing steep valley sides at each meander.

8.8 The ancient development of Irish rivers

Superimposition

Many Irish rivers have a long history. About 135 million years ago Ireland was covered by a warm, shallow sea. Chalk deposits were laid down at this time. They covered the older, folded sandstone and granite rocks below.

Later, much of Ireland was uplifted out of the sea and was weathered and eroded. The streams that formed at this time were the earliest ancestors of the rivers we see today.

The Rivers Barrow, Slaney, Nore, as well as the south-flowing parts of the Rivers Suir, Blackwater, Lee and Bandon, all flowed south across the chalk landscape because the land they travelled over tilted towards the south. These rivers are called **consequent streams** because their flow is a result (consequence) of the slope of the land.

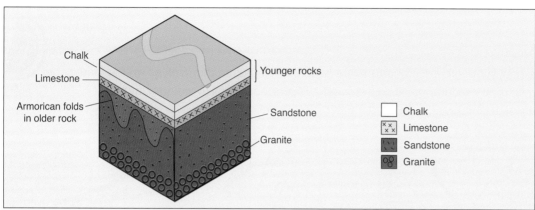

Fig. 57 A river flows over rock layers which are then removed by erosion.

When these rivers had cut down through the chalk, they began to erode the older rocks underneath. These older rocks were made of folded sedimentary sandstone rocks.

The rivers were able to cut down into the landscape that was much older than the rivers themselves. The rivers cut across the ridges (anticlines) in the folded rocks below. They imprinted (**superimposed**) their drainage patterns on the older rocks below.

The Barrow cut down into the Leinster granite at Graiguenamanagh, County Kilkenny. The deep north–south gorges of the River Lee and River Blackwater are due to superimposition of their course upon east–west trending anticlines. The Inniscarra gorge north of Cork city is an example of an ancient consequent stream that also superimposed itself on an older landscape.

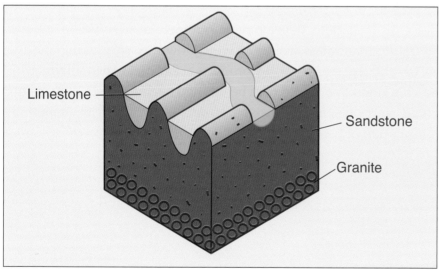

Fig. 58 Important Information: The river is now flowing over older rocks that have been exposed by erosion and weathering. The existing stream pattern has been superimposed on the newly exposed landscape.

See how some other European rivers have superimposed themselves on the landscape.
Log on to: www.durangobill.com/AncestralRivers/AncestralRiversIndex.html

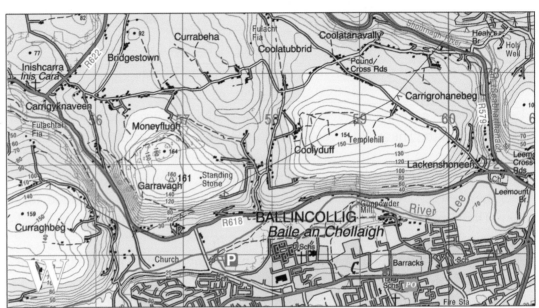

Fig. 59 The Shournagh River and the Inniscarra gorge in Cork show how rivers have cut across a ridge of sandstone. They have superimposed themselves on an older landscape.

Cycle of erosion and peneplains

The major theories of landscape development outlined a sequence of events whereby a newly uplifted landmass would be worn down by weathering and the agents of erosion (rivers, ice, sea, wind) to produce a flat plain (**peneplain**) with residual low hills. This landscape would then be uplifted again by earth movements and the cycle would start once more. Isostacy, eustacy and river rejuvenation all contribute to the formation of peneplains.

River capture of the River Suir

In parts of Munster and Leinster several rivers flow in a north-south direction (e.g. Rivers Barrow, Nore and Slaney). Other rivers in Munster (e.g. the River Suir) show unusual bends in their course. The Suir flows south for a distance and then suddenly turns to flow east towards the sea.

The unusual drainage system of this river can be explained by looking at the processes of superimposition and **river capture** – a part of the ancient development of Irish rivers.

1. The ancient south-flowing (consequent) Rivers Suir and Barrow cut down and both superimposed themselves into folded rocks that had an east-west trend.

2. A young east-flowing (subsequent/tributary) stream of the Barrow flowed in an east-west trending valley. This river entered the sea at Waterford.

3. By a process of headward erosion this younger subsequent stream of the Barrow met up with the south-flowing River Suir and captured its water. This created a sudden right-angled bend in the River Suir near Clonmel.

4. The point of capture is called an **elbow of capture**.

5. The beheaded River Suir is now much smaller than it once was, since it has lost much of its water to the subsequent stream. It is now too small for its valley. This river is known as a **misfit** stream (e.g. the River Blackwater south of Cappoquin).

6. The empty part of the valley south of the elbow of capture is known as a **windgap**.

7. In the past, the River Suir entered the sea at Youghal. Today, due to river capture it has a longer course and reaches the sea at Waterford.

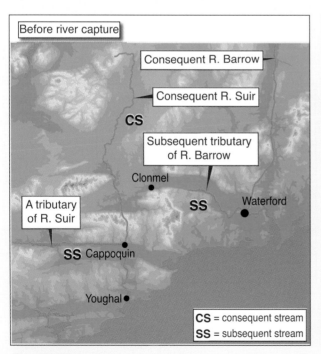

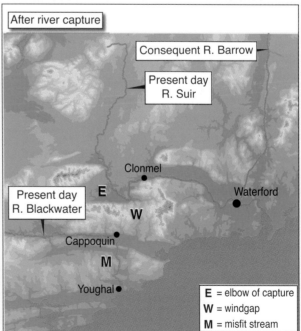

Fig. 60 Diagrams to show the course of the River Suir and River Blackwater

Questions

Chapter Revision Questions

1. (a) Explain four ways in which a river can erode the landscape.
   (b) Briefly examine the factors that influence a river's ability to erode the landscape.

2. Name and describe the processes of river transport.

3. Name and explain the factors influencing river deposition.

4. What is a graded profile? Why do graded profiles rarely occur in nature?

5. With the aid of diagrams, discuss the formation of two landforms found in the young stage of a river.

6. With the aid of diagrams, discuss the formation of two landforms found in the mature stage of a river.

7. With the aid of diagrams, discuss the formation of two landforms found in the old stage of a river.

8. (a) Explain the term drainage pattern.
   (b) Name and briefly account for the occurrence of any two drainage patterns.

9. With reference to a river you have studied, describe how humans have managed river processes.

10. Give an overview of the human and natural causes of flooding in an area you have studied.

11. Look carefully at the map to the right. Give a six-figure grid reference for the following landforms you can identify on the map.
    1. V-shaped valley
    2. Dendritic drainage pattern
    3. Tributary
    4. Watershed
    5. Mature stage
    6. Radial drainage pattern
    7. Young stage
    8. Waterfall

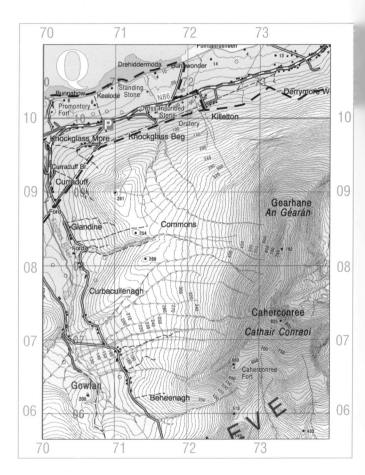

12. Copy and complete the table below using two landforms from each stage. The first one has been done for you.

Stage	Landform	Process	Irish Example
Upper Course	V-shaped valley	Erosion	River Nore
Middle Course			
Lower Course			

questions

13. (a) Explain the term river rejuvenation.
    (b) Why does river rejuvenation occur?
    (c) Discuss the formation of two landforms resulting from river rejuvenation. **(HL)**

14. With the aid of a diagram, explain the process of river capture. How has it affected the course of a named Munster river you have studied? **(HL)**

OL Short Questions

15. Examine the diagrams A, B and C below. Name each of the **three** river drainage patterns.

A

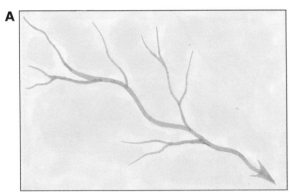

B

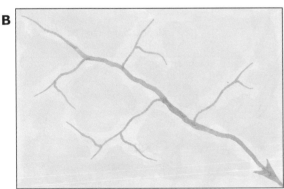

C

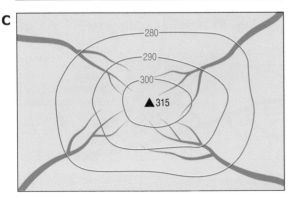

16. The OS map extract below shows a river valley.
    (a) Is the River Argideen in its upper or middle or lower course?
    (b) What name is given to the feature marked X on the map

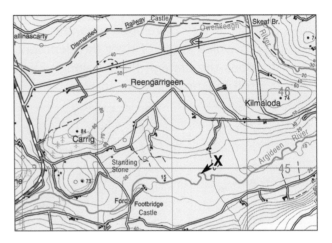

OL Long Questions

17. Select any one of the following surface processes: (a) sea/marine action; (b) river action; (c) glacial action; (d) mass movement.
    Explain the formation of any **two** Irish landforms caused by your selected process with the aid of diagrams.
    LC Exam Paper

18. With reference to an example which you have studied, describe and explain one way in which humans attempt to control river processes or marine (sea) processes or mass movement.
    LC Exam Paper

HL Long Questions

19. Examine how human processes can have an impact on the operation of one of the following natural processes: (a) mass movement processes; (b) river processes; (c) coastal processes.
    LC Exam Paper

questions

20. Examine the Ordnance Survey map below.
    (a) Draw a sketch map to show the drainage in this extract.
        Mark on and identify:
        (i) Two named rivers
        (ii) The flood plain
        (iii) A well-developed meander
    (b) To which stage of river development does the Elatagh River belong? Explain the reasons for your answer.

21. Isostatic processes involve adjustments to the balance between land and sea. Discuss how these processes have shaped the Irish landscape over time.

22. Examine, with the aid of a labelled diagram or diagrams, the processes that have led to the formation of any Irish landform of erosion of deposition of your choice.

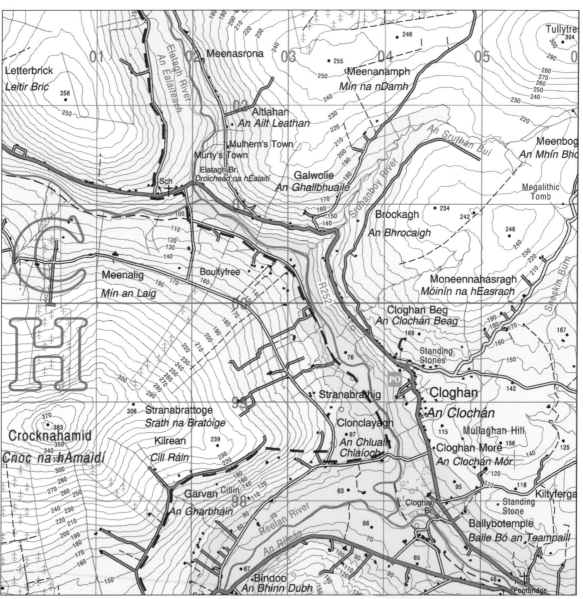

Chapter 9
Glacial Processes, Patterns and Landforms

At the end of this chapter you should be able to:

- **Understand how glacier ice is formed.**
- **Name and explain the processes of glacial erosion, transport and deposition.**
- **Identify glacial landforms on diagrams, maps and photographs.**
- **Describe the formation of glacial landforms.**
- **Identify locations around Ireland and the world where glacial landforms exist.**

Contents

9.1 Glaciation

9.2 The formation of glacier ice

9.3 How glaciers move

9.4 Types of glaciers

9.5 Glacial processes

9.6 Glacial landforms

9.7 The glaciation of Ireland

     Questions

If you are choosing this chapter to study in detail, you must be able to explain glacial processes, how the landforms are made, and be able to identify them on diagrams, maps and photos. The extra material you need to know is indicated by a green arrow. Higher Level students should study how landforms represent a balance between internal and surface forces. If you are not choosing this chapter, then you should be able to identify the landforms on diagrams, maps and photos and state the processes that made them.

Fig. 1 Glaciers in Alaska

9.1 Glaciation

Glaciation refers to the spread of great masses of ice across large areas of land and sea. There have been many ice ages (**glacials**) in the past. The warmer time between ice ages is known as an **interglacial**. We are now in an interglacial period that began about 10,000 years ago.

During the last ice age, which ended 10,000 years ago, 30% of the world was covered in ice. Today, just 10% of the world is covered in ice and this is shrinking fast as global warming continues.

Today, most permanent ice cover is found in Antarctica, Greenland, the Arctic Ocean and on high mountains such as the Alps, the Himalayas and the Andes.

9.2 The formation of glacier ice

A glacier can be thought of as a river of ice but, unlike rivers, glaciers are solid, much deeper and move more slowly. Glacier ice is formed when the build-up (**accumulation**) of snow is greater than melting (**ablation**).

As snow falls, the ice crystals are compressed (like squashing soft snow in your hand to make an icy snowball), pushing air out and creating a type of ice called **firn** or **neve**.

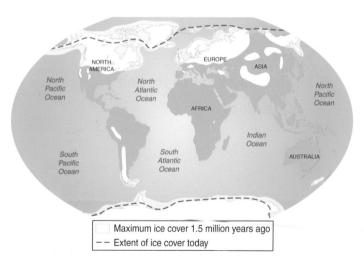

Fig. 2 The map shows the maximum ice cover 1.5 million years ago and ice cover today.

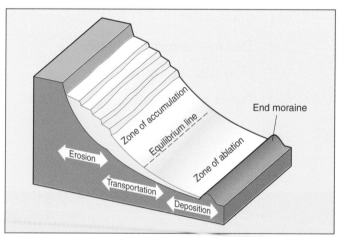

Fig. 3 The balance between accumulation and ablation (also called wastage) of ice in a glacier determines whether the glacier advances or retreats.

Over time, after a great weight of ice has accumulated (about 30 m), so much air has been removed by compression that the ice turns hard and blue. It takes 30–40 years for snow to form this dense glacier ice. Blue glacier ice is so hard that when armed with embedded rock fragments, it can bulldoze through rock and soil, completely reshaping the landscape.

Whether a glacier moves forward or retreats back up the valley depends on the balance between accumulation and melting. If more snow is added than is lost through melting, the glacier will move forward.

Fig. 4 Blue glacier ice

9.3 How glaciers move

Ice moves downhill because of the force of gravity upon the ice. The movement of glaciers involves the processes of:

1. Sliding (basal flow)
2. Plastic flow
3. Rotational slip
4. Gravity

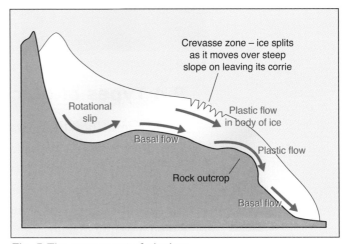

Fig. 5 The movement of glaciers

1. Sliding (basal flow)

The great weight of ice and pressure at its base will cause it to melt which allows the ice to slide along the valley floor and sides. The same effect is used in ice skating.

2. Plastic flow

If the glacier meets a large object in its path, such as a rock outcrop, ice will melt close to the object because of the increased pressure. This creates meltwater which allows the glacier to mould its way over and around the object.

3. Rotational slip

Ice can also move when the ice slips around a central point, much like a child on a slide when they reach the bottom of the steep bit. Rotational slip is very important in the creation of corries.

The longest glacier in the world is in Antarctica. It is the Lambert-Fisher Glacier and is over 700 km long and 64 km wide.

As the ice moves downhill it may move at different speeds over the landscape, causing huge cracks called **crevasses** to open and close on the surface of the ice. Imagine bending a chocolate-covered caramel bar slowly; the base stays connected but the chocolate surface cracks.

Fig. 6 Deep crevasse in ice

Fig. 7 These tunnels in a glacier at Mer de Glace in France are a tourist attraction. New tunnels are made each year as the ice moves downhill from the entrance ramp.

9.4 Types of glaciers

The accumulation of ice starts in hollows called corries high up in the mountains. This glacier type is called a **cirque** or **corrie glacier**. In Ireland Upper and Lower Lough Bray, County Wicklow contained corrie glaciers.

The continued accumulation of snow and ice makes the glacier build up inside the corrie until it spills out of the hollow and down into the valley below, where it is now called a **valley glacier**, for example the Lough Bray corrie glaciers spilled down into the Glencree Valley below. Valley glaciers are very common in the Alps today.

As valley glaciers advance onto lower lying land they meet and merge together to form a **piedmont glacier**. In Wicklow glaciers from the Glencree, Glenmacnass, Glendalough and Glenmalure valleys met and covered the land from the mountains to the sea.

Sometimes glaciers get so large that they cover whole continents and seas. They are then called **ice caps** or **ice sheets**. During the last ice age the ice sheet from the Arctic joined up with the valley and piedmont glaciers covering Ireland and much of North Europe.

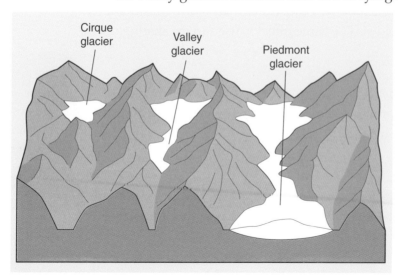

Fig. 8 Different types of glaciers

144

Fig. 9 Corrie glaciers, Chugach Mountains, Alaska

Fig. 10 A valley glacier, Mer de Glace, France

9.5 Glacial processes

A process is anything that happens to change the earth's surface.

Despite moving so slowly glaciers can shape the land using the processes of:

1. Erosion

2. Transportation

3. Deposition

In some areas one or more of these processes will be dominant, for example in mountain regions erosion is more common. On lowlands, deposition is more common as melting is more likely to take place here because it is warmer. Transportation can happen in both the uplands and lowlands.

These different processes produce some of the most spectacular scenery in Ireland and the world. Erosional processes sculpt impressive rugged landscapes, while deposited material called drift forms the basis of a thriving agricultural industry and quarrying.

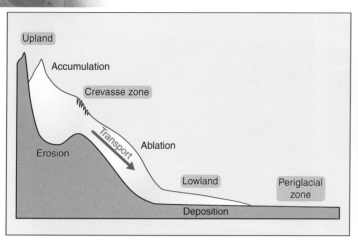

Fig. 11 Diagram and photograph to show accumulation, ablation and periglacial zones of a glacier in Alaska. The broken red line in the photograph shows where snow build-up (accumulation) gives way to melting (ablation). Above the red line fresh snow is whiter. Below the red line the melting ice is greyer in appearance.

Glacial erosion

Plucking

The weight of the ice puts incredible pressure on the base and sides of a valley. This causes the base and sides of the ice to melt, creating a thin film of meltwater for the ice to slide over. This meltwater seeps into cracks and crevices in the rock. When it refreezes it expands, crumbling the rock and sticking to it. Later when the ice moves it drags or plucks the rock fragments away. Plucking works in the same way as when you take an ice cube tray from the freezer and your fingers stick to it.

Fig. 12 Glacial striae, County Kerry

Abrasion

The plucked rock fragments embedded in the glacier act like sandpaper as the ice carries them. They scrape and gouge the landscape as the ice moves, creating deep scratches called **striations** or **striae**. Striae are very common on Irish glaciated landscapes and may help to indicate the direction of ice movement.

Glacial transport

The rock fragments plucked and abraded by the ice are carried along with it. This material is called **moraine**.

Moraine carried along while stuck to the bottom of the ice is called **ground moraine**. Moraine that finds its way into the ice through crevasses is called **englacial moraine**.

Rocks from the valley walls that are broken up by frost shattering (freeze-thaw action) fall onto the sides of the glacier to accumulate as **lateral moraine**.

You will learn more about moraines later in this chapter when studying depositional landscapes created by ice.

Fig. 13 Moraine deposited by ice in the French Alps

Glacial deposition

All material deposited by ice as it melts is called **drift**. There are two types of drift.

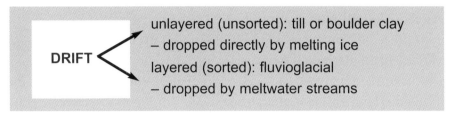

Fig. 14 below shows the various zones involved in glacial environments. Different processes are dominant in each.

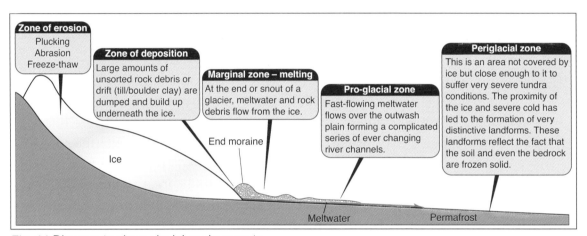

Fig. 14 Diagram to show glacial environments

9.6 Glacial landforms

Landforms made by glacial erosion

There are many landforms created by glacial erosion. They are listed below.

> **REMEMBER!**
>
> **You need to name, explain and apply the glacial processes involved in your explanation of landform formation.**

	Landform	Example
1	Corrie/cirque	Upper and Lower Lough Bray, County Wicklow. Devil's Punchbowl, County Kerry
2	Arête	Between Upper and Lower Lough Bray, County Wicklow
3	Pyramidal peak	Carrauntoohill and Brandon mountains, County Kerry. The Matterhorn in Switzerland
4	U-shaped valley	Glendalough and Glenmacnass, County Wicklow
5	Ribbon lake	Glencar, County Sligo
6	Truncated spurs	Glencree, County Wicklow
7	Hanging valley	Glendalough, County Wicklow
8	Fiord	Killary Harbour, County Mayo/Galway. Sogne Fiord, Norway

Corrie/Arête/Pyramidal Peak

Main processes: freeze-thaw, nivation, rotational slip, plucking, abrasion

Example: Corrie – The Devil's Punchbowl, County Kerry

Arête – Mount Brandon, County Kerry

A corrie or cirque is an armchair-shaped hollow high up in the mountains. Corries are the birthplace of all glaciers. If two corries form back to back, a knife-edged ridge called an **arête** is formed between the two corries. Freeze-thaw action makes the arête sharp and jagged. There are several arêtes visible from the road between Tralee and Dingle via the Conor Pass in County Kerry.

Where a number of corries form around a high mountain, continued erosion of their back walls creates a **pyramidal peak**, e.g. the Matterhorn in Switzerland.

IN DEPTH – Corrie

> **All In Depth sections contain material you need to know if you are studying this chapter in detail.**

At the beginning of the ice age, snow started to accumulate on the mountain tops in hollows on sheltered north and northeast facing mountain slopes.

Freeze-thaw action occurred on the rocks above the hollows which were filled with patches of snow. This created rock fragments which then fell onto the snow or were washed under it by summer meltwater.

Over time, the rock fragments were incorporated into the ice. Continued build-up of snow squashed it to form firn and blue glacier ice, which further deepened and widened the hollow by plucking and abrasion. The process of creating a hollow like this is called **nivation** or **snow patch erosion**. The weight of the ice eventually becomes so great that it slides by rotational slip and pulls away from the back wall of the hollow. However, some ice remains attached to the back wall, creating a deep crevasse called a **bergschrund.**

When the ice age was over the corrie filled with water, creating a lake called a **tarn.**

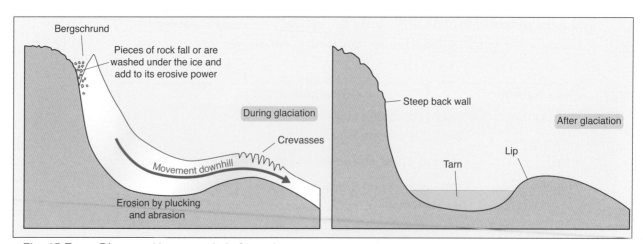

Fig. 15 Exam Diagram: How a corrie is formed

Fig. 16 As the ice moves out of the corrie, its surface is stretched and this causes the ice to split into smaller crevasses on the ice surface (like splitting a chocolate-covered caramel bar described earlier). This is the main crevasse zone. However, because the ice moves at different speeds in different places crevasses form in many areas across its surface.

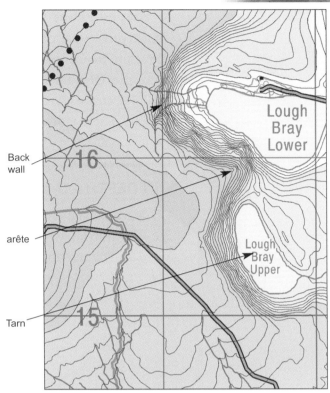

Fig. 19 Corries, arêtes and tarns at Upper and Lower Lough Bray, County Wicklow

Fig. 17 The corrie and tarn at Upper Lough Bray, County Wicklow. Look at the map in Fig. 19 and work out which direction the photographer was facing when the above photograph was taken.

Fig. 18 The largest corrie in Ireland is Coumshingaun in the Comeragh Mountains. Its back wall is 700 m deep. The helicopter flying on the left-hand side of the photograph is dwarfed by it.

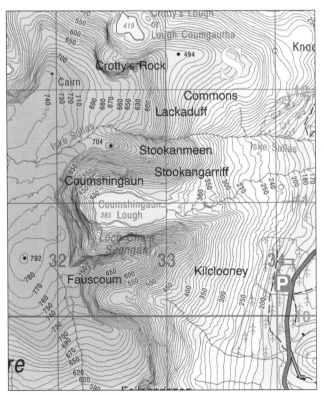

Fig. 20 Coumshingaun area showing corries and an arête

U-shaped valley and associated landforms

Main processes: deepening and widening of existing river valleys by plucking, abrasion, freeze-thaw action.

Example: Glendalough, County Wicklow

When corrie glaciers move downhill, they travel into existing V-shaped river valleys. They widen and deepen these valleys to create wide, flat-floored U-shaped valleys.

IN DEPTH – U-shaped valleys and associated landforms

The ice movement causes friction which heats and melts the bottom layer of the ice. This thin layer of meltwater seeps into rock layers, refreezes and sticks to pieces of rock. The moving ice will pluck out the loose rock fragments. This ice, armed with jagged rock fragments, abrades the valley, widening and deepening it.

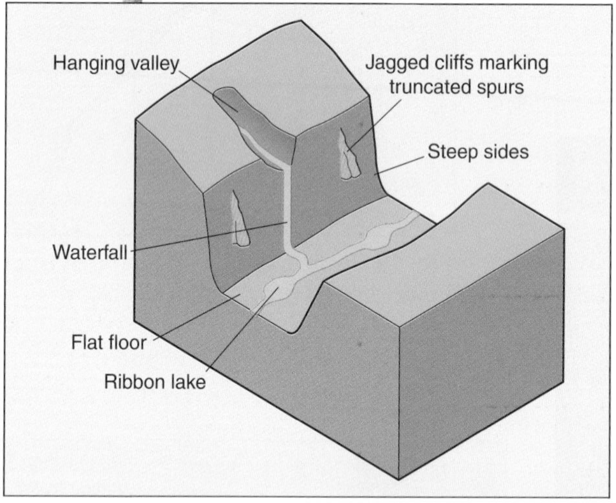

The moving ice cuts straight through the valley cutting away everything in its path. It erodes the bases of interlocking spurs, cutting them off and leaving **truncated spurs**. These are visible as jagged cliffs along the sides of the U-shaped valley.

Well-developed U-shaped valleys are also called **glacial troughs** and have distinct characteristics of lateral and vertical erosion – **steep headwalls**, **truncated spurs**, **hanging valleys** and **ribbon lakes**.

Fig. 21 Exam Diagram: A U-shaped/glaciated valley

Fig. 22 U-shaped valley, also called a glacial trough, at Glendalough, County Wicklow

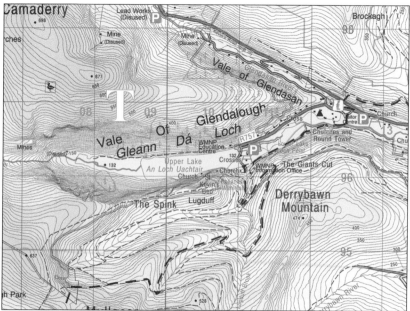

Fig. 23 U-shaped valley, a hanging valley and ribbon lakes

Hanging valleys are the valleys of former river tributaries which were glaciated.

Tributary glaciers were smaller so they contained less ice than the main valley glacier, and therefore they did not erode as deeply into their valley. When the ice age ended they were left perched, or hanging, above the main valley. Hanging valleys are often marked by a waterfall, e.g. Pollanass above Glendalough.

Fiords are formed if a glacial trough is flooded by rising sea levels after the ice age, e.g. Killary Harbour on the Galway/Mayo border and Sogne Fiord in Norway.

Fiords are deepest at the landward end. At their mouth there is often an underwater lip which can be a hazard to ships and submarines.

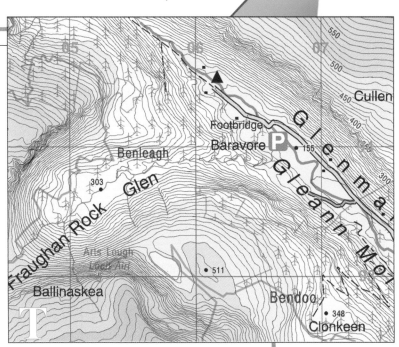

Fig. 24 Glenmalure hanging valley

ACTIVITY

Find the spot heights in Fraughan Rock Glen and at Baravore using Fig. 24. Work out the difference in height between the hanging valley floor and the floor of Glenmalure Valley.

Fig. 25 Killary Harbour, a fiord looking west from the road north of Leenaun.

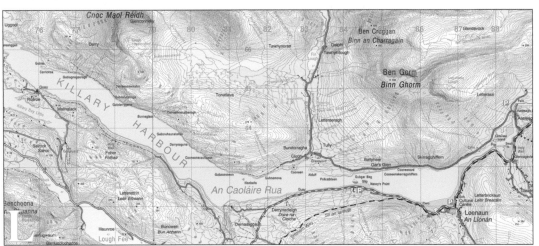

Fig. 26 Map showing Killary Harbour – an Irish fiord.

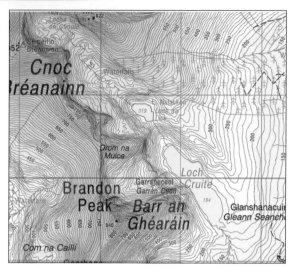
Fig. 27 Map to show ribbon lakes in County Kerry.

Fig. 28 Ribbon lakes, Mount Brandon, County Kerry.

Ribbon lakes formed where soft rocks occurred on the valley floor which were more easily eroded by plucking and abrasion. The hollows created are known as **basins**. After the ice age, the basins filled with water and were joined by a stream to form a chain of small lakes called ribbon lakes or **paternoster lakes**. These are seen in Glendalough, County Wicklow and Glenbeigh, County Kerry.

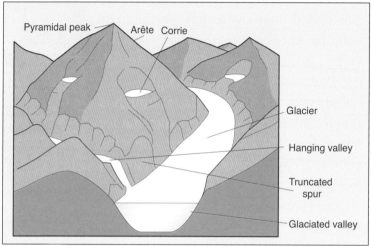
Fig. 29 Exam Diagram: Glaciated landforms in an upland region

Landforms made by glacial deposition

When a glacier melts (ablation) it deposits its load. Any material dropped by ice is called drift. This drift can be large amounts of unlayered (unsorted) rock debris (**till** or **boulder clay**), ranging in size from large boulders to clay, sand and dust grains.

Drift can also be sediments dropped by **meltwater**. These are called **fluvioglacial** deposits. The meltwater and rock debris that flow from the front (**snout**) of the glacier are layered (sorted) and shaped to make distinct landforms which are called fluvioglacial landforms. These are dealt with in more detail later in the chapter.

	Landform	Example
1	Boulder clay plain	The Central Plain
2	Moraine	Glendasan Valley, County Wicklow
3	Drumlin	Strangford Lough, County Down to Clew Bay, County Mayo
4	Erratic	Scottish granite on the east coast of Ireland

Boulder clay plains

Main processes: plucking, melting, transportation, deposition
Example: The Golden Vale, Munster

Fig. 30 Cliff in West Clare made of boulder clay

IN DEPTH – Boulder clay plains

Boulder clay, or glacial till, is an unsorted ground moraine which was dropped across the landscape by the retreating glaciers. Boulder clay is a mixture of soil and rocks. Most people think of ice as white and clean but in fact it is often covered with rock and full of broken pieces of rock. Sometimes you can hardly see the ice at all. This debris falls out as the ice melts. As the ice rapidly melted, boulder clay up to 30 m deep was deposited across the Irish landscape, providing a deep, well-drained and fertile soil in certain regions. Similar deposits are found in Europe, e.g. the North European Plain.

Moraine

Main processes: mass movement from valley sides, transport, melting, deposition.
Example: Glendasan Valley, County Wicklow
As mentioned earlier, any material carried on, in or under the ice is called a moraine. When the ice melts this material is deposited on the land and forms ridges of stone and boulder clay which, depending on their location in the valley, have different names (see Fig. 31).

Fig. 32 Moraines being carried by glaciers in Glacier Bay, Alaska

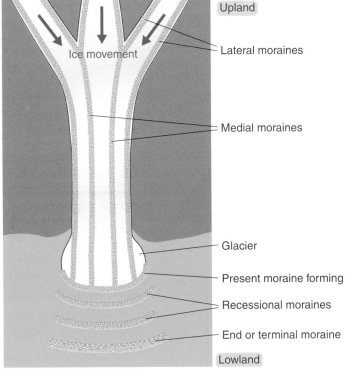

Fig. 31 Exam Diagram: The different types of moraine

IN DEPTH – Moraines

Freeze-thaw action on the mountainsides above the ice created debris which fell onto the top and sides of the glacier. This debris added to the plucked material and was held close to the valley side by the ice. Once the glacier melted this debris fell to the ground at the valley sides, blanketing it in a gently sloping ridge of unsorted stones and boulders called **lateral moraines**. **Englacial** and **ground moraine** as well as **medial moraine** are carried to the snout of the glacier and deposited there as **end moraines**. Meltwater streams flow through and out of this end moraine. The very large South Ireland end moraine sweeps across Ireland in a crescent shape from South Wicklow to the Shannon estuary.

As the ice melts, the glacier retreats. When it stops it will start depositing smaller ridges of debris at the front. These are **recessional** moraines.

Medial moraine: This ridge of debris is formed where two lateral moraines meet at the junction of two glaciers. Large glaciers may have many medial moraines visible as dirty-looking stripes on their surface. The moraine is carried further down the valley by the main glacier until it is deposited at the front (snout) of the glacier.

End (terminal) and recessional moraines: An end moraine is a crescent-shaped ridge of debris, which marks the furthest point reached by the ice.

Drumlins

Main processes: plucking, melting, friction, deposition.

Example: County Monaghan

These landforms are small, oval-shaped hills made from boulder clay ('drum' meaning small hill). They range in size from 25 to 100 metres high , 0.5 km wide and 1 km long. One end is steep (known as the **stoss side**) and faces the direction of ice movement, the other end has a gentler slope (the **lee side**). In Ireland the drumlin belt runs from Strangford Lough, County Down to Clew Bay, County Mayo.

IN DEPTH – Drumlins

Drumlins are formed beneath the ice when an ice sheet is heavily laden with boulder clay and is melting but still able to advance or **surge**. Friction between the ground and the ice causes the load to be deposited. As the ice advances it moulds the deposited material into these distinctive egg-shaped mounds.

Some drumlins have a large boulder at their centre and are called **rock drumlins**. Rock drumlins form where the large boulder causes extra friction as it gets in the way of the ice, causing deposition around it. Drumlins tend to occur in large groups called **swarms** and the resulting landscape is often called a **basket of eggs landscape**.

Fig. 33 A drumlin near Monaghan

Fig. 34 Exam Diagram: A drumlin

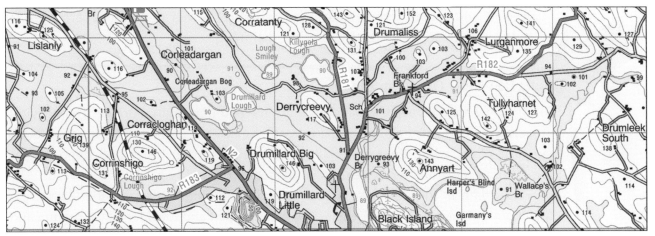

Fig. 35 Map to show drumlins, County Monaghan

ACTIVITY

Look at the map and answer the questions.
1. What is the direction of ice movement shown by the drumlins?
2. Choose five drumlins and work out their average height.

Erratics

Main processes: plucking, transportation, melting, deposition
Example: the Burren, County Clare
These are large boulders that have been picked up by the ice in one area, then transported long distances before being deposited on a landscape which may have a completely different rock type. Many are left in a precarious position perched on a hillside, e.g. near Lough Duff, Black Valley, Killarney. A large perched block is seen at Carrigacareen near Kenmare, County Kerry. Many are found on the Burren. Many erratics of Scottish origin are found across Ireland.

Fig. 36 An erratic, County Clare

Landforms made by fluvioglacial deposition

Landforms created by meltwater flowing under and out of glaciers are known as fluvioglacial landforms. These are all depositional landforms.

	Landform	Example
1	Outwash plain	The Curragh, County Kildare
2	Esker	Esker Riada, Clonmacnoise, County Offaly

Outwash plains

Main processes: melting, transportation, sorting, deposition

Example: The Curragh, County Kildare

Outwash plains are the most extensive of fluvioglacial deposits. They are large areas of sand and gravel which have been deposited across the landscape by glacial meltwater flowing from the snout of the melting glacier.

IN DEPTH – Outwash plains

Sand, gravel and clay were washed through the end (terminal) moraine. The heaviest gravels were deposited closest to the retreating glacier, leading to the formation of an outwash plain, while finer materials were carried further away and deposited as loess/limon, creating fertile, easily cultivated farmland, e.g. the Paris Basin. The outwash plain is thickest close to the terminal moraine. In Ireland the Curragh is underlain by sands and gravels so is very well drained and ideal for sheep rearing and horse racing but not good for arable farming, unless well fertilised.

Eskers

Main processes: melting, transportation, sorting, deposition.

Example: The Esker Riada

Eskers are long winding ridges of **stratified** (layered) sands and gravels created by rivers of meltwater flowing beneath melting ice sheets.

IN DEPTH – Eskers

When the ice was melting rapidly, streams of meltwater flowed under the ice, making tunnels. The meltwater carried large quanities of sand and gravels, which were deposited on the floor of the tunnels. This deposition usually happened when the stream lost energy as it left the tunnel. The heaviest load was dropped first with the lighter sediment deposited on top. Over time, many layers of deposits built up.

When the ice age was over, these deposits were revealed as snake-like ridges of sorted sands and gravels, winding across the landscape and running across hills and valleys. These esker ridges are usually between 20–30 m high and are very different in composition to the surrounding landscape.

Over time, weathering and mass movement reduced the height of eskers making them perfect for routeways. The ancient route An tSlighe Mhór was constructed on esker deposits extending from Galway to Dublin known as the Esker Riada. Today, part of the Dublin–Galway rail line runs upon the Esker Riada.

Fig. 37 An esker deposited by the Brúarjökull glacier in Iceland

Fig. 38 The Kilcormac Esker, County Offaly

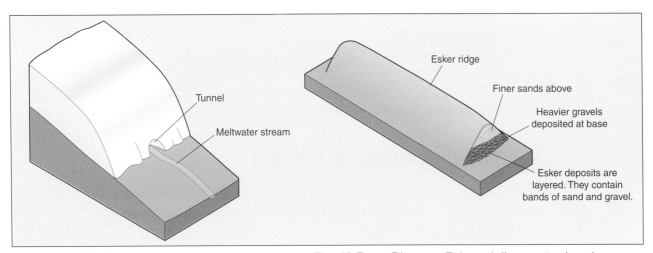

Fig. 39 Esker formation: Meltwater streams deposit sand and gravel under the ice as they flow. Over time, a winding ridge of sand and gravel is exposed as the ice retreats. See enlarged esker ridge diagram in Fig. 40.

Fig. 40 Exam Diagram: Enlarged diagram to show how eskers are formed from layers of sand and gravel.

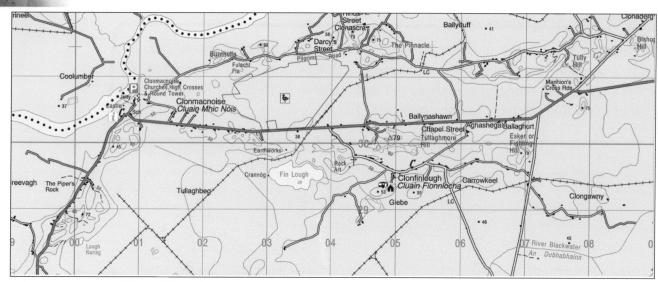

Fig. 41 Map of eskers around Clonmacnoise, County Offaly. Note how the roads and settlements (modern and ancient) are located on or near the eskers. The roads in particular follow the esker routes. This area is part of the 'Shannon Callows' flood plain area which is flooded each winter. Eskers have provided dry point settlements for over one thousand years in this area.

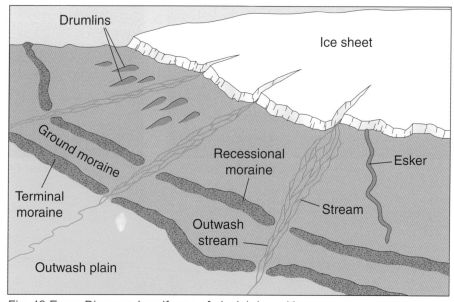

Fig. 42 Exam Diagram: Landforms of glacial deposition

Higher Level Students should study landforms associated with changes in sea level and land level caused by glaciation. These landforms are explained in Chapters 8 and 10. Higher Level students must study section 8.7 in Chapter 8 OR section 10.7 in Chapter 10.

9.7 The glaciation of Ireland

Europe has had four major ice ages. The last two of these reached Ireland. The first to cover Ireland is called the **Munsterian Ice Age,** which began about 175,000 years ago and lasted for 75,000 years. It was followed by an interglacial which lasted 30,000 years.

The next ice age to affect Ireland is called the **Midlandian Ice Age.** It started 70,000 years ago and lasted for about 60,000 years, ending nearly 10,000 years ago. Ireland was at its warmest about 5,000 years ago.

The Munsterian glaciation

The climate of Europe cooled 175,000 years ago and thick ice sheets spread from Europe and Scotland, covering all of Ireland except for the highest peaks. These peaks stuck up above the ice sheets as **nunataks**. They were weathered by freeze-thaw action. Carrauntoohill is an example of a nunatak.

The Midlandian glaciation

The climate cooled again 70,000 years ago and another ice sheet spread across Ireland. This ice sheet only reached as far south as a line from Wicklow to the Shannon estuary. The South Ireland end moraine marks the furthest point reached by this glacier (see Fig. 44). The Midlandian glacier bulldozed over the earlier Munsterian deposits, re-depositing them in the midlands. The eskers we see today across the midlands were formed at this time. Drumlins were created in the north and central lowlands. Till was deposited across the central lowlands. Local ice caps developed in the Wicklow, Mourne, Cork and Kerry Mountains due to the colder climatic conditions there.

   This ice age in Ireland ended 10,000 years ago. From 10,000–7,000 years ago it was still fairly cool, leading to coniferous forest growth. From 7,000–4,000 years ago the climate got warmer, a little like today's Mediterranean climate, and the vegetation developed into deciduous oak forest. The first people arrived at around this time and the climate remained relatively warm. This forested countryside remained almost unchanged until the arrival of the first farmers around 3,500 BC. They cleared the forests to grow crops and rear animals.

   From 1,200–1,700 AD there was a slight drop in temperature, leading to a mini ice age. This did not have an impact on the landscape but it affected the economy and society. From the eighteenth century to the present day the climate has remained somewhat similar to today's climate.

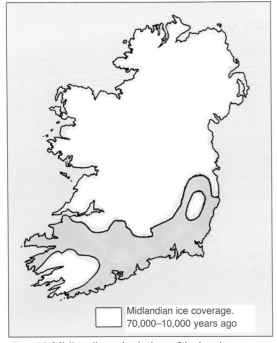

Fig. 43 Midlandian glaciation of Ireland

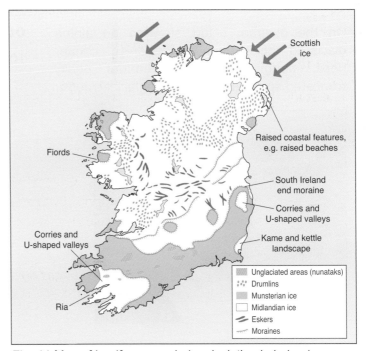

Fig. 44 Map of landforms made by glaciation in Ireland

Chapter Revision Questions

1. Explain how glacier ice builds up.

2. What are the main types of glacier?

3. How do glaciers move?

4. (a) Name and draw two landforms of glacial erosion.

   (b) Describe in detail the formation of the landforms you named in part (a).

5. Name and describe the processes of glacial erosion.

6. Name and draw two landforms of glacial deposition and describe in detail their formation.

7. Discuss the formation of fluvioglacial landforms. In your answer refer to two named features.

8. Look at the map below and label the landforms of glacial erosion 1–4.

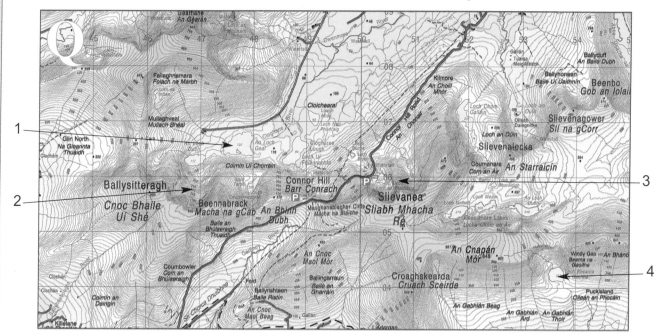

9. On the diagram below showing an alpine glaciated region, identify the arête, cirque, fiord, hanging valley, pyramidal peak, truncated spurs, and U-shaped glacial trough.

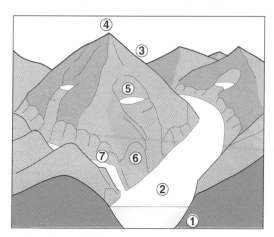

OL Short Questions

10. Which of the following glacial features is present at V on this extract from an Ordnance Survey map?

    Corrie/Cirque or Arête or Pyramid Peak:

    _____

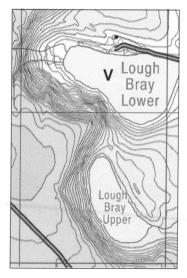

11. Study the Ordnance Survey and photograph extracts below and answer the following questions.
    (a) Name the glacial feature marked X on the map.
        Write the correct name: _____
    (b) Name the glacial feature marked Y on the photograph.
        Write the correct name: _____
    (c) Were features X and Y formed by the process of erosion or deposition?

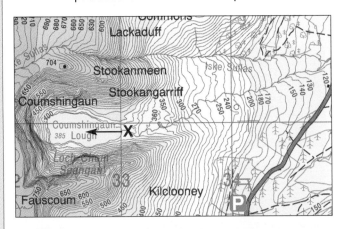

OL Long Questions

12. Select any **one** of the following surface processes:
    (a) Sea/marine action
    (b) River action
    (c) Glacial action
    (d) Mass movement
    Explain the formation of any **two** Irish landforms caused by your selected process with the aid of diagrams.

    LC Exam Paper

HL Short Questions

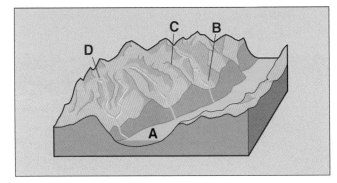

13. Examine the diagram above of a glaciated landscape. Match each of the following landforms with its correct letter in the diagram: hanging valley; cirque/corrie; glaciated trough; arête.

14. Examine the diagram below showing some glacial landforms.
    Insert the labels A to D in their correct places in the table below the diagram.

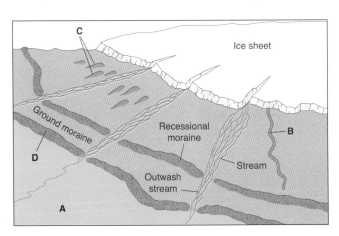

Esker	
Terminal Moraine	
Outwash plain	
Drumlin	

15. Examine the Ordnance Survey map extract below. Write the answers to the questions in the spaces provided.

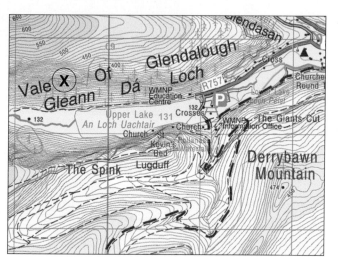

(i) The height above sea level of the surface of the Upper Lake in Glendalough is: _____ metres.

(ii) What type of glacial lake is the Upper Lake?

(iii) What is the correct name for the feature found at X?

Tick the correct box.

U-shaped Valley ❑   Corrie ❑

Pyramidal Peak ❑

(iv) The glacier which shaped the Upper Lake moved out of the basin in which of the following directions?

Tick the correct box.

North ❑   North Eastwards ❑

West ❑   South Eastwards ❑

HL Long Questions

16. (a) Identify the glacial landforms in the two photographs below.
    (b) Name the process which formed each landform.
    (c) Explain the formation of each landform and give an Irish example of each.

17. Examine, with the aid of a labelled diagram or diagrams, the processes that have led to the formation of any one Irish landform of erosion or deposition of your choice.

questions

Chapter 10
Coastal Processes, Patterns and Landforms

At the end of this chapter you should be able to:

- **Name and explain the coastal processes of erosion, transport and deposition.**

- **Identify coastal landforms on diagrams, maps and photographs.**

- **Describe the formation of coastal landforms in Ireland.**

- **Describe how human activities affect natural coastal processes.**

- **Discuss how our coastline is under threat from natural and human influences and describe some of the methods used to protect it.**

- **Explain how changes in sea levels affect coastal landforms. (HL)**

Contents

10.1   The Blue Planet

10.2   Waves

10.3   Marine processes

10.4   Landforms of marine erosion

10.5   Landforms of marine deposition

10.6   Human interaction with coastal processes
        Case Studies: North Bull Island, County Dublin
                       Courtown north beach, County Wexford

10.7   Isostatic and eustatic processes **(HL)**
        Questions

If you are choosing this chapter to study in detail, you must be able to explain marine processes, explain how the landforms are made and be able to identify them on diagrams, maps and photos. The extra material you need to know is indicated by a green arrow. Higher Level students should study how landforms represent a balance between internal and surface forces. If you are not choosing this chapter to study in detail, then you should be able to identify the landforms on diagrams, maps and photos and state the processes that made them.

Fig. 1 **The blue planet**

10.1 The Blue Planet

Our planet is a water world. The ocean covers 71% of the surface area of the globe and makes up over 90% of all habitable space on Earth. No wonder that Arthur C. Clarke, scientist and writer, once remarked that it was 'inappropriate to call this planet, Earth, when clearly it is ocean'.

> **Marine processes**
> A process is anything that changes the landscape. Marine processes are erosion, deposition and transport. These are performed by the action of waves, tides and currents.

10.2 Waves

If the earth were a football the average depth of the ocean would be no more than the thickness of a piece of paper, and even the deepest ocean trench would only be a dent of one third of a millimetre deep.

The wind blowing across the surface of the sea creates waves. The ability of waves to shape the coast is influenced by the strength of the wind and the length of time it blows. If a gentle breeze blows, wavelets appear. If the breeze stops, so do the waves. Stronger winds produce larger waves which may last for hours and travel long distances.

The size of waves is affected by the **fetch**, which is the distance a wave has travelled before it reaches land. Large fetches produce bigger waves because the wind has had longer to blow over the surface of the sea, creating bigger swells, e.g. the west coast of Ireland.

Around the Irish and British coast are a series of weather buoys which can be accessed from the Internet. They will tell you the height of the waves and their frequency as well as other weather information.

> Find out what the waves are like now. Log on to www.marine.ie/home/publicationsdata/data/buoys

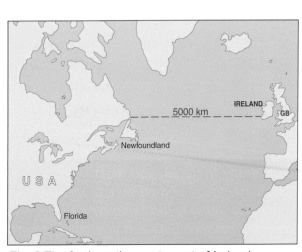

Fig. 2 The fetch on the west coast of Ireland

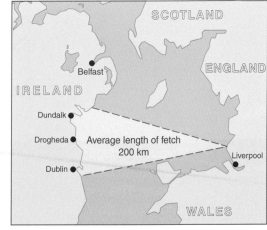

Fig. 3 The fetch on the east coast of Ireland

Fig. 4 Wave sailing in strong winds Belmullet, County Mayo

Factors controlling wave height over open water

wind speed

wind duration

fetch

When waves break, water rushes up the beach. This is known as the **swash**. Some of the water will seep into the sand, the rest returns to the sea as the **backwash**.

Swash leaves material on the beach.

Backwash removes material from the beach.

Fig. 5 Swash and backwash

Constructive waves (spilling breakers) – building up our coastline

Some waves have a powerful swash that can carry debris up the beach but have little energy left in the backwash to drag the debris away again. These are called constructive waves. A wide sandy beach is the best evidence of deposition by constructive waves. Constructive waves break some distance from the shore, and the surf rolls in gently up the beach.

Fig. 6 Constructive waves (spilling breakers)

Destructive waves (plunging breakers) – destroying our coastline

Destructive waves have great strength, large fetches and can erode soft coastlines very quickly. Destructive waves occur during storms and rough, high tide conditions. They plunge powerfully against the coastline. Their backwash digs into the land removing large quantities of rock, sand and earth. They may throw large stones up on the shore creating a storm beach. Destructive waves are very effective where the beach is steeply sloping. Coastlines change rapidly during storm conditions as beaches are removed and cliffs eroded. During winter storms in 2005, destructive waves at Brittas Bay, County Wicklow exposed a 200-year-old schooner which had been buried under 3 metres of sand.

Destructive waves normally curl over, forming a tunnel until the wave breaks.

Fig. 7 Destructive waves (plunging breakers)

Destructive waves	Constructive waves
High frequency (10 – 15 per minute)	Low frequency (under 10 per minute)
Backwash is stronger than the swash	Swash is stronger than the backwash
Removes beach material	Deposits beach material
Tall waves which drop down forcefully onto the shore	Long low waves spill gently over the beach

Fig. 8 Differences between destructive and constructive waves

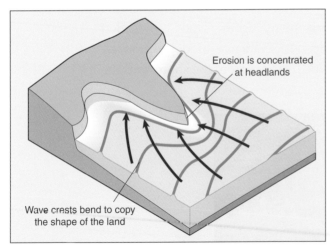

Erosion is concentrated at headlands

Wave crests bend to copy the shape of the land

Fig. 9 The part of the wave in shallow water moves more slowly than the part of the wave in deeper water. Therefore, when the depth of water under a wave crest varies along the crest, the wave bends.

Wave refraction

Wave refraction is the bending of waves. In Fig. 9 the headland is further out to sea than the bay and the water around it is shallower. At first, the waves approaching the coast are straight. Friction with the sea bed causes the part of the wave near the headland to slow down, while the rest of the wave carries on at the same speed. This difference in speed along the wave makes it curve towards the headland. This is called wave **refraction**. The constant curving of the waves concentrates erosion at the headlands, leading to the presence of cliffs, caves, arches and stacks.

10.3 Marine processes

Processes of marine erosion

The sea erodes the coastline in several ways.

Hydraulic action

The crushing force of tonnes of water in each wave wears the land away. The pressure exerted by Atlantic waves in winter average nearly 10,000 kg/m^2. Hydraulic action is most effective on soft coastlines such as Louth, Dublin and Wexford.

Abrasion

Waves throw stones and sand against the coast wearing it away. Abrasion is most effective at high tide and during storms.

Air compression

As waves break against the coast, air is trapped and compressed in small crevices in rocks. When the wave moves away, the air is released. This expansion and compression shatters rock.

Attrition

The load carried by the waves is itself worn down by constant rolling and knocking together. This is why beach cobbles are usually well rounded. Ultimately, sand is formed in this way.

Solution

Salts in sea water can dissolve rock by chemical means. Chalk and limestone coasts are most easily eroded this way.

Processes of marine deposition

Deposition occurs when the sea loses its energy. Waves, tides and local currents combine to drop sand and shingle at particular locations.

The conditions required for deposition are:
1. Gently sloping beaches which reduce wave energy.
2. Shelter from strong winds and currents creating calmer seas.
3. Constructive waves allowing sand to settle on the beach.

Many bays and inlets have these conditions, allowing beaches and other depositional features to form there.

Processes of marine transport

Huge amounts of material are carried along our coastlines each day. Waves and currents are constantly moving sand along the coast due to a process called longshore drift.

Longshore drift (littoral drift)

This is the movement of material along the coast. It occurs because the coastline is irregular and waves do not break parallel to the coast (wave refraction). The swash moves sediment up the shore at an angle and the backwash pulls the sediment back out to sea at a right angle to the shore.

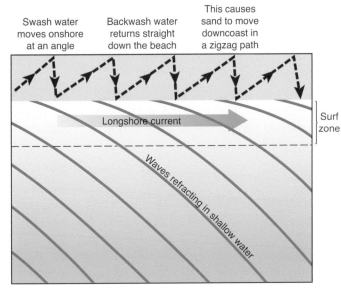

Swash water moves onshore at an angle

Backwash water returns straight down the beach

This causes sand to move downcoast in a zigzag path

Longshore current

Surf zone

Waves refracting in shallow water

Fig. 10 Exam Diagram: Longshore drift

The result of longshore drift is that much of the sea's energy is spent moving material up and down the shore. This is why a sandy beach is the best natural protection a coastline could have from sea erosion.

Breaking waves also produce currents which flow parallel to the shore. Where the waves break (**surf zone**) the water is turbulent and carries fine sand grains in suspension and rolls larger pebbles along the sea floor. These local currents along the shore can be very powerful and can carry swimmers along parallel to the coast quite quickly.

10.4 Landforms of marine erosion

REMEMBER!

You need to name, explain and apply the coastal processes involved in your explanation of landform formation

Landform	National Example
1. Cliffs	Slieve League, County Donegal
2. Wave-cut platform	Burren coastline, County Clare
3. Bay	Dundalk Bay, County Louth
4. Headland	Howth Head, County Dublin
5. Cave	Kilkee, County Clare
6. Blow holes	Hook Head, County Wexford
7. Sea arches	Ballybunion, County Kerry
8. Sea stacks	Stags of Broad Haven, County Mayo

Cliffs and wave-cut platforms

Main processes: abrasion, hydraulic action, air compression, solution, attrition, undercutting, collapse

Example: Cliffs of Moher, County Clare.

Cliffs are landforms of marine erosion. They are steep slopes formed where the land meets the sea. They can form in hard and soft coastlines.

IN DEPTH – Cliffs and wave-cut platforms

The erosional processes of hydraulic action, abrasion and air compression combine to exploit weaknesses in a rock face looking out to sea to form a **notch** or overhang. The notch is enlarged until the weight of the unsupported rock above is so great that it collapses. A steep cliff is formed.

The fallen debris lies at the bottom of the cliff, protecting it from further erosion. Gradually the hydraulic force of the sea removes this debris depositing it on the sea bed some distance out to sea. This accumulation of debris is called a **wave-built terrace**.

Over time, the repeated collapse of the rock at the cliff face causes it to **retreat** inland. Eventually the force of the sea is unable to erode a notch this far inland and mass movement, such as **slumping**, takes over as the primary cause of cliff formation.

The original base of the cliff is left as a rocky shore in front of it. This may be exposed at low tide. It is called a **wave-cut platform**.

The structure of the rock plays an important part in determining the type of cliff that is formed (vertical or sloping). Rocks with layers that are horizontal (See Fig. 12) or dipping towards the sea are easily undercut and collapse frequently. Cliffs with vertical faces are formed.

Cliffs made from unjointed rock such as granite or schist are harder to erode and form more gently sloping cliffs, e.g. Slieve League in Donegal.

Soft coastlines made of glacial till are the least resistant to the erosive power of the sea. Every tide can wash soil from the base of these cliffs and heavy rainfall may cause slumping, e.g. Killiney, County Dublin.

Actively eroding cliffs are characterised by a lack of vegetation on their steep faces and well-developed notches or signs of recent slumps.

> **All In Depth sections contain material you need to know if you are studying this chapter in detail.**

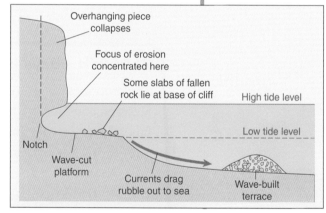

Fig. 11 Exam Diagram: Cliff formation

Fig. 12 Hard coastline on Inis Mór, Aran Islands, County Galway. Note wave-cut platform and cliff.

Fig. 13 A soft coastline with slumps, Port Strand, County Louth.

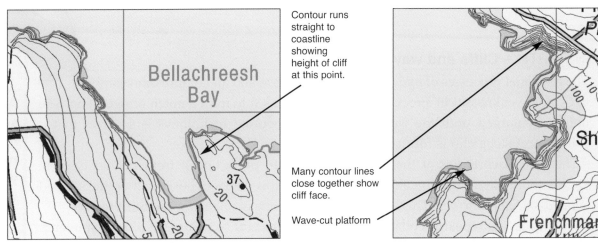

Contour runs straight to coastline showing height of cliff at this point.

Many contour lines close together show cliff face.

Wave-cut platform

Fig. 14 OS maps showing cliffs and wave-cut platforms in County Donegal

Bays and headlands

Main processes: hydraulic action, abrasion, air compression

Example: Galway Bay and Black Head, County Clare

Bays and headlands are landforms of marine erosion.

Bays are large curves (indentations) in the coast, while headlands are areas of land that jut out into the sea. These features form when bands of soft and hard rock are found along the coastline.

IN DEPTH – Bays and headlands

The processes of marine erosion such as hydraulic action, air compression and abrasion combine to attack the different rock types along the coast. Soft rock, e.g. limestone is eroded more quickly, creating a curve in the coast. Hard rock, e.g. granite, is eroded more slowly. It stands out of the coast as a headland. As waves bend around the coast (**wave refraction**) erosion is focused on the headlands. Eventually, large bays are created. Bays may contain beaches formed when constructive waves deposit rock debris. As the bay is eroded further into the land the sea has less energy and deposition continues to occur forming a **bay head beach.**

Dublin Bay formed because the soft limestone was eroded more quickly than the resistant metamorphic rocks of Bray Head and Howth Head.

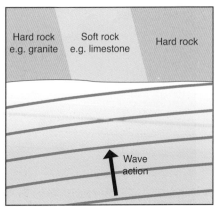

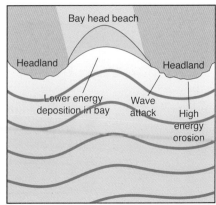

Fig. 15 Exam Diagram: The formation of bays and headlands

Fig. 16 Bay and headland at Silverstrand, County Wicklow

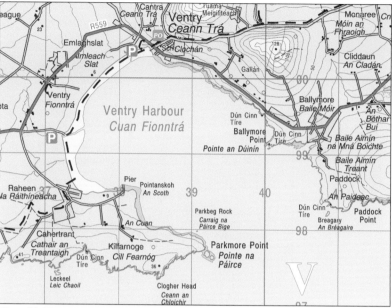

Fig. 17 Map to show bays and headlands in Ventry, County Kerry

Caves, arches, stacks and stumps

Main processes: hydraulic action, abrasion, air compression, solution.

Example:

1. Small caves are found in the cliff face at Loughshinny, North County Dublin.
2. Arches are found at Hook Head, County Wexford.
3. Stacks are found along the Clare coastline near Kilkee and also along the Sligo and Mayo coasts, e.g. Downpatrick Head.

Caves are hollows in rocky cliff faces and headlands. Large caves do not form in soft coastlines.

IN DEPTH – Caves, blowholes and sea stacks

Hydraulic action, abrasion and air compression combine to enlarge existing joints and lines of weakness in a rock face.

Air compression is very effective. As the waves smash against the rock, air is compressed in the lines of weakness in the rocks and released hundreds of times in an hour. This weakens and shatters the rock, creating small hollows. Once formed, a hollow is enlarged to form a **cave**. Now the combined forces of marine erosion continue to deepen the cave. Solution and air compression can also cause the formation of a tunnel in the roof, known as a **blowhole**.

If two caves form either side of a headland, they may join up to form an **arch**. Over time, weaknesses in the roof of the arch are attacked by the sea and weather and the roof may collapse leaving a **sea stack**.

Eventually marine erosion and weathering will wear the stacks down until they are **stumps** barely visible above the water. It is then they are most dangerous to boats.

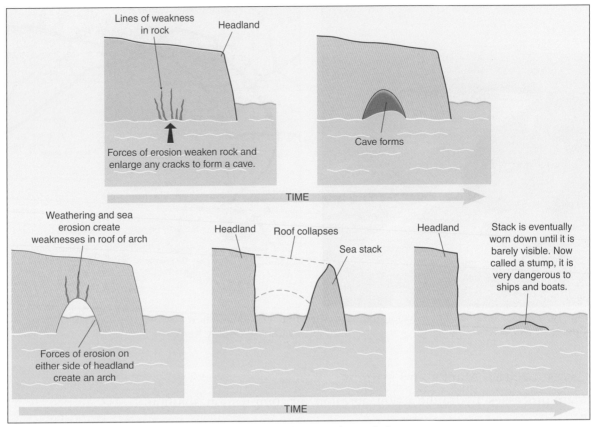

Lines of weakness in rock

Headland

Forces of erosion weaken rock and enlarge any cracks to form a cave.

Cave forms

TIME

Weathering and sea erosion create weaknesses in roof of arch

Forces of erosion on either side of headland create an arch

Headland

Roof collapses

Sea stack

Headland

Stack is eventually worn down until it is barely visible. Now called a stump, it is very dangerous to ships and boats.

TIME

Fig. 18 Exam Diagram: The formation of caves, arches, stacks and stumps

Fig. 19 Sea stacks in the Algarve, Portugal.

Fig. 20 An arch in the Algarve, Portugal.

Fig. 21 The Cliffs of Moher, County Clare. Note the debris at the base of the active cliffs.

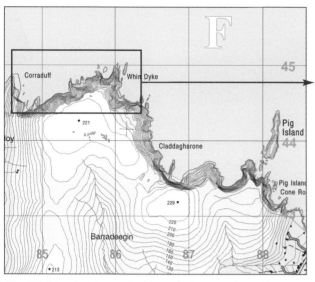

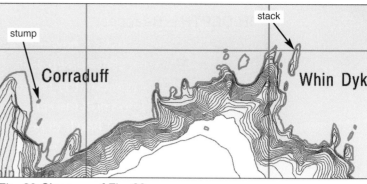

Fig. 23 Close-up of Fig. 22

Fig. 22 Map to show stacks and stumps along the Sligo coast

10.5 Landforms of marine deposition

Feature	National Example
1. Beach	Tramore, County Waterford
2. Storm beach	Doonbeg, County Clare
3. Sand spit	Inch Strand, County Kerry
4. Sand bar	Tacumshin, County Wexford
5. Lagoon	Lady's Island, County Wexford
6. Tombolo	Castlegregory, County Kerry

Fig. 24 A beach with pebbles and stones

Beaches

Main processes: constructive waves, longshore drift, deposition

Example: Tramore, County Waterford.

Beaches are landforms of marine deposition.

Constructive waves and longshore drift leave large deposits of mud, sand, shingle and larger stones as beaches on our coast. All around the Irish coast there are numerous beaches, many of which are major tourist attractions.

For a beach to form there must be:

1. A sheltered area to trap sediment.

2. Longshore drift to transport material to the beach.

3. Constructive waves to deposit beach material between the high and low tide marks.

Many bays provide these conditions and the beaches that form there are known as bay head beaches.

IN DEPTH – Beaches

Constructive waves have a powerful swash which drags sediment (**beach fabric**) up the shore. The wave slows down as it travels up the shore and some of the water seeps (percolates) into the sand. The backwash is weak and unable to drag larger pebbles back down to the sea. However, it can carry finer particles of sand and mud. Over time constructive waves sort/arrange the beach deposits. Heavier stones are left high up on the **backshore**, while finer sand and mud is left closer to the low tide mark on the **foreshore**. Large stones are only carried by storm waves and are deposited at the top of the beach as **storm beaches**. On a typical beach some or all of the following landforms may be found.

1. Berms: Long steps or terraces which form on shingle beaches in summer when constructive waves push beach sediment into long low ridges. Berms mark the junction between the backshore and the foreshore.

2. Cusps: Crescent-shaped hollows formed where shingle changes to sand. Cusps form as a result of complex wave actions which sort heavier material into crescent-shaped patterns. Cusps generally occur on pebble beaches. They form on beaches where the wind blows mainly at an angle to the beach.

3. Runnels and ridges: Runnels are broad depressions in the sand of the foreshore, ridges are gentle rises in it. If you have ever walked out to sea in shallow water and it gets deeper for a while then shallower, you have walked across a runnel and ridge. They are formed by the action of constructive waves.

Longer stretches of beach tend to lie on the east coast of Ireland while on the west coast most beaches are found in small bays. This is because the west coast of Ireland is exposed to the full force of the destructive Atlantic waves, so sheltered bays and inlets are the only calm places in which beaches can form.

In general, beaches may be divided into two zones. The backshore and the foreshore. The beach gets slowly flatter as you walk from the backshore to the foreshore.

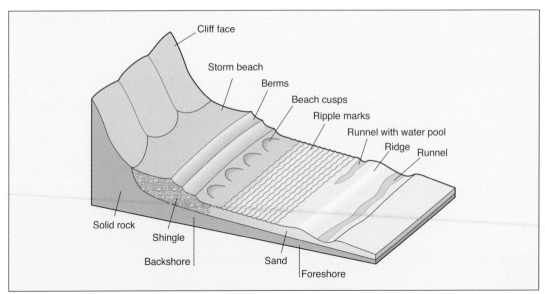

Fig. 25 Exam Diagram: **Some landforms that may be found on a beach**

Fig. 26 The photograph shows some well-developed cusps on a shingle beach in County Louth.

Fig. 27 A beach in a sheltered bay in County Donegal

Sand spits

Main processes: longshore drift, constructive waves

Example: Inch Strand, County Kerry.

Sand spits are landforms of marine deposition. They are long deposits of sand attached to the land at one end. Portmarnock and North Bull Island in Dublin are well-known beaches which also happen to be sand spits.

Sand spits are created when the process of longshore drift is interrupted in some way either by a change in the shape of the coast or by human activity such as building a sea wall. They are commonly found attached to headlands.

IN DEPTH – Sand spits

Where the coast changes direction longshore drift is unable to move material further along the coast and the material is deposited at this point. Longshore drift continues to pile sand up here. Eventually a long ridge of sand extends out to sea and may be exposed at low tide.

Over time the spit builds up, becoming visible at high tide. Vegetation may grow, its roots stabilising the sand. Wind action may create sand dunes on the spit. Most spits have wide sandy beaches and dunes. Behind the dunes on the landward side a salt marsh may develop.

Wave action and local currents often make the end of the spit curve, e.g. Inch Strand, County Kerry. One of Ireland's best studied sand spits is the North Bull Island in Dublin. See the case study on page 181.

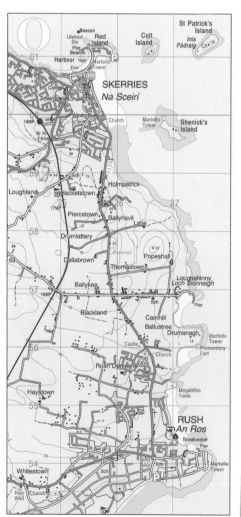

Fig. 28 Map showing bays, headlands and beaches between Rush and Skerries, County Dublin

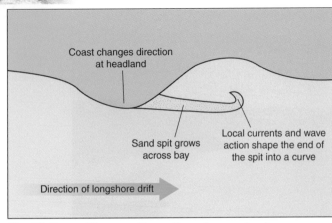

Coast changes direction at headland

Sand spit grows across bay

Local currents and wave action shape the end of the spit into a curve

Direction of longshore drift

Fig. 29 Exam Diagram: Formation of a sand spit

Onshore winds

Sand dunes

Sea   Beach   Lagoon   Marsh   Sea

Fig. 30 Cross section of a typical sand spit. Note the sand dunes marked on the spit. These formed as the wind blew across the wide sandy beach. When the tide is out the bay behind the spit is uncovered as mudflats. Not all spits have lagoons and marshes.

Fig. 31 Important Information: Map to show sand spits at Dooey, County Donegal. Note where the spit is connected to the land. This is where the coast changes direction and turns into Ballyness Bay.

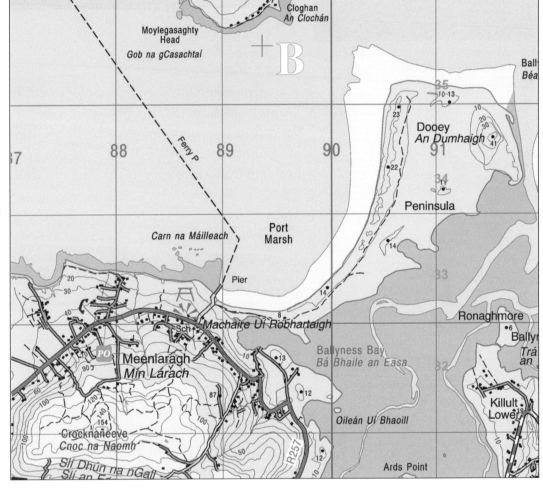

Tombolo

Main Processes: longshore drift, wave refraction, deposition.

Example: Sutton, County Dublin and Castlegregory, County Kerry.

A tombolo is a sandbar or sandspit that connects an island to the mainland. A tombolo is a landform of marine deposition. Tombolos are common around the west coast of Ireland and are made of shingle, sand and stone.

IN DEPTH – Tombolos

Tombolos are formed in two ways by the action of wave refraction and longshore drift. Firstly, as waves approach the shallow water near an island they slow down and begin to wrap around (refract) the island. The wave patterns caused by the island trigger longshore drift currents on each side of the island. These longshore drift currents then collide in the sheltered area between the island and the mainland. This causes deposition to occur leading to the formation of a ridge of sand or shingle. Over time the ridge connects the island to the mainland and a tombolo has formed (Fig. 32).

Secondly in some places an island is located in the path of the prevailing longshore drift current. Longshore drift produces a sand spit where the coastline changes direction. The sand spit may grow along the coast until it reaches an island forming a tombolo (Fig. 33).

Tombolo deposits are often layered with coarser sediments at the base and finer sands at the top of the tombolo. Tombolos are easily eroded by storms and destructive waves. They are often reinforced to provide access to islands for tourists and the local population who may live on the island.

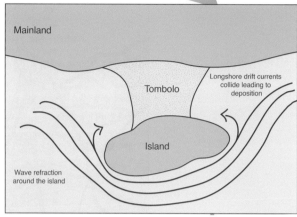

Fig. 32 Exam Diagram: The formation of a tombolo (a)

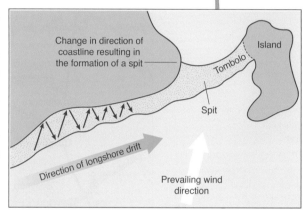

Fig 33 Exam Diagram: The formation of a tombolo (b)

Fig. 34 A growing tombolo visible at low tide at Shenick's Island near Skerries, County Dublin. See map on page 178.

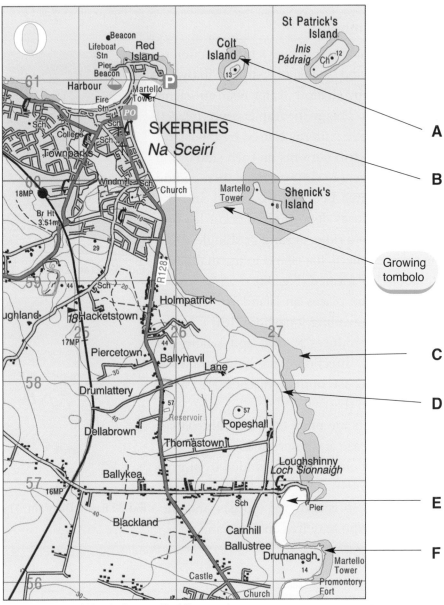

Fig. 35 Map of North County Dublin coast

Landform	Letter	Grid Reference	Formed by erosion or deposition
Cliff			
Tombolo			
Beach			
Sea stack			
Wave Cut Platform			
Headland			

10.6 Human interaction with coastal processes

> You must study human interaction with river processes OR coastal processes OR mass movement processes

Coastal protection methods

Humans have interacted with marine processes of erosion, deposition and transport. In order to protect the coastline and prevent dangers to shipping, many methods of coastal management are used. These often affect the natural processes of erosion, transport and deposition.

Methods used to protect the coast fall into one of two groups: soft methods or hard methods.

Fig. 36 Human activities affect coastal processes.

Soft methods encourage deposition

Soft methods are designed to encourage beaches and dunes to form or get bigger. They may trap sediment moving along the coast or deflect waves to redirect the transport of sediment in order to keep harbours free of sediment.

Soft methods usually work to strengthen the natural processes already at work in the sea, for example beach and sand-dune formation and longshore drift.

The following structures are built to do this:

Fences in sand dunes: encourage build-up of wind-blown sand in dunes

Mats: placed in front of dunes trap sand and encourage plant growth

Beach nourishment: sand is pumped onto a beach to build it up.

Groynes: trap sand

Fig. 37 Beach nourishment in Andalucia in Spain. The sand is pumped onto the shore from the boat in the background.

Hard methods prevent erosion

These usually work to resist the force of the sea. They are carefully engineered structures designed to protect the coast from storm waves and general wave action.

The following structures are built to do this:

Sea walls: built to prevent erosion of valuable sea front, e.g. Tramore sea wall

Rock armour: 1–2 tonne boulders placed in front of the coastline or at an existing sea wall. They absorb the energy of the waves, e.g. Templetown Beach, County Louth.

Revetments: sloping banks built to absorb the energy of the sea, e.g. Balagan Point, County Louth.

Breakwaters: concrete walls built some distance offshore to reduce the force of the waves before they hit the coast, e.g. a breakwater is planned for Courtown Beach, County Wexford.

Gabions: wire mesh cages filled with large stones placed at the base of cliffs to absorb the energy of the waves, e.g. Newcastle Beach, County Wicklow.

Fig. 38 Tetrapods protect the harbour wall at Kilmore Quay, County Wexford. They are designed to reduce the power of waves.

Fig. 39 Gabions and rock armour, Newcastle Beach, County Wicklow

Fig. 40 Groynes at Rosslare Strand, County Wexford. Work out the direction of longshore drift in this photo.

Fig. 41 Sea wall at Lahinch, County Clare

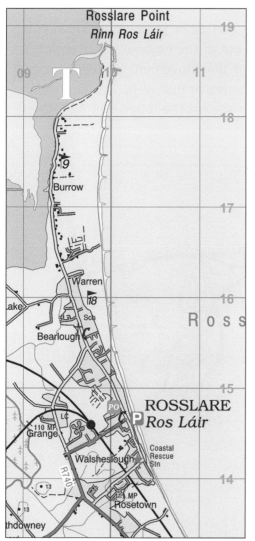

Fig. 42 Map of Rosslare Strand to show groynes built along a sand spit

Fig. 43 Rock armour and groynes protect this beach. Groynes are very effective methods for widening a beach and protecting the coast. Similar groynes are planned for Courtown Beach, County Wexford. Look at the photo of Rosslare strand. Can you work out the direction in which longshore drift is carrying the sand?

> The east coast of Britain has some of the highest erosion rates in the world. Losses of up to 25 m a year have been recorded. Hundreds of villages have disappeared into the sea since Roman times.

North Bull Island, County Dublin

The North Bull Island is a good example of how humans have changed the natural processes of coastal transportation and deposition in Dublin Bay. The North Bull Island is a low-lying, dune-covered sand spit running parallel to the coast between Clontarf and Sutton in the northern half of Dublin Bay. The word 'bull' is adapted from the word 'ball' which in the eighteenth century meant 'sandbank'.

How have human activities affected natural coastal processes at the Bull Island?

- The island is approximately 200 years old and was formed as a result of the building of the North Bull Wall by Captain Bligh. At one time, the natural process of longshore drift carried sand and silt southwards across Dublin Bay and often blocked the port. Ships frequently ran aground on the sand banks deposited in the area.

case study

case study

The North and South Bull Walls were built between 1818 and 1824 to prevent Dublin Port choking with silt. The walls increased the tidal flow in and out of the harbour which kept the port clear of sand. However, the North Bull Wall blocked the movement of sediment by longshore drift. As a result sand was deposited against the North Bull Wall. This deposition resulted in the creation of sand dunes and a salt marsh up against the North Bull Wall. Over time this deposition created the North Bull Island.

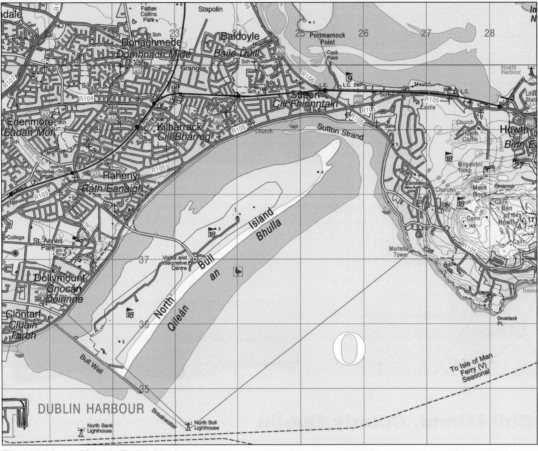

Fig. 44 Map of North Bull Island

The island now extends five km in length and is about one km wide. A well-developed dune system is established which runs along the length of the island. On the seaward side is Dollymount strand, on the leeward side is a lagoon and salt marsh. At low tide the bed of the lagoon is exposed as mudflats which provide vital winter feeding grounds for migratory wildfowl such as Brent Geese from the Canadian Tundra and Iceland.

North Bull Island is still growing but storms can erode the seaward edge.

The main human pressure on the island is erosion of the sand dunes due to visitor traffic. Anything between 1,500 and 4,000 people visit per day in summer.

Human Impact on Coastal Deposition Processes in Dublin Bay

Before the Bull Walls were built	After the Bull Walls were built
Deposition occurred in the sheltered mouth of the River Liffey.	Deposition occurred beside the North Bull wall forming Bull Island.
Sand bars shifted frequently and endangered shipping.	Bull walls increased speed of tidal flow of water keeping the mouth of the River Liffey clear of sediment and preventing sand bar formation.
The harbour was only 1.8 m deep.	The harbour is now 6 -12 m deep.

Human Interaction with the Sand Dunes on Bull Island

1. Quad bikers may illegally ride over the dunes, wrecking them.

2. Cars park on dune edges damaging them.

3. Cars parking on the beach may compact the sand making dune growth difficult.

6. People walk over dunes looking for a sunbathing spot damaging marram grass and thus causing erosion.

4. Litter from thousands of beach users has to be managed.

5. To decorate their fairways and greens golf clubs may use non-native plants which may 'escape' into the natural vegetation on the island.

case study

Fig. 45 Bull Island, Dublin, looking south across Sutton tombolo

For an ecological view of the oceans log on http://www.eco-pros.com/oceanhome.htm

Courtown north beach, County Wexford

Courtown Beach is a good example of how human activities have protected the coast from natural erosion processes.

- In County Wexford erosion rates are some of the highest in the country, up to two metres per year in places. Severe erosion of more than 1 m per year affects 13 km of Wexford coast.

- Courtown is a major tourist centre in the county. The tourist industry in the Gorey/Courtown area has been built up around the Blue Flag beach at Courtown.

- Coastal erosion of the beach at Courtown has been a major problem. Action has had to be taken to protect the beach. In addition, the dune and backshore area is an area of scientific interest. Any further dune erosion will lead to the loss of significant areas of tourist and amenity land as well as environmental damage to the adjacent woodland area.

Fig. 46 Location map of Courtown

Soft coastal protection methods

- Soft methods work with nature rather than resist it. Wexford County Council used a variety of soft engineering techniques including dune reclamation, sand fencing and marram grass planting in an attempt to trap sand and slow the erosion of the beach and dunes.

- Winter storm waves overwhelmed many of their attempts to protect the shore. The council then had to use hard rock banks (revetments) and rock armour in order to prevent the immediate threat of further coastal erosion. Soft engineering techniques may be used on the dunes north of the river delta where erosion rates are lower and there is less pressure on the beach and backshore area.

Fig. 47 Revetments and rock armour protecting the coast at Courtown, County Wexford

- Several alternative beach protection methods have been considered but not constructed:
  1. Beach nourishment
  2. Groynes
  3. Offshore breakwaters

No method on its own would be enough to cure the problem. The council has considered a number of options to provide the most suitable method of protecting this valuable stretch of coastline.

Some of the options that were identified by initial surveys of the coast at Courtown are described below.

Beach nourishment

- This is when sand is added to the beach to replace that removed by longshore drift. Sand is pumped onto the beaches from sites under the sea off the coast. However, a beach nourishment scheme would be affected by the process of longshore drift. The rate of loss of beach material would be such that the maintenance cost would be too high.

Groynes

- These walls are built at right angles to the shoreline and placed in a line stretching up and down the beach. They trap sediment carried by longshore drift.

case study

A system of groynes could be used to stabilise the problem. However, during severe storms at Courtown, sediment would be carried out to sea. Either a regular renourishing programme or the use of specially shaped groynes would be required. Any groyne system makes access difficult along the beach, however, and it is therefore unlikely to be acceptable on such an important recreational beach. Groynes have been used successfully further down the coast at Rosslare Strand.

> Archaeologists have found evidence of many villages that existed along the Wexford coast. They are underwater today.

Offshore breakwaters

- Breakwaters are concrete walls placed some distance offshore. Tidal conditions at Courtown make the use of offshore breakwaters to control sediment movement an attractive option. The breakwater would slow the rate of longshore drift and allow the beach to grow.

- As well as controlling the longshore drift, offshore breakwaters have the advantage of reducing the energy of waves reaching the beach during storms, thus reducing erosion.

So what is happening at Courtown?

- Between €5–€6 million is being spent building three offshore islands to protect the coast and encourage the deposition of beach material. A new 250-berth marina is also planned. Until it is constructed several hundred metres of rock armour have been put in place to prevent further degradation of the coast.

- Funding for the project comes from the European Union under its Interreg IIIA scheme which offers financial assistance for projects in Ireland and Wales.

higher level

10.7 Isostatic and eustatic processes

> Landforms represent a balance between the action of internal and surface processes. Isostatic processes involve adjustments to the balance between land and sea. This balance may change over time.

In some coastal areas of Ireland (e.g. Donegal, Antrim) beaches and cliffs are visible in the landscape high above the present sea level. In other areas, parts of the coastline have been submerged beneath the sea (e.g. Shannon Estuary). The formation of these unusual coastal features is linked to the effects of huge ice sheets which covered the land during the last glaciation and the changes in sea level that have occurred since. Two processes occur which lead to changes in land and sea level.

Eustatic changes

Eustacy is the process whereby **sea level rises or falls** relative to the land. During an Ice Age the sea level drops because rain and river water is locked away in ice sheets on land and does not reach the sea. This lowers sea levels across the world. When the ice melts, large volumes of meltwater flow into the sea and cause global rises in sea levels. Such widespread changes in sea levels are called **eustatic sea level changes**. Coastal areas that are drowned by rising sea levels due to eustatic sea level change are known as **submerged coastlines.**

Isostatic changes

Isostacy is the process whereby the **land rises or falls** relative to sea level. The earth's solid crust floats on the more liquid mantle below in the same way that a piece of wood floats on water. The weight of huge ice sheets on the land can cause the earth's crust to push into the mantle, in a similar way to someone pressing onto a block of wood or a plastic float in water and holding it down. When the ice is removed the crust slowly returns to its original level raising the land out of the sea. Imagine someone removing their hand from the wood/float and letting it settle at its usual level in the water. Only the area of land affected by this ice may be raised from the sea so that sea level changes are local not global in extent. These local changes in sea level are called **isostatic sea level changes**. They may also happen when tectonic plates collide and cause uplift of land in certain areas, e.g. fold and block mountains, or when a great weight of overlying rock is removed. Coastal areas that are raised from the sea by isostacy are known as **emerged coastlines.**

Fig. 48 What will happen to the springs when the dog gets up?

In many areas of the world, the isostatic uplift or rebound of land out of the sea is greater than the subsequent rise in sea level caused by melting ice sheets. For example around the Baltic Sea in Scandinavia and Hudson Bay in Canada, sea cliffs and beach ridges are now found nearly 300 m above the present sea level!

Isostatic uplift of land is still happening. The northern Baltic Sea is rising nearly one centimetre a year. This may not sound like much, but it adds up to one metre per century which can impact on port towns and shipping.

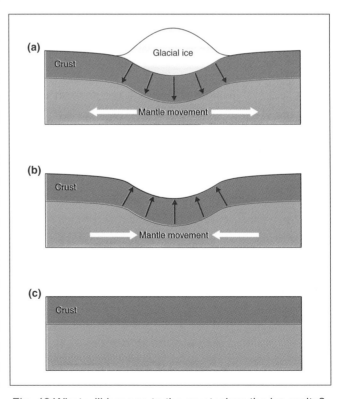

Fig. 49 What will happen to the crust when the ice melts?

higher level

187

higher level

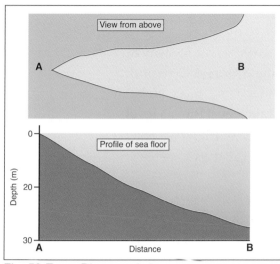

Fig. 50 Exam Diagram: A ria

1. Landforms associated with drowned/submerged coastlines

(a) Rias

A ria is a drowned river valley, e.g. Kenmare Bay in County Kerry and Shannon Estuary in County Limerick/Clare.

Rias form where sea levels rise relative to the land either as a result of eustatic sea level change (where the global sea levels rise) or isostatic sea level change (where the land sinks). When this happens coastal valleys which were previously at sea level become submerged/flooded. The result is often a very large estuary at the mouth of a relatively small river. Rias are common across south-western Ireland and Europe, e.g. the mouth of the River Severn in the UK and the north Brittany coastline of France.

(b) Fiords

Fiords are drowned glaciated valleys, e.g. Killary Harbour in County Mayo. They are formed when a glacier cuts a U-shaped valley by plucking and abrasion into the surrounding bedrock. In countries such as Norway and Greenland the glaciers flow into the sea so their glaciated valleys open into the sea. When ice sheets melt, the meltwater flows into the sea and causes the sea level to rise which then floods the U-shaped valley.

Fiords generally have a sill or rise at their mouth caused by the previous glacier's deposition of a terminal moraine. In many cases these cause extreme tidal currents and rapids at the entrance to the fiord.

Rias and fiords have several differences:

- Rias get shallower towards the land.
- Fiords get deeper towards the land.
- Rias are V-shaped and wider at their mouths with gently sloping sides.
- Fiords are long and narrow with steeply-sloping sides.
- Fiords have a submarine sill at their entrance.
- Rias do not.

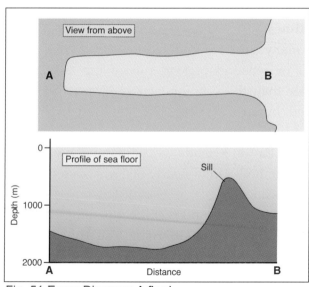

Fig. 51 Exam Diagram: A fiord

2. Landforms associated with raised/emergent coastlines

(a) Raised beach/Marine terrace

A raised beach or a marine terrace is an emergent coastal landform of deposition. Raised beaches/marine terraces represent an ancient shoreline now exposed above sea level, e.g. near Ballyhillin, Malin Head, County Donegal.
They form because of the land rising due to isostacy.

During a period of glaciation (ice age) great ice sheets cover the land. Coastal landforms such as beaches continued to form by the action of constructive waves in sheltered bays unaffected directly by the ice sheet.

When the ice melts the huge weight of ice is removed from the land which is then gradually uplifted out of the sea due to isostacy. The beaches which once marked the ice age sea level are now raised above the present day sea level and form wide terraces. New beaches now form but at a lower level than before.

Fig. 52 A raised beach near Ballyhillin, County Donegal

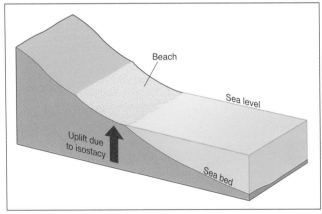

Fig. 53 Exam Diagram: Formation of a beach during a period of glaciation

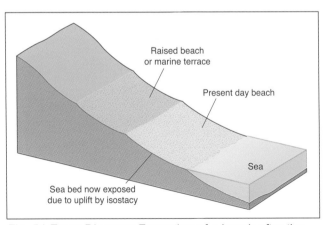

Fig. 54 Exam Diagram: Formation of a beach after the ice melts

(b) Raised cliffs and wave-cut platforms

Raised cliffs, caves and wave-cut platforms are also emergent coastal landforms, e.g. Portbradden, County Donegal. They are erosional coastal landforms which existed during the last ice age. They formed in the same way that modern cliffs and caves are formed. The marine processes of erosion such as air compression, hydraulic action and abrasion attacked the coast forming notches, cliffs, wave-cut platforms and caves.

After the huge mass of ice was removed at the end of the Ice Age, the land was uplifted due to 'isostatic rebound'. The cliffs, caves and wave-cut platforms were raised above the level of the sea.

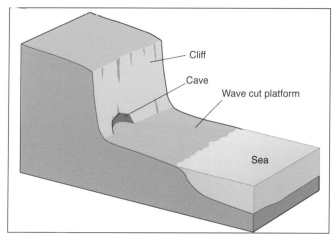

Fig. 55 Formation of a cliff and a wave-cut platform during a period of glaciation

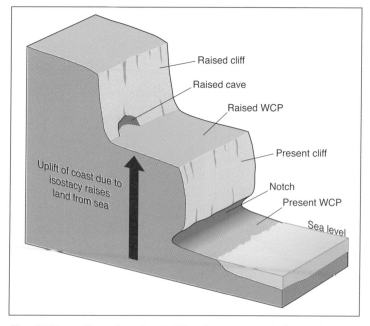

Fig. 56 Formation of a raised cliff and wave-cut platform after the ice melts

Chapter Revision Questions

1. Explain the characteristics of constructive and destructive waves.

2. Name and explain three processes of marine erosion.

3. When does marine deposition occur and what conditions are necessary for it to take place?

4. With the aid of a diagram explain the process of longshore drift.

5. Explain the process of wave refraction.

6. Describe, giving examples and referring to the processes involved, the formation of three of the following landforms of marine erosion: cliff, cave, sea stack, arch.

7. Describe, giving examples and referring to the processes involved, the formation of the following landforms of marine deposition: beach, tombolo, sand spit.

8. The North Bull Island is an example of how nature and people can co-exist. Outline the pressures on the island and measures taken to reduce human impact.

9. What is the difference between hard and soft coastal protection methods?

10. Using an area of coastline you have studied, describe the impact of coastal erosion and some measures taken to protect against it. What may influence the decision of a county council to spend money on coastal protection?

11. Explain the terms isostatic and eustatic sea level changes. **(HL)**

12. Name and describe the formation of two landforms made by isostatic processes. Draw a diagram of each. **(HL)**

OL Short Questions

13. Examine the photograph which shows a coastal region.
    (a) Name **two** features of deposition that you can see.
    (b) Are the waves here more likely to be constructive or destructive?
    (c) Name **two** ways in which a coastal area like this is of economic benefit to people.
    LC Exam Paper

14. The following features are the result of ice, river or sea action. In the case of each feature listed, state which of the agents (ice, rivers or sea) formed it: waterfall; interlocking spur; esker; blowhole; cirque/corrie.
    LC Exam Paper

15. Match the processes A–E with the landforms 1–5.

Process	Landform
A. Air compression	1. Cave
B. Hydraulic action	2. Beach
C. Deposition	3. Sand spit
D. Longshore drift	4. Rounded beach pebbles
E. Attrition	5. Cliff

16. (i) Examine the photograph above and then pair each of the landforms in the table below with the correct letter in the diagram.

Landform	Letter
Sea Arch	
Sea Cave	
Sea Stack/Stump	
Cliff	

(ii) Read the statement below and place an X in the correct box.
"All the landforms in the photograph above were formed by marine deposition."

a False ☐   b True ☐

17. Study the map and photograph extracts that follow and answer the questions.
(i) The feature marked X on the map joins Omey Island to the mainland. Was it formed by deposition or erosion?
(ii) Name the feature marked Y on the photograph.
(iii) Was it formed by deposition or erosion?

(iv) Read the statement below and place an X in the correct box.
"The river in the photograph is in the middle or lower course and meandering."
a False ☐   b True ☐

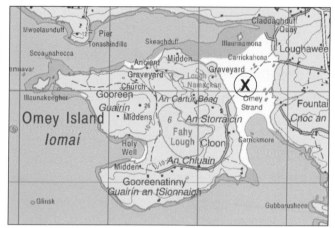

OL Long Questions

18. Select any **one** of the following surface processes:
    (a) Sea/marine action
    (b) River action
    (c) Glacial action
    (d) Mass movement.
    Explain the formation of any two Irish landforms caused by your selected process with the aid of diagrams.
    LC Exam Paper

19. Describe and explain how humans attempt to control **one** of the following surface processes:

    • River processes

    • Coastal processes

    • Mass movement

HL Long Questions

20. Examine how human processes can have an impact on the operation of **one** of the following natural processes:
    (a) Mass movement processes
    (b) River processes
    (c) Coastal processes.
    LC Exam Paper

21. Explain any **two** processes of erosion for each of the following: rivers, ice, sea.

22. (a) Identify **one** erosional and **one** depositional landform evident in the photograph on the top right.
    (b) Describe and explain the process at work in the formation of any one of these landforms.

23. With the aid of a labelled diagram, examine the processes that have led to the formation of any **one** Irish landform of your choice.

24. Isostatic processes involve adjustments to the balance between land and sea. Discuss how these processes have shaped the Irish landscape over time.

Chapter 11

Mass Movement Processes, Patterns and Landforms

At the end of this chapter you should be able to:

- Explain what mass movement is.
- Name and explain the factors that affect mass movement processes.
- Describe how mass movements are classified.
- Describe examples of each type of mass movement.
- Use case studies to illustrate the impact of mass movement on people.
- Use case studies to show how people cause and control mass movement.

Contents

11.1   What is mass movement?

11.2   Factors affecting mass movement

11.3   Classifying mass movement

Case Studies: Lahars in Colombia

Landslides in Venezuela

11.4   Human influence on mass movement

Case Studies: The impact of overcropping in China

Deforestation causes landslide in Indonesia

The Derrybrien bog flow/bog burst, County Galway

Questions

If you are choosing this chapter to study in detail, you must be able to explain mass movement processes, how the landforms are made, and be able to identify them on diagrams, maps and photos. The extra material you need to know is indicated by a green arrow. Higher Level students study how landforms represent a balance between internal and surface forces. If you are not choosing this chapter, then you should be able to identify the landforms on diagrams, maps and photos and state the processes that made them.

11.1 What is mass movement?

Mass movement is the movement of material downhill under the influence of gravity.

The action of weathering (mechanical and chemical) and erosional processes create soil and scree which lie on the surface of the earth. This loose material is called **regolith**.

For mass movement to occur a slope must be present, whether gentle or steep. Some mass movement is so very slow that it cannot be seen happening, while other types of mass movement are very fast and devastating.

Mass movements are often triggered. These triggers may be natural or man-made.

Natural triggers
1. Torrential rains
2. Heavy snow
3. Earthquakes and volcanoes

Human triggers
1. Building road cuttings across hillsides
2. Placing waste material on unstable slopes
3. Quarry blasting
4. Deforestation
5. Skiing in soft snow

Fig. 1 The LaConchita landslide of 1995 in Ventura County, California

11.2 Factors affecting mass movement

Several factors encourage mass movement to happen.
1.   Gravity
2.   Slope
3.   Water
4.   Vegetation
5.   Human activities
6.   Type of material

1. Gravity

Gravity helps stick the regolith (soil) to a slope or move it downhill. The speed of movement is proportional to the weight of the regolith to be moved and the steepness of the slope. Heavy particles on a steep slope will move more quickly.

2. Slope

Steep slopes result in fast movements such as avalanches.

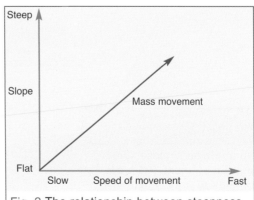

Fig. 2 The relationship between steepness of slope and the speed of mass movement

3. Water

Water adds weight and helps the regolith slip downhill. When the regolith is saturated it slides easily over the ground beneath it.

4. Vegetation

The absence of vegetation increases the risk of mass movement on hills. Roots lock soil particles together, absorb water and shield the ground from rain. This prevents slippage and reduces the chance of mass movement occurring.

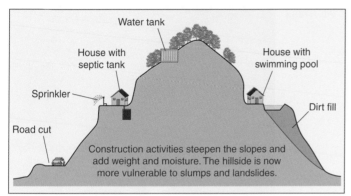

Fig. 3 A variety of human activities can trigger mass movement.

5. Human activities

People can increase the risk of mass movement occurring by:

(a) undercutting hillsides for road and railway construction.

(b) building on unsafe areas such as landfills.

(c) building structures on slopes.

6. Type of material

This can range from loose rock, soil, snow or turf, all of which can move downslope.

11.3 Classifying mass movement

There are several ways of classifying mass movements.

They can be grouped according to:

1. Speed (fast, slow)   **2.** Water content (wet, dry)

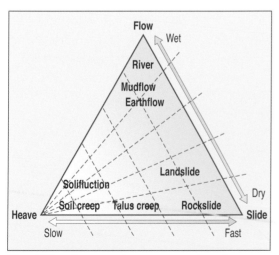

Fig. 4 The diagram above summarises the various types of mass movement. From this, we can see that a mudflow is a wet and fast type of mass movement. A rockslide is a fast, dry type of mass movement.

Type of mass movement	Examples
1. Very slow	Soil creep and solifluction
2. Fast and wet	Mudflows, lahars, bog bursts/flows, landslides and slumps
3. Fast and dry	Rock falls, avalanches

Very slow mass movements

Soil creep

Main processes: freeze-thaw action, wetting, drying

This is a very slow but continuous movement of soil downhill. It is common on grassy slopes in Ireland. Soil creep occurs so slowly you cannot see it happening, but it leaves tell-tale evidence behind.

Evidence of soil creep

Once you know what to look for, evidence of soil creep is easy to see and it is quite widespread across Ireland.

1. Terracettes (small steps) in grassy slopes

2. Cracks in roads parallel to the slope

3. Tilted telegraph poles

4. Soil bulging against the upslope side of a wall on a hill

5. Burst stone walls

6. Tilted fence posts

7. Tree trunks curved as they try to grow straight up but their roots are moving downhill.

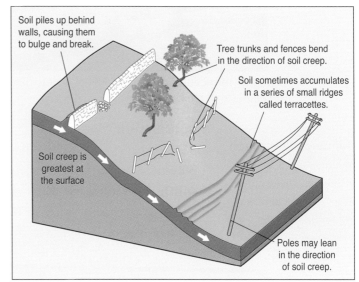

Fig. 5 Evidence of soil creep

IN DEPTH - Soil creep

Soil creep occurs due to the combination of two processes.

1. Alternating wet and dry periods

2. Freeze-thaw action

During rainy weather soil grains expand (hydration) and are pushed up and away from each other. As the soil grains dry out during dry weather they shrink (dehydrate) and as they move closer to each other they roll slowly downhill. Repeated wetting and drying causes the gradual movement of soil downhill. Soil piles up against walls or forms **terracettes** and may cause fences and poles to tilt.

During colder weather frost can cause the upward movement of soil as the ice expands. When the soil thaws, the soil grains move slowly downhill.

All In Depth sections contain material you need to know if you are studying this chapter in detail.

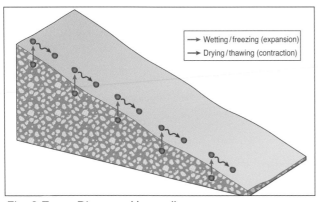

Fig. 6 Exam Diagram: How soil creep occurs

Fig. 7 Terracettes: A small-scale but widely distributed landform of mass movement.

Fig. 8 Tree tilted due to soil creep in Gortin, County Tyrone

Solifluction

Main processes: summer melting of permafrost, sliding

Solifluction is a slow, wet form of mass movement. It produces landforms called **solifluction lobes.** Solifluction has probably not occurred in Ireland since the last ice age. It is common today in permafrost slopes close to ice sheets (**periglacial areas**) such as Iceland, Canada and the Tundra areas of the world.

> The deepest permafrost in the world is found in Siberia. The ground is frozen to a depth of more than 300 m.

IN DEPTH - Solifluction

Fig. 9 Solifluction lobes in Siberia, a landform created by mass movement

Solifluction occurs in areas where there is **permafrost**, that is where the ground is frozen to a depth of several metres below the surface. During the summer the top metre or so may thaw out. The permafrost below prevents meltwater seeping down and so the topmost layer is a soggy mix of tundra vegetation and water. If this mix occurs on a slope it flows slowly downhill a bit like honey off a spoon and leaves behind curved bulges of debris called solifluction lobes.

Fast and wet mass movements

Fast and wet mass movements 'flow' downhill like liquids but once they stop moving they become completely solid, making the rescue of buried people very, very difficult.

All wet mass movements contain a lot of water and are often triggered by heavy rain.

Mudflows

Main processes: heavy rain, flooding

These are the most dangerous mass movements. They are slurries of mud, loose rock and water. They quickly gather speed and volume as they flow downhill. As they move, air, water and earth are mixed together and become an unstoppable river of debris. Mudflows can move many kilometres wiping out everything in their path. They occur on bare slopes with gradients greater than 25°, e.g. Brazil.

Lahars

Main processes: volcanic eruption, snow melt/heavy rain, flooding

Example: Mount St Helens, USA

Lahars occur when volcanic ash mixes with large amounts of water. The excess water can come from torrential rain during an eruption or from snow melted from the top of an erupting volcano.

IN DEPTH - Lahars

Lahars follow the landscape (**topography**) closely. Valleys become well-known paths of repeated lahar events. Lahars have the density of wet concrete and can travel at speeds of 40–100 km/h. Some have been recorded as reaching 300 km/h, e.g. the Mount Pinatubo eruption in the Philippines in 1991.

When Mount Pinatubo erupted again in 1995 lahars did massive damage to farmland and roadways. The lahars left deposits which were up to four metres thick in places.

Mass movement in South America

1. Lahars in Colombia

● This most damaging lahar occurred in 1985 on the Colombian volcano, Nevado del Ruiz. This volcano had created several devastating lahars in the past and it was a disaster waiting to happen. The town of Armero had been built on older lahar deposits that had flowed down the valley of the River Lagunillas in 1845.

● In 1985 when the volcano erupted again the heat of the lava melted the snow and ice on top of the mountain. The combination of ash, rock, meltwater and torrential rain created a lahar 30 m high travelling at 80 km/h down along the same river valley. This lahar hit the town of Armero, burying it under 8 m of mud and killing 23,000 of the 24,000 people in Armero. The lahar hit at midnight when many of the residents were asleep – they had no chance to escape.

Fig. 10 Location map of the Nevado del Ruiz volcano and the town of Armero in Colombia

● The most tragic thing is that with proper planning this disaster would never have happened. Today the paths of lahars are mapped and predicted around many of the world's active volcanoes and (in developed countries at least) strict planning laws prevent settlement in risk areas.

case study

Fig. 11 The Armero Lahar of 1985

Landslides and slumps

Main processes: a trigger, gravity
Example: South-east Brazil
These occur when rock or sediment suddenly moves downhill along well-defined surfaces which may be flat or curved. The common term for them is **landslide**.

Fig. 12 A slump on the Louth coastline

IN DEPTH - Rotational slumps

Rotational slumps are very common in Ireland along soft coastlines made of glacial till. In a rotational slump, a slab of earth slips along a curved surface and rotates back on itself as it slides downslope. Water helps the slump or landslide to occur by reducing the sticking ability (**friction**) of the soil particles. Coastal areas are often at risk from rotational slumps as the sea undercuts the base of such cliffs.

Rotational slumps may be observed along the Louth coastline north of Clogher Head. Every winter landslides/slumps occur on soft coastlines around Ireland. The rail link between Dublin and Greystones has been damaged in this way.

Fig. 13 Exam Diagram: A rotational slump

Fig. 14 Landslide at Greystones, County Wicklow

2. Landslides in Venezuela

- Torrential rains which fell on the north of Venezuela in 1999 caused massive landslides. Thousands of homes and buildings were destroyed and approximately 190,000 people were evacuated and lost their houses. An estimated 30,000 were killed.

- The international airport of Caracas was temporarily closed and the coastal road was destroyed or closed at many locations. The economic damage was estimated at over €2.3 billion.

- Environmental damage after the massive landslides left the area at risk of future mass movement because of the removal of vegetation and trees.

- This disaster was one of the most devastating natural disasters ever recorded in the country. The infrastructure (roads, water supplies, sanitation, electricity, harbours) was badly affected for months after the rains.

Fast and dry mass movements

Avalanches

Main processes: gravity, weight of snow, a trigger
Example: Swiss Alps
Avalanches are considered to be dry mass movements because the snowflakes act as dry particles. Avalanches occur when huge masses of snow and ice fall down mountainsides at great speed (up to 400 km/h). The study of avalanches is critical in the Alps where millions of skiers use the slopes each year.

IN DEPTH - Avalanches

Snow on a mountain builds up in layers. These layers stick to each other with varying degrees of strength. An avalanche occurs when the weight of fresh snow causes layers of snow underneath to slide over each other. On an avalanche-prone slope a very small additional load, such as the weight of a single skier, can trigger an avalanche. Huge slabs of snow fall down the mountain at great speeds.

Certain weather conditions can increase the risk of avalanches occurring. Fresh snow and wind create the greatest avalanche danger.

To reduce the threat, avalanches are deliberately triggered. Explosive charges are placed in large snow accumulations. They may be dropped from the air or are fired by artillery.

Victims of avalanches are mostly skiers, snowboarders and mountaineers. The winter reports of the Swiss Federal Institute for Snow and Avalanche Research clearly show that most avalanches are triggered by sporting activity on the mountain slopes. On the basis of statistics over the last 55 years, one can say that on average 26 people are killed by avalanches – the white death – in Switzerland every winter.

Avalanche frequency is increasing because of the growth of extreme sports like heli-skiing where skiers are dropped off from helicopters onto unofficial (**off piste**) ski runs.

Fig. 15 It is important that people stay on official ski runs. Off-piste skiing can lead to avalanches.

Fig. 16 Avalanche in Northern Pakistan

Find out more about avalanches. Log on to http://www.cln.org/themes/avalanches.html This is an American-based site that has links to other avalanche pages.

Rock falls

Main processes: weathering, a trigger, gravity

Example: The Conor Pass, County Kerry

In mountainous areas where bare rock is exposed to weathering, earthquakes and repeated frost action may trigger rock falls. Blocks of rock fall from steep slopes. Individual blocks may fall away from (or slide down) well-developed bedding planes or joints. The falling pieces bounce and roll downhill. Over time the debris from rock falls can build up into scree (talus) slopes. Active scree slopes are characterised by angular blocks and an absence of vegetation. In this case the old saying is true – rolling stones really don't gather any moss!

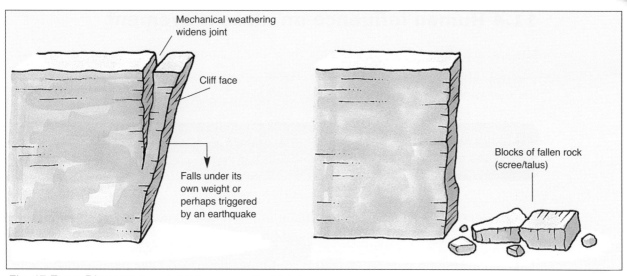

Fig. 17 Exam Diagram: A rock fall from a vertical joint

Fig. 18 Scree slope and rock fall at Glendalough, County Wicklow

Higher Level Students should study landforms associated with changes in sea level and land level. These landforms are explained in Chapters 8 and 10. Higher Level students must also study section 8.7 in Chapter 8 OR section 10.7 in Chapter 10.

Fig. 19 A rock fall in Cheddar Gorge, England and a close-up of the fallen rock.

11.4 Human influence on mass movement

Human activities can lead to an increase in mass movement. Landslides and soil erosion are more frequent as a result of over-grazing, overcropping and deforestation.

> You must study human interaction with river processes OR coastal processes OR mass movement processes

1. **Over-grazing** occurs when too many animals are allowed to graze an area of land. This damages soil structure and plants.

2. **Overcropping** occurs when land is continuously farmed in an unsustainable way. This reduces soil nutrients and destroys the structure of the soil, making it less fertile and easy to erode.

3. **Deforestation** occurs when large areas of forest are cut leaving a bare landscape. Forests provide natural protection for soil from rain and wind and so prevent mass movement.

Other human activities such as blasting and placing waste material on unstable slopes also cause mass movement as the following case studies show.

case study

Human activities trigger mass movement

1. The impact of overcropping in China

- Overcropping occurs when land is continuously farmed. It is not left fallow or refertilised properly. This causes the removal of nutrients from the soil. It also destroys the structure of the soil, making it loose, dry and infertile. Mass movement and erosion agents can then easily remove this soil.

- Overcropping and soil erosion is a major problem in parts of China, which has lost more topsoil than any other region on the planet. Over 4 million hectares of cropland was lost to soil erosion and removal in the last 20 years. This soil provided food for approximately 45 million people and was equal to 3% of China's total agricultural production.

> The population of China is expected to increase by at least three hundred million people by 2020.

- Overcropping happened for the following reasons:

  1. The rapid economic development in East Asia since World War II has led to massive urbanisation and industrialisation.

  2. Rapid population growth has also increased the demand placed on China's farmland.

  3. Towns and cities have spread into the surrounding countryside, which was formerly farmland. In just 33 years an area of cropland the size of all the cropland in France,

Germany and the Netherlands was converted to urban use. Therefore the amount of farmland was reduced. The remaining farmland was even more intensively cultivated, leading to overcropping.

4. This remaining farmland was used and reused so often that it could not recover its lost nutrients, so it became loose and dusty. Soil on even the gentlest of slopes started to move downhill by mass movement, some barely noticeable, others as landslides. These remove vast quantities of topsoil so that bare, vacant scars are left where once there was fertile soil.

5. Marginal and forested land on hills was increasingly used for agricultural land. The land was cleared for farming but soil quickly slipped, blew away or was washed downslope. The clearance of the tree cover removed the tree roots which had originally kept the soil anchored to the ground and protected it from strong winds and heavy rain.

6. The demand for higher yields to feed the growing population continues and increases the use of artificial fertilisers and pesticides. Too much of these reduce the health of the soil, pollute the region's rivers with toxic agricultural run-off and make the region more vulnerable to floods, further soil erosion and landslides.

2. Deforestation causes landslide in Indonesia

The article below shows how deforestation and its effect on mass movement was reported in Sumatra.

Nias Natural Disaster Caused By Deforestation
– 50 Bodies Recovered

'Floods and landslides hitting Nias Island in North Sumatra since Monday (30/7/2001) have been closely connected with deforestation at the Masio River's mouth to clear the grounds for a patchouli field,' said North Sumatra Governor, T. Rizal Nurdin, after receiving a report from the islanders when he was on an observation trip to the disaster area.

'This disaster is a lesson for us to treat nature more carefully,' the governor stressed.

Reports from before the disaster mentioned that deforestation on Nias Island was happening at an alarming speed. Trees were felled to develop a plantation, but the main objective was to get valuable timber from the cleared woods. These acts are done by timber barons from Medan who use the local population as a source of cheap labour.

114 people died. Getting help to the area was difficult because roads were destroyed by the floods, bridges collapsed under the stress of the raging waters and parts of the highway crumbled when the saturated soil gave way and slid down to sea, leaving a gap in the highway.

Medan, Kompas Online

case study

● This article highlights the problems of deforestation in underdeveloped regions of the world. Timber is an important source of income and logging companies recruit villagers to fell trees. Poor people see this as a great opportunity to raise their standard of living. The forests seem endless and huge areas are indiscriminately cut.

● Today, over two million hectares of forest are felled every year. Unprotected forest areas are almost completely cleared. Forests are cut to supply the plywood, pulp and paper industries.

● After the trees are gone the soil is left unprotected and the frequency of mass movement increases.

EXERCISE

Name the countries marked 1–5.

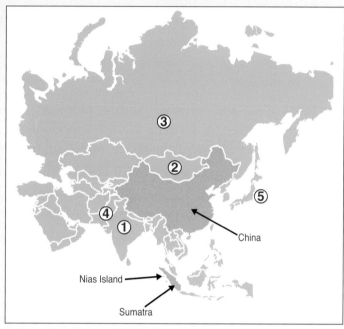

Fig. 20 **East Asia and Russia**

Poor people

Lush forest

Timber company...

...chance to earn money

Forest cleared

Ground left bare + exposed

Heavy rains → instability

Devastating landslides

Fig. 21 **The link between deforestation and mass movement**

case study

3. The Derrybrien bog flow/bog burst, County Galway

Fig. 22 The Derrybrien bog flow in County Galway

- In October 2003 a bog flow (bog burst) occurred near the village of Derrybrien, County Galway. A combination of human activity and heavy rainfall triggered the burst.

- This bog flow began within the site of a large wind farm development. The development area covers most of the summit of one of the main peaks in the Slieve Aughty Mountains. The area is covered by blanket bog to a depth of between 2.5 to 5.5 m.

- While digging the foundations for the wind turbines, waste peat was piled up in unstable areas of the site. Bog drainage ditches were also blocked by these waste piles, allowing water to build up and adding to the weight of the bog on the hillside.

- At first a large mass of bog moved downhill for a distance of 2.5 km. Two weeks later during heavy rain, the bog then travelled more than 20 km along the Derrywee River and entered a major fishing lough, killing more than 100,000 fish. Drinking water was polluted for weeks and had to be supplied by tanker to residents in the area. Roads were severely blocked restricting travel.

Fig. 23 Bog piles up at a house in Derrybrien.

- Many people used the event to protest against wind farms in general, but in fact poor site management and not wind farms themselves were to blame for the bog flow.

Chapter Revision Questions

1. Name the **six** factors that affect mass movement. Briefly explain the effect each factor has.

2. What are the **three** types of mass movement? Name two examples of each type.

3. (a) With the aid of a diagram explain how soil creep occurs. Describe the evidence that may be visible in the landscape if soil creep has happened.

   (b) What is solifluction? Where does it occur? Describe the signs left in the landscape by the solifluction process.

4. Explain the term, avalanche. How are avalanches triggered? What weather conditions increase the possibility of an avalanche?

5. Explain with the aid of a diagram how a rotational slump occurs.

6. Explain the following terms with reference to examples you have studied: mudflow, lahar, bog flow, soil creep.

7. Using examples you have studied, discuss how human activities can influence mass movement.

OL Short Questions

8. Examine this diagram of mass movement.

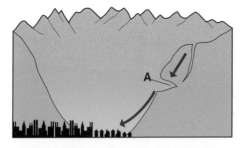

   (a) What type of mass movement could occur here?

   (b) What human activity at the area marked A could trigger a mass movement?

9. (a) Match each of the images below with the correct term:
   - Scree   ❑
   - Terracettes   ❑
   - Avalanche   ❑

   (b) State whether each image is as a result of mass movement or weathering.

A

B

C

OL Long Questions

10. Select any **one** of the following surface processes: sea/marine action, river action, glacial action, mass movement.
    Explain the formation of any **two** Irish landforms caused by your selected process with the aid of diagrams.
    LC Exam Paper

11. With reference to an example which you have studied, describe and explain **one** way in which humans attempt to control river processes or marine (sea) processes or mass movement.
    LC Exam Paper

12. Slope, vegetation, water, human activities: choose **two** of these factors and explain how they influence mass movement.

13. Describe and explain any **one** process of mass movement.

HL Long Questions

14. Describe and explain how humans attempt to control **one** of the following surface processes:
    • River processes
    • Coastal processes
    • Mass movement.
    LC Exam Paper

15. Suggest a method of classifying mass movement.

16. Describe and explain **one** mass movement process that you have studied.
    LC Exam Paper

questions

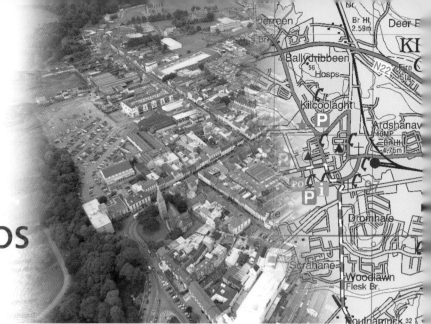

Chapter 12

OS Maps
and Aerial Photos

At the end of this section you should be able to:

- **Use a variety of skills to read and interpret information provided in OS maps and aerial photographs.**

Contents

12.1   OS map-reading skills

12.2   Map interpretation

12.3   Aerial photo skills

12.4   Aerial photo interpretation

        Questions

KEY THEME

Map and aerial photograph interpretation are key geographical skills which can be applied to a wide variety of geographical topics.

12.1 OS map-reading skills

A map represents a scaled-down plan of parts of the earth's surface. In this section you will learn to use the following OS map skills:

1.	Scale	5.	Distance	8.	Area
2.	Legend	6.	Height	9.	Cross sections
3.	Direction	7.	Slope	10.	Sketch maps
4.	Co-ordinate systems		

1. Scale

> Map scale is the relationship between a unit of length on a map and its corresponding length over the ground.

There are three different ways of describing scale.

1. **Statement of Scale:** The statement of scale is written below the scale bar on the legend on the map. On the scale bar in Fig. 1, the statement of scale is 2 centimetres to 1 kilometre.

2. **Linear** or **graphical scale:** Linear scales allow you to convert map distance to actual distance on the ground. You will use this scale bar later in the chapter.

3. **Representative fraction (RF)**: A representative fraction indicates how many units on the earth's surface are equal to one unit on the map.

RFs may be shown as an actual fraction (e.g. $\frac{1}{25,000}$) but are more usually written as a mathematical proportion with a colon (i.e. 1:25,000).

So 1:50,000 means that for every 1 unit measured on the map there are 50,000 units on the ground. For example, if 1 centimetre on the map = 50,000 centimetres on the ground, then 1 centimetre = 500 metres (50,000 cm) and 2 centimetres = 1 kilometre (100,000 cm).

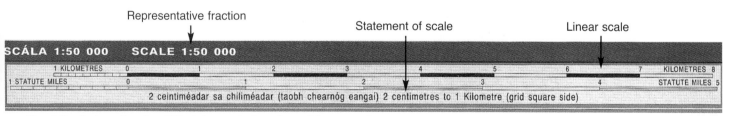

Fig. 1 Scale bar showing RF, statement of scale and linear scale

Maps of different scales are used to show different levels of detail:

(a) Small-scale maps

These maps show **large areas with little detail,** e.g. a map of the whole world is at the scale of 1:100,000,000.

A world map shows the names of countries and some larger capital cities, but it does not include minor cities, towns or villages.

A weather map on the TV news is also a small-scale map – it shows a large area in little detail, e.g. Europe. This is because the weather covers a large area and very little detail is needed on the names and functions of the towns on a weather map.

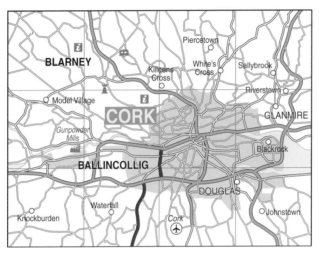

Scale: 1 to 250,000

Fig. 2 This is a car atlas map extract of Cork city at a scale of 1:250,000.

Scale: 1 to 1,100,000,000

Fig. 3 This is a world atlas map extract of North America at a scale of 1:100,000,000.

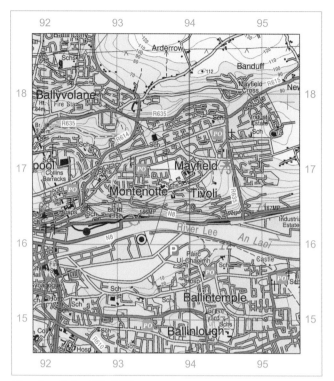

Scale: 1 to 50,000

Fig. 4 This is an OS map extract of Cork city at a scale of 1:50,000.

Scale: 1 to 1,000

Fig. 5 This is an urban town plan of Dundalk at a scale of 1:1,000.

(b) Large-scale maps

These maps show **small areas in greater detail,** e.g. town plans (1:1,000)

These maps may show street names, rivers, mountains, hills and all major historical sites. Others may be of such a large scale that the shape, number of your home and every lamp post in your street will be printed on the map.

ACTIVITY

Look at Figs. 2, 3, 4 and 5.

1. For **each** give the RF and the statement of scale.
2. Rank the maps in order of scale – largest scale first.
3. Which map shows most detail? Write one reason for your answer.
4. Which map shows least detail? Write one reason for your answer.

2. Legend

The symbols that appear on OS maps are explained on a page called a legend or a key.

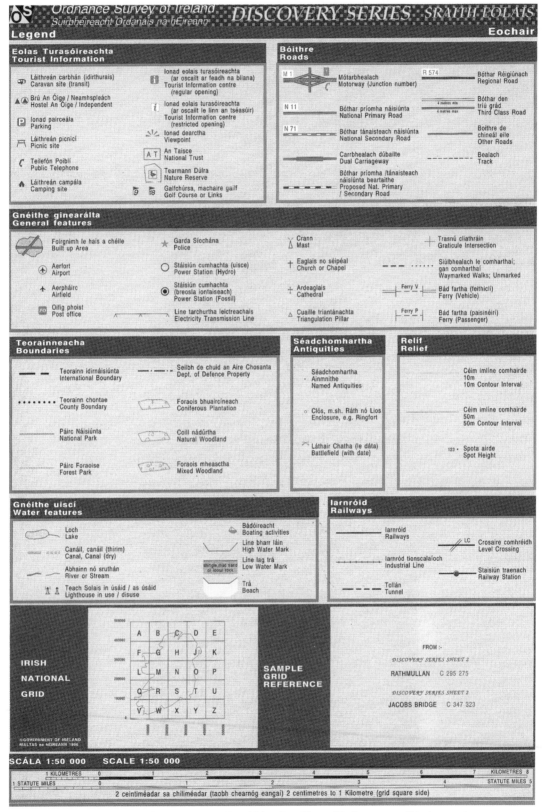

Fig. 6 Legend from an OS map. You should be familiar with items on this legend.

3. Direction

Compass directions are used to give directions on maps.

When you hold the map so that the writing on it is the correct way up, the top of the map is pointing north. In the Leaving Cert Exam, an arrow with an N marked on it is often used to show north on the OS map.

You should learn the directions of the compass on Fig. 7.

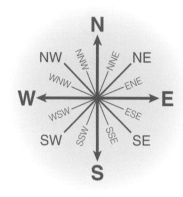

Fig. 7 Directions on a compass

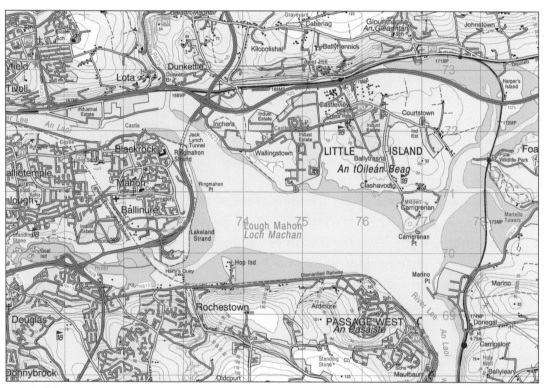

Fig. 8 OS map extract of Cork city

MAP SKILLS EXERCISE

1. In which direction is the post office at Passage West from Little Island?
2. State the direction from the railway station at Fota Wildlife Park to Blackrock.
3. Which direction is the journey from the Jack Lynch Tunnel to the railway station near Carrigaloe?
4. State the direction of the journey to the post office on Little Island from Rochestown.
5. In which direction is the journey from the golf course at Douglas to the post office at Passage West?

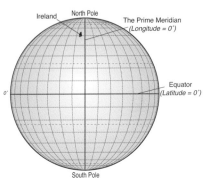

Fig. 9 Lines of latitude and longitude

4. Co-ordinate systems: latitude, longitude, Ireland's National Grid and grid references

Latitude and longitude

Lines of latitude and longitude provide a global scale location. Lines of latitude are drawn horizontally across the globe and are numbered every 10 degrees north or south of the equator. They are also known as **parallels**.

Lines of longitude are drawn vertically from pole to pole and are numbered every 15 degrees east or west from the Prime Meridian (0°). The Prime Meridian passes through Greenwich in London.

The National Grid

The National Grid locates places in Ireland. It divides the country into 25 squares or **sub-zones**. Each square is labelled with a letter from the alphabet, A to Z (no letter I). Each letter represents an area in the country. Looking at Fig. 10, you can see that Dublin is in sub-zone O, Cork is in W, Sligo is in G and Galway City is in M. Identify the sub-zone in which you live. Sometimes more than one sub-zone letter may appear on the map extract you are using (see Fig. 12 on page 217).

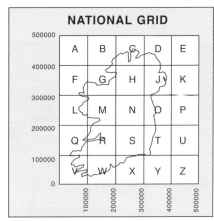

Fig. 10 The National Grid of Ireland

Each sub-zone is divided into 100 equal parts numbered 00 to 99. Each part is marked by vertical lines called **eastings** and horizontal lines called **northings**. These are the blue lines you see on your OS map extract.

Each easting and northing line has a number. By using these co-ordinates or **grid references**, you can find the exact location of any place in Ireland.

Grid references

To give an exact location on the National Grid, we use grid references. This involves 'finding LEN'.

L = Identifying the sub-zone **L**etter.

E = Reading the **E**asting co-ordinate (vertical lines).

N = Reading the **N**orthing co-ordinate (horizontal lines).

> Always read eastings first! Walk along the corridor (easting) and then go up the stairs (northing).

Fig. 11 Sub-zone letter, eastings, northings

1. Four-figure grid references

This gives a less detailed location for large areas or features which are quite easy to see on the map, e.g. a lake, a forest, a large town.

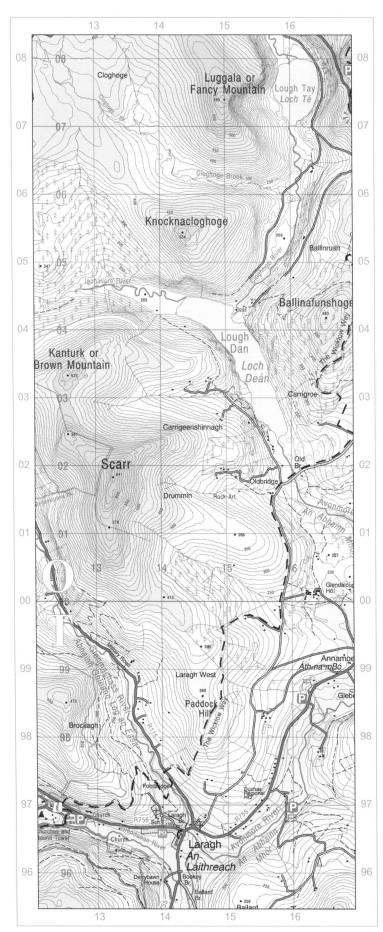

Fig. 12 OS map, County Wicklow

On Fig. 12:

The location of Lough Dan is sub-zone = O

Easting co-ordinate = 15

Northing co-ordinate = 03

Therefore, the location of the lake of Lough Dan is O 15 03.

MAP SKILLS EXERCISE (A)

1. What is located at O 14 05?
2. Locate the following as four-figure grid references.
   (a) Lough Tay.
   (b) Forest on the east of Lough Dan.
   (c) The village of Laragh at the intersection of all of the valleys.

Six-figure grid references

This type of grid reference gives a more exact location. It can locate specific landforms, sites or services on the map, e.g. an oxbow lake, ringfort or post office.

The same basic method is used to get this grid reference as is used to get a four-figure reference but an extra two numbers are added. These numbers are the further division in tenths of the distance between any two eastings or northings.

On Fig. 12:

The post office at Laragh is located at sub-zone = T

Easting = 140

Northing = 966

Therefore, the post office at Laragh is T140 966.

MAP SKILLS EXERCISE (B)

1. What is located at T 163 987?
2. What is located at O 150 O74?
3. Give a six-figure grid reference for the car park to the west of Laragh.
4. Give a six-figure grid reference for the top of Scarr mountain south-west of Lough Dan.

5. Distance

There are two ways to calculate the distance between two places on a map.

1. Straight line method.
2. Curved line method.

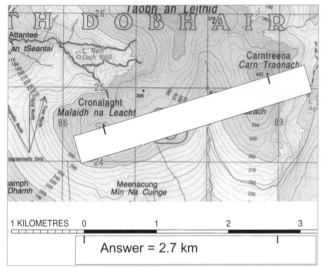

Fig. 13 How to get the straight line distance from Cronalaght to Carntreena in County Donegal

1. To measure straight line distance (as the crow flies) between two points:

(a) Place the edge of a piece of paper on the two points on the map.

(b) With a pencil make a mark on the paper's edge where it touches the two points.

(c) Place the marked paper edge along a linear scale bar and read the distance.

(d) Using the scale bar, count the number of full kilometres to the right of the 0 mark.

(e) Place any remaining measurement to the left of the 0 mark to get the tenths of the kilometre for an exact distance.

Short cut: If the map is 1:50,000 in scale, use a ruler to measure the distance between the 2 points in centimetres and divide by 2. This will give the answer in kilometres.

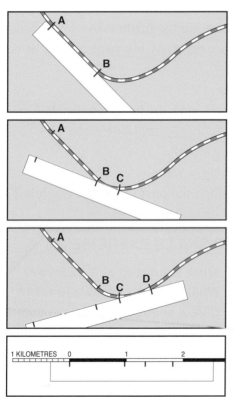

Fig. 14 How to get the curved line distance between two points

2. To measure curved line distance between two points:

This usually involves measuring roads, rivers or coastlines. In order to measure a curved line distance, break the distance into a series of small straight sections which you will mark on the edge of a strip of paper.

(a) Find your starting and finishing points on the map.

(b) Place the edge of a strip of paper on the starting point on your map. Mark the paper at this point. Line up the edge of the paper with the road or rail line to be measured.

(c) Make another mark on the paper and map where the road line moves away from (or under) the paper.

(d) Keeping the marks you made on the map and paper together, turn the paper to meet the road underneath and mark the next section of straight line.

(e) Repeat the procedure until you reach the end of the distance to be measured.

(f) Find the distance by measuring it along the linear scale as you did for the straight line distance.

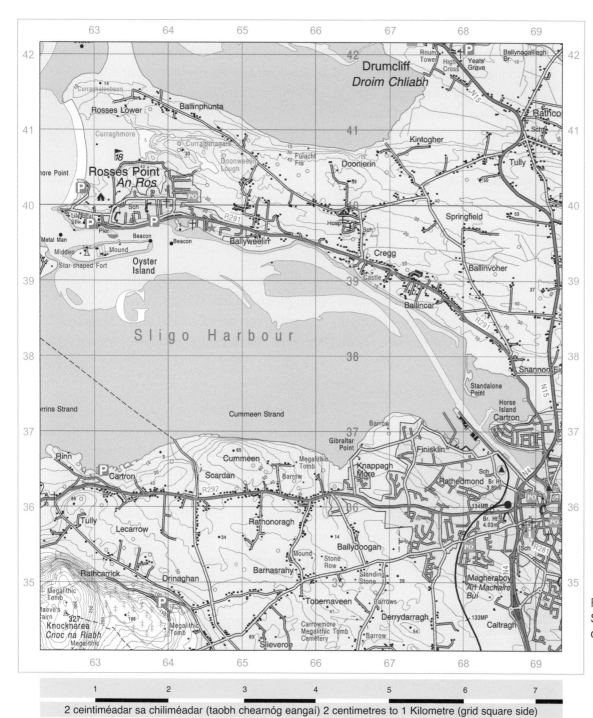

Fig. 15 OS map of
Sligo used to
calculate distance

2 ceintiméadar sa chiliméadar (taobh chearnóg eangaí) 2 centimetres to 1 Kilometre (grid square side)

Using the map above, answer the following questions:.

1. Calculate the straight line distance in kilometres between the following places:

(a) The railway station at G 687 361 and the camp site at G631 401.

(b) The railway station in Sligo and the youth hostel at G 685 365.

(c) The parking place in Rosses Point village and the parking place at Yeats' Grave.

2. Calculate the distance in kilometres:

(a) Along the R291 from Rosses Point to the junction with the N4/N15 at G692 367.

(b) Along the rail line from the railway station south to where it leaves the map.

219

6. Height

Heights above sea level in Ireland are measured in metres above a base line taken at Malin Head. This headland is used as the base line location because a headland can be an open area of sea and thus gives a more accurate sea-level reading. This base level is called **Ordnance Datum (OD)**.

Height can be shown on maps in the following ways:

(a) Colour layering.

(b) Contour lines.

(c) Spot heights.

(d) Trigonometrical station/Triangulation station.

(a) Colour layering

Colour codes are used to distinguish height throughout OS maps. These colours give an immediate view of the lowland and highland parts of the map. Elevations below 100 metres are dark green changing to light green between 100 and 200 metres. This then changes to light brown above 200 metres and stronger shades of brown for each 100 metres above this.

(b) Contour lines

These are lines which join all points of the same height above sea level (or OD). They are shown at intervals of ten metres apart on OS maps.

As well as height, they also show the shape and slope of the land. Contour lines placed close together indicate steep land.

(c) Spot heights

Spot heights show the height/elevation of particular points. Usually these heights mark all mountain/hill tops. They are drawn as a black spot with a number beside it representing its height in metres.

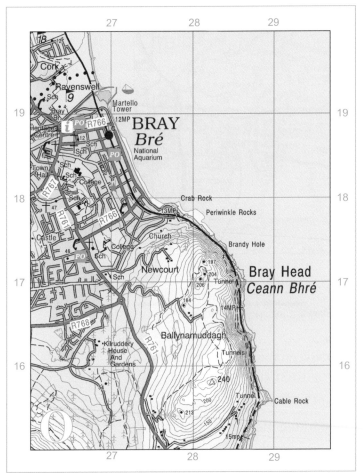

Fig. 16 Different ways of showing height on an OS map

Height (m)		Name	Symbol
700-800			
600-700		Contour line	—150—
500-600		Spot height	● 240
400-500		Triangulation station	△ 240
300-400			
200-300			
100-200		Fig. 17 Colour layering and symbols showing height on OS maps	
0-100			

(d) Trigonometrical stations/triangulation stations

These fulfil the same role as spot heights except they are marked as open triangles on the map with the height written beside them. They are located on specific places which were important to surveyors in the past. The surveyors built a pillar to hold surveying equipment at the point marked. These stations usually show the highest peaks in a mountain range and have had further importance to communication systems in the country as TV, radio and phone masts are often constructed at these points.

> **MAP SKILLS EXERCISE**
>
> **Look at Fig. 16 on page 220.** Name and locate an example of each method used to show height on this OS map.

7. Slope

Contour lines can be used to work out the shape of the land, e.g. gentle slopes, steep slopes. They also show the shapes of river, marine and glacial landforms such as V-shaped valleys, cliffs and corries.

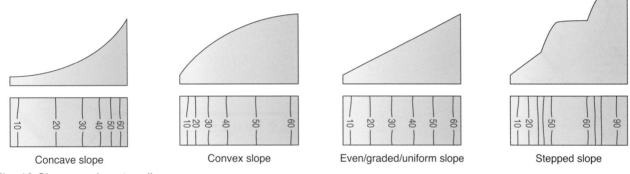

Fig. 18 Slopes and contour lines

Concave slopes have a steep upper section (contour lines close together) and a gentle lower section (contour lines widely spaced).

Convex slopes have a gentle upper section (widely spaced contours) and a steep lower section (contour lines are closely packed together).

Even, graded or uniform slopes have contours that are spaced evenly.

Stepped slopes have contours that show a combination of flat and steep sections. **Steep slopes** have contours that are close together.

Gentle slopes have contours that are quite far apart.

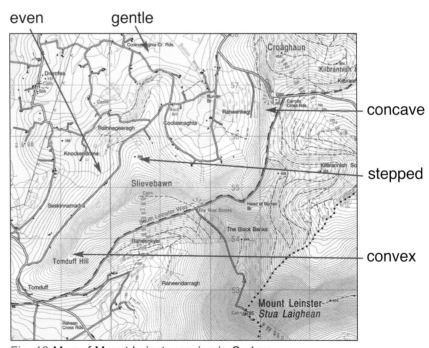

Fig. 19 Map of Mount Leinster region in Carlow

8. Area

Remember:
Each grid square is 1km².

To calculate the area of a rectangular region:

1. Count the number of full grid squares across the top of the map.

2. Count the number of full grid squares up the side of the map.

3. Multiply the two figures. That is the area in square kilometres.

In Fig. 20, the area of the whole map is 4 x 4 grid squares = 16 km².

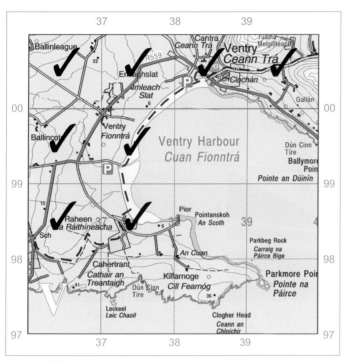

To calculate the area of an irregularly-shaped region:

(e.g. forest park, a lake, mountain range):

1. Count and place a tick in each complete grid square within the region.

2. Any square more than half covered by the region you are looking at is counted as one full square.

3. Add the two together. That is the approximate area in square kilometres.

The area of map covered by land on the Ventry map is 8 km².

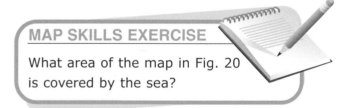

MAP SKILLS EXERCISE

What area of the map in Fig. 20 is covered by the sea?

Fig. 20 OS map of Dungarvan

9. Cross sections

A cross section is a side view of the landscape. It also shows whether one place can be seen from another (**intervisible**) or if there is a mountain in between.

To draw a cross section, you will need graph paper, a sharp pencil and a strip of paper.

1. Place the edge of the strip of paper along the line of the section to be drawn (**A–B**).

2. Mark the beginning and end of the section. If contours are tightly spaced, mark every 50 m.

3. Mark all the contours on the edge of the paper, noting the heights of each point.

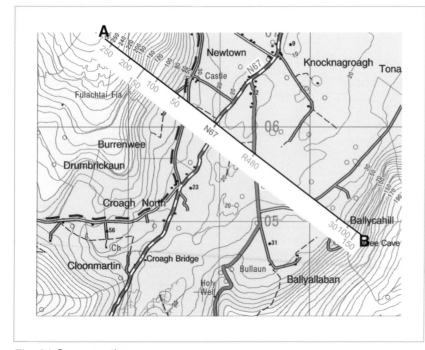

Fig. 21 Cross section

4. On a sheet of graph paper, draw a base line the same length as the section you have just drawn (X-axis). Transfer all the markings and heights from your paper onto the base line.

5. Choose a vertical scale: In Fig. 22 the scale used is 2 cm = 100 m.

6. Draw a vertical line (Y-axis) at the left-hand edge of the base line and mark the vertical scale along this line. (2 cm = 100 m)

7. Using the heights marked on the base line, mark with a point each height using the vertical scale.

8. Join all the points.

9. Write the vertical scale you have selected (e.g. 2 cm = 100 m) and the horizontal scale (taken from the OS map) which is usually 1:50,000.

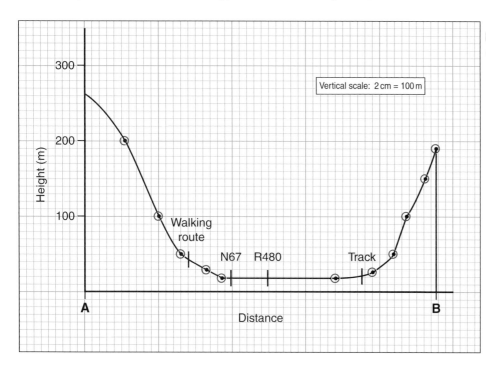

Fig. 22 Drawn cross section of Fig. 21

Vertical scale: 2 cm = 100 m

Remember:
Always have a pencil, eraser, ruler and graph paper to do your sketches. A final sketch should always be the same shape as the original but not the same size. The sketch will always be smaller than the original. A sketch should never be traced.

10. Sketch maps

How to draw a sketch map to **half scale**.

1. Count the number of grid squares across the top of the map and divide by two. This is the length in centimetres of the top and bottom of your frame.

2. Count the number of grid squares up the side of the map and divide by two. This is the length in centimetres of the left and right sides of your frame.

3. Using graph paper and a ruler, draw the frame of your sketch in the same shape as the OS map.

4. Using a light pencil, divide the map and sketch into three evenly-spaced rows and three evenly-spaced columns. Use these rows and columns to draw the items in the correct position and proportion.

5. Put a title and sub-zone letter on your sketch.

6. Mark the coastline and major lakes if shown.

7. Mark and label only what you have been asked to draw in the question.

8. Use a key to explain your colour code, labels and symbols if used.

9. Draw a north arrow and state the scale. If the scale of the map is 1:50,000, then half scale is 1:100,000.

10. Roads, rivers and rail lines should be represented by drawing a single line and then colour coded accordingly.

(See Figs. 23 and 24 below.)

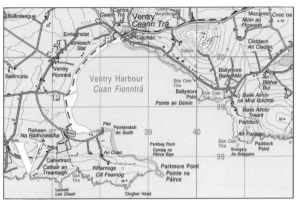

Fig. 23 OS map of Ventry Harbour

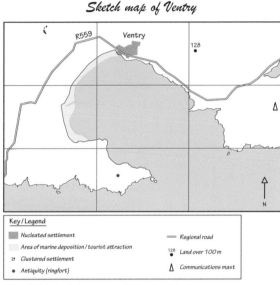

Fig. 24 Sketch map of Ventry Harbour

12.2 Map interpretation

Map interpretation involves a description and explanation of the patterns and shapes shown using symbols. Using any OS map as an example, you can see evidence of physical processes, human settlement and/or transport infrastructure. (See Legend, page 214.)

Symbol recognition involves recognising symbols that represent historical sites, functions, land uses, communications/transport, infrastructure and other features.

Pattern recognition involves identification of landforms (see Chapters 8–11) and description of site and situation of settlement.

Symbol recognition

Many features are shown on an OS map using symbols. These symbols are explained on a page called a **legend** or **key**. All maps contain legends.

Using OS maps and their legends, you can describe:

1. Relief and landscape features
2. Antiquities
3. Settlement patterns
4. Land use and function

1. Relief and landscape features

The map below shows a variety of coastal, glacial and fluvial landforms.

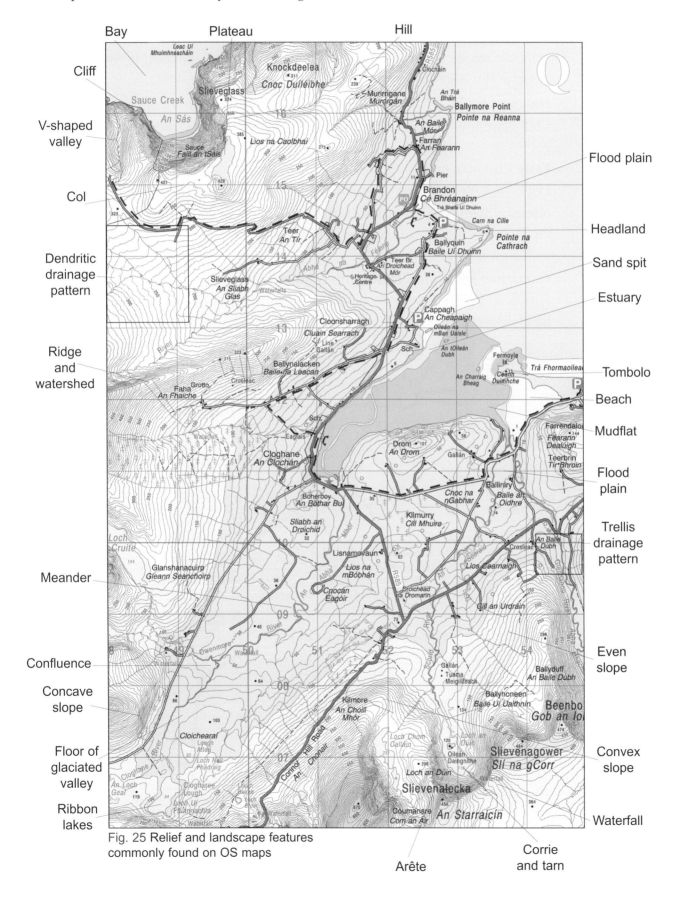

Fig. 25 Relief and landscape features commonly found on OS maps

2. Antiquities

Stone Age: 4000BC to 2400BC

Megalithic tombs, stone circles, cairns, rock art, middens.

Bronze Age: 2400BC to 600BC

Standing stones, dolmens, Fulacht Fia, barrows (burial mound), stone rows, copper mines and wedge tombs.

Iron Age: 600BC – 600AD

Crannóg, hillfort, ring fort, stone forts, promontory fort, Ogham stone, souterrain, togher.

Early Christian era: Sixth - Eleventh century

High cross, holy well, monastic site, round tower, graveyard, cross-inscribed stone.

Norman/Medieval: Twelfth - Thirteenth century

Castle, keep, motte and bailey, moat, walls, tower house, abbey, gate, place names with a prefix, e.g. Baile, Bally.

Plantation: Sixteenth - Eighteenth century

Fortified houses, demesne, towns with landlord's name, e.g. Charleville, Randalstown.

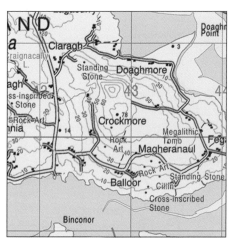

Fig. 26 OS map of Doagh Island in County Donegal showing ancient settlements

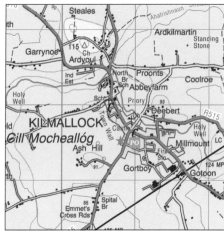

Fig. 27 OS map of Kilmallock, County Limerick showing ancient settlements

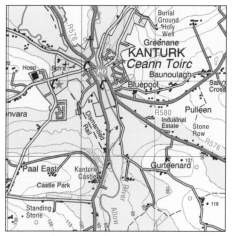

Fig. 28 OS map of Kanturk in County Cork showing ancient settlements

3. Settlement patterns (rural)

Individual buildings/houses in rural areas are represented on OS maps as small black squares. Settlements can be one of these four patterns:

(a) Linear/Ribbon

(b) Clustered/Nucleated

(c) Dispersed/Scattered

(d) Absence of settlement

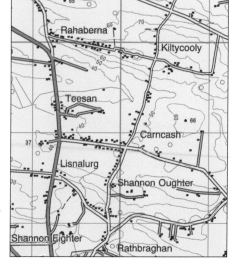

Fig. 29 Linear settlement in County Sligo

(a) Linear/Ribbon

This is the most common pattern seen in rural areas. Houses run along either side of roads. Linear settlement develops because services such as electricity, water and sewage are installed and supplied more cheaply along roadsides.

Many houses are built on sites made available by farmers as they sell off sections of their land. These sites with road frontage are more valuable.

(b) Clustered/Nucleated

In this case, houses are close to each other. This pattern may occur because people in the past settled around a water source – a spring or well – or in an easily-defended site (e.g. castle).

In the eighteenth century, people tended to cluster close to landlord estates (demesnes) because they also worked on the estate. Over time, many grew in size to become villages and towns, e.g. Adare, County Limerick.

As the size of the cluster grew, the pattern was relabelled as nucleated, because a definite centre, usually due to a market function, developed. In these built-up urban areas it is impossible to show every building. Therefore, nucleated settlements are shaded grey on the map.

(c) Dispersed/Scattered

In this case many houses/buildings are scattered across the map.

Relief, aspect, altitude, access to a water supply and soil quality are the greatest influences on this pattern. There are often isolated houses on large farms in lowland areas with fertile soils. In upland areas dispersed settlement occurs due to relief, aspect and poor soil quality.

(d) Absence of settlement

The most common reasons for absence of settlement in an area are: annual flooding on a river flood plain, areas of poor drainage, northerly aspect, steep high ground, good agricultural land where there are many large fields, forested areas and coastal areas with erosional landforms.

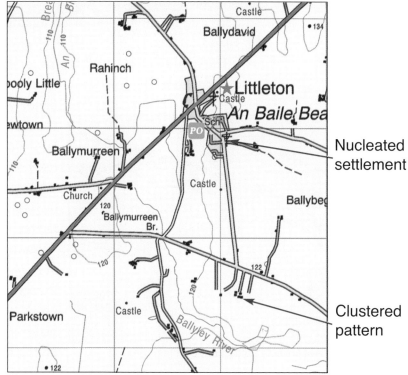

Fig. 30 Clustered and nucleated settlement in a rural area of County Tipperary

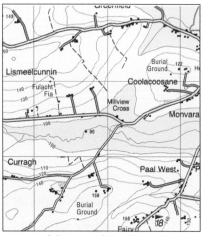

Fig. 31 OS map of the Kanturk, County Cork, region showing dispersed or scattered settlement

You should always note any places on a map where there is no settlement and try to account for the absence.

In summary, all of these settlement patterns reflect aspects of the physical, social, economic and historical environment.

In the past, water supply was one of the most important locational factors for settlement. In some cases, the settlement may have become depopulated at a later date due to emigration or an ageing workforce, e.g. the deserted village of Achill Island.

The quality of the land is also an important factor – people prefer to live in fertile areas where they can grow crops and raise livestock. However, due to historical factors such as the Plantations (sixteenth century) and the Famine (1845–48), often the most unproductive land was settled by the native Irish as the best land was used for planter estates.

Modern settlement is less influenced by physical factors and more influenced by social and economic factors such as transport routes.

From a historical point of view, careful examination of a map can indicate that certain areas were attractive for settlement in the past and nearby areas continue to grow. Some settlements continue to grow from their historic roots, as ruins such as town walls are marked on the map as antiquities.

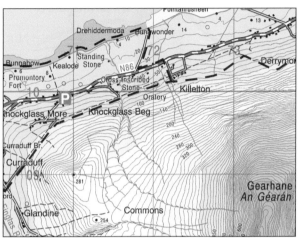

Fig. 32 Absence of settlement on steep ground

4. Land use and function

A variety of land use and functions can be identified by their symbols on OS maps.

Land use means what is actually built/found on a piece of land, e.g. a school or farm. Function means what service the building/land provides, e.g. education, agriculture.

Use the table below to improve your skills at recognising land use and functions on OS maps.

OS Map Symbol	Land use	Function (Ricepots)
☩ ✝ ● Abbey ● Priory ● Church	Cathedral – modern Church – modern Abbey – historic Priory – historic Church – historic	Religious
⚑₁₈ ⛵	Racecourse Golf course Boating activities	Recreation

Fig. 33 OS map symbols, land uses and functions

OS Map Symbol	Land use	Function (Ricepots)
Demesne	Estate house	
	Houses	
	Built up area	Residential
	Power station (thermal)	
	Power station (HEP)	
Ind. Est.	Industrial estate	Industry (secondary economic activities)
	Central Business District	Commercial
Sch	School	Education
Coll	College, University	
	Fishing port	Economic Activities (primary)
	Farm land	
	Forest (coniferous)	
	Quayside	Port
	Shipping channel	
A T	National Parks	Open spaces
	Camping site	Tourism
	Caravan site	
	Hostels	
	Marina, slipway	
	Tourist information office	
	Walking path	
	Nature reserve	
	Motorway	Transport
	National Primary route	
	Regional road	
	Railway Station	
	Airport	
	Canal	(historic transport land use)
	Garda station	Services
Fire St	Fire station	
	Communications mast	
Hosp	Hospital	

Fig. 33 cont/d OS map symbols, land uses and functions

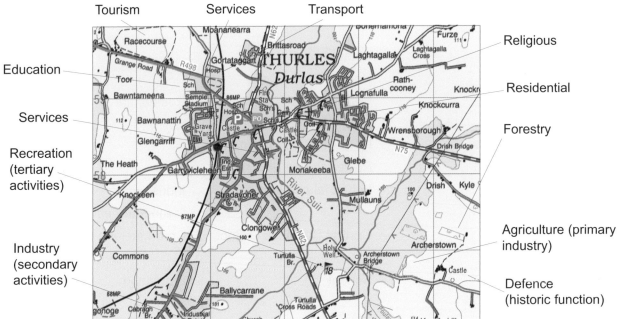

Fig. 34 Land use and function on an OS map for Thurles in County Tipperary

Functions change over time

Transport networks develop and change. This can often be seen on an OS map. The table below summarises the types of transport and when they were in use in the past.

TABLE OF TRANSPORT TYPES	
Canals	1700s-1800s for transport of goods and people. Modern use is for tourism and recreation.
Railways	1800s – present
Roads	1600s – present
Airports	1950s – present
Shipping	Viking times – present ports

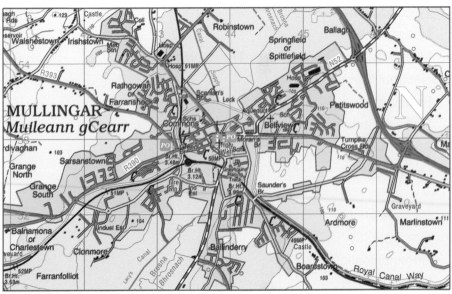

Fig. 35 OS map of Mullingar showing different modes of transport

ACTIVITY

Look at Fig. 35.

1. Identify the different types of transport in Mullingar.

2. What evidence is there that the transport network has developed over time?

3. In your answer, name each type of transport, give the grid reference of its location and state its time of development in the past.

12.3 Aerial photo skills

Photographs taken at different altitudes and angles can give us more up-to-date information than even the most recent of OS maps. Using maps and photos together helps us to build a better picture of an area.

Aerial photographs are taken from an aeroplane or helicopter. They show the present, but can also indicate features from the past that are invisible from the ground, e.g. ancient crop marks, overgrown/demolished ancient settlements.

Aerial photos can be of two types: **vertical** and **oblique**.

~ **A vertical photograph** is taken when the camera points directly down over the subject matter of the photograph. The scale on this type of photo is the same across the image (i.e. true to scale). **Use compass points to find the location.**

~ **An oblique photograph** is taken when the camera is pointing at an angle to the ground. It gives a side view of objects so they have depth, making them easier to identify. Oblique photographs can be **low oblique** (no horizon visible) or **high oblique** (horizon is visible). **Use left, right, foreground, centreground and background notation to find location.**

Fig. 36 Example of high oblique photo – Ballymun, Dublin

Fig. 37 Example of low oblique photo – Blanchardstown roundabout, Dublin

Finding location on aerial photos

Location on vertical photos

AERIAL PHOTO SKILLS EXERCISE

Look at Fig. 38.

Complete this exercise in your copybook.

1. Storage tanks are located in the _____ of the photo.

2. Busaras is located in the _____ of photo.

3. A residential area is located in the_____ of the map.

4. Ships are tied up in the _____of the photo.

Look at Fig. 39.

Locate: (a) The caravan park.

    (b) The lake.

    (c) The forest.

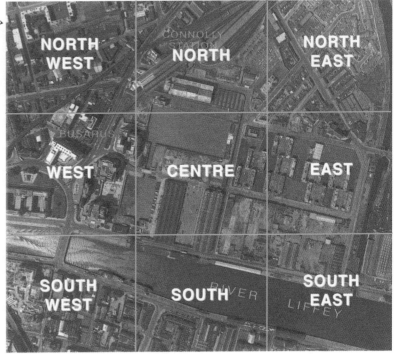

Fig. 38 Vertical photo of Dublin city

Location on oblique photos

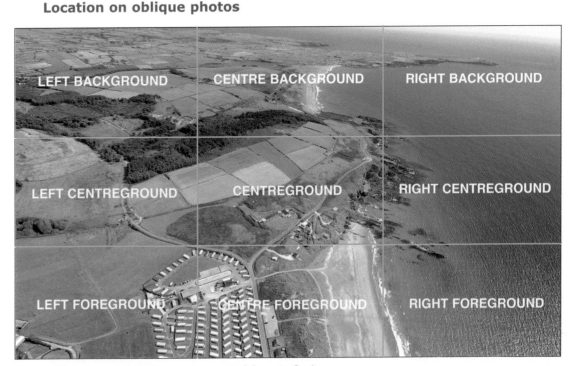

Fig. 39 Oblique photo of the south coast of County Cork

Working out direction using a map and photo

To find out which way the camera was pointing when the picture was taken, use the following method:

1. Identify two major landmarks. For example, in Figs. 40 and 41 below, a lake and a meandering river are visible.
2. Draw a line joining the landmarks on the photo.
3. Draw a line joining the same two landmarks on the OS map.
4. By comparing the direction of the line on both the map and the photo, it should be possible to calculate the direction in which the camera was pointing.

Fig. 40 View from the head of the Glendalough valley above the upper lake.

Fig. 41 Map of Glendalough, County Wicklow

12.4 Aerial photo interpretation

Using aerial photos you can see and describe land use and function, street pattern, house types, traffic management, historic developments and time of year.

Land use: rural and urban

From a photo, you can see rural landscapes and identify details such as what type of farming is carried out on the land. For example, uplands are likely to have sheep rearing. Lowland river areas are more likely to have pasture or cereal crops.

Irregular and smaller fields under grass imply pasture and livestock farming. The field colour, size and shape also indicate the agriculture type, e.g. green grass means pastoral farming, glasshouses indicate market gardening.

The table on the next page shows main land uses and examples of buildings that might be visible on aerial photos.

Function

The term **function** refers to the services provided for a town's residents and for those in its hinterland (the land surrounding the town) and rural areas.

The function of some buildings will be easy to identify due to buildings and structures nearby, e.g. a large building with basketball courts, tennis courts and large playing fields around it usually depicts a school or leisure centre.

Each function you identify must be supported with clear evidence from the photo based on the buildings and land uses you can see.

Function (ricepots)	Landuse Photo Evidence
Religious	Church, graveyard, abbey, convent, cathedral, round tower
Residential	Housing estates, playgrounds, apartments, terraced/detached housing
Recreation	Pitches, parks, river/coastal walks, playgrounds, golf courses, racetracks, beach, leisure centre, marina
Industrial (secondary economic activities)	Industrial estates, factories, warehouses, chimney stack, mill, power lines
Commercial	Shops, terraced multi-coloured buildings with large ground floor windows, car parks, shopping centres, petrol stations, market square, mart, CBD
Education	Schools, colleges, playgrounds, pitches, tennis courts, car parks
Economic activities (Primary: farming, fishing, forestry, mining)	Fields (crops, grazing land), glasshouses, quarry, forest, port, trawlers, dock side, quay
Port	Harbour, ships, boats, yachts, docks/quayside, container parks, cranes
Power generation	Large building with pylons and overhead cables, chimney stacks, dams and reservoirs, wind farms
Open spaces	Greenfield and derelict sites, car parks, parks
Transport (tertiary economic activity)	Roads, car parks, bridges, railway lines, railway station, port, canal, canal locks, river, airport
Tourism (tertiary economic activity)	Physical and man-made attractions, beaches, forestry, river, mountains, golf course, horse riding, boating, caravans, camping site, interpretative centres.
Services (tertiary economic activity)	Garda station, radio mast, hospital, banks, court house, jail, offices
Defence (in the past)	Castle, town walls, fortified house, town wall gates

Fig. 42 Aerial photo of Drogheda

AERIAL PHOTO SKILLS EXERCISE

Identify and locate 4 land uses and 4 urban functions visible in this photo.

Town street layout

Town layout or settlement shape can be clearly shown by drawing a simple sketch of a photo of the area. If used with a town plan, streets on the photo can also be named. Older settlements tend to have narrow, winding streets and are quite random with little planning. Modern settlements and housing developments/estates show clear order in their planning and design.

The main street of Irish country towns is usually easy to identify due to the common use of bright multi-coloured paint on the walls. Large front windows indicate shopfronts. There may also be more traffic on this road or the road may be pedestrianised.

Fig. 43 Aerial photo of town street layout – Sligo

AERIAL PHOTO SKILLS EXERCISE

Draw a sketch map of Sligo to show the street pattern visible in the photograph opposite.

Fig. 44 House types in a Dublin suburb

House types

You should be able to identify one or more of the following house types from a photo:

1. Detached
2. Semi-detached
3. Bungalow
4. Terraced
5. Apartments

AERIAL PHOTO SKILLS EXERCISE

Name and locate **two** different house types in Fig. 44.

Traffic management and congestion

Fig. 45 Traffic management in Sligo

TRAFFIC CONGESTION BLACK SPOTS	METHODS USED TO SOLVE TRAFFIC CONGESTION	HOW THESE METHODS WORK
Junctions	Roundabouts	Increase traffic flow at junctions.
Schools	Yellow boxes	No entry unless exit free. Reduce congestion.
Shopping centre exits		
Narrow streets	Double yellow lines	No parking. Keep roads clear for traffic.
Streets with parking	Off street parking	Keep roads clear for traffic.
Churches	Car parks	Keep roads clear for traffic.
Traffic lights	Park and ride centres	Reduce number of commuter cars.
	One-way streets	Reduce congestion on narrow streets.
	Bus lanes	Reduce bus journey times.
	Pedestrian streets	Reduce accident/congestion in shopping streets.
	Bypasses	Reduce 'through traffic' in city centre.
	Traffic lights	Control traffic at junctions used by pedestrians.

Historic development

The historic development of a town can also be seen from a photograph.
The table below shows some structures, their age and past functions.

TIME	BUILDING	FUNCTION/USE
6th century: Early Christian	Church ruin	Religious services
12th–13th century: Norman	Castle, priory	Defence, religion
16th–18th century: Plantation	Market square	Trade
19th century–21st century	Mills, canals	Industry, transport
	Shopping centre	Business
	School	Education

Fig. 46 Historic development of Carlow

Using photos to place new developments in an area

In the Leaving Cert Exam, you may be asked to choose a suitable site for a new
development by carefully examining a photograph. All new developments need
space but some need more than others. Consider the following when making your
decision:

1. Are greenfield or brownfield sites available? Greenfield sites are usually found
   on the edge of towns. They are larger and cheaper to buy and redevelop. They
   are usually farmland that has been rezoned for another use.

Brownfield sites already have some buildings on them and are found in towns. These cost more to buy and redevelop and do not have as much space but are often in profitable, accessible locations in towns.

2. Traffic – consider parking/access/deliveries/lorries/cars.

3. Noise – consider the noise levels from people or machinery/traffic/day and night noise levels.

4. Pollution – consider the effects of pollution in the air, water, noise, light (lights disturb people at night).

5. Is there a workforce, market and transport infrastructure close by?

New developments	Possible location
Swimming pool	Close to town, near schools, housing estates.
Computer factory	Greenfield site outside towns with good transport links.
Leisure centre	Close to town/in town.
School	Near residential areas and away from busy roads.
Shopping centre	Large brownfield site in town or on edge of town on large greenfield site.
Industrial estate	Edge of town away from residential areas, good transport links.
Multi-storey car park	Brownfield site in town.
Hospital	Close to town, near housing, room for car park and easily accessible.

AERIAL PHOTO SKILLS EXERCISE

Look at the photo. Choose a suitable location for the development of a new leisure centre. Give two detailed reasons for your answer.

Fig. 47 Aerial photo of Drogheda

Drawing sketch maps of aerial photos

1. Draw a frame in the same **shape** as the photograph, i.e. landscape, portrait.

2. Divide the sketch into three equally spaced columns and three equally spaced rows.

3. Sketch in the items that are listed in the question you are answering. For example, if the question mentions a church, make sure you include the church in your sketch.

4. Draw the **outline** of areas of land use. For example, if there is a housing estate in the photograph, do not draw each house in the estate. In the example below, the residential land use is represented by coloured shapes and these shapes are explained in the key.

5. Use block colour neatly.

6. The items you draw in your sketch should be in the same position and have the same relative sizes on the sketch as in the photo. For example, if an area of forestry is in the left background of the photo, it should be in the left background of your sketch. If it covers a small area on the photo, it should cover a small area on your sketch. This is why the grid is drawn on the sketch – to help you position and size items correctly.

7. Use a key to explain any symbol or colours in your sketch. Make sure you give a title to your sketch.

8. Always use graph paper.

Fig. 48 Aerial photo of Drogheda

Fig. 49 Sketch map of aerial photo

Uses of maps and photos

PHOTOS CAN SHOW:

Actual buildings, their relative sizes and positioning

Derelict sites available for redevelopment

Relative ages of buildings

Areas of traffic congestion/traffic management

A small area in great detail

Land use

Street patterns

Time of year

MAPS CAN SHOW:

Large areas

Accurate detail

Distances between places

The shape of the land (relief)

Aspect/altitude of a place

Road numbers and their classification

Exact locations

Urban functions (schools, hospitals, post offices)

PHOTOS CANNOT SHOW:

Large areas except from a great height which then loses image detail

Slopes clearly

Accurate scale – in the case of oblique photos. Oblique photos make near objects look bigger than they really are

Building functions clearly – in the case of vertical photos

The names of important buildings

Exact locations

MAPS CANNOT SHOW:

The actual land use, except by interpretation

Derelict sites

Individual buildings in built-up areas on the (1:50,000) scale map

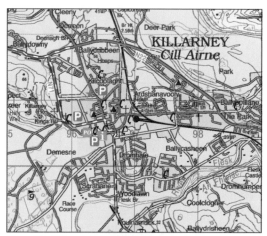

Fig. 50 OS map of Killarney

Fig. 51 Aerial photo of Killarney

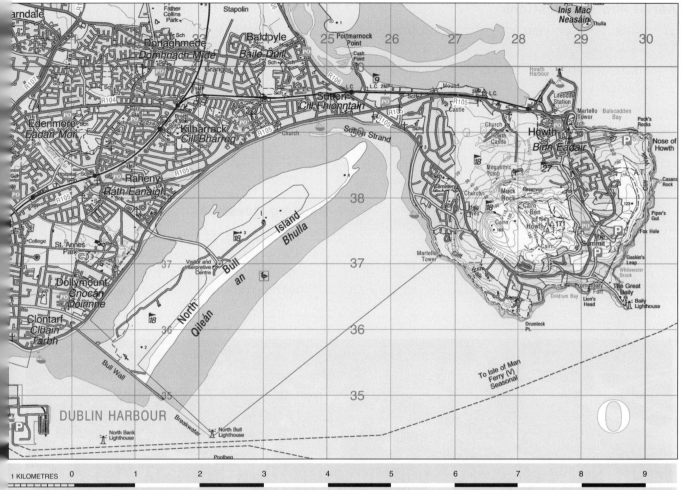

1 KILOMETRES 0   1   2   3   4   5   6   7   8   9

2 ceintiméadar sa chiliméadar (taobh chearnóg eangaí) 2 centimetres to 1 Kilometre (grid square side)

Chapter Revision Questions
OS Map Questions

1. State the scale of this map and give the representative fraction.

2. Calculate the area of sea south of northing 40.

3. Calculate the straight line distance between the post office in Baldoyle and the Post Office in Howth village.

4. Calculate the distance in kilometres along the railway line between the stations at Howth and Raheny.

5. Describe, with reference to the map, **three** land uses and their functions visible on this map.

6. Identify the coastal landforms at:
   (i)   Bull Island
   (ii) O298 376
   (iii) O233 367
   (iv) O287 367
   (v)   Drumlick Point

7. Give six-figure grid references for five different antiquities shown on the map.

8. State the direction travelled from:
   (i)   The Great Bailey lighthouse to the lighthouse in Howth harbour.
   (ii) Clontarf boating marina to Sutton boating marina.
   (iii) The North Bull lighthouse to the post office in Baldoyle.

9. Draw a cross section of Howth from (a) spot height .3m (O265 387) to (b) the 18-hole golf course at O275 378.

10. Draw a sketch map of the OS map extract. Mark and identify the following;
    (i)   The third class road network
    (ii)   the village of Howth
    (iii) any two post offices
    (iv)   a beach
    (v)   the highest point on the map
    (vi)   the railway lines
    (vii) a car park.

Aerial Photos Questions

1. What time of year was this photograph of Carlow taken?

2. State the type of photo (low oblique/high oblique/vertical).

3. Draw a sketch map to show: the street pattern, the river, the castle, an area of redevelopment and an area of religious land use.

4. Name, describe and locate **three** different land uses visible in this photograph.

5. Name, describe and locate three different functions of the town of Carlow.

6. Describe the variety of residential land use visible in this photograph.

7. The area in the centre background is being redeveloped. Suggest a suitable use for this piece of land. Give one reason for your answer.

8. 'The buildings visible on the photograph show that Carlow has a long history.' Use the photograph to support this statement.

9. A large church and a castle are to be seen in this photograph. Using the correct reference system, describe their location.

HL Long Question

10. Draw a sketch map half the length and half the breadth of the photograph. On it show and name any three different land-use zones within the town.

LC Exam Paper

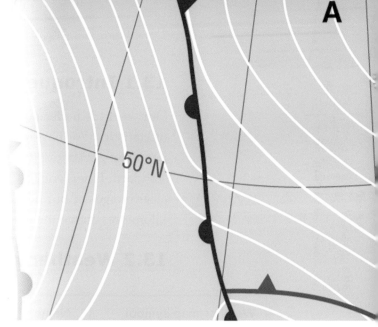

Chapter 13

Weather Maps, Satellite Images and Graphical Skills

At the end of this chapter you should be able to:

- Identify, explain and interpret symbols on weather maps and charts.
- Read and interpret a variety of charts and tables showing statistical data.
- Draw a variety of graphs to Leaving Certificate Exam standard.
- Use satellite images to examine large areas of the earth's surface.

Contents

13.1 Introduction

13.2 Weather maps and charts

13.3 Representing statistical data on graphs and charts

13.4 Drawing graphs for the Leaving Certificate Exam

13.5 Satellite images

Questions

KEY THEME

Interpretation of weather maps and satellite images is a key geographical skill. Graphing skills can be applied to a wide variety of geographical topics.

13.1 Introduction

Our world is increasingly represented by maps, satellite photos, graphs and tables of statistics. We have access to data that was once available only to highly skilled people in government. Today, cars are sold with global positioning systems (GPS) as standard. Emergency teams use satellite charts to pinpoint search areas. Zoomed-in, clear images of our homes and landscapes can be taken from satellites hundreds of kilometres above the ground.

13.2 Weather maps and charts

Weather map symbol	Name	Weather conditions
	Cold front	Produces quite heavy rain, often in sudden showers which soon pass. Big, towering cumulus and cumulonimbus clouds form. Winds tend to be quite strong and gusty along cold fronts. Feeling cool.
	Warm front	Clouds change from high cirrus to low, thick stratus cloud as front approaches. Weather is overcast and grey. Air pressure drops. Feeling warmer.
	Warm sector (The zone between a warm and cold front.)	Heavy stratus cloud covering the sky. Drizzle and rain lasting several hours. Misty, mild damp weather.
	Occluded front	Thick stratus clouds, overcast grey skies with showery rain.
H	High pressure (anticyclone)	In summer, warm, dry cloudless sunny skies. Very calm winds. In winter, cold but sunny weather, clear skies, calm winds.
L	Low pressure (depression)	Changeable weather depending on what type of front is passing over at the time. Usually cloudy, wet and windy.

Fig. 1 Weather maps and charts

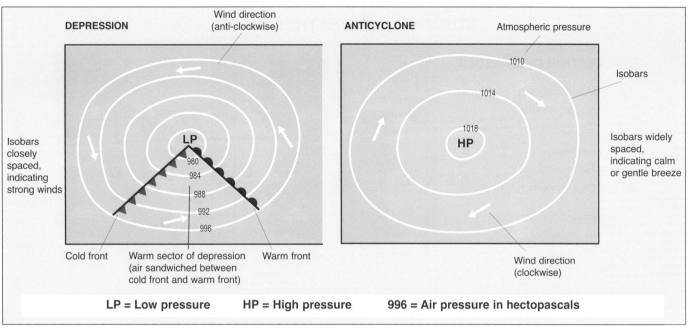

Fig. 2 Synoptic chart of depression and anticyclone

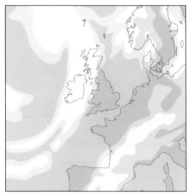

Fig. 3 Cloud cover for the low (depression) shown in Fig. 4

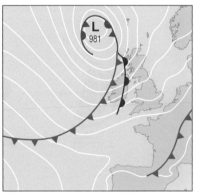

Fig. 4 Synoptic chart for the depression (low) shown in Fig. 3

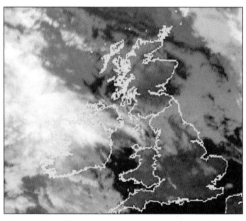

Fig. 5 Satellite image of weather situation from Met Éireann

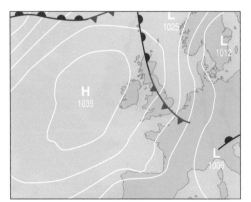

Fig. 6 Synoptic chart for the anticyclone (high) shown in Fig. 7

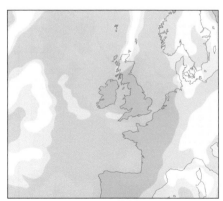

Fig. 7 Cloud cover for the high (anticyclone) shown in Fig. 6

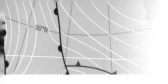

SUMMARY OF WEATHER MAPS

EXPLANATION OF SYMBOLS

- ↖31 = Wind direction and wind speed in km/h
- ⓿ = Temperatures in degrees Celsius
- ☀ = Fair weather
- ⛅ = Cloudy with bright spells
- 🌧 = Rain
- 🌦 = Showers

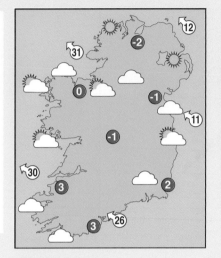

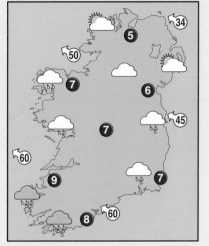

Weather in brief
Mainly dry but cold tonight.
Widespread ground frost.
Low of +3 to -2 degrees.

Tomorrow
Rain spreading countrywide from the south tomorrow.
High of 5 to 9 degrees.
Dry at first. Wet and windy later.

Fig. 8 Summary of weather maps

A variety of maps and charts are used to show the weather. Log on to: www.met.ie for a closer look.

Always quote the units of measurement when stating weather conditions, e.g. 1012 mb.

1. Examine the weather and cloud maps A to D and answer the questions that follow:

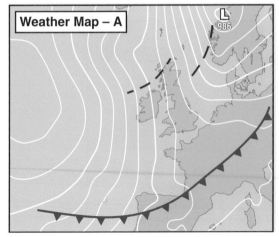

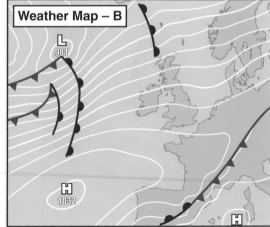

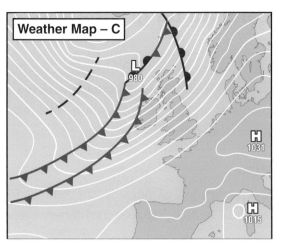

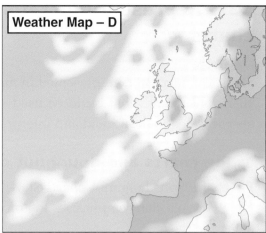

(a) Categorise the type of weather front over Central Europe in Weather Map A.

(b) State the barometric pressure of the anticyclone in Weather Map B.

(c) Is Ireland experiencing strong or light wind conditions in Weather Map C?

(d) Which of the Weather Maps A, B or C is represented by Cloud Map D?

2. The Atlantic Weather Chart below shows a weather situation in June.

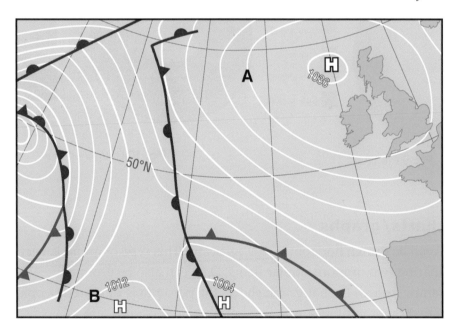

Examine the chart and answer the questions which follow:

(i) Is Ireland under the influence of a depression or an anticyclone?

(ii) Name the type of line at A on the map.

(iii) What is the barometric pressure at B on the map?

(iv) Which of the descriptions below best describes weather conditions over Ireland?
Tick the correct box.

Continuous light or heavy rain ❑

Showers with strong winds ❑

Calm dry weather with warm temperature ❑

13.3 Representing statistical data on graphs and charts

Statistical data can be represented in many ways. This section contains a variety of charts and graphs that could be used in the Geographical Investigation. You may also be asked to draw, read and interpret them in an exam.

1. Pie charts and doughnut charts

Pie charts and doughnut charts show the proportions of parts to the whole. In Fig. 9, the pie chart emphasises the proportion of bedload shapes at different sites along the river.

Pie charts are used to emphasise important elements.

Doughnut charts are similar to pie charts but contain more than one set of data.

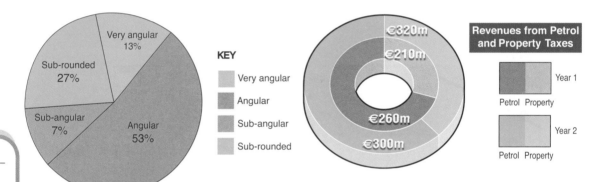

PIE CHART

Fig. 9 Pie chart

DOUGHNUT CHART

Fig. 10 Doughnut chart

EXERCISE

Examine Fig. 10. What was the value of taxes from petrol in Year 1 and Year 2?

2. Bar charts/graphs

Bar graphs can be drawn horizontally or vertically. This type of graph is very useful when comparing two or more similar items. Data can also be grouped.

In the example below, the bar graph shows the percentage of retired people living with a severe illness, an illness or in need of frequent hospital care.

VERTICAL BAR CHART

Fig. 11 Vertical bar graph showing the percentage of retired people in the USA with an illness and their age.

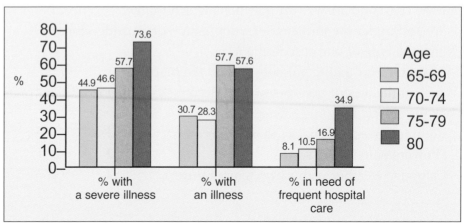

EXERCISE

Examine Fig. 11.

(a) State the percentage of people who are 80 years old with
(i) a severe illness and (ii) in need of frequent hospital care.

(b) State the age group with the lowest percentage of people with
(i) an illness and (ii) a severe illness.

In the example below, the horizontal bar chart shows how many years of life are lost to AIDS in each of the 20 countries listed and the percentage of adults with AIDS in each of these countries.

HORIZONTAL BAR CHART

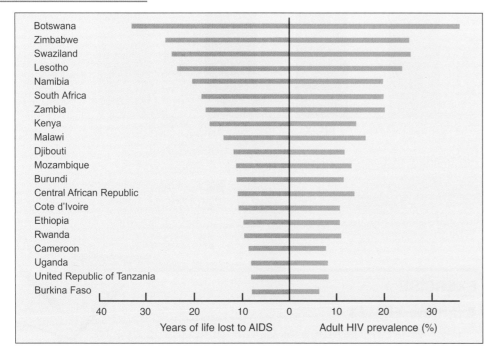

Fig. 12 This horizontal bar chart shows years of life lost to AIDS and the percentage of adults living with AIDS in 20 countries.

EXERCISE

Examine Fig. 12.

(a) State the percentage of adult HIV prevalence in Zambia.

(b) State the years of life lost to AIDS in Botswana and Rwanda.

Stacked bar charts show more than one set of information in each bar.
The bar chart below shows sources of air pollution in Victoria, Australia and percentage rates of how heavily these sources are polluting the air.

STACKED BAR CHART

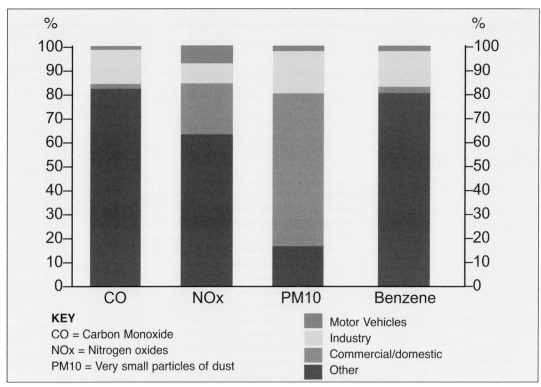

Fig. 13 Stacked bar chart showing air pollution sources in Victoria, Australia

EXERCISE

Examine Fig. 13.

(a) What percentage of CO air pollution is due to (i) industry and (ii) other sources?

(b) What percentage of PM10 pollution is due to commerical/domestic sources?

(c) What percentage of Benzene pollution is due to motor vehicles?

3. Trend graphs

Trend graphs show trends in a set of data **over time**, e.g. population growth, birth rates and death rates. They can also show the relationship between two variables. This trend graph shows how much fuel the US used from 1980 to 2004 and how much fuel it is likely to use from 2004 to 2030.

TREND GRAPH

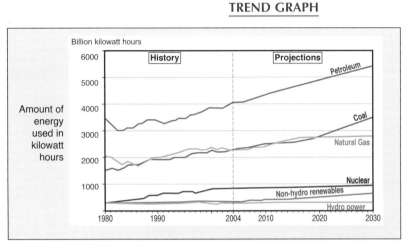

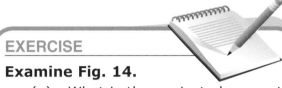

EXERCISE

Examine Fig. 14.

(a) What is the projected amount of energy use provided by petroleum in 2022?

(b) What was the actual amount of energy use provided by coal in 1994?

Fig. 14 Trend graph showing US energy consumption in kilowatts, 1980 – 2030

4. Triangle graphs

This type of graph is often used in relation to soil structures, water contents and mass movements.

TRIANGLE GRAPHS

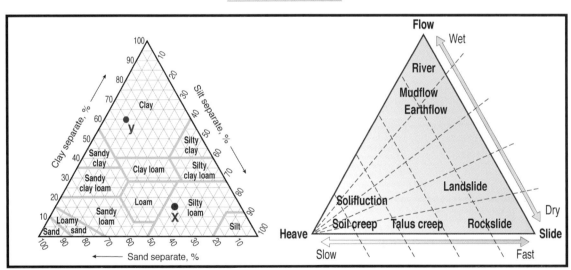

Fig. 15 Triangle graph showing soil composition and mass movement chart

Fig. 16 Triangle graph showing mass movement classification

In Fig. 15, the soil marked X has 30% sand, 55% silt and 15% clay. This makes it a silty loam. In Fig. 16, a mudflow is a fast, wet, flowing type of mass movement.

EXERCISE

Examine Fig. 15.

(a)   What is the composition of the soil marked Y?

(b)   What is the name of the soil with the following composition: 15% silt, 70% sand, 15% clay?

5. Scatter plots

Scatter plots show clusters of data and the relationships between two variables, e.g. bedload roundness and distance from a river's source.

SCATTER PLOTS

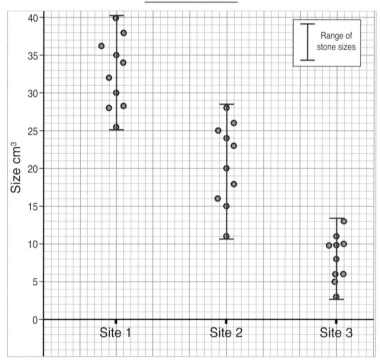

Fig. 17 Scatter plot showing bedload size of 10 stones at three sites along a river

EXERCISE

Examine Fig. 17.

(a)   What is the range in stone sizes at sites 1, 2 and 3?

(b)   What is the average size of stones at site 2?

(c)   Find the average size of stones at each site and plot the data as a trend graph of site against average size.

6. Climographs

Climographs combine bar graphs and trend graphs to show two different sets of data on one chart. Sometimes each side has a different scale, e.g. in Figs. 18 and 19, temperature is shown in degrees Celsius on the left-hand scale and rainfall is shown in millimetres on the right-hand side. The bars indicate the level of rainfall and the lines indicate temperature.

CLIMOGRAPHS

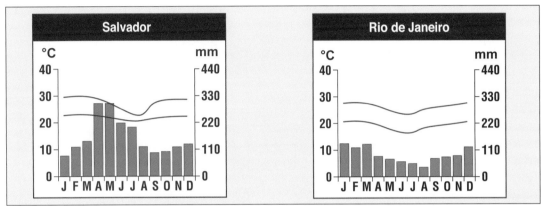

Fig. 18 Climograph showing the climate of Salvador, Brazil

Fig. 19 Climograph showing the climate of Rio de Janeiro, Brazil

EXERCISE

Examine Fig. 18.

   (a)   What is the average temperature in Salvador in February?

   (b)   What is the average rainfall in millimetres in Rio de Janeiro in January?

7. Radar charts

Radar charts compare the values of a number of sets of data.

RADAR CHARTS

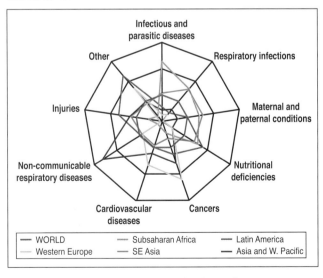

Fig. 20 A radar chart showing infectious diseases around the world

EXERCISE

Examine Fig. 20.

In which region do most people die from:

   (a)   non-communicable respiratory diseases?

   (b)   infectious and parasitic diseases?

   (c)   cancers?

In Fig. 21 we see the direction from which the wind is blowing and the percentage frequency of wind direction.

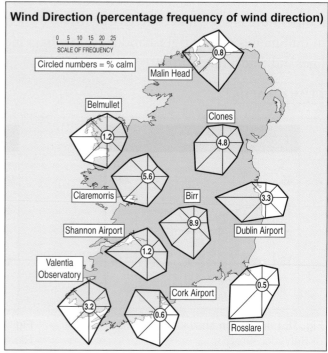

Fig. 21 A radar chart showing wind direction

SKILLS EXERCISE

For Dublin Airport:
- State the percentage of time for which the winds were westerly.

For Rosslare:
- State the most common wind direction. For what percentage of time did this wind blow?

For Valentia Observatory:
- State the percentage of time for which winds were:
  (i) southerly.
  (ii) easterly.

8. Wind roses

Wind roses are used to present wind speed data and wind direction data that have been collected over time, so that the dominant wind pattern for a particular area can be determined.

Wind roses are also useful as they project a large quantity of data onto one graphical plot.

The length of each 'arm' is proportional to the amount of time for which that wind speed was observed from that direction. The different colours on each arm indicate the wind speed. For example, in the wind rose in Fig. 22 most winds came from the south to south-west as indicated by the length of the two longest arms. Winds with higher wind speeds came from the west and south-west as indicated by the orange at the end of the arms.

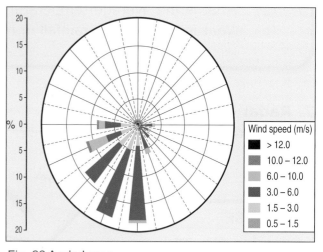

Fig. 22 A wind rose

SKILLS EXERCISE

In Fig. 22 calculate the percentage of days with wind speeds between 3–6 metres/second from the south-west.

9. Choropleths

Choropleths are maps on which information is presented using a colour-coded system.

CHOROPLETHS

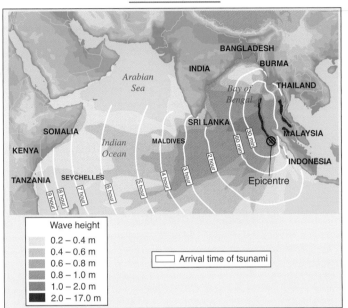

Fig. 23 The area affected by the tsunami that hit South-East Asia, December 2004

ACTIVITY

Examine Fig. 23.

(a) How many hours after the earthquake did the tsunami reach:

(i) Sri Lanka? (ii) Somalia?

(b) What was the height of the wave at these two locations?

13.4 Drawing graphs for the Leaving Certificate Exam

To draw a graph representing data from a table, follow the guidelines given below. These guidelines are based on the Leaving Certificate marking scheme.

1. Always put a **title** on your graph. The title can be copied from the title on the data table given in the question.

2. Always use **graph paper**. There are often marks awarded for the use of graph paper. Ask the exam supervisor for this paper.

3. If drawing a bar or trend graph, make sure the **axes** of your graph are drawn with a ruler and **labelled**. Ensure that the **scale** is carefully shown. If drawing a pie chart, use a compass to draw the circle and carefully mark the centre.

4. **Accurately** show the information from the data table using bars/points/sectors.

5. There are often marks available for overall **presentation**. Neatness gets you marks! Use colour wisely. Do not scribble with biro to colour a bar or pie sector.

Which graph to use?

1. Trend graphs show **changes over time**.

2. Bar charts, graphs and pie charts show **comparisons** or **single sets of data**.

3. Pie charts are more time consuming to draw, so use a bar chart instead unless specifically asked for a pie chart.

Drawing a trend graph

Atmospheric CO_2 – Ireland

The table below refers to the amount of CO_2 in the atmosphere in Ireland.

Year	1980	1985	1990	2000	2002
Metric tons per capita	7.7	7.5	8.7	11.2	10.9

Use graph paper to draw a graph that shows the data in the table above.

(30 marks)

Leaving Certificate Paper, OL

Marking Scheme – Drawing a graph for 30 marks

Graph paper used	4 marks
Vertical axis labelled	3 marks
Horizontal axis labelled	3 marks
5 items at 4 marks each	20 marks

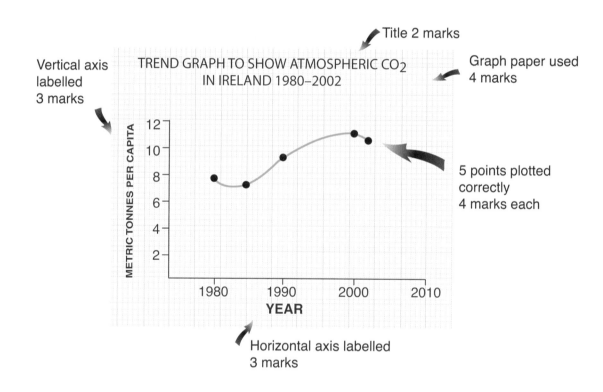

Drawing a bar graph

Employment Structure

Examine the table below, showing the percentage of people in employment in various economic sectors in Ireland (1984–2004).

SECTOR	YEAR	
	1984	2004
Primary	24%	6%
Secondary	31%	28%
Tertiary	45%	66%

Using graph paper, draw a graph suitable to illustrate this data.

(20 marks) Leaving Certificate Paper, HL

Marking Scheme – Drawing a graph for 20 marks

Title or chart named	2 marks
Use of graph paper	2 marks
Scaled axis	2 marks
6 bars/points plotted (at 2 marks each)	12 marks
Overall presentation (neatness and key)	2 marks

Accept bar chart / histogram / trend graph / scatter graph / pie chart etc.

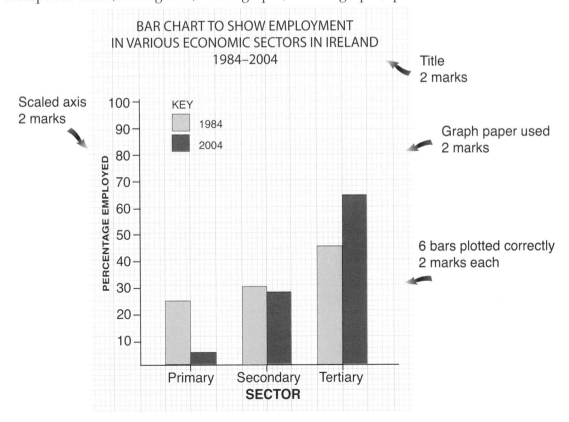

BAR CHART TO SHOW EMPLOYMENT IN VARIOUS ECONOMIC SECTORS IN IRELAND 1984–2004

Title 2 marks

Scaled axis 2 marks

Graph paper used 2 marks

6 bars plotted correctly 2 marks each

Overall presentation – 2 marks

Drawing pie charts

Use the worked example below to help you draw pie charts.

Sample Question: Draw a pie chart to represent the data in the table shown below. This table shows the shape of 15 stones sampled at Site 1 of the Whitewater River, County Down.

Stone No.	Shape	Stone No.	Shape
1	Angular	9	Very angular
2	Sub-rounded	10	Sub-angular
3	Sub-rounded	11	Angular
4	Angular	12	Sub-rounded
5	Very angular	13	Angular
6	Angular	14	Angular
7	Angular	15	Sub-rounded
8	Angular		

Pie Chart to show the shape of 15 stones from Site 1, Whitewater River

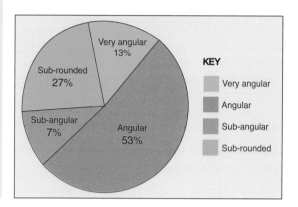

Answer: 15 stones must be shared out amongst 360 degrees of the pie. Therefore, each stone is: 360/15 = 24 degrees.

Make a rough table to work out what size each segment of the pie will be.

Shape category	No. of stones	Portion of the pie chart (degrees)
Very angular	2	2 x 24 = 48 degrees
Angular	8	8 x 24 = 192 degrees
Sub-angular	1	1 x 24 = 24 degrees
Sub-rounded	4	4 x 24 = 96 degrees

To draw the pie, you must use a compass, protractor and graph paper. Mark the centre of the circle clearly as marks are given for neatness and accuracy.

Start by drawing a horizontal line from the centre to the left edge of the pie using your protractor. Draw all segments from this line in a clockwise direction. Label or use colours to show all the pie segments. Provide a key and title.

Pie Chart Exercise

Draw a pie chart to represent the data in the table below:

Traffic survey: vehicles per hour passing along Mary Street, Dublin City.

Types of vehicle	Number of vehicles
Motorbikes	40
Cars	230
Vans	60
Buses	5
Cyclists	25

13.5 Satellite images

Satellite photos are used in many situations. Disaster areas, urban growth, hurricanes, ground cover, deforestation, sea surface temperatures, wave heights, volcanic activity, forest fires and the greening of the planet at springtime can all be seen by satellites. In the Leaving Cert exam you will be expected to identify landforms and events on satellite images.

Use the following website to browse satellite images that may be useful to you: www.earthobservatory.nasa.gov

Fig. 24 Before and after the Indian Ocean tsunami in December 2004

Fig. 25 Hurricane Katrina approaching the coast of Florida, USA

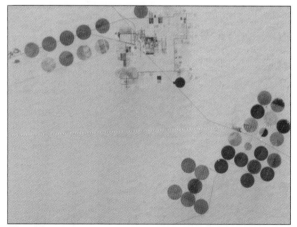

Fig. 26 Irrigation in the Sahara desert

Chapter Revision Questions are covered *within* Chapter 13

OL Short Question

1. Examine the population graphic for the Republic of Ireland (State) and Cork-South Central 2006 and answer the questions in the spaces provided.

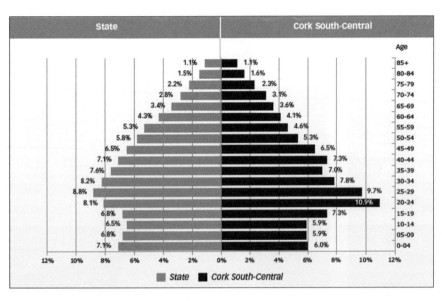

(i)   In which age group is the greatest overall percentage of population in the State?

(ii) What is the total percentage of the population in the 35-39 age group in Cork South-Central?

(iii) What percentage of Cork South-Central's population is over 65 years?

(iv) What is the difference in population in the 20-24 age group between Cork South-Central and the State?

HL Short Questions

2. The table and graph below give information on rainfall and run-off, gathered over a twelve-month period.

Month	J	F	M	A	M	J	J	A	S	O	N	D
Rainfall (in mms)	150	130	100	100	75	60	50	50	80	90	120	120
Surface run-off (in mms)	120	120	65	60	45	30	20	15	30	50	80	90

Answer the questions below.

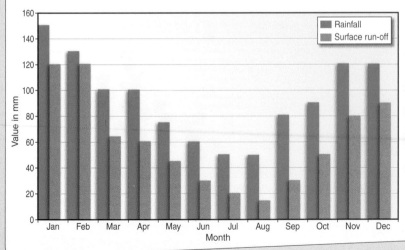

(i)   In how many months did rainfall exceed 80 mm?

(ii) Calculate the average monthly rainfall for the last three months of the year.

(iii) Name the month when rainfall and surface run-off were closest.

(iv) Select the most likely explanation for run-off being almost equal to rainfall in that month:
(a)   the ground was very dry
(b)   evaporation was low
(c)   the soil was very wet

LC Exam Paper

3. Examine the triangular graph which shows the employment structure in three countries, A, B and C. Complete the table on the right. *LC Exam Paper*

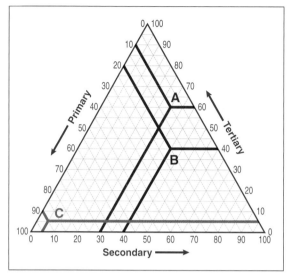

Employment Structure	Country
Primary 20%, Secondary 40%, Tertiary 40%	
Primary 90%, Secondary 5%, Tertiary 5%	
Primary 10%, Secondary 30%, Tertiary 60%	
Which country would appear to have the most developed economy?	

4. Examine the table on the right, showing GDP in the European Union.

Answer the following questions:
(i) Which country had the highest average GDP in both 1995 and 2000?
(ii) Which country had an average GDP that did not change from 1995 to 2000?
(iii) How many countries had an average GDP lower than the EU average in 2000?
(iv) By how many points did Ireland increase its GDP between 1995 and 2000?

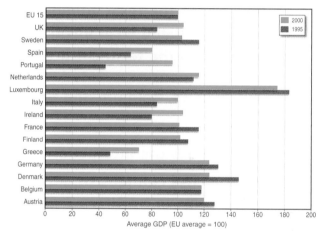

LC Exam Paper

5. Match **each** weather map symbol in Column A with its description in Column B.

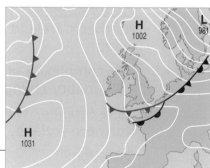

Column A

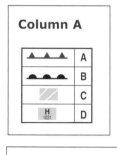

Column B

Warm Front   = 1
Isobars   = 2
Anticyclone = 3
Cold Front   = 4

____ = A   ____ = B
____ = C   ____ = D

LC Exam Paper

HL Long Question

6. Examine the table below, showing selected unemployment statistics for 2004.

Country	Unemployment rate (% of adult population)
Austria	3.8%
Estonia	9.7%
France	9.5%
Latvia	14.6%
Poland	16.1%
Spain	10.5%

Using graph paper, draw a graph suitable to illustrate these data. *LC Exam Paper*

Chapter 14

The Concept and Complexity of Regions
– Physical, administrative and cultural regions

At the end of this chapter you should be able to:

- Define the term region.
- Identify the categories into which regions can be classified.
- Explain how climate and landscape can be used to define a region.
- Define the term administrative region and explain how central and local government is organised in Ireland and France.
- Define the term cultural region and discuss the characteristics of regions associated with particular languages or religions in Ireland, Belgium and the Islamic world.
- Discuss how language regions in Ireland have changed over time.
- Discuss the interaction among cultural groups and political regions.
- Discuss changes to political boundaries and their impact on cultural groups in Northern Ireland and Poland.

Contents

14.1 The concept of a region

14.2 Physical regions

14.3 Administrative regions

Case Studies: Functions of local and central government agencies in Ireland and France

14.4 Cultural regions

Case Studies: Ireland, Belgium, Northern Ireland and the Islamic world

14.5 The complexity of cultural regions – Boundary changes

Case Studies: The Gaeltacht, Northern Ireland, Poland

Questions

KEY THEME

A region is an area of the earth's surface that is distinctive in some way. Regions can be identified by one or more human and/or natural characteristics, e.g. cultural or landscape. Boundaries of regions can change over time. These changes affect cultural groups. The study of regions illustrates the geographical complexity of the interaction between economic, cultural and physical processes.

14.1 The concept of a region

A region is an area with a characteristic (or characteristics) that sets it apart from other areas, making it distinctive or unique in some way, e.g. the Sahara desert in Africa or the 'sunny south east' of Ireland. A region can be identified on the basis of a variety of characteristics such as its landscape, climate, economic development, language, religion or government.

The edges of regions often overlap and these areas share characteristics found in neighbouring regions, e.g. language. People may move between regions bringing their way of life with them and introducing it to the people of their adopted region.

Types of regions

Regions can be grouped into five categories: physical regions, administrative regions, cultural regions, nodal/urban/city regions and socio-economic regions. In each category, we can identify different types of regions which are shown below with examples.

TYPES OF REGIONS IN EUROPE		
Physical regions	Climate	Cool temperate – Ireland
		Mediterranean – Mezzogiorno, Italy
	Geomorphic (landscape)	Upland – Munster Ridge and Valley province
		Lowland – Paris Basin, North European Plain
		Rock type – the Burren, County Clare
Administrative regions	Local authorities	Dublin City Council, town councils
		French *départements*
	EU administrative regions	Ireland's South and East region
		Border Midlands West (BMW) region
Cultural regions	Language	Ireland – Gaeltacht, Belgium – Flanders, Wallonia
		Basque region of Northern Spain
	Religion	Northern Ireland, Islamic World
Nodal / urban / city regions		Dublin
		Paris
Socio-economic regions	Core regions (wealthy)	Urban – Paris, Dublin, Randstaad
		Industrial – Milan, Turin, Genoa, Ruhr
		Agricultural – Paris Basin, North Italian Plain
	Peripheral/less developed regions	BMW region, Mezzogiorno, Northern Norway
	Regions of industrial decline	Sambre Meuse Valley, Belgium
		North coast of Spain, Drogheda

14.2 Physical regions

1. Climatic regions

These are areas of the world that experience a particular climate. Climatic regions tend to be large in size, covering entire countries and sections of the globe. For example, the Tundra climate encircles the earth north of the Arctic Circle. It is found in all countries that have land in this zone. So Canada, Greenland, Northern Norway, Northern Sweden, Northern Finland and Russia are united in one climatic region – the Tundra climatic region.

Climate is an important physical factor that influences the distribution and type of natural vegetation, human activities and animal species found in a region. For example, we tend to associate camels, cacti and nomadic tribes with deserts.

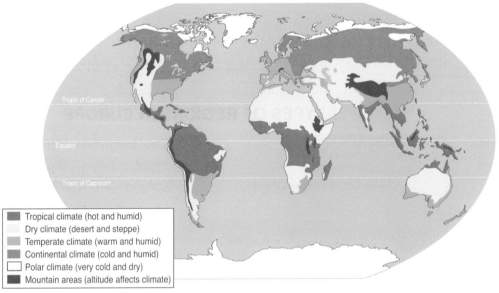

Tropical climate (hot and humid)
Dry climate (desert and steppe)
Temperate climate (warm and humid)
Continental climate (cold and humid)
Polar climate (very cold and dry)
Mountain areas (altitude affects climate)

Fig. 1 The world's main climatic zones

Climates on earth can be divided into hot, temperate and cold climates. Within these three divisions, there are further subdivisions.

HOT CLIMATES	TEMPERATE CLIMATES	COLD CLIMATES
Equatorial	Cool temperate oceanic	Tundra (sub-arctic)
Savanna	Warm temperate oceanic	Boreal (coniferous forest)
Monsoon	(Mediterranean)	
Desert	Cool temperate continental	

Cool temperate oceanic climate – North-west Europe: Ireland

Ireland and north-west Europe have a cool temperate oceanic climate.

This type of climate is found on the western sides of continents in a zone between 40 to 55 degrees north and south of the equator. Therefore, Ireland has mild winters (average 6°C in January) and moderately warm summers (average 15°C in July). Rainfall is frequent throughout the year (1,500 mm), with more rainfall in winter.

Ireland's climate is influenced by several factors, including latitude, the sea, south-westerly winds and the movement of frontal depressions.

(a) The influence of latitude on Ireland's climate

Ireland is located between 51.5° and 55.5° north of the equator. This influences the amount of sunshine and the temperatures that we experience throughout the year. At this latitude, the polar and tropical air masses meet and have an important influence on our climate.

(b) The influence of the sea on Ireland's climate

The sea warms and dampens the prevailing south-westerly winds and keeps the coast free of ice in winter.

The sea acts as an enormous storage heater. The sea warms up slowly in spring and summer and holds this heat until the winter. Throughout the winter, the sea gradually loses the warmth it picked up earlier in the year.

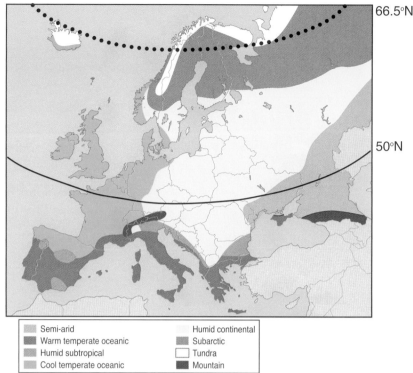

Fig. 2 Climatic zones of Europe

This keeps our land temperatures much higher than they should be given our latitude. Without the influence of the sea, average winter temperatures in Ireland could be 10 degrees colder. The warm ocean current – the **North Atlantic Drift** – keeps the water warm and prevents it from freezing, as well as being a source of heat for the south-westerly winds.

In summer, the land heats quickly and the sea is relatively cold. Sea breezes blowing onshore in the afternoons keep summer temperatures down.

In the central part of Ireland, away from the sea's influence, temperatures are slightly more extreme, with average summer temperatures of 16°C and in winter of 2.5°C.

(c) The influence of south-westerly winds on Ireland's climate

The prevailing south-westerly winds blow across several thousand kilometres of the Atlantic Ocean before reaching Ireland. The winds pick up moisture and heat from the warm water as they travel. This influences Ireland's temperatures and precipitation levels.

This prevailing wind picks up water vapour by evaporation on its journey across the ocean. When the moist air reaches land, it is forced to rise above the mountains along the west coast, causing **relief rainfall**. This is the reason why levels of precipitation in the west of Ireland are more than treble (2,800 mm) that of the eastern part of the country (800 mm).

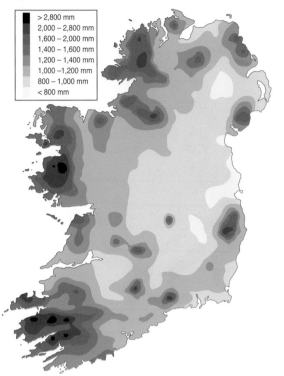

> 2,800 mm
2,000 – 2,800 mm
1,600 – 2,000 mm
1,400 – 1,600 mm
1,200 – 1,400 mm
1,000 – 1,200 mm
800 – 1,000 mm
< 800 mm

Fig. 3 Average rainfall in Ireland

Note the high rainfall levels over the upland areas

(d) The influence of frontal depressions on Ireland's climate

Over Ireland, cold (**polar**) and warm (**tropical**) air masses meet forming the **polar front**. Movement of the polar front creates disturbances in the atmosphere called **depressions** or lows.

These depressions move across the Atlantic Ocean from west to east causing frequent, often rapid changes in the weather, i.e. daily changes in air pressure, temperature, cloud cover, wind speed, wind direction and precipitation. Ireland lies in the path of these depressions causing our weather to change from day to day. Depressions cause rain to fall throughout the year.

The rainfall created in these depressions is called **frontal rainfall** and is the most common type of rain to fall in Ireland. See page 244.

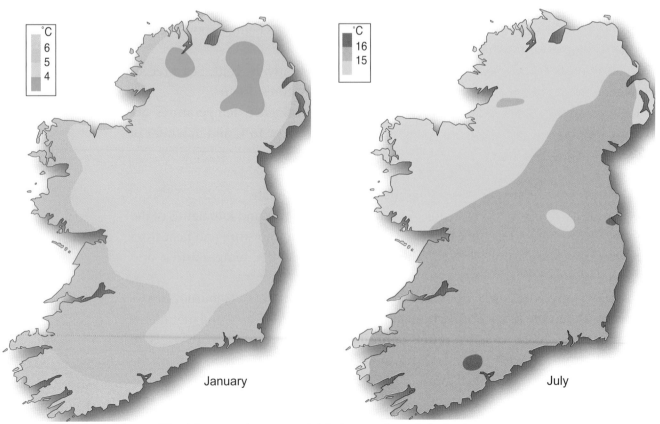

°C
6
5
4

January

°C
16
15

July

Fig. 4 Average January and July temperatures in Ireland

Fig. 5 Location of Birr and Valentia weather stations

AVERAGE WEATHER CONDITIONS FOR VALENTIA COUNTY KERRY

TEMPERATURE	jan	feb	mar	apr	may	jun	jul	aug	sep	oct	nov	dec	year
mean temperature (°C)	6.8	6.6	7.6	8.9	10.9	13.3	14.8	14.8	13.5	11.5	8.7	7.6	**10.4**
number of days with ground frost	7.5	7.1	6.1	4.3	1.1	0.1	0.0	0.0	0.2	1.1	4.5	6.8	**38.8 (total)**
SUNSHINE (hours) mean daily duration	1.24	2.09	3.03	5.00	5.48	5.07	4.32	4.30	3.37	2.32	1.43	1.10	**3.23**
RAINFALL (mm) mean monthly total	166.6	123.0	122.9	76.2	89.6	79.2	74.0	110.8	123.8	156.4	148.3	159.2	**1,430.1**

AVERAGE WEATHER CONDITIONS FOR BIRR, COUNTY OFFALY

TEMPERATURE	jan	feb	mar	apr	may	jun	jul	aug	sep	oct	nov	dec	year
mean temperature (°C)	4.6	4.8	6.1	7.9	10.4	13.2	14.9	14.6	12.6	10.1	6.4	5.4	**9.3**
number of days with ground frost	17.0	15.1	13.6	11.8	6.1	1.2	0.1	0.2	2.0	4.9	13.0	15.0	**100 (total)**
SUNSHINE (hours) mean daily duration	1.36	2.18	3.11	4.38	5.19	4.48	4.15	4.09	3.35	2.40	2.02	1.25	**3.20**
RAINFALL (mm) mean monthly total	75.9	54.0	61.3	52.5	61.7	55.2	59.1	77.6	70.6	83.5	74.1	78.6	**804.2**

2. Geomorphic regions (landscape)

There are many regions around the world that have unique landscapes.

You have already studied karst regions (regions associated with limestone rock such as the Burren – Chapter 7, page 93) and a region associated with particular rock structures, such as the Munster Ridge and Valley province. (See Chapter 4, page 57).

The final geomorphic region you will study is the North European Plain.

The North European Plain

The North European Plain is a lowland region covering more than half of Europe. It includes Poland; northern Germany; southern Scandinavia; Belgium; the Netherlands; northern and western France; and the Romanian, Bulgarian and Hungarian plains. Several physical factors combine to make the North European Plain one of the most densely populated areas of Europe.

Soils

During the last ice age (**glacial period**), continental ice sheets covered parts of this region. Wherever the glaciers stopped, they deposited great quantities of rock, sand and soil as moraine and boulder clay.

Strong winds blew across these deposits and lifted fine sands and silts, redepositing them across the southern edge of the plain as **limon**, or loess. Limon makes a very fertile soil. As a result, it is heavily cultivated, e.g. Paris Basin.

Climate

The climate of the North European Plain is generally mild and moist, adding to the agricultural prosperity of the region. Rainfall is evenly distributed throughout the year and temperatures are moderate.

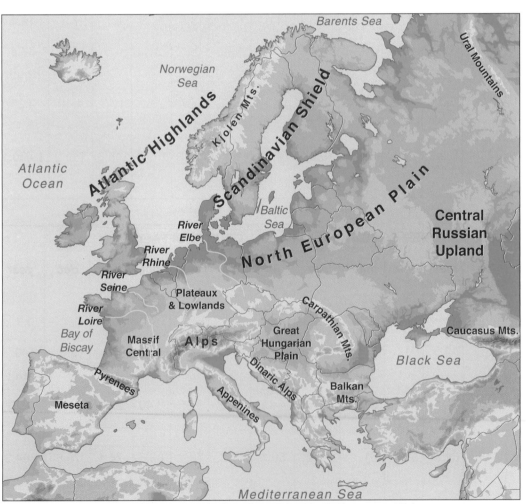

Fig. 6 Physical regions of Europe – the location of the North European Plain

Fig. 7 Satellite photo showing the North European Plain and other geomorphic regions

Drainage

Many large rivers such as the Seine, the Rhine, the Elbe and the Loire flow across the region in a north-westerly direction, providing fertile alluvium, natural communications and trade routes.

Relief

The lowland landscape (**topography**) has allowed intensive commerical agriculture and the development of one of the world's most efficient transportation networks. Major roads, railways, rivers and canals stretch across the plain linking major cities such as Paris and Berlin.

The plain is at the heart of European industrial power. Coal and iron ore deposits lie beneath the glacial sediments in Germany, Poland, France and Belgium. The rivers, soils, climate and abundance of mineral/metal resources helped the region become highly industrialised, attractive for settlement and one of the most densely-populated areas in Europe.

Find out more about geomorphic regions in Europe. Log on to www.worldatlas.com/webimage/countrys/eulnd.htm

14.3 Administrative regions

> *Administrative regions* are areas controlled by local or central government agencies. Local agencies are town councils and county councils. Central agencies are government departments.

We will examine two case studies – Ireland and France.

Functions of local and central government agencies in Ireland

(a) At local level

Local government agencies deal with motor taxation, local courts, housing, water supply, refuse collection and disposal, road repair and the running of public parks, swimming pools and other public leisure facilities such as libraries. The ability of the local government to carry out its functions depends upon the levels of financial support provided by the central government.

• Local government in Ireland occurs at three levels: town level, county/city level and regional level.

At town level: Eighty town councils throughout Ireland carry out a representative role for their town and a range of local government functions, e.g. Bray Town Council, Clonmel Town Council.

At county/city level: Thirty-four county/city councils are the main providers of local government services. There are 29 county councils throughout Ireland and five city councils, e.g. Wicklow County Council, Waterford County Council.

THE RESPONSIBILITIES OF LOCAL AND CENTRAL GOVERNMENT AGENCIES

Local government	Central government
1. Motor taxation	
2. Planning and provision of housing	The provision of larger, more expensive national services, such as:
3. Refuse collection and disposal	
4. Road repair	
5. The maintenance of recreational facilities, e.g. public parks, swimming pools and other public leisure facilities such as libraries	1. School buildings
6. Water supply and sewerage	2. Road construction
7. Heritage issues	3. Hospitals
8. Local courts	4. Courts
9. Environmental protection	
10. Health and education, e.g. clinics and VECs	

Funding for services

The funding for the services listed above is provided by local and central government sources, including:

1. Rates on commercial and industrial buildings.
2. Income from goods and services (housing rents, planning fees).
3. Exchequer grants from the central government.
4. Internal capital receipts (sale of houses, land).
5. Borrowing.

(b) At regional level

On a larger scale, the EU divides Europe up into many administrative regions in order to allocate funds for projects such as road building and farm improvement.

● In the past, eight **regional authorities** in Ireland co-ordinated some of the county/city and town activities, e.g. Mid East Regional Authority, South East Regional Authority. They monitored the way in which EU structural funds were used. Regional administration in Ireland was modified when the eight regional authorities were grouped into two large **regional assemblies.** This grouping into two assemblies (the Border Midlands West [BMW] and South East [SE] regions) occurred in 1999 in order to maintain extra EU funding for the poorer regions of Ireland, i.e. the BMW region.

These two assemblies have three functions:

1. To encourage the co-ordination of the provision of public services in their areas.
2. To manage new regional projects such as infrastructure supply and social development schemes.
3. To monitor the implementation of all EU funding.

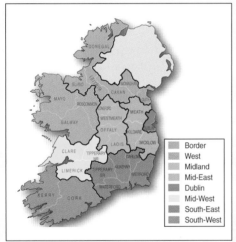

Fig. 8 The original eight regional authority areas in Ireland

Fig. 9 The two regional assembly areas in Ireland today

● The European Union also provides money for the development of services and infrastructure. See Fig. 10 below.

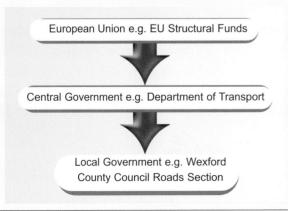

Fig. 10 Levels of government administration in Europe

For more information on local government, log onto www.irlgov.ie

case study

Functions of local and central government agencies in France

Like Ireland, France also has a three-level (tier) local government administration system. The three levels are the *commune*, the *département* and the *région*. Each level is a distinct legal body, responsible for funding and providing the same types of local services and projects as in Ireland.

Communes

These date from 1789 and are the oldest form of local authority in France. They are responsible for water supply, lighting, park maintenance and primary school buildings. Over 36,000 towns and villages are communes, each with an elected mayor and assembly. They are similar in size to small Irish towns, villages and parishes. Most communes have less than 1,000 people. Central government is urging smaller *communes* to merge together to increase efficiency.

Départements

These were created in 1790 – a year after the French Revolution. They are responsible for planning, public housing, car tax, secondary schools and colleges, roads, health and social services. There are 100 *départements* in France (96 in Europe, 4 overseas). All have a similar size and shape. The head of each *département* is the *préfet* (governor). The *préfet* is the government's representative in his/her local *département*. Similar to Irish counties, each *département* is identified by a two-digit number which is used on car number plates and postcodes.

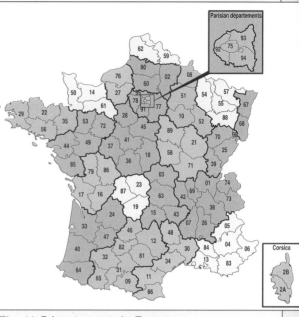

Fig. 11 *Départements* in France

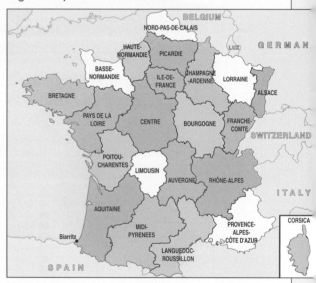

Fig. 12 *Régions* in France

Régions

These were formally created in 1982 to decentralise government services and decision making. They are responsible for regional planning and economic development as well as funding schools and colleges across the region. There are 26 *régions* (22 in France and 4 overseas). Each *région* has a unique cultural identity, e.g. Brittany. Decisions are made by the *Conseil Régional* (Regional Council) whose members are elected every six years. They are similar to Irish provinces.

Find out more about France. Log on to
http://geography.about.com/library/maps/blfrance.htm

14.4 Cultural regions

> Regions where people share a specific language, religion and/or way of life are called cultural regions.

Language

Language is an essential part of a country's tradition and culture. In many countries, there is an official state language; however, people may also speak a local version of it (a **dialect**) or a completely different language to the official national language.

Historical conquest, colonisation, missionary work and migration have been responsible for the spread or destruction of many languages across the world. Some languages take on influences from other regions and local dialects emerge. For example, the German spoken in Switzerland is very different from the German spoken in Germany.

Cultural regions associated with language: Ireland

(a) Gaeltacht regions in Ireland

The Gaeltacht is a group of regions in Ireland where Irish is spoken in the community and in the home. It is a cultural region based on its language. Other cultural activities associated with the Irish language include *sean nós* singing, set dancing, *céilís* and story telling. The Gaeltacht region is unique because it is the last surviving remnant of an ancient Indo-European language. Irish began in Central Europe around 400 BC and is the third oldest written language after Greek and Latin. Irish is most closely related to Welsh and Scots Gaelic.

Fig. 13 Road sign in Irish in County Donegal

Location of Gaeltacht areas

- The Gaeltacht is a dispersed region of seven separate geographic areas and eight offshore islands. These Irish-speaking communities are found on the western and south-western seaboards of Ireland, covering extensive areas of Counties Donegal, Mayo, Galway, Cork and Kerry. The Gaeltacht is a rural region with a population of about 91,862 (2.1% of Ireland's population) of which about 60% (54,000) of the residents are fluent in Irish and use the language in the community and at home. Donegal is the largest Gaeltacht area in Ireland. An Daingean (Dingle) in County Kerry is the largest Gaeltacht town, with a population of over 1,500 people.

The Formation of Gaeltacht Areas

- Following independence from Britain in 1922 only about 18% of people spoke Irish on a daily basis. In 1925 the Free State government recognised that there were both Irish and semi-Irish speaking districts in 15 of the 26 counties. Therefore they established the **Commission for Irish Speaking Districts** (Coimisiún na Gaeltacht). In 1926 this

Commission established the boundaries for the Gaeltacht based on the numbers of people speaking the language. At that time the region consisted of over 250,000 people who were categorised into **Fíor** (true) Gaeltacht regions (over 80% speaking Irish) and **Breac** (partial) Gaeltacht regions (25% - 79% speaking Irish).

Today the Department of Arts, Heritage, Gaeltacht and the Islands has responsibility for promoting the cultural, social and economic wealth of the Gaeltacht region. It has provided government funding to develop the Gaeltacht economy, to stop depopulation and to preserve the Irish language, culture and traditions. In 1980, **Údarás na Gaeltachta** was established. It is the organisation responsible for the economic, social and cultural development of the Gaeltacht. The overall objective of Údarás na Gaeltachta is to ensure Irish remains the main language of the region and is passed on to future generations.

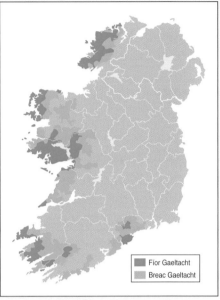

Fig. 14 Gaeltacht areas of Ireland in 1926

Factors affecting the Gaeltacht region

Several physical and human factors have combined to make the Gaeltacht a unique cultural region based on its language. These factors include relief, soils, history, infrastructure, services, population, government and EU support.

Physical factors

The Gaeltacht regions are the most remote, scenic and rural parts of the country. They generally have mountainous relief, high rainfall and poor soils. The infertile, acidic, peatland soils covering much of the Gaeltacht area leads to limited farm incomes. The harsh remote physical landscape has limited economic development. These factors have led to out-migration of younger people, leaving older Irish speakers in isolated communities. This has had two effects: firstly the number of Irish speakers is declining and secondly the role of Údarás na Gaeltachta in attracting industry to the region is made even more challenging.

Human factors

The existence of Gaeltacht regions of Ireland is not just the result of government policy but of Ireland's history.

Irish was the first language spoken by the majority of the population until the time of the Plantations in the sixteenth century. During the Plantations, large areas of Irish farmland were given to British landlords by the British authorities. Many Irish famers were forced to leave their land and move to the more remote and less fertile lands of the

Fig. 15 Donegal, a Gaeltacht region

western counties ('to Hell or to Connacht'). This led to the survival of the language in the Gaeltacht regions we see today in Donegal, Kerry and Mayo.

Decline of Irish language regions

- **Historic reasons**

During the Plantations of the sixteenth century, English, Scottish and Welsh planters did not have enough settlers to work their new farms in Ireland. Therefore they employed Irish labourers who quickly had to learn the English language in order to communicate and gain employment. The Irish language rapidly experienced social, economic and regional marginalisation and its use thus declined.

- As English rule strengthened in Ireland during the seventeenth and eighteenth centuries Irish survived only in the western coastal regions. By the end of the eighteenth century, less than 50% (4 million) of the population spoke only Irish and these were the poorest rural dwellers.

- During the Great Famine (1845-1848), the high death rate and mass emigration led to a dramatic reduction in numbers of Irish speakers in the country. By the end of the famine only 1.5 million people spoke Irish in the country and these were mainly concentrated in Munster and Connacht. Economic, political and business life was conducted through English and the Irish language continued to be associated with poverty. National schools taught through English with the result that many people had little or no understanding of the language.

- **Modern Reasons**

In the twenty-first century the main threat to the survival of the language in Gaeltacht regions is in-migration of non-Irish speakers and the influence of English-speaking media such as satellite TV and the internet.

- Today, Irish culture is strongly influenced by television, music and fashion from English-speaking countries such as Britain and America. This influence contributes to the decline in the use of the language in the Gaeltacht on an everyday basis, therefore shrinking the Gaeltacht region.

- During the economic boom of 1990 - 2008 there was a period of in-migration to the Gaeltacht regions. This has had a negative impact on the language in the area as many of the people moving into the Gaeltacht did not speak Irish. The Connemara Gaeltacht, for example, is under continued pressure (even during economic recession) from the urban expansion of Galway city and the subsequent influx of non-Irish speakers into the Gaeltacht area. In the past many non-Irish speakers bought holiday homes in the area, resulting in an increase in the cost of property. This has priced many young Irish-speaking locals out of the market, forcing many of them to settle outside of Gaeltacht regions. However, with the decrease in property prices since 2008 this trend may reverse.

case study

case study

Support for Irish language regions
Organisations supporting the Irish language

Foras na Gaeilge
Promotes the use of Irish across Ireland

The GAA
Promotes the use of Irish in all their sporting and social activities

Údarás na Gaeltachta
Promotes the economic and social development of Gaeltacht areas

Support for the Irish language today

The Irish Language Act
A law ensuring the provision of public services and documents through Irish, e.g. driving licences

TG4 and Raidió na Gaeltachta
Use Irish in their TV and radio programmes

Gaelscoileanna
Supports the development of Irish-speaking schools

- Encouraging Irish speakers to remain in the Gaeltacht is important to the survival of the Gaeltacht as a cultural region. The government recognises this by providing unique financial support to Gaeltacht families. These include: a grant paid to families in the Gaeltacht who can satisfy the Department that Irish is their usual spoken language, a grant paid to qualified families in the Gaeltacht to accommodate learners of Irish while they attend recognised Irish Colleges and grants paid to qualified applicants in the Gaeltacht to build new houses and to improve existing houses. Annual assistance is available for organisations working to maintain the Irish language in the Gaeltacht. Grants are also paid for cultural events in which the Irish language has a central role or that will benefit the Irish language and the cultural and social life of Gaeltacht areas.

- The creation of the dedicated Irish language station TG4 in 1996 has encouraged more Irish language programmes. Cúla4 is an Irish language children's TV station. Raidió Na Gaeltachta broadcasts 24 hours a day and has an average listenership of 150,000. *Foinse* is the biggest Irish language weekly newspaper.

- The increase in the numbers of Irish language schools, na Gaelscoileanna, and provision of summer colleges in Gaeltacht areas all continue to promote Irish language, culture and traditions. The youth organisation Óige na Gaeltachta Teo was founded in 2006 to promote and develop services, through the medium of Irish, for young people in the Gaeltacht.

- A 20-year national strategy (2010-2030) has been implemented by the government with the aim of increasing to 250,000 the number of people using Irish on a daily basis outside of the education system.

Cultural regions associated with language: Europe

(b) Belgium's language divide

Belgium (population of 10.6 million people) is a linguistically divided country. The division of the population by language has led to political, social and economic division of the country. An official language line stretches across the country separating Dutch-speaking **Flanders** from French-speaking **Wallonia**. The people in each region rarely mix.

Fig. 16 The Belgian linguistic divide

- Southern Belgium is known as Wallonia. It is a French-speaking region. Here people are more liberal, socialist and Catholic. The main cities are Namur, Liège and Charleroi. Locals are known as Walloons. Wallonia was once a wealthy industrial region based on its coal resources but since the 1960s it has undergone economic decline and has a high unemployment rate (20%).

- In northern Belgium or Flanders people speak Flemish – a variation of Dutch. Sixty per cent of the Belgian population is Flemish. Here people are also Catholic but are more republican and conservative in their outlook. Flanders had an economy mainly based on agriculture with little industry but since the 1960s Flanders has undergone economic growth and accounts for 87% of Belgian GDP. The main cities are Antwerp and Ghent. The capital city, Brussels, is located in Flanders. Brussels is officially bilingual but most people there speak French.

- The language line was established in 1917 and led to the formation of the two government administrative regions – Wallonia and Flanders. (See Fig. 16.) Both Wallonia and Flanders have their own governments. A third region, the East Cantons, is German speaking. This region is in the east and is centred on the towns of Malmedy and Eupen. It also has its own government. The regions control 40% of all public spending and are responsible for roads, urban projects, health services, the environment and education. Representatives from each region are elected to the Belgian national government.

Factors leading to the division of Belgium
Physical factors – Location, resources

Flanders' economy was based on its fertile farmland. This led the region to be perceived by the Walloons as poor and economically underdeveloped. This gave the French-speaking Walloons a sense of superiority over the Flemish.

● Flanders has access to the North Sea and beyond via the port of Antwerp. This has been a major advantage in attracting industrial development to the region. This gives economic strength to the Flemish desire for independence.

● Wallonia's wealth was originally based on coal reserves in the Sambre-Meuse Valley. This coal led to the development of iron- and steelworks that provided employment and wealth for the region up to the 1960s. This provided economic power to Wallonia over Flanders.

● Wallonia is closer to the industrial regions of France and Germany. This provided an important market for its coal and was a source of wealth during the Industrial Revolution. When the coal ran out in the 1960s, the region lost its wealth and became an unemployment blackspot with social problems as a result. This has reversed the social and economic fortunes of the Walloons.

● **Human factors – History, government**

Before 1830 Belgium was part of the United Kingdom of the Netherlands. The southern states included Flanders and Wallonia which were collectively known as Belgium. However the Dutch King, William I, favoured the Dutch speakers of the Netherlands. The French-speaking Walloons resented his attempt to make Dutch the official language of government.

● When the French Revolution occurred it spurred the Walloons to seek Belgian independence from the Netherlands but they brought Flanders with them. Belgium became an independent state and French became the national language.

● French domination of economic and industrial life in Belgium between 1830 and 1940 led to increasing resentment amongst the Flemish against the Walloons. The mainly agricultural Flemish people felt like second-class citizens in their own country even though they were in the majority. By 1930 laws were enacted that made Flemish the language of government, education, road signage and the courts in Flanders. Brussels became bilingual.

● In 1980 the constitution was revised to form the federal government in Flanders, Wallonia and Brussels. Each region now has social and political autonomy from each other but is represented at the national Belgian government.

● The cultural division of Belgium due to language has many effects on the daily life of the population. The people in each region rarely mix. Each region has its own schools which follow different subject curricula. There is no national University of Belgium. Each region has its own shops, transport networks, soccer teams, TV stars and radio stations. Government press conferences and publications are in both languages. Walloons who wish to buy property in Flanders are required to take a language exam to show they can speak Flemish. Before they take office, politicians have to pass a language exam to show they can speak both languages.

The Brussels region faces difficult challenges because of the language differences. Brussels is in Flanders but is mainly French speaking. It is the centre of the EU government. People from Wallonia have moved to Brussels for work. In the eyes of the conservative Flemish many towns around Brussels are being 'colonised' by French speakers. In primary schools Flemish- and French-speaking children are educated separately, often in the same buildings. Public libraries must have equal numbers of Dutch and French books. Political meetings in Flanders must be in Dutch even if all those present are French speakers. Should Flanders seek independence it would want Brussels to be its capital city.

Interaction between cultural groups and political regions - Belgium

Belgium was established as a political state in 1830. It is a monarchy. The present King Albert II presides over a federal Belgian state. Each state elects representatives to the Belgian government. Belgium is a member of the EU and the people elect representatives to the EU government. Athletes represent Belgium at international games and events. However, the cultural differences between the Walloons and Flemish people are threatening the continued existence of the Belgian nation.

The difficulty is that people see themselves as either Flemish or Walloon before they consider themselves Belgian. The formation of a national government involving agreement between the Walloons and Flemish has always been difficult as each side wants to increase its power in the national government. Talks to form a new government usually last many months and governments may last only a few months. In the 2010 elections, the Flemish separatists won the majority of seats. They had canvassed in favour of an independent Flanders and the end of the Belgian nation.

Many argue in favour of Wallonia becoming independent or part of France and for Flanders to become independent or part of the Netherlands. But it is not as simple as that. There are two major issues. If Flanders becomes an independent state what would happen to Brussels – a mainly French-speaking city within Flanders? Brussels is an economically important city that generates 20% of Belgian GNP. Also the population of Wallonia would not necessarily merge completely with France. There are many German speakers in the region. If Belgium does break up, Wallonia may break up as well, with part of it preferring to go to Germany, part of it to the Grand Duchy of Luxemburg (GDL) and part of it to France. Issues of the monarchy's future role as well as many political decisions would need to be discussed.

Many leading commentators believe that these cultural differences will see 'Belgium' as a nation die and that it will eventually become a **confederation** (an association of sovereign states) with four states: Flanders, Wallonia, Brussels and the East Cantons (the German-speaking region).

279

Religion

Religion can also make regions unique. Religion can shape group identity and act as a unifying force but equally it can be a source of social conflict and strongly divide people.

This world map (Fig. 17) showing distinct religions is very generalised as it is difficult to show minority groups on a large-scale map. However, as a broad guide to the location of religions, it is useful. Judaism, Christianity and Islam originated in the Middle East. Hinduism and Buddhism have their roots in the Indian sub-continent.

Political expansion, conquest, colonisation and missionary work were responsible for the distribution of religions worldwide, e.g. the teachings of Mohammed (Islam) stimulated the Arab world into a phase of religious and cultural expansion. Christianity was spread with the help of European political expansion in the Americas. Today, migration, population growth and conversion contribute to the expansion of religions.

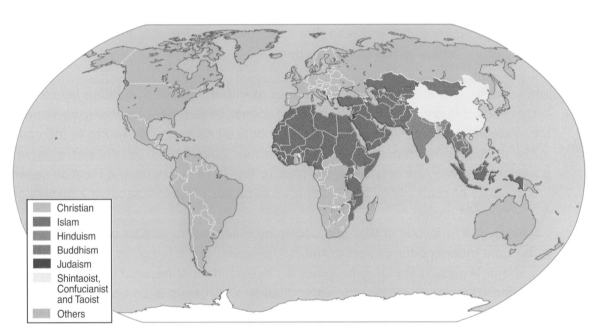

Fig. 17 Religions of the world

Cultural regions associated with religion

(a) Ireland – Protestantism in Northern Ireland

Northern Ireland can be seen as a separate region based on the distribution of the Protestant and Catholic religions.

- The concentration of Protestants in this region owes its existence to the **plantation** of the area during the sixteenth and seventeenth centuries. These settlers (planters) came from Scotland and England.

- Their Protestant religion was a unifying cultural force which separated them from the native Irish Catholic inhabitants. Over time, their religion became associated with their political struggle to remain part of the United Kingdom as expressed today in unionism and loyalism. Catholicism became associated with the struggle to re-unify Ireland as expressed today in republicanism and nationalism. Gradually, several counties in Northern Ireland developed majority Protestant populations.

- Today, areas with a strong Protestant tradition tend to be urbanised areas such as north Armagh, north Down, Antrim and north Derry. In most of these areas, up to three quarters of the population claim a Protestant identity.

- In Belfast and other large urban areas, there are distinct zones in which either Protestants or Catholics live. In Catholic areas, e.g. west Belfast, these zones are often marked by kerbstones painted green, white and orange as well as wall murals of the tricolour or scenes of Irish history, e.g. the Easter Lily, the 1916 Rising.

- In Protestant areas, e.g. east Belfast, the kerbstones may be painted red, white and blue and murals of the Queen or William of Orange are painted on the walls. In Belfast, the Peace Line – a physical division built across roads and between housing areas – separates these areas to minimise sectarian violence.

- Sport is another aspect of everyday life which can reveal an affiliation with either Catholicism or Protestantism in Northern Ireland. Catholics tend to support GAA, Glasgow Celtic F.C., Cliftonville and the Republic of Ireland soccer team, while Protestants tend to support Glasgow Rangers F.C., Linfield and the Northern Ireland soccer team.

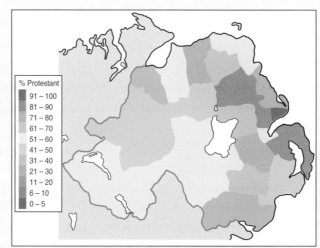

Fig. 18 Distribution of the Protestant religion

- Integration is slowly improving in schools, but it is still an issue in areas where children are sent to schools reflecting their religion. In certain areas, children are conscious of wearing football jerseys as it implies their religious affiliation, which could lead to hostility.

281

case study

(b) The Islamic world

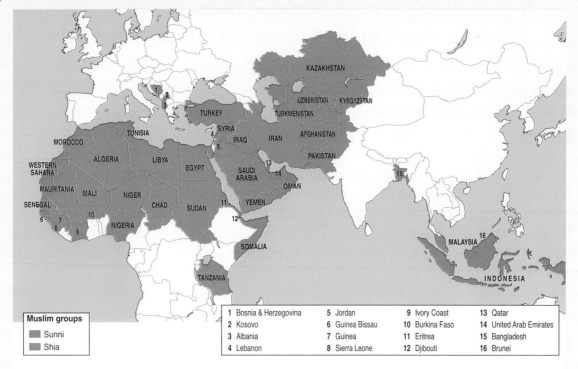

Muslim groups
- Sunni
- Shia

1	Bosnia & Herzegovina	5	Jordan	9	Ivory Coast	13	Qatar
2	Kosovo	6	Guinea Bissau	10	Burkina Faso	14	United Arab Emirates
3	Albania	7	Guinea	11	Eritrea	15	Bangladesh
4	Lebanon	8	Sierra Leone	12	Djibouti	16	Brunei

Fig. 19 The Islamic world is divided into Shia and Sunni religious regions.

- In 570 AD, the prophet Mohammed founded the religion known as Islam. Followers of Islam are called Muslims. Approximately 20% (more than one billion) of the world's population is Muslim.

- Within 100 years of the death of Mohammed, the Muslim Empire stretched across Central Asia, east to India and west to Spain, all as a result of a jihad or holy struggle. Muslim armies conquered vast areas of land. They drew up treaties with these conquered people which gave local religions the status of 'protected minorities'. However, many of the conquered people quickly converted to Islam.

- Muslim merchants and travellers introduced Islam into the Indian sub-continent, especially present-day Pakistan and Bangladesh. Islam spread further east into Malaysia, Indonesia and the Philippines. Local people were impressed by the advanced culture of the Muslim traders; intermarriage between locals and Muslims quickly became acceptable.

- During the Middle Ages, there were regular conflicts between Christians and Muslims. These Crusades were organised by Christian leaders to regain conquered territories but the only real success was in Spain which today is a Christian country.

- Followers of Islam are divided into two groups called Sunni Muslims and Shia Muslims. The origin of these groups dates back to just after Mohammed's death when the question of leadership and religious control led to a division between the followers of Mohammed.

- The majority of Muslims are Sunni Muslim. Shia Muslims are more common in Iran, Southern Iraq, Libya and Pakistan, although many countries have both groups. Such divisions seem likely to persist in the continuously evolving Muslim world.

- All Muslims follow the teachings written in the Qur'an (Koran). The Qur'an contains the basic beliefs (The Five Articles of Faith) of Islam and strict guidelines for Muslim daily life (The Five Pillars of Faith).

- All Muslims attach great importance to the idea of belonging to the family of Islam. Religion is central to everyday life in Muslim communities. A typical day involves worshipping in a mosque and praying five times a day whilst facing in the direction of Mecca. Mecca, a city in Saudi Arabia, is regarded by Muslims as the holiest city in the world.
  Muslim customs differ among countries and local traditions, e.g. in Saudi Arabia women are obliged to remain completely covered by wearing a burka, while in other countries, women must keep only their hair covered with a scarf when outside the family unit. Arranged marriages are also quite common in Muslim countries.

- Muslims are not allowed to drink alcohol or gamble. When entertaining, men and women tend to socialise in different parts of a building. Certain foods are forbidden to Muslims, e.g. pork.

Fig. 20 A mosque – a Muslim place of worship

14.5 The complexity of cultural regions – Boundary changes

Boundaries and the extent of regions may change over time. Many changes have been made to largescale political boundaries, e.g. the partition of India to create Pakistan, the creation of Israel in the Middle East or the division of Yugoslavia into separate states.

On a smaller scale, changes to political constituencies in Northern Ireland during the 1920s had an impact on the political power of Catholics. On a similar smaller scale, changes to Gaeltacht boundaries could affect funding in that region.

Changes to political boundaries, whether at national or at constituency level, can have an impact on the cultural groups living in the affected regions.

You will study three case studies – (a) the Gaeltacht, (b) gerrymandering in Northern Ireland and (c) border changes in Poland.

Boundary changes to language regions

(a) The Gaeltacht Regions of Ireland

As we have seen, the Gaeltacht as a distinctive cultural region was not officially established or mapped until 1926. As the exact boundaries of that region were never accurately defined and people move around, the boundaries have undergone some changes.

Fig. 21 Gaeltacht areas of Ireland in 1926

Fig. 22 Gaeltacht areas of Ireland in 2011

case study

- Since 1926 the numbers of people speaking Irish in the Gaeltacht region as their everyday language has dramatically changed. Figs. 21 and 22 (1926 and 2010) clearly show the dramatic changes in the Gaeltacht boundary. The changes to these boundaries reflect the impact of physical but more especially human, socio-economic and historic factors.

- Prior to the formal establishment of the Gaeltacht regions, the decline in the area and numbers speaking Irish throughout the island was due to the growing dominance of English in everyday social, educational and business life and mass emigration as already discussed (See page 275).

- The size of the 1926 Gaeltacht was considerably reduced in 1956 following economic emigration and a review of Gaeltacht boundaries. Other minor changes have since occurred:
  - The inclusion of Clochán-Bréanann in County Kerry in 1974.
  - The inclusion of a part of West Muskerry in County Cork.
  - The creation of a new Gaeltacht area (Baile Ghib and Rath Chairn) in County Meath in 1935.
  - The inclusion of Baile Ghib and Rath Chairn into the Gaeltacht regions in 1967.

- Today sections of the 1926 Breac Gaeltacht (25% to 79% fluent speakers) have completely disappeared. Fíor Gaeltact areas (over 80% fluent speakers) are also shrinking and survive only in former Breac Gaeltacht areas in isolated, small, mainly coastal communities.

The effect of changes to Gaeltacht boundaries

- Many areas that witnessed a decline in the language since 1926 ceased to be part of the Gaeltacht in the 1956 mapping. This reduced Gaeltacht regions to 7 areas in the state's 26 counties. A new Gaeltacht region was created at the Rath Cairn and Baile Ghib Gaeltacht in County Meath in 1935. An organised migration of 41 families from Connemara, County Galway to County Meath took place. In exchange for the properties they left behind, each family was provided with a house, 22 acres of land, basic livestock and farm implements. A national school was also built. A new Irish speaking area gradually developed. It was not recognised as an official Gaeltacht area until 1967. Today the area has profitable farmland, a thriving Irish language and an industrial estate.

- Any future reduction in the area of present Gaeltacht regions could have an economic impact on the people living there. They are currently in receipt of grants payable to Irish speakers. They may lose these grants if their homes are no longer located inside any redrawn Gaeltacht boundaries.

case study

(b) Gerrymandering in Northern Ireland

Gerrymandering means to unfairly change the boundaries of an electoral constituency in order to give one candidate, political party or group an advantage over others.

The term gerrymander was first used in America in 1812. The governor of Massachusetts, Elbridge Gerry, changed the boundaries of the electoral constituencies of his state in order to benefit his own political party, the Republican Party. It was noted that one of the districts was shaped like a salamander. One quick-witted person observed that it was more like a gerrymander, and a new political term was born!

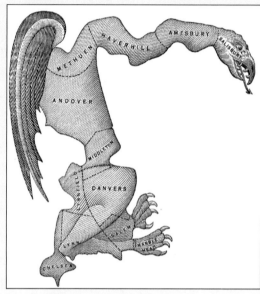

Fig. 23 The original Gerrymandering cartoon, which appeared in the *Boston Herald* shortly after Governor Gerry altered the constituency boundaries of Massachusetts.

In Northern Ireland during the 1920s, changes to political boundaries were introduced to ensure that elections would produce a unionist majority. If the political boundaries were not changed by gerrymandering, certain electoral areas would have produced a Catholic majority giving them political power – this was a result the unionists did not want. This system was used in particular in Derry city which had a majority Catholic population but returned a unionist majority in various elections.

The impact of this was to reduce the political power of the Catholic population in areas of the North. Gerrymandering led to the creation of a Protestant-controlled corporation governing a majority Catholic population. This system of 'vote rigging' is no longer in practice in Northern Ireland.

Today, gerrymandering is still an issue in the United States. Modern census techniques now use computers and sophisticated Geographical Information Systems to draw constituency districts. The results of these are still challenged by political parties who want to maximise their votes in particular areas.

Find out how gerrymandering can happen. Log onto:
http://geography.about.com/library/weekly/aa030199.htm

(c) Boundary changes in Poland

Poland is an excellent example of a country that has undergone many changes to its political boundaries. These changes have had a considerable impact on the ethnic composition of its population.

Before the Second World War

● Poland's borders have changed many times throughout its history. After the First World War, Poland was a much bigger country than it is today (see Fig. 24). Until the end of the 1930s, Poland had a variety of ethnic groups such as Catholic Poles, Jews, Armenians, Germans, Dutch, Ukrainians and Orthodox Christians.

   Its borders were east of its present location.

After the Second World War

● In 1939, Poland was invaded by Nazi Germany. The Nazis killed about 3.5 million Polish Jews and more than one million Polish Catholics. Devastated by war and with the population reduced from 35 million to 23 million, Poland became a Communist state under Russian influence.

   After the Second World War, new boundaries were designed for Central Europe by Stalin, Churchill and Roosevelt (the leaders of Russia, Britain and the United States) at the Yalta conference.

The result was:

1. Poland lost a third of its pre-Second World War land area, which was taken over by the Soviet Union.

2. The Allied Powers (i.e. Russia, Britain and the USA) gave Poland a large part of eastern Germany.

Pre-Second World War Poland
---- Modern borders

Fig. 24 Pre-Second World War Polish borders marked in white. Red shows modern borders of Poland and its neighbours.

Fig. 25 Poland 2011

The Second World War dramatically reduced Poland's former ethnic diversity. Massive migrations of Polish refugees occurred as they left Soviet- and German-owned lands. Many Germans left and moved west.

Hundreds of thousands of Ukrainians were forced to leave Poland to settle in the Soviet Union. Most of the Jews who survived the Holocaust emigrated to Israel or to the USA.

As a result of this mass migration, modern Poland has a very small population of ethnic minorities – roughly 5% in total. This figure is made up of Germans (who live mostly in south-west Poland), Belarussians (who live in eastern Poland) and Ukrainians.

Chapter Revision Questions

1. What is a region?

2. Name five different types of regions. Give an example of each.

Climatic Regions

3. Use the world map and table on page 264 to name and locate an example of (a) a hot climate (b) a temperate climate (c) a cold climate.

4. What do the following countries have in common? North Canada, Greenland, North Finland.

5. Name Ireland's climate and give a general description of it referring to rainfall and temperature in your answer.

6. Name and explain four influences on Ireland's climate.

7. Why is it wetter in the west of Ireland than in the east?

8. Name two air masses which meet close to Ireland.

9. What effect does the polar front have on Ireland's climate?

10. Look at the map of European climates and answer the questions that follow:
    (i) Identify the type of climate that occurs in north-west Europe.
    (ii) How does the North Atlantic Drift influence the climate of north-west Europe?
    (iii) Describe the rainfall and temperature of north-west Europe. Write three sentences on each.

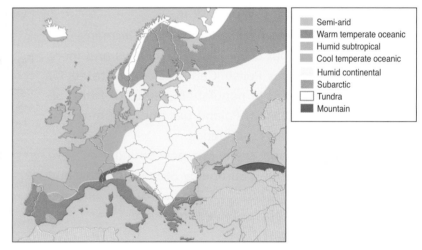

	Semi-arid
	Warm temperate oceanic
	Humid subtropical
	Cool temperate oceanic
	Humid continental
	Subarctic
	Tundra
	Mountain

11. Explain the term geomorphic region.

12. Match each of the region types in Column A with its description in Column B.

Column A	Column B
A Geomorphological regions	**1.** Local councils/corporations/constituency boundaries/county divisions etc
B Cultural regions	**2.** Less-developed regions/core regions/peripheral regions/regions of industrial decline
C Administrative regions	**3.** Regions based on distinctive landforms e.g. karst landscapes/ridge and valley landscape/plains etc
D Socio-economic regions	**4.** Regions that are associated with language and religion

Administrative regions

13. What are administrative regions?

14. How do local government and central government agencies differ in their administrative responsibilities?

15. Briefly describe the three levels of administration in Ireland.

16. Name two of the services provided by each level of administration in Ireland. How are the services funded?

17. Name and state the functions of the two Irish regional assemblies.

18. Draw an outline map of the counties in the BMW regional assembly area and in the SE regional assembly area.

19. Briefly describe each of the following in relation to the administrative regions in France: *commune*, *département*, *région*.

Cultural regions

20. The Gaeltacht is a cultural region in Ireland.
    (i) Draw a sketch map to show the location of Gaeltacht regions in Ireland.
    (ii) Describe two problems facing Gaeltacht regions.
    (iii) How does the Irish government support Gaeltacht regions?

21. Name two languages spoken in Belgium.

22. How has the economic importance of Flanders and Wallonia changed over time?

23. How has the Belgian government recognised the importance of the two cultures in Belgium?

24. State three everyday effects of the language divide on the people of Belgium.

25. What event in Irish history brought the Protestant religion to Northern Ireland?

26. Which areas of Northern Ireland are most closely associated with the Protestant religion?

27. What areas of the world are associated with Islam?

28. How was Islam spread across Asia?

29. Name the two major divisions within the Islamic faith.

30. Name three Muslim customs.

31. 'Cultural regions may be identified using one or more characteristics.' Explain this statement using an example from Ireland AND Europe.

32. 'Cultural regions may experience social tensions with national governments.' Discuss this statement, referring to a region you have studied.

OL Short Questions

33. Match each type of region with the correct example in the spaces provided.

LC Sample Paper

Type of region	
Economic peripheral	A
Economic core	B
Language	C
Administrative	D
Climate	E

Example	
Cool Temperate Oceanic	1
Gaeltacht	2
County	3
Ireland's BMW	4
Dublin	5

A	
B	
C	
D	
E	

questions

questions

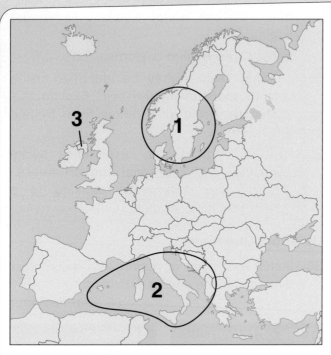

34. Examine this map of regions in Europe.

    (a) Name the regions numbered 1 to 3:
        1. _____
        2. _____
        3. _____
    (b) How many counties are contained in Region 3? _____

LC Sample Paper

OL Long Questions

35. Examine the development of **one** Irish or non-Irish cultural region you have studied.

HL Short Questions

36. From your study of regional geography, identify an example of any **four** of the following types of region:
- Climatic region
- Administrative region
- Cultural region
- Socio-economic region
- Nodal/city/urban region

LC Sample Paper

37. Identify an example of each of the following types of regions:
- An economic core region
- A resource-decline region
- A culture (language) region
- A climatic region

LC Sample Paper

HL Long Questions

38. 'A region is an area which may be identified by one or more characteristics.'
Briefly explain this statement, using a sketch map to illustrate an example or examples.

LC Sample Paper

39. Examine this map of Europe. In your answer book, associate **each** of these descriptions with the letters A,B,C,D:
- An administrative region
- A region defined by language
- An economic core region
- A geomorphological region

LC Sample Paper

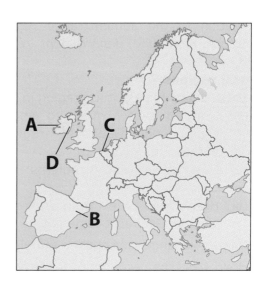

40. 'Culture is an important factor in defining some regions.' Examine the above statement with reference to any region you have studied.

LC Sample Paper

41. Examine two factors which have influenced the development of distinct cultural divisions in a European region which you have studied.

LC Sample Paper

Chapter 15

The Concept of a Region
– Socio-economic regions

At the end of this chapter you should be able to:

- Define the term **socio-economic region**.

- Discuss the characteristics of each type of socio-economic region and name an Irish and European example of each type.

- Discuss the cause and impact of industrial decline in an Irish and European region.

- Discuss the importance of EU funding to socio-economic regions.

Contents

15.1 Socio-economic regions

15.2 Regions of industrial decline –
      Case Studies: Drogheda, County Louth and the
                       Sambre-Meuse Valley, Belgium

15.3 EU funding for socio-economic regions
      Questions

KEY THEME

A region is an area of the earth's surface that is distinctive in some way. Regions can be identified by one or more human and/or natural characteristics, e.g. socio-economic regions. Regions can be of various sizes.

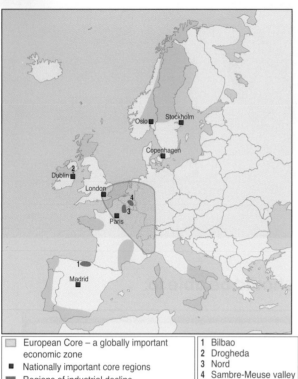

☐	European Core – a globally important economic zone	
■	Nationally important core regions	
■	Regions of industrial decline	
☐	Peripheral, less developed regions	

1	Bilbao
2	Drogheda
3	Nord
4	Sambre-Meuse valley

Fig. 1 Socio-economic regions in Europe

15.1 Socio-economic regions

Socio-economic regions are regions that have unique social and/or economic characteristics. They may be important urban industrial and service centres or they may lack industrial development and be centres of low population with few services. Some socio-economic regions are problem areas because they have high unemployment levels. This may be due to declining industrial development or the presence of conditions that do not attract modern industry.

Socio-economic regions such as the eastern coast of North America and South-East Asia have become globally important, influencing employment levels and industrial performances in countries thousands of kilometres away. This is part of the **globalisation** of world trade.

We will study three types of Irish and European socio-economic regions.

(i)   Core regions

(ii)   Peripheral / Less developed regions

(iii) Regions of industrial decline

Core regions:	Ireland – The Greater Dublin Area
	Europe – The Paris Basin
Peripheral/ Less developed regions:	Ireland – The Border Midland West Region (BMW)
	Europe – Mezzogiorno, Italy
Regions of industrial decline:	Ireland – Drogheda – Decline due to business competition
	Europe – Sambre–Meuse Valley (Belgium) – Decline due to depletion of resources

Factors affecting socio-economic regions

Physical Factors	Human Factors
Climate Relief Drainage Soils Resources	Population Transport Government EU policy History

(i) Core regions

Core regions are generally **accessible wealthy** areas. They have physical and urban factors that attract settlement and industry, i.e. they possess many natural resources such as coal or fertile land. They tend to have a climate that supports intensive agriculture and are often lowland areas easily accessible by road, rail, canal, river and sea. Core regions are also highly urbanised and are centres of business, services, government administration and decision making. They are usually centres of high population density.

Core regions are also often centres of further education,

research and development. They are favourite locations for industry because they have all the positive factors that attract industrial development, such as skilled workers, an educated population, efficient transport networks, large markets and access to services and power supplies. Migration into these regions is common, as incomes in core regions are usually higher than elsewhere.

Globally important core regions include: north-east America, south-east Asia and Japan. In Europe, a globally important core region stretches across several countries. The London–Milan axis stretches from northern Italy through central Germany, into northern France and the Netherlands and west across to the Greater London Area. South-west from this zone lies the national core zone of Spain around Barcelona. Within the European Union, incomes in core regions are 10% higher than the EU average.

Each country may have its own core region to which people are attracted. These are known as **national core** regions. The **Greater Dublin Area** is Ireland's national core region. In Chapters 17 and 19, we will study this region and the **Paris Basin** as examples of two core regions.

(ii) Peripheral/less developed regions

Peripheral/less developed regions can be regarded as poor socio-economic regions. They have physical and human factors that discourage settlement and economic activity.

They are often remote mountainous areas, with few resources and poor soils. They are usually inaccessible with a poor transport infrastructure and low population density. They suffer from out-migration. Peripheral regions have few services and are not favoured as industrial locations.

Peripheral areas are more dependent on primary activities than core regions. Farming, forestry and fishing are important sources of employment. Many industries in peripheral regions suffer from higher transport costs that reduce their ability to compete successfully in the marketplace, leading to closure.

Because of these disadvantages, governments offer incentives to businesses to locate in these areas.

1	Greater Dublin area	4	Stockholm	7	Paris
2	Manchester-London axis	5	Scania-Copenhagen	8	Catalonia
3	Oslo lowlands	6	Rotterdam-Ruhr-North Italian Plain axis	9	Madrid

Fig. 2 **Core regions of Europe**

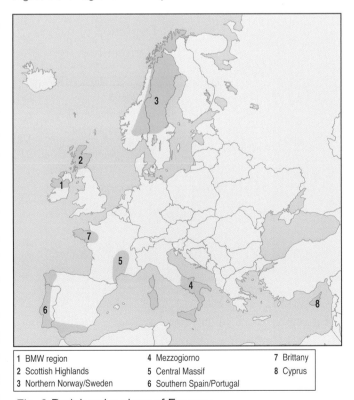

1	BMW region	4	Mezzogiorno	7	Brittany
2	Scottish Highlands	5	Central Massif	8	Cyprus
3	Northern Norway/Sweden	6	Southern Spain/Portugal		

Fig. 3 **Peripheral regions of Europe**

Those industries that choose to locate in a peripheral region tend to be branch plants of multinational companies, leaving the area vulnerable to closure and to decisions made in core areas.

Peripheral regions are usually coastal and/or mountainous areas with beautiful scenery. Because of this, tourism is very important in these regions and is often based on outdoor activities such as golf, fishing, walking and water sports.

Peripheral regions are areas of higher unemployment levels and lower incomes than core regions. Within the EU, incomes in peripheral regions are 10% lower than the EU average. They have few higher educational facilities and poorer health services.

Examples of peripheral regions in Europe are Andalucia (Spain), the **Mezzogiorno** (southern Italy) and northern Norway. In Ireland, the **BMW** region is considered to be a peripheral region. We will study the BMW (Ireland) in Chapter 16 and the Mezzogiorno region (Italy) in Chapter 18.

(iii) Regions of industrial decline

In several areas of the world, industrial regions which were once major economic centres have declined in importance and currently face many problems.

These areas are characterised by high unemployment, derelict buildings, urban decay and out-migration.

Causes of industrial decline

There are two main reasons for industrial decline in a region.
(a) Depletion of natural resources.
(b) Competition from other regions with cheaper business costs.

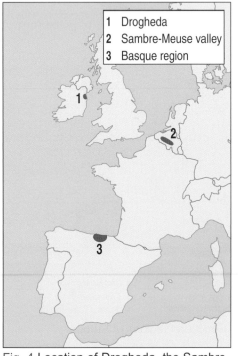

Fig. 4 Location of Drogheda, the Sambre-Meuse Valley and the Basque region

1 Drogheda
2 Sambre-Meuse valley
3 Basque region

(a) Depletion of resources

In Europe, the industrial region of the **Sambre-Meuse Valley** in Belgium and **Bilbao** in the Basque region of northern Spain both declined in importance because local coal and iron ore deposits were depleted. These centres were very important industrial areas up until the mid-twentieth century. When the resources were used up, industries closed and these regions became centres of high unemployment, social deprivation and derelict landscapes.

(b) Competition

Ireland never experienced an industrial revolution and therefore lacked the large-scale industrialisation found in Europe, although several Irish counties, towns and cities had important industrial functions, e.g. Drogheda and Cork city. In the 1970s, after Ireland joined the European Economic Community (now called the EU), Irish manufacturing companies in various cities closed because

of the availability of lower-priced products from European manufacturers. High unemployment rates and emigration occurred. The town of **Drogheda**, once a bigger port than Dublin, is an example of an urban region that declined in industrial strength. Today, it is becoming a dormitory town for Dublin and a retail centre.

15.2 Regions of industrial decline

(a) Drogheda, County Louth

International competition and economic recession caused a major decline in the industrial base in Drogheda in the mid 1970s.

The town has a long, proud, industrial history based on its port function close to the mouth of the River Boyne. Until the mid 1980s, Drogheda had a wide variety of industries.

Early industrial strength

- In the 1500s, most of Drogheda's trade was with Liverpool. Yarn and linen were major exports and Drogheda Port was more important than Dublin Port at that time. By the eighteenth century, it was the fourth largest town in Ireland after Dublin, Cork and Waterford. It exported grain and linen. In the early 1800s, the Drogheda Steam Packet Company was founded and the Drogheda railway viaduct was built.

Fig. 5 Location map of Drogheda

- Drogheda was famous for its textiles industry. Raw cotton from Dublin, Glasgow and Liverpool was brought to Drogheda where it was spun and bleached in the textiles factories. At its peak, there were up to 20,000 hand weavers in Drogheda and the surrounding area.

- Four linen mills existed in the town. Each employed over 700 people. By 1972, one of these mills – the Greenhills Mill – was famous worldwide for its sheets and towels which were exported to Japan, America, China and Europe.

- As well as textiles, Drogheda had a thriving ironworks and shipbuilding company, which built engines for the Brazilian railway and vats for the Guinness brewery in Dublin.

case study

Case study

- Other industries in the town included the Donaghy & Son Boot Factory (which made over 8,000 pairs of boots a week), the Drogheda Gas Company and the Drogheda Fertiliser Company.

- The Drogheda Oil and Cake Mills produced ingredients for biscuits, margarine and soap, accounting for almost 15% of the exports revenue from Drogheda Port.

- Before the decline in industry, over 50% of the population was employed in manufacturing.

The 1970s – a time of decline for Drogheda

- The 1970s were a time of economic depression throughout the world, largely due to the Middle East oil crisis. Ireland's economy faced many problems and all areas of the country were affected, including Drogheda. In addition, after Ireland joined the European Economic Community (EEC) in 1973, Drogheda's industries found it increasingly difficult to compete with similar products being manufactured within and outside the EEC.

- This competition contributed to the closure of these traditional industries by the 1980s. This decline was not confined to Drogheda. Across Europe, the traditional industries of iron, steel and textiles declined in many countries. Drogheda became an unemployment blackspot with unemployment rates as high as 30% in certain areas.

The Middle East Oil Crisis of the 1970s began when Arab leaders of oil-producing countries in the Middle East refused to export oil to Western countries. These leaders wanted to penalize Western countries for their involvement in Arab-Israeli conflicts. The fear that Western oil reserves would run out sparked panic – and massive increases in the price of petrol – in many Western countries, including Ireland.

Industry in Drogheda today

- Drogheda has not yet regained the reputation it once had as a manufacturing town. However, 31% of its workers are employed in manufacturing compared to 19% in the rest of Ireland.

- There are several modern industries. Drogheda Concentrates, one of the main employers in the town today, produces the concentrate for Coca Cola soft drinks. Becton Dickinson produces medical equipment and Premier Periclase makes magnesia for the ceramics industry. Several small-scale light engineering businesses operate around the town. These companies were attracted by the educated workforce, transport,

Fig. 6 Industrial decay in the old port area of Drogheda

access to a large market and EU membership. Many foreign firms outside the EU used Ireland's EU membership as an entry point to the large EU market.

Plans to overcome the challenge of industrial decline

Plans have been put in place to overcome industrial decline and promote Drogheda as a modern business and retail centre.

Fig. 7 Drogheda is now promoted as a business and retail centre.

1. **The Business Park**

   The Industrial Development Authority (IDA) has built a Business and Technology Park close to the M1 Motorway. An impressive business infrastructure, good supply of labour and easy access to Dublin and Belfast help to make Drogheda an ideal location for investment by multinational companies.

2. **The River Boyne**

   The Boyne is playing an important role in the redevelopment of Drogheda. The derelict buildings of the old oil and cake mills have been redeveloped and turned into a new shopping centre. New apartments have been built beside the Boyne and a new bridge has been placed over the river. Green areas beside the river have been cultivated and redeveloped for recreation (e.g. walking paths have been placed alongside the river).

3. **Retail centre**

   Drogheda became a retail centre with the opening of the M1 retail park in 2005. Two new shopping centres, a new hotel and conference centre also opened. These provide the services and employment needed in this rapidly growing satellite town.

Modern advantages favouring Drogheda as an industrial location

Road Links: Drogheda is located on the M1 motorway linking Dublin and Belfast.

Rail: Drogheda is on the Dublin/Belfast rail line. Freight services including container and refrigerated transport and heavy haulage facilities are available in the area.

Air: Dublin Airport is 30 minutes from Drogheda by motorway. The airport provides connections to all major European and North American centres.

Fig. 8 Drogheda's redevelopment

297

case study

Fig. 9 A retail centre in Drogheda

Seaports: Drogheda has its own port which has been expanded and modernised and is now able to handle containerised shipping.

Labour force – Young, educated and skilled

- The population of Drogheda has experienced a rapid growth in recent years to reach 29,000 people. Many people have moved to Drogheda to take advantage of its easy access to the facilities of Dublin city while benefiting from much lower housing costs.

- Drogheda is within commuting distance of Dublin; consequently, there is a growing pool of highly skilled workers based in the town and travelling to work in Dublin and Dundalk. Many of these would prefer employment opportunities in the town.

ACTIVITY

Look at the OS map below.

1 Name and explain two possible impacts of the motorway route on people and business in the Drogheda region. Refer to the map in your answer.

2 Suggest a suitable location for the development of a new retail park. Explain three reasons for your decision.

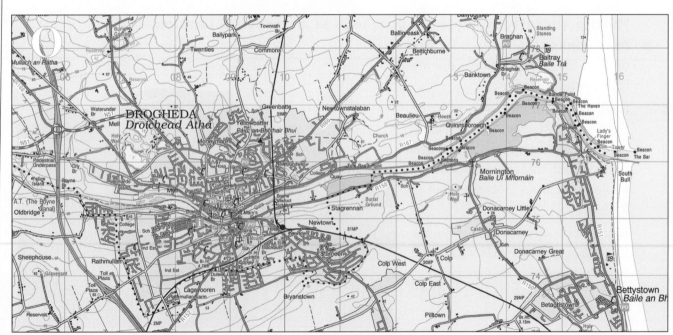

Fig. 10 Map extract of Drogheda

(b) The Sambre-Meuse Valley, Belgium

Early industrial strength

During an industrial revolution in Belgium in the late 1880s, 150 kilometres of the Sambre-Meuse river valley in Wallonia, southern Belgium was the industrial core region of the country. The Sambre-Meuse valley was an industrial region based on coal mining and the traditional heavy industries of iron and steel, engineering and chemicals. The size and success of the industrialisation was due to large deposits of coal, iron ore, lead and zinc that were exposed by the river as it cut its valley into the land.

The main coalfields were Borinage, Charleroi and Liège. This region had traditionally been known as the Black Country due to the presence of so many coal tips and smoke stacks. Its industrial wealth allowed Wallonia to dominate the economy of Belgium from the beginning of the 1800s to the mid 1960s. At its peak, over 120 mines employing more than 120,000 people produced roughly 30 million tonnes of coal each year.

The 1960s: time of decline for the Sambre-Meuse region

Over time the coal seams were exhausted and coal production declined steadily from an output of over 30 million tonnes in 1955 to just over 2 million tonnes in 1988. Any remaining seams were deep, faulted and badly fractured creating higher extraction and production costs. Added to this was competition from cheaper imports of coal from America and Poland. By the mid 1960s the European Coal and Steel Community (ECSC), of which Belgium was a founding member, stated that only efficient coalfields in member states should remain open. This led to the collapse of coal mining in the Sambre-Meuse region. By the end of the 1960s the region had become a problem region of industrial decline. Over 50,000 jobs were lost between 1960 and 1973. The last mine closed in 1992.

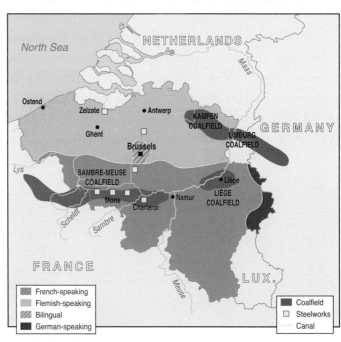

Fig. 11 Coalfields in Belgium

case study

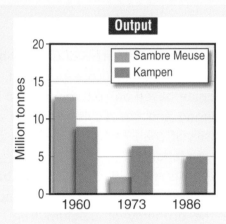

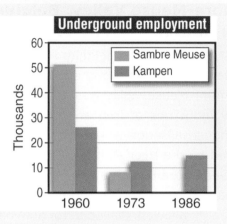

Fig. 12 The bar chart shows the decrease in employment and production in the Sambre-Meuse mines. Kampen is a coalfield north of the Sambre-Meuse Valley.

Problems of industrial decline

The traditional industries of engineering and chemicals that depended on coal as a raw material also declined. They could not compete with the modern petro-chemical industries and integrated steelworks located near the coast at Zelzate in Flanders. These new factories were offered cheap greenfield sites, lower labour costs, room to expand and non-unionised labour. They were linked by canal to the North Sea ports of Antwerp and Terneuzen through which American and Polish coal and iron ore from Sweden and West Africa were imported.

From the 1960s Wallonia rapidly experienced high unemployment (over 20%) and had a significantly lower GDP per capita than Flanders. The outdated factories, poor infrastructure, derelict buildings and unsightly spoil heaps were not an attractive environment for new investment. It quickly became a depressing place in which to live with few recreational facilities. Unemployment forced the migration of many Wallonian workers from the region, seeking work in the capital city of Brussels and in the newly-emerging modern industries in Flanders. Liège survived the worst effects of the decline in coal mining as it produced more specialised goods, e.g. weapons and crystal glass, and so **industrial inertia** prevented their closure. It also had a variety of industries not related to coal.

Fig. 13 Derelict landscape in Charleroi. This old coal mine has since been converted into a mining museum.

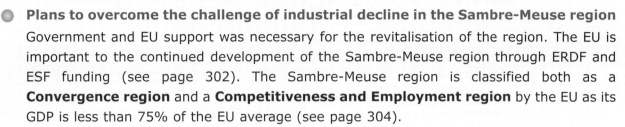

Plans to overcome the challenge of industrial decline in the Sambre-Meuse region

Government and EU support was necessary for the revitalisation of the region. The EU is important to the continued development of the Sambre-Meuse region through ERDF and ESF funding (see page 302). The Sambre-Meuse region is classified both as a **Convergence region** and a **Competitiveness and Employment region** by the EU as its GDP is less than 75% of the EU average (see page 304).

The European Structural funds programme for 2007 – 2013 has allocated a budget of €15 billion for improving growth, investment and employment in these regions. The Belgian government is spending its share of this funding to encourage investment in the region by:

- Offering low-interest loans, grants and tax incentives to private and foreign industry to encourage investment in the region.

- Setting up worker retraining schemes, improving transport links to the region and cleaning up the derelict environment.

- Building new intergrated steelworks at Liège and Charleroi using coal from the Kampen coalfield in Flanders and iron ore imported through Antwerp, Europe's second largest port.

- Providing improved river, canal and motorway links between Liège, Charleroi, Rotterdam, Ostend, Brussels and Cologne. The upgrading of Charleroi airport improved international access to the region, encouraging more industrial development.

- Undertaking environmental improvement schemes to clean up the scarred, run-down coalmining landscape of Charleroi.

- Encouraging new industries, e.g. newer modern industries manufacturing chemicals are locating their plants in the Sambre-Meuse region. These chemical industries produce ammonia, fertilisers and a variety of plastics, paints, soaps, cosmetics, detergents and pesticides.

Revitalisation of the Sambre-Meuse region continues today in an attempt to reclaim some of the former wealth and industrial status it had in the past.

15.3 EU funding for socio-economic regions

The European Union (EU) is a very important human factor influencing the development of all member states. All socio-economic regions receive funding from local and central government. However, as well as domestic government support, funding from the EU is made available to all 27 member states. Various **Structural** and **Cohesion** funds are allocated by the EU as part of its regional policy to tackle the economic and social imbalances between states and within states. These funds are used for development of infrastructure, telecommunications, education and human resources and to support research and development.

Structural and Cohesion funds account for over one third of the EU budget. The overall budget for 2007 – 2013 is €347 billion.

EU Structural and Cohesion Funds

All EU regions are eligible for funding under the various **Structural funds** and poorer regions receive extra funding and support through **Cohesion funds.**

Structural funds

Four EU Structural funds help reduce regional imbalance in all 27 states.

1. The European Regional Development Fund (ERDF). This fund is used to promote economic and social equality within the EU by reducing the imbalances between regions or social groups. It funds the modernisation of industry and also invests in infrastructure and environmental protection in all EU regions.

2. The European Social Fund (ESF). This funds job creation schemes and improves access to the labour market. It also funds schemes to help disadvantaged people enter the workforce. The New Era awards for students to access further education is funded by the ESF.

3. The European Agricultural Guidance and Guarantee Fund (EAGGF - Guidance Section). This fund helps the agricultural sector in all regions. Money is distributed to all EU farming regions through the Common Agricultural Policy (CAP). CAP is a major source of income for EU farmers. (See page 304).

4. The European Fisheries Fund (EFF). This money is used to support the fisheries industry in the EU. Money is distributed to fishing communities through the Common Fisheries Policy (CFP). It is used to conserve fish stocks and develop the fisheries infrastructure (see page 304).

Cohesion funds

This fund is spent on the least-developed member states who have a Gross National Income (GNI) of less than 90% of the EU average. It covers all 12 new member states as well as Greece and Portugal. The Cohesion fund contributes to environmental issues and trans-European transport networks.

> All EU member states receive Structural funds. Only the poorer EU regions receive Cohesion funds as well.

Allocation of Structural funds for 2007-2013

Prior to EU enlargement to 27 states, structural funding was allocated to Objective 1, 2 and 3, Interreg, Urban and Leader regions. Since enlargement these regions have been reclassified as **Convergence, Regional Competitiveness and Employment** and **European Territorial Cooperation regions.**

The Structural and Cohesion funds contribute to these three types of regions, aiming to reduce the economic and social inequalities between the states/regions.

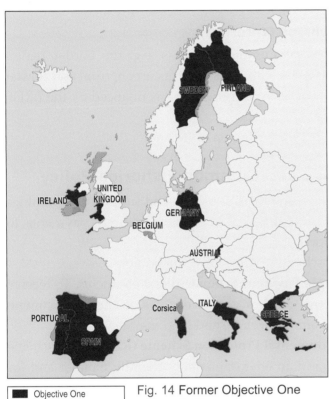

■ Objective One	
■ Phasing out (until 2005)	
■ Phasing out (until 2006)	

Fig. 14 Former Objective One regions in Europe

■ Convergence regions	
■ Phasing-out regions	
■ Phasing-in regions	
■ Competitiveness and employment regions	

Fig. 15 The EU's new system of support for under-performing regions

Convergence regions

Convergence regions include all 12 new EU member states and parts of existing poorer peripheral member states, most of which are farming regions, e g. Cornwall, Wales, north Portugal and southern Spain. Funding also helps existing states to phase out of this category, e.g. Scotland, northern Greece.

It is financed by the Structural and the Cohesion Funds. The budget allocated to this objective is €283.3 billion, representing 81.5 % of the total Structural funds available.

Funding to convergence regions aims to speed up their economic development allowing the region to grow, e.g. roads and educational centres. It applies to the less-developed EU member states and regions where GDP per capita is **below 75%** of the EU average.

Competitiveness and Employment Regions

The **Regional Competitiveness and Employment region** covers all regions of the EU territory, except those in the Convergence region. Its funding improves the job opportunities and economic attractiveness of these regions, e.g. South and East Ireland, France and Germany. It also includes 'phasing in' regions which had convergence status, but which have become wealthier due to financial support, e.g. the BMW and parts of northern Spain. This 'phasing in' policy will continue until 2013. The funding, €55 billion, comes from the Structural funds.

European Territorial Cooperation Regions (Interreg)

This aims to improve co-operation across all European borders, e.g. the border region between Northern and Southern Ireland. It deals with issues such as urban, rural and coastal development or improved transport links between countries. This is financed by the ERDF with a budget of €8.7 billion.

This funding is especially important to the Border region of Ireland.

The Common Agricultural Policy and Common Fisheries Policy

The **Common Agricultural Policy (CAP)** is a system of subsidies and support programmes for agriculture funded by the EU Structural funds. CAP combines direct payments to farmers together with price/market supports.

Farmers can apply for several payment schemes. Three are outlined here.

The majority of farmers receive the **Single Payment Scheme** (direct payment). To receive a payment under this scheme farmers must follow a variety of rules on the environment, public health, animal health, plant health, animal welfare and land maintenance.

Some farmers apply for the **Rural Environmental Protection Scheme (REPS)**. This scheme is designed to reward farmers for farming in an environmentally friendly manner and for making environmental improvements to existing farms. CAP reform 2009 – 2013 will make farmers spend 10% of their EU subsidies on projects to improve the countryside. Farmers in lands that are classified as **Less Favoured Areas** can apply for a further CAP payment. These farmers face disadvantages preventing them from fully using their land, e.g. harsh climatic conditions, mountains or where preservation is required for environmental or tourism purposes.

Fig. 16 Farmers can apply for an additional CAP payment if their land is classified as being in a Less Favoured Area. Examples of a less favoured area include farms where there is mountainous terrain.

The CAP helps reduce Europe's reliance on imported food but has led to over-production and the creation of 'mountains' and 'lakes' of surplus food and drink. Due to these problems the CAP is currently being reformed. Milk and other farm production quotas are being phased out. The arable 'set-aside' policy will also be removed. Up until recently farmers were leaving some land fallow to prevent surpluses accumulating but that land will now be put back into production. Conservationists say set-aside has been very beneficial for wildlife.

The **Common Fisheries Policy** is the EU's system for the management of fisheries and aquaculture. It is funded by Structural funds. The CFP sets rules governing the size of fleets, the size of fish catches and how and where fishermen can operate. It also ensures fishermen get a fair price for their catch. The CFP is also responsible for research into fish stocks, regulating conservation of fish stocks, development of ports and fish processing plants as well as safety. Preventing illegal fishing is also an important part of fishery protection.

Fig. 17 The Common Fisheries Policy sets rules governing the management of fisheries and aquaculture in all EU member states.

Under the CFP, EU fishermen have equal access to member states' waters. Access to Ireland's 10 km coastal zone is confined to Irish-registered fishing vessels and vessels from Northern Ireland. In the 10 – 20 km coastal zone access is limited to some Irish and some EU vessels. From 20 – 320 km access depends on quota entitlements. Every December the EU Council negotiates arrangements for managing fish stocks. These negotiations set the **total allowable catches (TACs)** and quotas for each fish species caught by each fishing state.

Special arrangements apply to the **Irish Box** – a large area (100,000 km²) off the south and west coast of Ireland. The time spent in this area is capped for all fishing vessels to protect important young fish.

Fig. 18 Each year fish stocks are analysed to help the EU Council decide the total allowable catches and quotas for each fishing species.

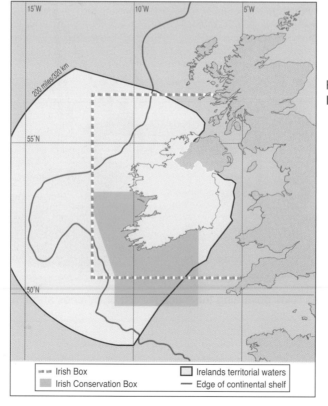

Fig. 19 The Irish Conservation Box and Ireland's territorial waters

Chapter Revision Questions

Socio-economic regions

1. Name the three types of socio-economic regions.
2. What is a core region?
3. Explain three characteristics of core regions.
4. Name one Irish and three European core regions.
5. What is a peripheral / less developed region?
6. Explain three characteristics of peripheral / less developed regions.
7. Name three European and one Irish peripheral region.
8. Explain the terms Structural Fund and Cohesion Fund and describe their uses.
9. What are Convergence regions?
10. Name and explain the funds available to help Convergence regions in the EU.
11. Explain how the CAP and the CFP affect Ireland.
12. Explain the following term: region of industrial decline.
13. Explain two characteristics of regions of industrial decline.
14. Name two European and one Irish region of industrial decline.

Drogheda, Sambre-Meuse and industrial decline

15. What industries were associated with Drogheda in the past?
16. What led to the modern decline of industrial activity in Drogheda?
17. What advantages does Drogheda offer to attract industrial development today?

OL Short Questions

18. Look at this map that shows the household disposable income per head in Ireland in 2002.

    (a) Identify the county with the highest disposable income.

    _____

    (b) Name the **three** counties with the lowest disposable income.

    (i) _____

    (ii) _____

    (iii) _____

    (c) Name **one** reason why these counties have such a low disposable income.

    _____

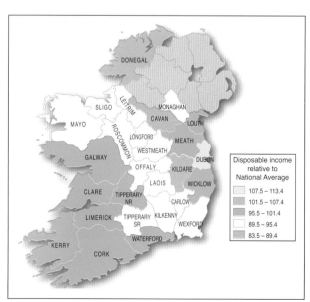

LC Exam Paper

OL Long Questions

19. 'Some regions have experienced economic decline.' Discuss the causes of economic decline with reference to an example you have studied.

HL Short Questions

20. Look at this map of Europe. Match the number on the map with a letter given for different types of regions in the list below.

Letter	Description	No.	Example
A	A core economic region		
B	A peripheral region		
C	A cultural region		
D	A climatic region		

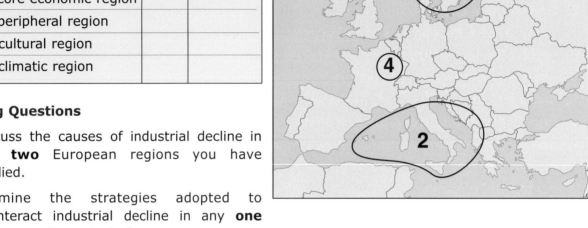

HL Long Questions

21. Discuss the causes of industrial decline in any **two** European regions you have studied.

22. Examine the strategies adopted to counteract industrial decline in any **one** region you have studied.

23. Name and describe **one** economic challenge facing a European region you have studied.

Chapter 16
The Dynamics of Regions (1)
– An Irish Peripheral Region

At the end of this chapter you should be able to:

- Describe the Border Midlands West (BMW) as a peripheral/less developed socio-economic region.
- Name and describe the physical and human characteristics of the BMW region.
- Describe primary, secondary and tertiary activities in the BMW region.
- Describe the population characteristics of the BMW region.
- Outline some government plans to reduce regional inequality in Ireland.
- Explain the impact of economic recession on regional planning in Ireland.

Contents

16.1   The BMW region – physical and human factors/characteristics, economic
                 activities and human processes
16.2   Regional inequalities in Ireland
16.3   The impact of economic recession on Ireland's economy and on regional planning
        Questions

KEY THEME

The study of regions shows how economic, human and physical processes interact in a particular way. This can be demonstrated by examining contrasting Irish regions.

Fig. 1 The BMW and GDA regions

Introduction

We have already examined the concept of a region in Chapters 14 and 15, using examples in Ireland and Europe.

Ireland has many different regions. Almost every county has some distinctive characteristic that sets it apart from others. The Drumlins of Monaghan, the high mountains of Kerry, the sunny south-east of Wexford and the Gaeltacht areas of Donegal – these are just some of the regions in Ireland.

In this chapter we will look at the Border Midlands West (BMW) – a peripheral/less developed socio-economic region.

16.1 The BMW region – physical and human characteristics, economic activities and human processes

A peripheral/less developed region in Ireland

The BMW region is made up of 13 counties. It has just over one quarter (1.13 million) of Ireland's population and occupies almost 48% of the land area of the state.

The three areas of the BMW region have several factors in common.

1. They are rural areas with low population densities (25–30 people per km^2).
2. There is a high dependence on primary activities.
3. Short and long-term unemployment are above the national average.
4. The transport infrastructure is underdeveloped.
5. There are low employment levels in services.
6. A high proportion of people are classified as rural poor.
7. Industrial development is based on multinational company branch plants.
8. There are high levels of out-migration.

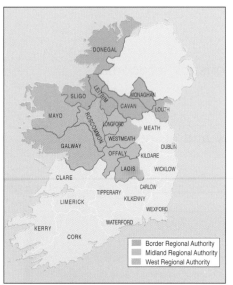

Fig. 2 The BMW region

The BMW region is not as urbanised as the GDA. Only 32% of its population live in settlements of more than 1,500 people compared to the national average of 58%.

Galway city is the main urban centre in the region: other larger towns have experienced population growth due to rural to urban migration, e.g. Castlebar and Sligo.

The BMW has good economic potential. It has an unspoilt environment, very little congestion and many areas of outstanding natural beauty, particularly its mountains and coastline. The labour force in the BMW region represents almost 25% of the national labour force. However, unemployment rates remain high, particularly along the western seaboard. We will now examine the physical and human factors that influence the development of the BMW region.

Physical characteristics/factors influencing the development of the BMW region

1. Climate

Like the rest of Ireland, the BMW has a cool, temperate, oceanic climate.

Across the region, the influence of the sea and relief can be seen in rainfall and temperatures. The higher relief creates cooler wetter conditions than in the GDA, especially in the western part of the BMW region where average annual rainfall in some mountainous areas can at times exceed 2,500 mm.

Average July temperatures are 14°C (Belmullet) and average January temperatures are 5.7°C (Belmullet). Away from the warming influence of the sea, there is more frost inland. Clones in County Monaghan experiences twice as many days with ground frost (99 days) as Belmullet in County Mayo. Average annual rainfall varies from 928 mm in Clones to 1,150 mm in Belmullet. This variation is due to the influence of relief and the rain shadow effect.

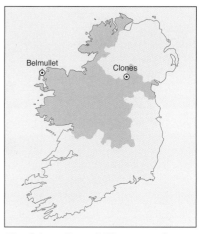

Fig. 3 Location of Clones and Belmullet weather stations in the BMW region

2. Relief and drainage

The region has a varied relief of mountains, lakes and lowlands.

Mountainous ground is located in Donegal (A: Derryveagh Mountains, B: Bluestack Mountains), Mayo (C: Nephin Beg Range) and Galway (D: Croagh Patrick, E: Mweelrea) where the landscape is dominated by metamorphic rocks.

These mountains were formed during the Caledonian mountain building period 400 million years ago.

Lowlands are found around Lough Mask in County Galway, the edges of Lough Swilly in County Donegal and south of Connemara. Much of the lowlands are unsuitable for agriculture because they are poorly drained boglands or have thin soils, particularly in parts of Laois, Offaly and Westmeath.

The coastline is made of headlands and sheltered bays (indented), due to erosion by powerful Atlantic Ocean waves. Clew Bay is a major feature created as a result of rising sea levels after the last Ice Age which flooded the Drumlin landscape, creating its well-known islands. Killala Bay in County Mayo is a ria.

Fig. 4 BMW – Rivers, mountains and lakes

Killary Harbour on the border of Galway and Mayo is an important sheltered fiord.

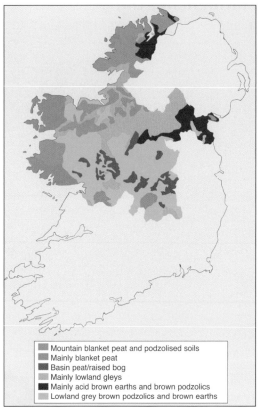

Mountain blanket peat and podzolised soils
Mainly blanket peat
Basin peat/raised bog
Mainly lowland gleys
Mainly acid brown earths and brown podzolics
Lowland grey brown podzolics and brown earths

Fig. 5 Soils of the BMW region

3. Soils

Soils in the BMW region are varied and generally of poor quality, compared to the GDA. From Fig. 5 we can see that BMW regions have more peat and gley soils while the Midlands has areas of raised bog as well as fertile brown earth soils.

Heavy rainfall has led to leaching of soils and the creation of podzol soils which have a hard pan and are poorly drained.

As a result of glacial deposition, the Border region has boulder clay soils and a Drumlin landscape with several large lakes (e.g. Lough Erne). In Connemara, glacial erosion has removed the soil cover, leaving a landscape of lakes and shallow peat soil. In East Galway, the limestone parent rock has led to the formation of shallow soils.

The drainage basin of the River Shannon around Clonmacnoise has fertile alluvial soils but is often flooded and as a result has a unique **callow** landscape of flooded meadows.

Fluvio-glacial deposition has left several **eskers** running across the landscape which provide well-drained dry areas (the **Esker Riada**).

Human characteristics/factors influencing the development of the BMW Region

Physical factors also interact with several human factors affecting the BMW region. These factors combine to influence the primary, secondary and tertiary activities that occur in the BMW region. Three main human factors that affect the BMW region are: **population, transport infrastructure** and **government/EU policies**.

1. Population characteristics of the BMW region

The area has a lower than average population density (32 people per km^2 compared to 60 per km^2 nationally). Leitrim has the lowest population density in Ireland with just 18 people per km^2. The low population density is due to the mountainous relief, poor soils and the impact of out-migration of young people from the region.

This low population density prevents economic development across the region because employers prefer to locate where they can find a large labour force. The western region has the largest urban centre (Galway) and the greatest concentration of high-tech industry attracted by the good quality road and air links and by the graduates of UCG and GMIT. The western region was projected to experience a 21.7% growth in population by 2031 due to the availability of jobs in the biotech industry. However economic recession may reduce this estimate. Services are concentrated in the urban centres, e.g. Castlebar, Dundalk

Fig. 6 The poor soils and mountainous relief of the BMW has contributed to a low population density.

and Galway. This will encourage uneven economic growth in the BMW region. Overall the population of the BMW region is projected to grow by 7.8% (over 75,000) by 2031 although it is not known how much impact economic recession will have on this estimate. The population could decrease due to out-migration of newly unemployed people.

2. Transport infrastructure

Transport infrastructure in the BMW region is underdeveloped. This influences the location of industry in the region and the allocation of government and EU funds for transport development. The NDP had focused on providing better road and rail links to the region and motorway links are now complete between Galway and Dublin as well as Dublin and Belfast. Road access to Sligo has also been upgraded. These improvements will aid economic development in the BMW region by reducing transport costs and improving access.

Fig. 7 Rail links to the BMW region have been improved but transport infrastructure is still underdeveloped.

3. Government/EU policy

Through various departments the Irish government allocates Irish and EU funds to help the economic and social development of the BMW region (see Chapter 15.) CAP, CFP and government funds are especially important to the BMW region where much of the employment is based directly or indirectly on the primary sector. Some of the most important departments and their funding are outlined below.

Fig. 8 Connemara in County Galway is classified as a Less Favoured Area.

(a) The **Department of Agriculture, Fisheries and Food** is responsible for the promotion and development of agriculture, food, forestry and rural development. It allocates CAP, CFP and a range of government payments to farmers and fishermen in the BMW region. The CAP Single Payment Scheme subsidises crop, land and headage payments to farmers. Three out of four farms in the BMW now qualify for this scheme. Around €26 million is targeted to those sheep, goat, dairy and beef farmers in the BMW who are in areas classed as less favoured e.g. the Mullet Peninsula, County Mayo.

This department is also involved in forestry management offering training, afforestation grants and woodland/forest environment protection schemes. This is important to the BMW region as many counties have poor soils (e.g. Leitrim) and farmers add to their incomes by converting their land to forest.

Fishing is funded by BIM (Bord Iascaigh Mhara) through the CFP, which is responsible for developing the Irish Sea Fishing and Aquaculture industries. It is especially important for funding and supporting infrastructure development at Killybegs port in County Donegal.

Fig. 9 The Department of Agriculture, Fisheries and Food allocates CAP and CFP payments to fishermen and farmers in the BMW region.

(b) The **Department of Communications, Energy and Natural Resources** has responsibility for the energy sector in Ireland. This department regulates, protects and develops Irish natural resources and aims to maximise the benefits to the State from exploration for and production of Irish oil and gas resources. This is especially important to the exploitation of the Corrib gas field in Mayo and for wind farms in the BMW region.

(c) The **Industrial Development Authority (IDA)** is responsible for the attraction and development of foreign investment in Ireland. This is necessary in attracting foreign investment away from Ireland's core southern and eastern regions to the less attractive peripheral BMW. Grants and tax incentives are offered to attract investment. Galway is the main centre of foreign investment in the BMW region. FÁS is also an important organisation in providing training and support for Irish workers.

(d) Údarás Na Gaeltachta funds the economic and social development of the Gaeltacht regions in the BMW, e.g. Donegal.

Primary activities in the BMW region

Agriculture

The wet climate, varied relief and poor soils are an obstacle to the development of agriculture in the region. As a result, much of the land in the region is classified by the EU as disadvantaged for farming.

Farm incomes are substantially lower in this region than in the GDA. In order to make a living, 50% of farmers in the midlands-west region have an 'off-farm' job. This is due, in general, to poorer land, smaller farm size and older farmers. In Donegal, for example, 46% of farmers are over 55 years of age. Farms in the BMW region are smaller and more **fragmented** (scattered about the countryside) than the national average (37.1 ha) thereby increasing production costs. The smallest farms are found in Counties Mayo and Monaghan, where 21.8 hectares is the average size of a farm.

Farm production is based on pastoral farming, especially sheep, in the upland areas and cattle rearing on lime-rich soils found on lower ground. The boulder clay of the Border region is also used for pasture and cattle. Poultry and mushroom production are also found in Border counties (e.g. Monaghan) as they are not hugely dependent on ground quality. Because of the wet climate and steep relief, few cereals can be grown.

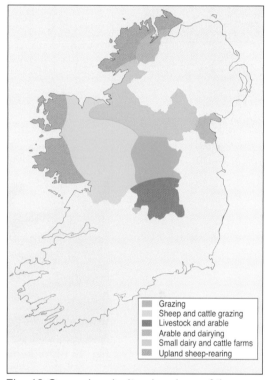

Grazing
Sheep and cattle grazing
Livestock and arable
Arable and dairying
Small dairy and cattle farms
Upland sheep-rearing

Fig. 10 General agricultural regions of the BMW region

Fig. 11 Pastoral farming in the upland areas of the BMW.

Fig. 12 Few cereals are grown in the west of Ireland due to the thin infertile soils.

The climate, relief and soils of the BMW region have combined to limit the region's production to pastoral mixed farming (sheep/cattle rearing) and forestry, unlike the GDA where a greater variety of tillage farming is possible.

Forestry

Many BMW farmers are part-time, supplementing their farm income with another job – often forestry – to make a living. By turning to forestry, farmers make more profitable use of their land. In Donegal, almost 14% of farmers had some forestry. Twelve per cent of the county is forested.

Galway, Mayo, Donegal and Leitrim have most forest cover due to the high percentage of marginal land (mountainous with poor soils). These regions are suitable for forestry because the mild, wet, Irish climate encourages rapid growth of coniferous trees such as Sitka Spruce and Scots Pine.

Fig. 13 BMW farmers often supplement their income by taking another job in forestry.

Fishing and aquaculture

The soils, relief and climate of the BMW region have combined to make agriculture difficult. As a result, people have turned to fishing. The west coast of the BMW region has a number of natural advantages for the fishing industry:

1. It is close to the rich fishing grounds of the North Atlantic.
2. It is influenced by the North Atlantic Drift ocean current which brings warm water and a variety of fish.
3. The sea is shallow and rich in plankton due to the wide, gently sloping continental shelf.
4. The indented coast provides natural, sheltered, pollution-free harbours.

Therefore, the fishing and aquaculture (fish farming) sector is a key source of income in the BMW region. The region has many small coastal and island communities where there are few other employment opportunities. This is due to geographic and economic factors, such as distance from centres of economic activity, low population density and poor agricultural land. These remote communities are unlikely to benefit

from the spin-off effects of manufacturing growth found in the larger urban centres of the region.

Within the BMW, Donegal is the most dependent on fishing. Killybegs in Donegal is the chief fishing port in Ireland. The value and tonnage of fish landed in Killybegs is greater than any other fishing port in the country. Fishing and related activities are estimated to be worth around €50 million to the local economy each year.

Donegal has the highest number of employees in the seafood processing sector (1,403). Killybegs is the centre of the Irish pelagic (open-ocean) fleet. These are large factory ships with refrigerated seawater tanks to hold the catch of herring and mackerel. They may fish up to 320 km off the coast. Over 60% (over 1,000 people) of employment in the Irish pelagic fishing sector is located in Donegal.

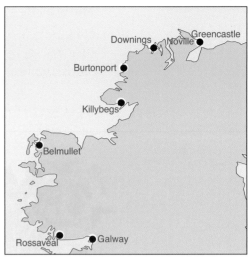

Fig. 14 Fishing ports in the BMW region

Aquaculture (salmon and shellfish) is an increasingly important economic activity in regions such as Mayo, with Clew Bay and Killary Harbour emerging as major producers who employ several hundred people. Sea trout are farmed in Clew Bay and at Inver Bay in Donegal. Killary Harbour is a major mussel cultivator.

The importance of fishing to the BMW region is clear from the fact that roughly 60% of funding from Bord Iascaigh Mhara for training in aquaculture, processing and catching is being spent in this region.

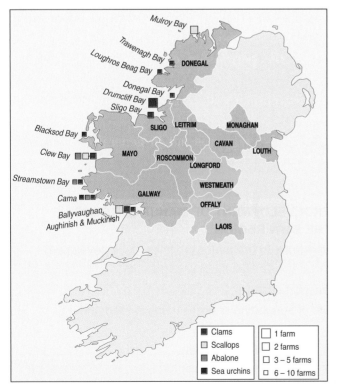

Fig. 15 Shellfish cultivation in the BMW region

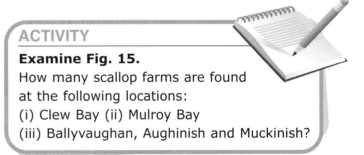

ACTIVITY

Examine Fig. 15.
How many scallop farms are found at the following locations:
(i) Clew Bay (ii) Mulroy Bay
(iii) Ballyvaughan, Aughinish and Muckinish?

317

Mineral Resources

Offshore resources, such as **gas**, are located in the Corrib gas field, 70 km west of Belmullet. The gas is located 3,000 m below the seabed under 355 m of water. When developed, the gas field will produce gas for about 20 years. It is approximately 70%

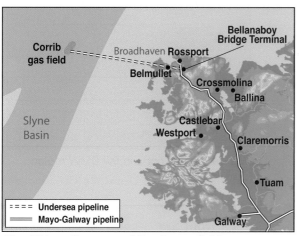

Fig. 16 Location map of Corrib gas field

the size of the Kinsale gas field. Bord Gáis is planning to build and operate a 150 km pipeline from Mayo to Galway, which will deliver gas from the Corrib gas field into the national network. There has been much controversy over planning permission, positioning and safety of the onshore processing plant and over-ground pipeline in parts of Mayo. In 2010 permission was granted for the final part of the pipeline to be constructed.

Peat is located in the raised boglands of the midlands. Before Kinsale Natural Gas came on stream in 1979, turf was Ireland's most important energy resource. The ESB's generating capacity for peat is 250 mw. Peat is supplied by Bord na Móna to the peat-fired power stations run by the ESB in Lanesborough and Shannonbridge.

Secondary activities in the BMW region

Reliance on a few industries such as food processing, timber processing and textiles is typical of the region. The BMW lacks variety (**diversity**) in its manufacturing base. The region has experienced uneven rates of industrial development. This means that the percentage of the labour force employed in unskilled occupations is higher in the BMW than the national average and the percentage employed in professional occupations is lower.

Industry (including building/construction) accounts for 40% of output in the region, similar to the national average.

Like many peripheral locations, the BMW region is not in general a favourable location for manufacturing.

> The high dependence on primary activities in the BMW region shows how the difficult physical landscape has controlled the type of economic activity carried out by people in the region.

REASONS FOR THE UNDERDEVELOPMENT OF MANUFACTURING IN THE BMW REGION

1. Poorly developed transport infrastructure (no motorway links / less developed).
2. Low population density.
3. Peripheral location (raising transport costs).
4. Lack of power supplies capable of supporting energy intensive (demanding) industry.
5. Small urban population (small labour pool and market).

The main centres of industry are Galway, Castlebar, Letterkenny, Sligo and Dundalk.

Galway is the only urban centre with a variety of modern **knowledge-based** industry, such as electronics, e.g. Hewlett Packard, Ingersoll Rand and Boston Scientific. This is due to the location of University College Galway which provides a skilled graduate labour force, a direct transport network to the east coast by air, rail, road or sea, a large urban market and the presence of serviced industrial estates for investors.

The Irish government recognises the importance of attracting industry to the BMW region and therefore offers grant assistance and tax incentives through the IDA to new industries. For example, the Gaeltacht region in County Donegal attracts the maximum level of grant assistance, averaging up to €14,000 per job.

Fig. 17 Manufacturing centres in the BMW region

The Medical Technology Industry in the BMW region

Ireland holds a cluster of medical technology (MedTech) industries. These companies manufacture specialist medical equipment used in hospitals across the world. Nine of the top ten global companies have a manufacturing base in Ireland, e.g. Becton Dickinson and Medtronic. Ireland employs the highest per capita number of medical technology personnel in Europe.

Many medical technology manufacturing and support companies have located in the BMW region of Ireland. Several human factors encourage medical technology industries to locate in this region:

- The labour force is young and educated. The BMW area has a population of over one million. Forty per cent of the population is under twenty-five years of age. Half of the school leavers in the region go on to third-level education. This provides an educated and skilled workforce for employers.
- The National Standards Authority of Ireland (NSAI) is globally recognised. Once the NSAI approves a product for sale a company can automatically receive EU-wide approval. This helps non-EU medical technology companies to rapidly gain access to the entire European market.
- The BMW area contains centres of excellence in bioengineering, laser applications, tool making and information technology. These service and supply companies provide the expertise needed to support the medical technology industry.
- Ireland offers a low 12.5% corporation tax on all trading activities. This low rate combined with a range of other tax advantages, such as research and development tax credits and patent royalty tax exemptions, means that locating in Ireland offers a financial advantage to medical technology companies.

case study

Merit Medical, Galway

- Merit Medical Systems, Inc. (MMSI) produces disposable medical devices used in hospitals worldwide. It employs 1,700 people with facilities in Galway, Utah, Texas, Virginia and the Netherlands.

- The products made include guide wires which are used to place medical devices into blood arteries and catheter devices to deliver fluids into veins and drain wounds as well as various syringe equipment. Merit is the market leader in these products. It supplies 40%-50% of the world market. In 2010 its sales increased by 16%.

- The Irish branch – Merit Medical Ireland Limited – was set up in Galway in 1994 and currently employs 250 people at this facility.

- The main inputs for the Galway factory are platinum, steel and plastic. Platinum is imported from South African mines through the UK by air and road. Plastics are imported from Salt Lake City, USA, by ship to Dublin and Galway. Steel is imported by ship and road from the UK. Products are manufactured in Galway and sent by container truck to Dublin, then by ship, air and road to the main markets in the EU, Eastern Europe and China.

- The manufacturing plant was located in Galway for several reasons:
  - Ireland has a skilled, educated workforce. NUI Galway provides skilled graduates.
  - Ireland's location provides access to EU and Asian Markets for the US company.
  - A suitable site was available.

- While some foreign-owned Irish companies have relocated to low-cost eastern European locations, Merit Medical Ireland has stayed and expanded its Irish operations because:
  - The total 'delivered cost' of Merit's Irish-made products is still lower than elsewhere.
  - The industry is highly regulated and therefore setting up another factory in a new location is costly and time consuming.
  - The response time between receiving orders and delivering the product is quicker in Ireland than elsewhere.
  - Ireland, and the BMW region in particular, have a supply of highly skilled and trained personnel. These would be hard to find and costly to train in a new location.

- In July 2010 Merit Medical invested €6.7 million in expanding its operation in Galway, creating 100 new jobs. As well as these 100 new positions in the plant, the extension project generated indirect jobs in construction and supply services which are important for the local economy in Galway.

Tertiary activities in the BMW

Communications/Transport

Transport and communications in the BMW region are affected by physical and human factors such as the mountainous relief and low population density. This means that the routes are often steep, winding and narrow due to having to travel over mountainous land and around lakes and bays. The low population density means that transport infrastructure is best developed along routes connecting the major urban centres/gateway towns of Galway, Sligo, Letterkenny, Dundalk, Mullingar, Athlone and Tullamore.

Many roads in remote areas of Mayo and Donegal are of poor quality and not suitable for heavy trucks. This prevents economic development in these areas. Rail links are absent north of Sligo and direct routes between some urban centres in the BMW region are not well developed. For example, if you want to travel by rail from Sligo to Dundalk, you must first travel to Dublin. These factors hinder economic development in the region by making commuting difficult and transportation of goods expensive and time consuming.

Public transport is underdeveloped with just 4% of the population using it to get to work compared to 11% nationally. Therefore there is a greater reliance on car ownership in the BMW region than elsewhere. The international airports are at Galway and Knock. Smaller airports are located at Sligo and Donegal.

An efficient transport infrastructure is essential to the continued economic development of the BMW region. The NDP has improved some transport facilities through the **Transport 21** programme. This ambitious scheme aims to develop an **Atlantic Corridor** of motorway and high quality dual carriageway linking gateway towns of Waterford to Letterkenny via Cork, Limerick, Galway and Sligo. However, while some motorways and dual carriageways have been started, economic recession has caused a delay in completing this project. At present none of the towns listed above are fully connected by these planned improved roads.

The peripheral location of the BMW region has led to the creation of many jobs based on teleservices. With high-speed internet access business can occur without the need for roads. Teleservice businesses such as recruitment agencies, call centres, ticket sales and tour operators depend on fast broadband services. There are several call centres in operation in the BMW region, e.g. the FBD customer support centre in Mullingar. Some companies provide technical support for call centres such as FCS in Galway.

Fig. 18 Part of the Atlantic Corridor in County Sligo

Tourism

Tourism in Ireland is an important tertiary industry. It generates over 200,000 jobs and close to €4.6 billion annually in revenue.

In the BMW region tourism is an economic activity dependent on physical processes. Tourism in the BMW region relies on the landscape as the scenic coasts, mountains, rivers and lakes attract both domestic and international tourists. Despite the scenic landscape, tourism in the BMW region in general has not grown as much as that in the GDA for a number of human and physical reasons.

1. Dublin Airport is the main entry point to Ireland. The majority of tourists stay in the GDA region rather than heading to the peripheral BMW area.
2. Ireland is now regarded as an expensive location to visit and this combined with economic recession has reduced tourist numbers,
3. Transatlantic aircraft are no longer required to stop at Shannon, a crucial hub for west coast tourism. This has reduced the number of tourists travelling on to the BMW region.
4. Transport and car hire are expensive in Ireland which discourages people travelling to the BMW region.
5. Rail infrastructure in the BMW region is underdeveloped. This prevents people travelling easily to the region from their arrival point in Dublin Airport and ferry ports.

Generally tourism in the BMW region is dependent on its scenic landscape and cultural activities, e.g. the beautiful coastal region of Sligo and Ben Bulben attract those interested in outdoor activities while concert events such as Electric Picnic in County Laois draw tens of thousands to the area.

Focus on tourism in north-west Ireland

Over 1.4 million tourists visited the north-west tourist region in 2009 generating €319 million for the economy. The majority of visitors came from Britain. The number of international tourists to the region has fallen dramatically due to the economic recession. In 2009 there were 403,000 international tourists visiting the north-west. But numbers of domestic tourists on staycations has increased since the economic recession rising from 736,000 in 2007 to 754,000 in 2009, generating €115 million.

Donegal and Sligo were the most popular destinations with 303,000 overseas visitors holidaying there contributing €85 million (as an **invisible export**) to the economy.

Tourism is very seasonal (May to August) in the north-west similar to the rest of Ireland except the Dublin region. The north-west has a wide variety of natural and manmade attractions for tourists. Like much of the BMW region, the north-west markets itself as a destination for tourists interested in outdoor activities and heritage. Events in Donegal include the 'Mary from Dungloe' festival and the Donegal International Rally.

The north-west is a region with varied scenic attractions ranging from the 600-

metre drop sea cliffs at Slieve League to the blue flag beaches of Bundoran and Rosses Point and picturesque towns and villages such as Sligo and the Glenties. Hotels in the region offer relaxing breaks with golf courses, health centres, spa clubs and leisure centres. Caravan, camping and self catering holidays are very popular in the area. Glenveagh National Park is a major attraction. The islands of Tory and Gola and many rivers and lakes (e.g. Gartan Lough) offer fishing and water sports holidays. Ben Bulben and Derryveagh mountains are used for outdoor pursuits, horse riding and hill walking.

Donegal's Gaeltacht region is attractive to tourists due to its history, culture and heritage. Donegal promotes its Irish culture with many traditional music and dance festivals held throughout the county each summer. Many tourists stay with friends and relatives (33%) while 6% stay in guesthouses, 30% do self catering and 12% stay in hotels.

To counteract its peripheral location, Donegal's tourist industry actively promotes the fact that access to the county is improving. It does this by offering fly/drive package holidays through Sligo and Donegal airports. In 2010, Fáilte Ireland established **Fáilte North West**, a new tourism development forum for the north west. It has a three-year plan aiming to identify and implement new measures to boost tourist numbers, especially overseas visitors. Measures include an investment of nearly €1 million for the development of key attractions such as Slieve League, along with another €1 million for walking and cycling routes in the county.

In addition, over €150,000 has been invested in the Historic Towns Initiative for Donegal Town and Ballyshannon and NDP funding is being used to develop the modern Discover Ireland Centre in Donegal Town.

Fig. 19 Glenveagh National Park, County Donegal

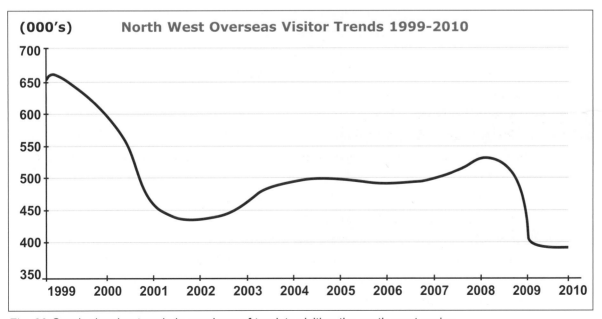

Fig. 20 Graph showing trends in numbers of tourists visiting the north-west region

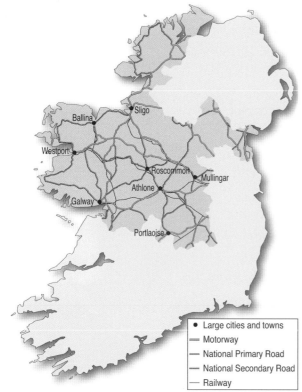

Fig. 21 Communications in the BMW region

Education

The percentage of the labour force that has completed second- or third-level education is 44% in the region compared with approximately 52% in the GDA.

The region provides 28% of national university students; however, only 13% of graduates from the BMW region are employed within the region. This **brain drain** is due to the lack of suitable job opportunities for an educated labour force.

Public services

Some public services have moved to the BMW region as part of the government decentralisation programme, e.g. the Department of Social Welfare offices in Letterkenny, County Donegal and the Department of Education offices in Athlone, County Westmeath.

Advantages the BMW region offers for economic development

Despite its problems, the BMW has many advantages for economic development:

1. Well trained and educated workforce.
2. High quality environment.
3. Lack of congestion.
4. Scope for development of industries based on local resources (e.g. forestry).

Fig. 22 Sligo town, County Sligo

People below the age of 15 and over 65 are classed as **dependents**.

Human processes in the BMW region

Within the BMW region, parts of the larger urban areas of Galway, Drogheda and Dundalk show symptoms of extreme disadvantage in terms of the level of unemployment and the provision of health and other social services.

Remote rural areas such as Connemara and the Donegal Gaeltacht areas, Inishowen, Leitrim, West Mayo and parts of Roscommon and Cavan show signs of **rural deprivation** such as low educational and skill levels, unprofitable farm holdings, unemployment and high dependency rates. These areas have traditionally been a region of out-migration, leaving older and younger **dependents** at home.

The BMW region has a lower population density than the GDA. Galway is the exception, showing an increase in population which reflects its position as an educational and manufacturing centre for the region. This highlights the relationship between economic and human processes.

The BMW is projected to gain 36,000 in net migration from the South and East region between 2002 and 2021. Much of this net migration will be to Galway.

16.2 Regional inequalities in Ireland

Several development plans have been introduced by the government in order to reduce the imbalance in wealth and economic growth between the BMW region and the South and East region in Ireland. These plans are financed by the government and/or EU funds. We will examine four of these plans.

1. National Development Plan (NDP)

The main aim of the NDP is to create **balanced regional development** throughout Ireland in a way that is economically, socially and environmentally sustainable. The budget for each plan changes. From 2000 to 2006 the budget was €57 billion. The 2007 to 2013 plan had a budget of €183.7 billion. However economic recession meant this budget became unaffordable. In July 2010 the NDP was revised. This revised plan runs from 2010 to 2016 and has a budget of just €39 billion (see table on page 331).

To encourage balanced regional development, the current NDP intends:

(a) To continue sustainable economic growth, maintain employment levels in Ireland and strengthen and improve Ireland's competitiveness amongst other countries.

(b) To provide a world-class economic and social infrastructure in transport, housing, health, education and environmental services.

(c) To promote the social inclusion of all people in the country, creating an ethnically and culturally integrated society and to provide services for the vulnerable members of Irish society.

(d) To support science and enterprise.

(e) To invest in education, skills and training.

Ninety per cent of the NDP's funding is provided by the Central Exchequer, i.e. through taxes.

The NDP identified five cities as engines of regional and national growth.

These are Dublin, Cork, Limerick, Galway and Waterford.

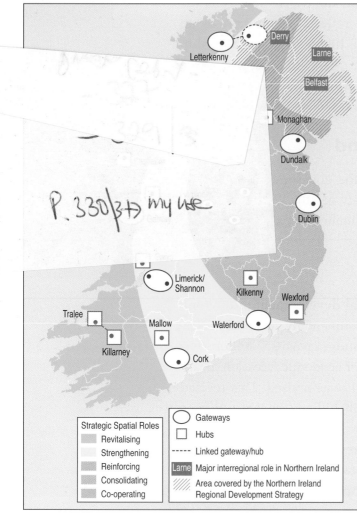

Fig. 23 Cities and towns identified as gateways and hubs

Strategic Spatial Roles
- Revitalising
- Strengthening
- Reinforcing
- Consolidating
- Co-operating

- ○ Gateways
- □ Hubs
- ----- Linked gateway/hub
- Larne Major interregional role in Northern Ireland
- Area covered by the Northern Ireland Regional Development Strategy

2. National Spatial Strategy (NSS) (2002–2020)

The NSS was developed to help implement the aims of the NDP.

The NSS is a 20-year strategy designed to enable each place in Ireland to reach its social, economic and physical potential, regardless of size or location. The NSS has identified certain cities and towns in Ireland as **gateways** and **hubs**. These gateways and hubs are being developed to prevent Dublin becoming the primary focus of the Irish economy. In turn, this will allow people living in other regions the opportunity to work and live in their local area. Rural areas around the gateway and hub centres will also develop.

The aim is that by spreading work opportunities throughout the country to identified gateway cities and hub towns, Dublin's growth can be controlled and people living outside the GDA can avail of the same services as those living within it.

The NSS provides guidelines on where industrial, rural and residential development takes place. It is also involved in deciding policies in relation to tourism, services and heritage issues.

Fig. 24 Cork city has been identified as a gateway city by the NSS.

CHARACTERISTICS OF GATEWAY AND HUB SETTLEMENTS

	Gateways	Hubs
1	A large urban population (of the order of 100,000 and above) set in a large urban and rural hinterland.	A significant urban population in the range of 20,000–40,000 set in an associated rural hinterland.
2	Wide range of primary/secondary education facilities and national or regional third-level centres of learning.	Primary and secondary education facilities with the option of third-level or outreach facilities.
3	Large clusters of national/international scale enterprises.	A mix of local, medium-sized and larger businesses serving local, regional and national/international markets.
4	A local point in transportation and communications terms: (a) on the national roads and rail networks, (b) within one hour of an airport either with international access or linking to one with such access, (c) adequate, reliable, cost-effective and efficient access to port facilities, (d) effective, competitive broadband access.	An important local centre in transportation and communication terms: (a) on the national road and rail or bus networks, (b) access to a national or regional airport, (c) adequate, reliable, cost-effective, efficient access to port facilities, (d) effective and competitive broadband access.
5	Integrated public transport with facilities for pedestrians and cyclists.	Effective local transport system with facilities for pedestrians and cyclists.
6	Regional hospital/specialised care.	Local and/or regional hospital.
7	City level range of theatres, arts and sports centres and public spaces/parks. Cultural and entertainment quarters.	Wide range of amenity, sporting and cultural facilities including public spaces and parks.
8	City-scale water and waste management services.	Effective water services and waste management arrangements.
9	Integrated land-use and transport planning frameworks.	Strategies for physical, social and economic development.
10	Phased zoning and servicing of land-banks in anticipation of needs associated with growth.	Phased zoning and servicing of land-banks in anticipation of needs associated with growth.
11	Strategic Development Zones.	Industrial and local business parks.

3. Transport 21 (2005 – 2015)

Transport 21 is the name given to the planned development of the **transport system** in Ireland, over the period 2005 – 2015. This investment covers improvements in national roads, public transport and regional airports.

Transport 21 aims to:

1. Increase accessibility to and from all regions.
2. Ensure the sustainability of transport services.
3. Expand the capacity of the current transport infrastructure.
4. Increase people's use of public transport.
5. Improve the quality of the transport infrastructure.

This will involve:

1. Upgrading the M50 motorway around Dublin.
2. Construction of a metro system in the Greater Dublin Area.
3. Building the Atlantic Corridor route from Donegal to Waterford.
4. Upgrading current rail routes (e.g. the Western rail corridor).
5. Reopening other rail routes (e.g. the Midleton rail commuter route).

Before economic recession led to the revision of Transport 21, the total estimated cost was €34.4 billion meaning that €9.4 million was to be invested in transport each day over its lifetime.

While some projects have been completed, others have been postponed due to economic recession, e.g. the Western Rail Corridor. The revised programme for 2010 to 2016 will now invest just €11.4 billion in transport infrastructure.

4. Decentralisation

This scheme was launched in 2003 to promote greater regional balance.

It was originally planned that a total of eight government departments and the Office of Public Works would move their headquarters from Dublin to other regions in the country. Only seven departments were expected to keep their headquarters in Dublin.

More than 10,000 civil servants and public service jobs were projected to relocate to 58 locations throughout Ireland, many of these to the BMW region. However, such is the attraction of the Dublin city region that few civil servants volunteered to move. In 2010 the decentralisation programme was severely reduced. Only 27 of the 92 planned moves had occurred, involving just over 3,000 civil servants.

The majority of decentralisation projects have been postponed.

Fig. 25 Upgrading of the M50 motorway is part of the Transport 21 investment programme.

The four plans described on pages 325 - 328 provide extra support to the BMW region in order to promote its social and economic development. Their impacts are summarised in the table below.

HOW THE NDP AIMS TO DEVELOP THE BMW

1. Development based on the BMW's natural resources and its tourism industry.
2. Improved access to the region as a result of the Transport 21 project.
3. Efforts to attract industries based on technology, where travel is 'electronic' and not physical, as a result of investment in electricity and broadband infrastructure.
4. Emphasis on improving services in order to keep people living and working in the region as a result of investment in health and education services.
5. Improved electricity supplies to attract more industry as a result of investment in the national electricity grid.
6. Investment in gateways, hubs, towns and rural areas.

HOW THE NSS AIMS TO DEVELOP THE BMW

1. Targeted investment in gateways and hubs in order to increase their appeal as places to locate industry and places to live.
2. Emphasis on locating industries in these gateways and hubs and other areas within the BMW in order to create jobs.
3. Monitored zoning of land to ensure there is a good balance of industrial, commerical, residential and recreational land.
4. Development of an efficient and coordinated transport system.
5. Improved cultural, sporting and recreational facilities within gateways and hubs.

HOW TRANSPORT 21 AIMS TO DEVELOP THE BMW

1. Improved rail and road network in the region (as mentioned in NDP aims).
2. Construction of the Atlantic Corridor linking Letterkenny, Sligo, Galway, Cork and Waterford. Roads along this route will be improved and new roads will be built (revised 2010).
3. Significant investment in city and nationwide bus services.
4. Improved Western rail corridor linking Galway to Limerick, including onward connections to Claremorris and the Dublin–Westport line (postponed 2010).

HOW DECENTRALISATION WILL HELP THE BMW

Many jobs were provided in small towns within the BMW region as a result of the relocation of some government departments to the region. For example, the relocation of 60 civil servants in the Road Safety Authority to Ballina in County Mayo has had an impact on other services and businesses in the town.

16.3 The impact of economic recession on Ireland's economy and on regional planning

Economic recession in Ireland began in late 2007. Recession has had wide-ranging impacts on people and the economy. Regional plans that looked affordable in 2007 can no longer be funded. The government had to modify its NDP and other schemes in response to the recession. Some economic and social impacts of economic recession on Ireland are outlined below.

- **On the construction industry:** In 2006 over 93,000 homes were built; by 2007 construction output peaked at just over €38 billion. This represented an astonishing 24% of total economic output for that year. However, some 140,000 jobs have been lost in the building industry since 2007. By 2010 the Irish Construction Industry Federation said less than 10,000 homes were built, putting Ireland at the bottom of the European construction chart.

- **On the national debt:** In 2005 the national debt was €38.5 billion; it had risen to €84 billion by 2010. This high level of debt led to an IMF/EU loan to support government finances.

- **On employment:** The unemployment rate was 4.2% in June 2005. Due to recession the unemployment rate rose to 13.7% in July 2010 (450,000). Men accounted for over 80% of the increase due to job losses in the male-dominated construction sector. The Department of Finance estimate that unemployment will reduce to a rate of 12.6% in 2011 and 11.8% in 2012.

- **On migration:** The recession forced people to leave the country to find work or to return to their native country after losing their job in Ireland. It also reduced the number of people moving to Ireland for work. The numbers of people leaving Ireland increased dramatically. In 2009 the number of emigrants from the State increased by over 40% from 45,300 to 65,100 (of this 18,400 were Irish nationals), while the number of immigrants declined from 83,800 to 57,300. These combined changes resulted in a return to net outward migration for Ireland for the first time since 1995. By 2010 Ireland recorded the highest net outflow of population in the EU at 9 per 1,000 inhabitants.

- **On Dublin Airport:** Passenger traffic at Dublin Airport fell by nearly 1.5 million in 2010 to 19 million as the economic recession continued. This represented a 20% decline on the 23.5 million passengers recorded in 2008. Passenger numbers at the three airports (Dublin, Shannon, Cork) declined by 13% to 26.1 million. However Terminal 2 was completed on schedule.

- **On Dublin Port:** As Dublin Port handles almost half of Ireland's imports and exports, trade levels at the port are a key barometer of what is happening in the economy. Dublin Port Company reduced its costs to its customers to such an extent that in 2010 costs were 10% lower than in 1988. Port trade decreased between 2007 - 2009 but returned to growth in 2010.

- **On regional planning:** The NDP 2007-2013 provided €75 billion for various infrastructure projects across the country. It became unaffordable due to the

economic crisis. Many schemes were stopped, postponed or reduced in size because the government could no longer afford to pay for them. A new plan, 'Infrastructure Investment Priorities 2010- 2016', was launched in 2010. It will spend just €39 billion on vital infrastructure across the country. The main cutbacks were in housing, roads, healthcare and education. The government's decentralisation programme was also severely reduced. Many Transport 21 projects were cut back. For example the completion of the Western Rail corridor linking Galway to Limerick has been postponed.

Despite the economic downturn the government continues to promote inward investment to Ireland. The IDA is promoting Ireland in the areas of technology, research and development. Currently 8 of the world's top 10 technology firms are based in Ireland. The expansion in 2010 of the European headquarters of food giant Kellogg's and Google proves to the global investor community that Ireland can outperform competitors in attracting and retaining multinational companies.

IMPACT OF ECONOMIC RECESSION ON NDP SPENDING

Sector	NDP expenditure planned for 2007 to 2013 (billion euro)	Revised NDP expenditure 2010 to 2016 (billion euro)	% change
Transport	32.9	11.74	-64%
Enterprise	3.22	3.79	14%
Agriculture	8.28	1.63	-79%
Housing	21.2	4.4	-79%
Education	25.7	4.2	-83%

Fig. 26 The IDA promotes Ireland in the areas of technology, research and development. Letterkenny is a gateway town.

Chapter Revision Questions

BMW

1. Using your atlas, draw an outline map of Ireland and mark the following: All the counties which make up the BMW; Rivers Foyle, Moy, Shannon, Erne and Corrib; the Twelve Bens, Derryveagh, and Nephin Beg Mountains; Donegal Bay, Clew Bay and Galway Bay; Letterkenny, Dundalk, Athlone and Galway City.

2. List the counties in the BMW region.

3. Name and explain **four** characteristics that make the BMW a peripheral region.

4. Name **two** mountains and **two** rivers in the BMW region.

5. Pick **two** areas within the BMW region and describe their soils and agriculture.

6. Discuss other primary economic activities, besides farming, which provide employment in the BMW region.

7. What natural and man-made factors contribute to the success of fishing in the BMW?

8. Name **three** industrial areas in the BMW region and describe the main reasons for the general underdevelopment of manufacturing in the region.

9. Describe the importance of the tertiary sector as a source of employment in the BMW region.

10. (i) What is the National Development Plan (NDP)?
    (ii) How does the NDP aim to help the BMW region?

11. (i) What is the National Spatial Strategy (NSS)?
    (ii) How does the NSS aim to help the BMW region?

12. (i) What is Transport 21?
    (ii) How does it aim to help the BMW region?

13. What steps are being taken by the BMW to attract industry to the region?

14. Name **two** gateways and **two** hubs in the BMW region.

15. Name and briefly explain **one** other plan financed by the government and/or the EU aimed at reducing imbalance between regions in Ireland.

16. Examine **one** challenge facing the BMW region in the future. Discuss one way in which this challenge might be reduced.

17. Outline the impact of economic recession on Ireland referring to a region you have studied.

OL Short Questions

18. The figures below show the tourist regions of Ireland visited by domestic tourists in 2004.

2004 – Regions Visited – Domestic Holidays	
	%
Dublin	13.9
Midlands-East	12.5
South-East	15.9
South-West	20.4
Shannon	11.3
West	17.9
North-West	8.1

A. IRELAND – DOMESTIC HOLIDAYS
    Use graph paper to draw a graph that shows the data in the table above.
    LC Exam Paper

HL Long Questions

19. **IRISH REGIONS**
    Draw an outline map of Ireland. Show and name the following on it:
    (i)   Any **one** Irish region that you have studied.
    (ii) Any **two** physical features in the region.
    (iii) **One** urban centre in the region.
    LC Exam Paper

20. Examine the development of primary activities in any **one** Irish region you have studied.

21. Examine the development of secondary activities in any **one** Irish region you have studied.

22. Examine the development of tertiary activities in any **one** Irish region you have studied.

Chapter 17

The Dynamics of Regions (2)
–An Irish core region and an Irish city/nodal/urban region

At the end of this chapter you should be able to:

- **Describe the Greater Dublin Area (GDA) as a core region.**
- **Name and describe the physical and human characteristics of the GDA.**
- **Describe primary, secondary and tertiary activities in the GDA.**
- **Describe the population characteristics of the GDA.**
- **Describe the growth of the Dublin city region and explain how this growth is being planned and controlled.**

Contents

17.1   The Greater Dublin Area – Physical and human factors/ characteristics, economic activities and human processes
        Case Study: Largo Foods
17.2   Planning policies for the GDA
17.3   City/Nodal/Urban Regions
        Case Studies: Dublin City Region
                        National Spatial Strategy (NSS)
        Questions

KEY THEME

The study of regions shows how economic, human and physical processes interact in a particular way. This can be demonstrated by examining contrasting Irish regions. The boundaries and extent of city regions may change over time.

17.1 The Greater Dublin Area (GDA)– – physical and human factors/ characteristics, economic activities and human processes

A core economic region in Ireland

Fig. 1 Location of the GDA – Dublin and Mid East regions

The Greater Dublin Area (GDA) includes Counties Dublin, Kildare, Meath and Wicklow as shown on Fig. 1 to the left. The GDA is a core economic region because:

1. It is a route focus/nodal point for Ireland's road, rail, air and river transport networks. The region contains an international airport and two seaports, Dublin and Dun Laoghaire.
2. Dublin city is the financial and administrative capital, as well as a major service centre providing national, governmental, health and educational services. It is also the country's biggest tourist destination.
3. The region has natural resources such as fertile brown earth soils and well-drained lowlands, leading to the development of profitable commercial agriculture. Its coastline provides sheltered harbours for the fishing industry and tourism.
4. It has a high population density and is an area of in-migration. It has 36% of the population (1.6 million) in just 12% of Ireland's land area.
5. Industry is attracted to this region because of its wealthy, educated population. In particular, Dublin city has become one of the world leaders in software development.
6. It has become one of the fastest-growing regions within Europe.

REASONS FOR THE DOMINANCE OF THE GDA IN THE ECONOMY

1. 80% of state-sponsored bodies are located in the GDA.
2. 70% of major public and private companies are located within the GDA.
3. All financial institutions have their headquarters in the GDA.
4. Dublin city is the capital city of Ireland.

All of the above are interdependent, making the region a major location in Ireland for inward investment.

Physical factors/characteristics of the GDA: climate, relief and soils

Climate

The climate of the GDA is drier than that of the BMW due to the rain shadow effect of the western mountains. Average annual rainfall is approximately 750 mm (Dublin Airport) which is almost 1,000 mm less than in the west. The Wicklow Mountains receive more rainfall because of their height, which encourages the formation of relief rain.

Average summer temperatures are similar to the BMW region with January averaging 5°C and July 15°C at Dublin Airport.

Relief and drainage

The region is low-lying and gently rolling (**undulating**) in the north and west. This is perfect for the development of commercial agriculture in the north of the region. The Dublin coastline is varied with headlands of metamorphic rock (Killiney Hill, Howth Head) and bays of limestone (Dublin Bay). Coastal erosion is a problem in Killiney and towards Bray, whereas deposition is occurring in Malahide and Rogerstown.

Several rivers cross the area, e.g. the Liffey, Boyne and Vartry.

Kildare and Meath are both low-lying counties with no major upland areas.

The steep ground of the Dublin Mountains forms a barrier to the development of roads and settlement.

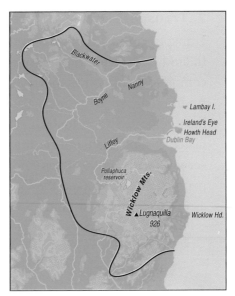

Fig. 2 **Relief map of Greater Dublin Area**

Soils

Unlike the BMW region where there is a variety of infertile soils, the GDA is mainly covered by fertile brown earth soils. Glacial deposition forms much of the boulder clay coastline. In North County Dublin, marine deposition has added sand to the brown earths making them suitable for intensive horticulture.

Infertile blanket peat is found on the uplands of the Wicklow Mountains.

Human factors/characteristics influencing the development of the GDA region

The physical factors affecting the GDA region that you have just read about interact with several human factors. They all combine to influence the primary, secondary and tertiary activities that occur in the GDA region. Three main human factors affect the GDA region. They are: **population, transport infrastructure** and **government/EU policy.**

1. Population characteristics of the GDA

The Dublin city area has a much higher than average population density (1,218 people per km² compared to 60 per km² nationally). However the average population density of the surrounding counties of the mid east region (Wicklow, Meath and Kildare) is 68 people per km² reflecting their more rural characteristics. The higher population density is due to the availability of work and the greater range of services such as health and education in the capital city and throughout the core region. The availability of a range of world-class third level education facilities such as Dublin City University and UCD attracts young people to the region. In turn, this educated population provides a skilled workforce for services and industry thus making the region attractive for continued economic development and investment.

2. Transport infrastructure

Transport infrastructure is better developed in the GDA region than elsewhere in Ireland. However, it still struggles to cope with the large volumes of business and commuter traffic. Transport costs are a major factor in location of industry and many traditional city centre industries, such as food processing and textile manufacturing have relocated to industrial estates on the edge of the city. Here, the M50 provides faster, cheaper transport to the airport and port. Provision of better public transport services such as the Luas and Dart have made the city centre more accessible to people and encouraged the location of financial services in city centre locations such as the IFSC and East Point.

3. Government/EU policy

Government allocation of national and EU funds to the GDA is important to the economic and social development of the region. CAP, Structural and Social funds are supplied to the GDA – as with the BMW. The GDA qualifies as a **competitive and employment** region (see Chapter 15, page 303).

With Dublin being the financial and administrative capital and the most densely populated part of the country, it is the natural focus for foreign and government investment. As so much development is focused on the national gateway city of Dublin, the other counties in the GDA do not contain gateway or hub settlements under the National Spatial Strategy. This is to ensure other regions beyond the GDA develop and allow the spread of the economic development across the whole country. Several government agencies are responsible for directing EU and government funds to the GDA region. They are briefly described on the next page.

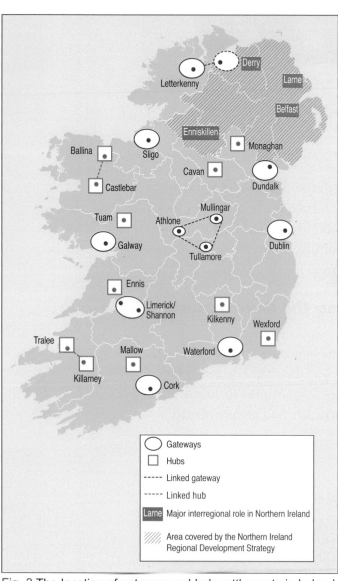

Fig. 3 The location of gateway and hub settlements in Ireland

1. The Department of Agriculture, Fisheries and Food is responsible for allocating CAP payments to the cattle and cereal farmers in Counties Meath, Kildare and Wicklow. Most funding is for research, development and modernisation of farms. Funding for horticulture is important for the north Dublin agricultural community. Farmers in the region have benefited from EU membership, sharing €12 billion allocated nationally in CAP funding for loans, training and advice up to 2013. This department also funds the extensive forest plantations especially in Wicklow through the Less Favoured Area payment scheme. The Common Fisheries Policy (CFP) funding is channelled through Bord Iascaigh Mhara (BIM) and is focused on the port of Howth.

Fig. 4 Cattle farmers in Counties Meath, Kildare and Wicklow receive funding for modernising their farms.

A smart economy uses the creativity of people to drive research and innovation in order to make products and services. A smart economy has secure energy supplies and protects its environment and society.

2. The Industrial Development Authority (IDA) attracts direct foreign investment from multinational companies to the GDA region. It promotes the government's policy to build a **smart economy** and to make Ireland a 'global innovation hub'. The IDA has a network of business parks in the GDA region: nine in Dublin and others in Navan, Bray, Arklow, Newbridge and Naas.

Fig. 5 Business park in the GDA

337

Primary activities in the GDA

Agriculture

There are over 19,000 farmers in the GDA, which is significantly less than the 123,000 farmers in the BMW. The quality of the soil and favourable climate mean farmers can make a better living from land in the GDA than those in the BMW. Farms are therefore large intensive commercial farms with an above average farm size of 42.3 hectares (the average size in the BMW is 26.7 hectares). Approximately 3% of the population in the GDA is employed in agriculture.

A number of physical and human factors influence the development of farming in the GDA region.

Physical factors

> Human and physical processes combine to produce a profitable commercial agriculture sector, making the GDA a core economic region.

- The mild maritime climate allows a long growing season for grass, making specialist beef farming the most common activity for the region.
  There are over 3,800 beef cattle farms in the region. Beef cattle are mainly produced on the boulder clay soils of County Meath. Many farmers receive young cattle from the BMW, fatten them and then sell them to the meat processors.
- There is a variety of fertile, well-drained loam, boulder clay and sandy soils in the region. This allows profitable cereal growing in Meath, greenhouse horticulture in Rush and Lusk in North County Dublin and cattle fattening across the GDA.
- The land is low lying and gently rolling which allows intensive mechanised agriculture in Meath and Kildare. In Wicklow, where land is mountainous, farms are small and sheep farming and forestry is more common.

Fig. 6 Farmers in the GDA can make a better living than those in the BMW due to better quality soil and a more favourable climate.

Positive physical factors (relief, soils and climate) allow for successful mixed grazing livestock, tillage and horticulture. Up to €53.1 million per annum has been earned from cereal production in the region and over €140 million per annum from cattle production. The drier, frost-free climate allows a longer growing season and outdoor vegetable production, lowering production costs.

Kildare is primarily an agricultural county with special emphasis on the bloodstock (horse) industry. The well-drained glacial outwash sand and gravel soils are world famous for breeding, rearing and training horses, e.g. the Curragh. Brown earth soils in **Meath** are good for the cattle and tillage farms there. The farms of lowland parts of **Wicklow** are also beef and tillage with any mountainous land used for sheep and forestry. A large part of the mountains and land of Wicklow is under national park lands.

The good quality soils and demand for fresh produce mean farmers in the GDA have not turned to forestry as an alternative source of income as is the case in the BMW region.

Human factors of capital, markets, transport, funding and education all mean farms are highly mechanised and yields are high. Farmers benefit from the large urban markets of Dublin, Drogheda, Arklow and Navan. The good transport links, low costs and short distances ensure fragile perishable fruit and vegetables arrive from the greenhouses to the markets in perfect condition. Such was the growth in the horticulture sector during the economic boom years that immigrant labour was used to make up the shortfall in labour supply. Since recession, cutbacks have meant a reduction in jobs and many labourers have left the sector. Farmers also receive funding from the EU where CAP contributes to the education and training of young farmers through Teagasc and the Department of Agriculture schemes.

Fig. 7 Horseracing and breeding are important industries in County Kildare.

	BMW	GDA
Number of farms: (Total farms for all Ireland 128,000)	68,000	9,300
Number of Farmers	123,700	19,200
Average Farm size (Av. for country = 32.3ha)	26.7	42.3ha
Value of farming by sector:	cattle €664.4 million sheep €91 million cereals €38.1 million	cattle €140 million sheep €25 million cereals €53.1 million

Fig. 8 Farm statistics for BMW and GDA regions

Forestry

The area under forestry in Dublin, Meath and Kildare is much lower than in Wicklow (1,583 hectares in Meath compared to 28,102 hectares in Wicklow). This is because the lowland counties have more fertile soils and the land is used for commercial agriculture. The Wicklow Mountains have thin acidic soils, wetter climate and steeper ground. Therefore forestry is a more productive use of this land than farming. However, overall few farmers in the GDA turn to forestry as an alternative to farming – which is in contrast to the experience of farmers in the BMW region.

Fishing

The fishing industry of the GDA is based at Howth. The value of fish landed at Howth ranks it in third place nationally, after Killybegs and Dunmore East. Dublin city is also ranked third in the number of people employed in fish processing (359) after Killybegs and Cork.

Dublin Bay Prawns account for 40% of the value of shellfish exports from Ireland. France, Spain and Britain are the main markets. In 2009, the value of Dublin Bay prawns landed at Howth was €7.3 million. In contrast to the BMW region the type of fish landed in the GDA is mainly demersal, e.g. plaice.

Fig. 9 The GDA's fishing industry is based at Howth.

Mineral resources

Since 1960 Ireland has had a string of significant lead and zinc metal discoveries, placing it firmly on the world stage as a country with lead and zinc deposits. The known deposits contain some 14 million tonnes (mt) of zinc metal, approximately 1.5% of the world zinc found to date.

Ireland is ranked first in the world in terms of zinc discovered per square kilometre and second in the world for lead discovered per square kilometre. Ireland has three underground lead and zinc mines in production. The largest of these is in the GDA region at Navan, County Meath (70 mt). This is the largest lead and zinc mine in Europe and employs over 600 people.

Secondary activities in the GDA

As with all core economic regions, the GDA has many physical and human advantages (factors) for the location of industry. Many of these advantages are concentrated in Dublin city.

Physical advantages include:

1. It is on the east coast of Ireland close to the UK and Europe.

2. Dublin Bay is a naturally sheltered harbour and has been a port location since Viking times. Dublin Port is the country's main port.

3. The hinterland of Dublin is fertile farmland, which provides a variety of raw materials for the food processing industries in the region.

Human advantages include:

4. Dublin city is the focus of Ireland's transport network. It is well connected to all parts of the country by road and rail. It also has international connections by air and sea through Dublin Airport and Dublin Port. Over one million trucks pass through Dublin Port each year.

5. The region has a high population density and a young population (43% are under 25 years of age), which provides a labour force and market.

6. Dublin is a national education centre making it an attractive location for knowledge-based industries such as software development.

7. Dublin is a service centre, providing support services for manufacturing, such as marketing and technical support.

8. People are generally wealthier in the GDA than elsewhere in Ireland, making the region attractive to producers of high-value luxury goods.

As in all core economic regions, the range of manufacturing in the GDA is wider than in peripheral regions, e.g. brewing, food processing, printing, clothing and electronics. There is a variety of manufacturing job opportunities in the GDA and no single industry has a major influence on the economy of the region. Should one industry close, there is a greater chance of finding another job in the GDA than would be the case in the BMW region. There is a variety of both modern and

traditional industries in the region. The Dublin region accounts for over 90,000 jobs in manufacturing.

As is typical of other core economic regions, the GDA is the location of many world renowned knowledge-based multinational companies such as Microsoft, IBM, Hewlett-Packard, Intel and Rank Xerox.

Food processing is also important in the GDA. Chocolate and biscuit-making factories are located here, e.g. Cadburys and Jacobs Fruitfield in Tallaght.

The Irish printing and publishing industry is based in Dublin. The Independent Newspapers site at City West is a 'state of the art' plant.

Metal fabrication and engineering, which support the construction industry, are also important in many small factories in the region, e.g. Wavin in Balbriggan.

Unlike the BMW region where manufacturing is concentrated in a few urban centres, in the GDA it is widely dispersed. For example, Intel is located in Leixlip, County Kildare and Oriflame is located in Bray, County Wicklow. However, the influence of transport is seen in the movement of industry away from its traditional location in the Dublin docklands to industrial estates and business parks close to the M50 motorway and Dublin Airport.

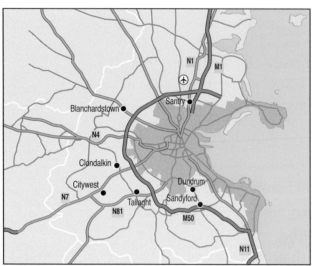

Fig. 10 **Business parks and industrial estates in Dublin**

Focus on the food processing industry in the Greater Dublin Area

There are several physical and human factors that have encouraged the development of the food processing industry within the GDA. Well known food producers are Cadburys (Coolock, Dublin), Tayto (Largo Foods in County Meath), Brennan's Bread (Walkinstown, Dublin), and Jacobs - Fruitfield (Tallaght, Dublin).

Physical factors

Climate: The region has a drier and warmer variation of the cool temperate oceanic climate and has very few frosty days. The annual soil temperature at Casement Aerodrome weather station is 10.9°C. The average rainfall is 545 mm. These moderate conditions mean that temperatures are high enough to support year-round growth of grass and it's not too wet to prevent wheat crop production.

Soils: The region has a variety of fertile soils such as brown earths, loam and sandy soils. These soils allow a variety of crops to be grown across the region such as potatoes, barley, wheat and vegetables. These provide raw material for the processed food factories such as Green Isle vegetables and Brennan's Bread companies.

Relief: The GDA has low-lying gently rolling land in Counties Kildare, Meath and north Dublin. This enables the use of machinery. Farms in these areas are some of the largest and most capital intensive in the country. In Kildare for example the average farm size is above the national average at 49.2 hectares.

Human factors

Government policy: The implementation of a new government programme called *Food Harvest 2020* aims to increase production in the agri-food sector. The aim of the programme is to increase the value of Irish food production exports to €12 billion by 2020. As part of this programme, farmers and processors are encouraged to use new technology, develop new products and find new food markets.

Market: The GDA has a population of over 1.6 million and is a wealthy core region in Ireland. As such it provides a market for producers who locate their factories in the region to reduce transport costs.

Labour force: The same population that provides the market also provides an educated workforce for companies looking for skilled and unskilled labour. This is an important factor affecting the location of the food processing companies in the region.

Transport infrastructure: The GDA has a well developed transport network including Dublin Airport, motorways (M50, M1, M7) and railways. Dublin Port is the main shipping point into and out of the country. The variety and efficiency of the transport network reduces travel costs and fuel consumption for producers and is an important influence on factory location.

Largo Foods, Ashbourne, County Meath

Largo Foods is an Irish company established in 1983. Largo Foods is the leading manufacturer and distributor of snack foods (crisps, snacks, peanuts and popcorn) in Ireland. The brands produced include Tayto, King, Hunky Dory, Perri and Sam Spudz. Largo Foods has production facilities in Ashbourne, County Meath and in Gweedore, County Donegal. Largo Foods employs 360 people in its Ashbourne plant. The company turnover in 2010 was worth €95 million. It produces about 15,000 tons of snack food products each year.

- Production of snack foods by Largo Foods demonstrates the international nature of the food industry in the Greater Dublin Area. Its markets are Irish and UK based. It distributes its products in mainland Europe. Transportation methods include intercontinental shipping and road haulage. Human factors such as personal links to the area influenced the location of the production facility.

Fig. 11 Largo Foods produces crisps, snacks, peanuts and popcorn.

case study

Location

Ashbourne is located 20 km north of Dublin on the N2 route-way. The company's founder Raymond Coyle was a local potato grower in Meath who supplied manufacturers of snack food brands, e.g. Tayto, King Crisps and Sam Spudz. He gradually expanded his business and now his company, Largo Foods, owns the brands he once supplied. He located his food processing business in his native area.

Raw materials and transport

The County Meath factory produces potato based snack-food products. Most raw materials arrive at the plant by lorry from Dublin Port. The main raw materials – potatoes – are supplied by Irish farmers in Meath, Dublin, Louth and Wexford. Ninety per cent of the potatoes are supplied from farms within 30 km of the plant. The products are cooked in sunflower oil produced from seeds grown in southern Europe (Italy, Spain, Hungary) which are then refined in the Netherlands. The sunflower oil is transported in lorry tankers by ship from Rotterdam. Other ingredients include maize grown in Argentina and shipped from Buenos Aires. Cassava (used in its Velvet Crunch product) is grown in Indonesia and delivered via Rotterdam. Rice is delivered by truck and ship from southern Europe. Maize, used in products like chip-sticks and onion rings as well as corn used to make popcorn, is grown in the Paris Basin region of France and delivered by ship and lorry. Corn is also supplied from Argentina and America.

Markets

As well as supplying products to the Irish market, 20% of its business market is located in the UK. The products are shipped from Dublin Port to the UK via Holyhead.

Production and packaging

The production process is highly automated with modern robotic machines cooking and packaging the snack foods. Packaging, manufacturing and food ingredients are important costs and the company aims to control them carefully. Seventy per cent of crisp packet material is produced in three plants in northern Italy; the rest is made in Ireland. Cardboard boxes used to transport the finished product are manufactured in Ireland.

Fig. 12 Packaging costs are carefully controlled in Largo Foods.

Tertiary activities in the GDA

The services sector is important to any core economic region. Because of its size and rapid growth, Dublin dominates tertiary activities in the GDA. However, certain services are much more important in the GDA than in the BMW region. For example, 21% of the workforce in Dublin is employed in professional services (finance, health care, teaching and legal work), reflecting the greater demand for such services in this region. In Donegal, this sector accounts for 17% of the workforce.

Transport and communications

The GDA is the transportation centre of Ireland. Roads, air transport, railway and inland waterway systems are focused on Dublin. Transport and communications-related work account for 9% of employment in the GDA reflecting the importance of this service sector. Due to the high population, the transportation network in the GDA is overcrowded and congestion is a problem. Major investment in rail, road and air links has occurred under the Transport 21 project.

This project aims to upgrade key routeways across Ireland and especially in the Dublin region. For example, Terminal 2 at Dublin Airport is completed and caters for over 15 million passengers per year. The Dublin Port Tunnel has reduced heavy traffic on city centre streets while the DART and Luas lines have been extended. The M50 upgrade and introduction of barrier-free tolling has reduced journey times along this key route around Dublin. Inter-city train links have been improved.

Within the city, Quality Bus Corridors (QBCs) have enabled faster bus journeys and the Dublin Bike Scheme has been a success with over one million trips recorded, reducing the need for car transport in the city centre. The completion of motorway links to Belfast (M1), Galway (M6) and Cork (M8) has made Dublin even more accessible; shorter journey times benefit both commuters and businesses.

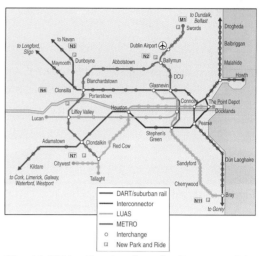

Fig. 13 GDA rail network under Transport 21

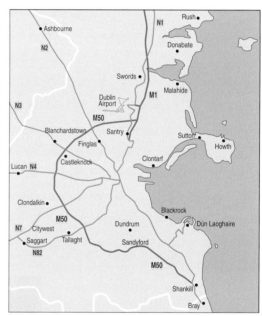

Fig. 14 National roads network in the GDA

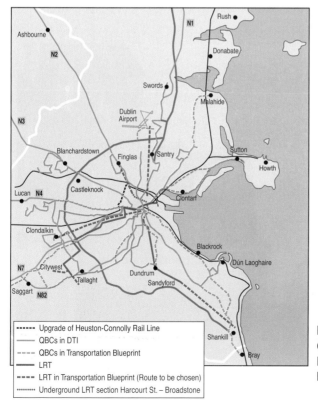

Fig. 15 The Dublin Transportation Initiative
QBC = Quality Bus Corridor
DTI = Dublin Transportation Initiative
LRT = Light Rail Transit (Luas)

Fig. 16 **Dublin Port Tunnel**

The GDA is also the communications capital of Ireland. The Information, Communications and Technology (ICT) sector is leading Ireland's **smart economy** with 7 of the world's top 10 ICT companies located in the GDA. Many companies have their European headquarters in the region. These companies rely on fast broadband services to run their global distribution, sales and financial service networks. For example in 2010 Kellogg's expanded its European headquarters in Swords, County Dublin.

Telesales is a growth sector in the GDA as a result of its broadband facilities. Hertz has located its European call centre in Swords, County Dublin. Google has two centres in Dublin. The City West business campus is the location for Ireland's National Digital Park. This park is being developed as a centre for e-commerce and technology companies who need high-speed digital communications.

Tourism

The tourism and hospitality sector continues to be a major economic force in the Irish economy, providing up to 200,000 jobs. In 2010 tourism generated €4.6 billion for the Irish economy.

There were over 5.6 million overseas visitors to the Republic of Ireland in 2010 – a decrease of over 11% on numbers for 2009 mainly due to the world economic recession. Two in every five Euros spent in Ireland by overseas visitors are spent in the Dublin region. Thirty-three per cent of tourists to the Dublin region are from mainland Europe, 25% are from the UK. The GDA is easily accessible through Dublin Airport with over 79 airlines operating to 207 destinations and over 450 flights per day. Ferry passengers use Dublin and Dun Laoghaire ports. The opening of Terminal 2 at Dublin Airport will be a further boost for Irish tourism.

Fig. 17 **Temple Bar in Dublin city, a popular tourist attraction**

The GDA region boasts a wealth of culture and activity holidays. Unlike the seasonal nature of tourism in the BMW, tourism in the GDA is a more 'year round' industry. However there is some variation in arrival patterns. Most UK visitors arrive between October and March, while visitors from Europe and America arrive in the summer. The scale of the GDA's tourism business is much greater than that of the BMW region because the majority of visitors to Ireland arrive into Dublin Airport.

As the capital city Dublin is a vibrant city with tourists arriving in all months. It is Europe's fourth most visited capital city. In 2009 over 5.5 million tourists visited Dublin city, generating €1.5 billion for the local economy.

Dublin city enjoys a reputation as an historical city with many museums, art galleries and historic buildings. It is equally famous for its literary tradition as home to writers such as Jonathan Swift, William Butler Yeats and James Joyce.

Dublin is marketed at high-spending tourists who want city-based holidays offering a variety of attractions ranging from castles (Dublin Castle) and churches (Christ Church and St. Patrick's Cathedral) to cafés and clubs. The capital is promoted as a short-stay destination for weekend city breaks, independent of the weather and has many repeat visitors. The attractions of modern Dublin include theatres (Gaiety), shops (Dundrum Town Centre), restaurants, and fashionable bars and music venues (the O2).

Dublin city is compact and easy to get around on foot or by road, rail, river taxi and tram. The recent Dublin 'rent-a-bike' scheme has been a huge success with over one million users within 12 months of starting operation. The annual Horse show in the RDS, rugby in Lansdowne Road's Aviva stadium, GAA at Croke Park and concerts in the O2 and other venues attract national and international visitors.

Beyond Dublin city, scenic walks, historic locations and active holidays are available. These tourist regions in the GDA are within easy reach of the capital with good road and rail links.

Fig. 18 The Ha'Penny Bridge at night, Dublin city

Fig. 19 Dublin Castle, a historic tourist attraction

Fig. 20 **The horseracing industry is important to County Kildare.**

The rolling landscapes of County Wicklow, the 'Garden of Ireland', offers 83 kilometres of hills and mountain walkways (e.g. the Wicklow Way), with scenic attractions such as Glendalough and Powerscourt Waterfall, as well as many blue flag beaches, e.g. Brittas Bay. County Kildare has a wide range of visitor attractions, with excellent angling and golf facilities. Kildare's countryside is home to Ireland's famous bloodstock and horseracing industries. The Curragh racecourse attracts many international visitors and racegoers throughout the year, especially to the classic flat Derby races. The Punchestown racing festival attracts the best international jump horses and riders and is similar in fame to the Cheltenham festival in the UK.

County Meath is Ireland's Heritage Capital. It is rich in history with castle ruins (Trim Castle), ancient stone circles and early Christian churches. It is the location for the world heritage site at Newgrange, which dates back to 3200 BC. The county is also host to the Irish Grand National horse race at Fairyhouse.

While the GDA has many positive factors attracting tourists, the economic downturn has been the most frequently listed negative factor quoted by tourism businesses. Tourism operators in the GDA blame high fuel costs and surplus hotel rooms for the downturn in their business. The volcanic ash cloud in 2010 was another negative factor affecting Irish tourism.

For more up-to-date facts and figures on tourism in Ireland log onto: www.failteireland.ie/Research-Statistics/Tourism-Facts

Other services

Employment in **public administration** (e.g. the Gardaí, government departments) accounts for a greater share of the workforce in Dublin city since it is the administrative capital of the country.

Health services are another important part of the tertiary sector. Core regions like the GDA need a variety of healthcare facilities. For example, Dublin has 6 private and 15 public hospitals which provide services to the region.

The majority of companies in the GDA operate within **international services** and **financial services.** These include multinational companies such as Intel, Hewlett Packard, Hertz and Citibank. Financial services have become a major growth industry in the region. The Irish Financial Services Centre (IFSC) in Dublin city employs over 6,000 people in 25 of the world's top 50 banks.

IT services in the GDA

The GDA has a variety of internet service providers who provide employment not just in software development but in finance, sales, supply chain management and human resources. The international high-tech services sector is developing rapidly and Ireland provides such services globally over the internet. The GDA is now the location of choice for the European headquarters of companies such as Google, Facebook, LinkedIn and eBay.

Within the GDA Dublin is becoming the information technology capital of Europe. The huge value of business by IT companies can be seen from the fact that software companies in Ireland increased their exports by six per cent during 2008-2010. IT services companies based in the GDA chose to locate in this area for the following reasons.

Fig. 21 There is a young educated workforce in the GDA.

Reasons for location of IT services companies in Ireland/GDA:
- A **young educated workforce:** In 2010 Ireland was first of ten European countries in a ranking of the percentage of the population with a third level qualification. Overall 44% of the population has a third level qualification.
- Dublin has **affordable office space.** Rents are now lower than ever in vacant office blocks built during the economic boom.
- **Government support** for industry and research & development (R&D): An attractive tax system, e.g. corporation tax is just 12.5% paid on profits compared to 41% in Japan, also helped to entice companies to locate here. Ireland also offers a 25% tax credit on R&D developments.
- **Industry-focused college courses:** Such courses are available in world-class universities and institutes of technology throughout Ireland. They ensure a continued supply of qualified graduates and the availability of ongoing management training.
- The massive 'server farms' of web service providers require expensive air conditioning which is cheaper to provide in the **mild Irish climate**.

The following IT services companies have all located in the GDA. Between them they employ almost 5,000 people.

- **Google** employs over 2,000 people. Based in Dublin's East Point Business Park and Barrow Street, many of the Dublin-based teams are engaged in supporting other Google offices across more than 25 countries in the Europe Mid East Asia (EMEA) region. Working in areas like finance, payroll, legal and HR, they also provide Google Maps and Google Local services as well as consumer products such as Gmail Calendar and advertising products such as AdSense.

- **eBay** employs more than 1,600 people at its Blanchardstown, County Dublin site together with PayPal, its online payment system. It employs people in customer service and personal account management.

- **LinkedIn** is a rapidly growing social networking service for business people with over one million new users per month. It has set up its international headquarters in Dublin. The jobs include a variety of business and technology roles, including positions in sales, marketing, finance and customer service. The company manages its international expansion from Dublin, working with teams in London and the Netherlands.

- **IBM** employs 200 people at its first-ever IBM Smarter Cities Technology Centre, located in Mulhuddart, west Dublin. It aims to revolutionise how cities provide services such as water and transport in the future. IBM already employs over 3,000 people in Ireland mainly in Dublin at its Technology Campus.

- **Hertz** employs almost 1,000 people at its European Shared Services Centre in Swords, County Dublin. The Swords offices provide centralised finance and customer support services to its European vehicle rental operations.

Fig. 22 Dublin is the chosen location for the international headquarters of well-known IT services companies.

Human processes in the GDA

The population of the GDA is 1.6 million people. The GDA is projected to account for 41% of the total projected national population of 5 million in 2021.

The number of young people (0-14 years) in the Dublin region is expected to increase by 26% by 2021. Between 2002 and 2021 it is predicted that births in the GDA will exceed deaths by 197,000.

There is a surplus of females in the region (20,000), which reflects the greater numbers of female workers in health and education. These patterns of change in the population mean that the government will have to invest in the provision of more childcare facilities and services for the elderly.

The number of people aged 45-64 in the Mid East region (i.e. Wicklow, Kildare and Meath) will double by 2021. At the same time, the number of older people (65 years and over) will increase by 75% in Dublin and by 133% in the Mid East region as a whole.

Dublin has become a cultural melting pot over the last decade. The number of religions practised in the county is increasing. Muslims, Hindus, Jews, Buddhists and others have places of worship in the city. There are two mosques in the city catering for the city's Islamic population. Because the government agencies dealing with immigration are located in Dublin, it is the first stop for many new immigrants to the country. Dublin has become a multicultural city. Overall, 15% of the Dublin city population are foreign nationals. Many stay in the GDA; others move to different regions, e.g. a significant number of Brazilians live and work in Gort, County Galway. National and secondary schools often have students from many different countries in their classes.

Fig. 23 There is a greater mix of cultures in Irish schools.

17.2 Planning policies for the GDA

As is the case for the BMW, the four plans (NDP, NSS, Transport 21 and decentralisation policies – see Chapter 16, pages 325-328) also affect the growth and development of the GDA.

HOW THE NDP AIMS TO DEVELOP THE GDA

1. Address traffic congestion and urban sprawl.
2. Maintain Dublin as a national gateway serving the whole country.
3. Build on the region's existing economic performance, improve jobs and reduce unemployment.
4. Develop tourism and promote social inclusion.
5. Maintain a viable rural economy.
6. Continue development of transport links to the rest of the country.

HOW THE NSS AIMS TO DEVELOP THE GDA

1. Enhance the competitiveness of the GDA so that it continues to perform on an international level as a driver for national development.
2. Monitor the growth of the Dublin city region (metropolitan area, i.e. city and suburbs).
3. Carefully manage Dublin as a gateway so that other areas have the opportunity to become similarly strong.
4. Manage the location of industry and zoning of land.
5. Integrate transport.
6. Develop the hinterlands of County Dublin, Meath, Kildare and Wicklow by concentrating on the strong and dynamic urban centres at Balbriggan, Navan, Naas, Newbridge, Kilcullen and Wicklow towns.

HOW DECENTRALISATION AIMS TO DEVELOP THE GDA

Planned relocation of government and Office of Public Works staff in Dublin to other areas of GDA. This should reduce some of the traffic congestion in Dublin and ease pressure on other services in the area. The offices listed for relocation within the GDA included:

1. Probation and Welfare Service, Garda Civilian HR unit, National Property Services Regulatory Authority and Coroner's Agency to Navan.
2. Revenue commissioners to Athy.
3. Department of Finance to Kildare.

Due to a review of the decentralisation programme many planned relocations have not occurred, e.g. Department of Finance to Kildare.

To find out more about regional planning in the GDA, log onto: www.spggda.ie

17.3 City/nodal/urban regions

We have already studied a variety of regions, such as climatic regions, cultural regions and socio-economic regions. A **city** is also unique and can be seen as a region. All cities serve their immediate surrounding areas (**hinterlands**) but city regions also include an area/zone of influence which may stretch beyond the immediate hinterland. Dublin is a city region whose zone of influence spreads beyond the city into the eastern, midland and border region (e.g. Gorey, Athlone, Ashbourne, Drogheda and beyond).

Cities develop because of the interaction of several factors such as defence, transport, water supply, food production, trade and industry. City regions continue to grow because they offer many advantages to people and businesses. For example, city regions have:

1. High standards of living.

2. Better health services than rural areas.

3. A variety of recreational facilities.

4. A skilled workforce.

5. A wealthy market for trade and industry.

For these reasons, city regions are areas of **in-migration** and are some of the fastest-growing regions in the world. Most city regions have well-defined zones of different land uses, e.g. **residential, industrial** and the **Central Business District (CBD)**. The majority of Europeans live in urban areas. There are over 25 cities in Europe with a population of more than one million.

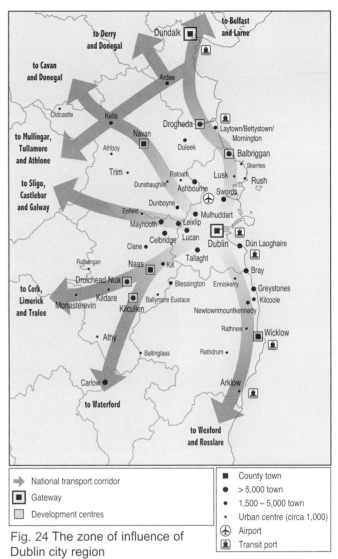

Fig. 24 The zone of influence of Dublin city region

In some countries (e.g. Ireland and France), the capital cities are more than twice as big as the next largest city in the country. These are termed **primate cities**. Dublin, for example, is more than six times larger than Cork.

In most urban areas, there is a **zone of transition** where buildings are in disrepair and awaiting redevelopment. There is great competition for space in urban areas. Intensive use of land has led to the construction of high-rise buildings in many cities.

City regions are important because they provide job opportunities and a wide range of services and goods to the people of the city and its hinterland. They also influence the social and economic development of areas beyond the city. The term **nodal point** applies to any region that is the focus of route-ways. All towns and cities are nodal points.

Fig. 25 Night-time lights showing the urbanisation of Europe

The zone of influence of city regions spreads beyond the city limits. Dublin city and its surrounding counties have a population of over 1.18 million people with a commuter belt of almost 90 km radius from the CBD. Paris has a population of 10 million with a commuter belt averaging 45 km radius from the CBD.

When groups of cities grow into each other, huge urban areas known as **conurbations** are formed. These regions are **polycentric**, containing several city areas that are of similar importance. Examples of conurbations include Manchester and Birmingham in the UK. The Randstadt in the Netherlands has a population of six million people which is made up of the merging of over six large towns and cities in a radius of 50 km. New York City is a metropolitan area which has a population of over 20 million people and covers a conurbation with a radius of 64 km.

City regions are also spreading into the surrounding countryside. This **urban sprawl** eats up valuable farm and recreational land and adds to commuter traffic problems. Controlling the future growth of city regions is important in every country.

The Dublin city region

The city of Dublin influences a large proportion of the eastern half of Ireland. The city of Dublin and its zone of influence is known as the **Dublin city region**. This region is not a fixed zone, although it is accepted that it now influences much of the eastern coast of Ireland (See Fig. 26).

The population of Dublin and the three surrounding counties (Meath, Kildare and Wicklow) is more than 1.6 million. It is estimated that the Dublin city region will have 42% (2.4 million people) of the national population by 2026.

Reasons for the growth of Dublin

Several physical and human factors have combined to promote the growth of the Dublin city region.

Fig. 26 The Dublin city region and its zone of influence

● **Physical factors encouraging the growth of Dublin**

The land to the north and west of the city is low-lying, gently rolling, fertile farmland with boulder clays and brown earth soils. These produce a variety of high-value crops such as vegetables and wheat. These crops are the basis of profitable farming and raw materials for the food-processing industries, which in turn provide employment.

Dublin is located at the mouth of the River Liffey. This has led to the development of a major port that is an important centre of economic growth and transport for the region.

The rapid economic growth of Dublin sets it apart from other regions in Ireland in several ways. Its problems are typical of many core economic regions in Europe.

● **Human factors encouraging the growth of Dublin**

Dublin is the capital city and centre of government administration, financial services and manufacturing. This attracts people to work in the civil service, financial institutions and many other businesses in the region.

The performance of this region is important for the economic success of Ireland as a whole. The average economic output per person is 108% higher in this region than the state average.

Dublin is the centre of the national transport network. Road and rail routes are focused on the city and this further promotes economic development in the city region.

Dublin has the state's largest port and airport. The volume of goods passing through Dublin Port was nearly 28 million tons in 2010, while Dublin Airport accounted for 65% of passenger traffic in 2010. The volume of goods and people entering the city transport network encourages continued growth of the city region.

case study

The effects of the growth of the Dublin city region

● **Urban sprawl**

Urban sprawl is the rapid growth of an urban area into the surrounding countryside. Urban sprawl is common around rapidly growing urban areas.

Dublin's earliest rural to urban expansion affected the traditional dormitory towns of Greystones, Malahide and Maynooth changing them from small villages to commuter towns because of their rail links. Such was the growth of Dublin in the 1970s and 1980s that new towns were built to accommodate the rising population.

● These **new towns** were built in Tallaght, Lucan-Clondalkin and Blanchardstown. In 1998 a new town, Adamstown, 16 kilometres south west of Dublin city centre, was planned to provide 10,000 houses and associated facilities such as schools, shops and public transport. By 2006 the first residents had moved. The town will eventually cater for over 20,000 people.

Despite these new towns, the Dublin city region has spread further into neighbouring counties. Towns such as Mullingar, Portlaoise, Gorey, Arklow and Navan all have large commuter populations.

Fig. 27 Urban sprawl leads to the loss of farmland.

● **Increased demand for water:** On average each person in the Dublin city region uses 150 litres of water per day. Such is the increase in demand for water in the city region (over 800 million litres per day will be required by 2031) that plans to pump water from the River Shannon are being developed.

● **Loss of valuable agricultural land:** Greenfield areas are built upon and this leads to an increase in demand for imported food as there is a reduction in available land for agriculture. It becomes difficult for farmers to expand their farms as they cannot afford to buy neighbouring land if it is zoned for housing.

- **Loss of wildlife habitats – hedgerows and wetlands:** Hedgerows provide essential living space for many species of animal, plant and insects. As land is built upon with houses and roads, this habitat is lost and the biodiversity of the area is reduced.

- **Traffic congestion**

Dublin is the sixth most congested city in Europe. Traffic congestion is worse in Dublin than any other city in Ireland. This is due to both the high levels of car ownership created during the economic boom years of 1990 to 2007 and the availability of so many jobs in secondary and tertiary businesses in this core socio-economic region. The number of cars on Dublin roads increased by over 3,000 in 2010. Traffic congestion increases air pollution. Businesses lose money due to increased fuel costs and journey times.

Fig. 28 Air pollution levels rise due to traffic congestion.

Several factors account for the high levels of congestion in the Dublin city region

- **Commuter traffic:** Urban sprawl in the Dublin city region means many workers travel into the city from towns up to 90 km away. This adds to congestion at peak times. Average speed in the city is expected to reduce to just 8 km/h due to congestion.

- **Lack of public transport:** While new transport developments have occurred – e.g. the Luas and Dublin Port Tunnel, quality bus corridors, cycle schemes and an increase of over 12% in the number of buses – people still find cars more convenient for transport. Dublin does not have the range of public transport facilities that a city of its size and population needs to tempt people away from using the car. The provision of a metro/underground rail system would reduce congestion in the future.

- **Historic street plan:** Like many cities Dublin streets were built to accommodate horse and carriages and not 40-tonne trucks. Many of the narrow and winding streets (e.g. Dame Street) are not wide enough for modern traffic and this has contributed to congestion. This has led to the ban on 5-axle lorries in the city centre.

Managing the growth of Dublin – a challenge for the future

1. Changes to Dublin council structures

Changes have been made to the administration of the city. These are the first such changes in over 200 years. The reason for the changes are:

(a) The Barrington report of 1991 showed that Ireland was at the bottom of the league table when it came to allocating powers and responsibilities to local government. This indicated that the central government was still too closely involved in making decisions that a local council could easily decide.

(b) The population and area of Dublin city was increasing to such an extent that it was becoming difficult for one county council to administer. For example, there was only one motor taxation office to deal with all licence and motor tax requests despite the fact that the number of car owners in the Dublin city region had increased dramatically.

(c) Decision-making structures were slow and this delayed the provision of services, e.g. council and affordable housing.

Find out more about the growth of Dublin. Log onto: http://www.dra.ie/ This is the website for the Dublin Regional Authority.

In 1993, the Local Government (Dublin) Act was passed in the Dáil. This allowed for the creation of three new councils to manage the region.

(a) **Dún Laoghaire-Rathdown County Council**

(b) **Fingal County Council**

(c) **South Dublin County Council**

2. Efficient use of existing land

If Dublin continues to spread physically into the surrounding counties, it will use up valuable agricultural land and lead to more traffic congestion. In order to control the physical spread of Dublin, the city planners have to make careful plans to use existing land more wisely. This is achieved by identifying unused and derelict sites in the city and preparing them for new development. Existing buildings can also be used more efficiently, e.g. apartments over shops.

Fig. 29 The new county councils created to accommodate the increase in population of the Dublin city area

Find out more about the administrations of the Dublin region. Log onto: www.fingalcoco.ie, www.dlrcoco.ie, www.sdcc.ie, www.dublincity.ie. These are the home sites for each of the county councils operating in the Dublin city region.

The National Spatial Strategy (NSS)

A policy to control the growth of Dublin

The NSS aims to balance the growth and development of Dublin by tackling growth in the metropolitan area (i.e. the city and its suburbs) and the hinterland (i.e. surrounding area) in the following ways.

1. In the metropolitan area

(a) Compiling a list of all derelict, vacant and underused land in the city to allow redevelopment for housing or other more efficient land use. This ensures that no land is wasted inside the city area.

(b) Ensuring the best use of existing housing. Shops often have unused apartment space above them. 'Living over the Shop' schemes were set up to encourage more people to live in the city rather than building on new ground in the suburbs.

(c) Some suburbs have large houses occupied by older people. Creating smaller houses for older people within these areas would make more family-size houses available.

(d) There are many old, inefficiently used warehouses in Dublin. These could be redeveloped and used more efficiently for newer businesses, e.g. the Docklands.

2. In the hinterland

(a) Develop existing towns such as Naas, Kildare, Drogheda and Arklow to draw people into jobs outside the city.

(b) Develop an efficient public transport network to provide easy access between these towns and the city. This will reduce traffic congestion.

3. Nationally

Improving the economic and social development of cities and towns around the country. Those cities and towns targeted are known as **gateway** towns and **hub** towns (see Chapter 16).

Fig. 30 This derelict factory could be a brownfield site for redevelopment.

questions

Chapter Revision Questions

GDA

1. What factors make the GDA a core economic region?

2. Name the counties which make up the GDA.

3. Describe the climate and relief of the GDA.

4. Write an account of the soil types and agricultural production within the GDA.

5. List and explain five factors which make Dublin an attractive location for industry.

6. Name and locate the different types of manufacturing to be found within the GDA.

7. Discuss tertiary activities providing employment within the GDA.

8. (i) Outline the importance of a good transport system to a core region.

   (ii) Explain how Transport 21 aims to improve Ireland's transport system.

9. Examine one challenge facing the GDA in the future. Discuss one way in which this challenge may be reduced.

10. The NDP and the NSS propose measures to address the challenges faced by the GDA. What are these proposed measures?

City/Nodal/Urban regions

11. What is a city region?

12. Name one Irish and one other European city region.

13. Why are city regions important?

14. What is a CBD?

15. What are conurbations? Name two.

16. What are the advantages of city regions?

17. Name two problems found in city regions.

18. What is a primate city?

19. What factors lead to the development of cities?

20. Why do city regions attract in-migration of workers and business?

The Dublin city region

21. What is the Dublin city region?

22. What is the population of the Dublin city region?

23. Describe the manufacturing industry in the GDA and BMW regions.

24. 'The scale of tertiary activity is greater in the GDA than in the BMW'. Describe three pieces of evidence to show this statement is true.

25. Discuss the tourism industry in the GDA region. In your answer, focus on a tourist destination and its attractions.

OL Long Questions

26. **IRELAND – REGIONS**
    Draw a sketch map of Ireland. On it mark and name:
    Two contrasting regions
    One major city or town in **each** region
    LC Exam Paper

27. Examine the development of **two** contrasting economic regions in Ireland.
    LC Exam Paper

28. Explain two reasons for the growth of one urban area in any region you have studied. Clearly state the name of the urban area.
    LC Exam Paper

29. (i) Name any one urban area in Ireland which you have studied.

    (ii) Explain one reason for the growth of that urban area.

    (iii) Describe one problem this growth has caused within that urban area.

HL Long Questions

30. **IRISH REGIONS**
    Draw an outline map of Ireland. Show and name the following on it:
    (i) Any **one** Irish region that you have studied.
    (ii) Any **two** physical features in the region.
    (iii) **One** urban centre in the region.
    LC Exam Paper

31. Examine the development of primary activities in any **one** Irish region you have studied.

32. Examine the development of secondary activities in any **one** Irish region you have studied.

33. Examine the development of tertiary activities in any **one** Irish region you have studied.

34. Regions can be defined by many factors including:
    - economic
    - human
    - physical

    Explain how any **one** of the above factors has defined an Irish region studied by you.

35. Examine the development of one urban area in any Irish region studied by you.

Chapter 18

The Dynamics of Regions (3)

– A European peripheral region

At the end of this chapter you should be able to:

- Describe the Mezzogiorno as a peripheral/less developed region.

- Name and describe the human and physical characteristics of the Mezzogiorno region.

- Describe primary, secondary and tertiary activities in the Mezzogiorno region.

Contents

18.1   The Mezzogiorno – Physical and human factors/characteristics

18.2   Economic activities and human processes in the Mezzogiorno

Questions

KEY THEME

The study of regions shows how economic, human and physical processes interact in a particular way. This can be demonstrated by examining two contrasting European regions.

18.1 The Mezzogiorno – physical and human factors/characteristics

A peripheral/less developed region in the Mediterranean

In Italy, the south or **Mezzogiorno** region is a less developed/peripheral region. It makes up 40% of Italy's land area and has 35% of its population, but it is one of the poorest regions in Italy. The Mezzogiorno is made up of the regions of Abruzzi, Campania, Molise, Puglia, Basilicata, Calabria, Lazio and the islands of Sicily and Sardinia.

Unemployment rates are high (20% in some regions) and the area has traditionally suffered from out-migration. It is also one of the least developed regions in the EU with GDP at less than 75% of the EU average. Billions of euros have been spent on the region through a scheme called the *Cassa Per Il Mezzogiorno* (see page 367) and through EU funding.

Despite this, in 2010 Italy was ranked 23rd out of 177 countries on the UN Human Development Index (HDI). Ireland was fifth.

The Mezzogiorno faces several problems, including illegal immigration, organised crime, corruption, high unemployment, low incomes and poor technical skills compared to the north.

Fig. 1 The regional divisions of Italy

The UN HDI measures achievements in terms of life expectancy, educational attainment and adjusted real income.

Physical factors/characteristics – climate, relief, drainage and soils

Climate

The Mezzogiorno has a Mediterranean climate. Summers are hot, sunny and dry. In Naples, daytime temperatures in July and August typically reach 29°C. In summer, the region is influenced by the Azores high pressure belt which has dry, stable, descending air causing cloudless skies and warm sunshine.

It is also influenced by the north-east trade winds which are hot and dry and cause drought throughout the region between June and September.

Winters are mild and moist with temperatures rarely falling below 11°C. Frost is rare. Most rain falls between October and March when the area is under the influence of Atlantic Ocean depressions and moist south-west winds. Rainfall averages between 500 mm and 900 mm and the western Mezzogiorno is wetter than the east due to relief rain (700 mm in Naples and 400 mm in Bari).

Fig. 2 Regions of the Mezzogiorno

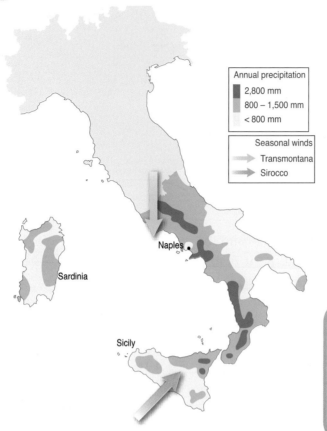

Fig. 3 Annual precipitation and seasonal winds in Naples and Sicily

In summer, **convectional rain** creates torrential downpours and thunderstorms. These often lead to mudslides causing soil erosion. The lowest rainfall occurs along the Adriatic east coast as it is in the rainshadow of the Apennine Mountains. Many parts of the extreme south are affected by the Sirocco (hot wind) from the Sahara.

EXERCISE

Look at the graphs below.
For Naples, state the maximum daily temperature and rainfall in June. For Sicily, state the maximum daily temperature and rainfall in June.

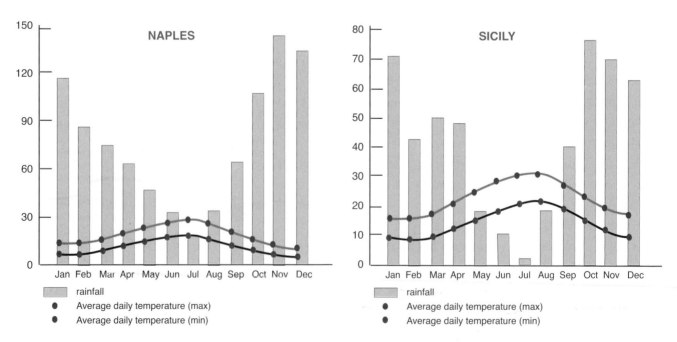

Fig. 4 Climate charts and rainfall measures for Naples and Sicily

Relief and drainage

The Apennine Mountains dominate the landscape of this region and are bordered by narrow coastlands. Eighty-five per cent of the region is classed as upland or mountainous (45% of total land area is steeply sloping). The mountains form the physical backbone of the Mezzogiorno. They are an extension of the Alpine fold mountains and vary from 40 km to 200 km wide. The mountains are made up of a series of limestone plateaus with granite outcrops in Calabria. The highest point is 2,015 m at Gran Sasso. The Apennine Mountains have had a considerable influence on the physical, social and economic geography of the region.

There are two main lowland regions. The Naples–Salerno lowlands are on the west coast. The Puglian lowlands are on the east coast. These lowlands are the most productive agricultural regions in the Mezzogiorno.

The coastal lowlands are mainly made up of poorly-drained mudflats and marshes, e.g. the Pontine Marshes south of Rome. In the past, these festered with mosquitoes. The marshes became a health hazard as well as being useless for farming due to poor drainage. Other natural hazards affecting the region are mudflows, avalanches, earthquakes, volcanoes, flooding and landslides.

The region is **tectonically active** – earthquakes and volcanoes are located at Vesuvius near Naples, at Mount Etna on Sicily and at Stromboli in the Lipari Islands close to Sicily. Stromboli is such an active volcano that it is called the 'Lighthouse of the Mediterranean'.

There are few rivers as much of the region contains permeable limestone. Rain and rivers quickly disappear underground through swallow holes. The few surface rivers present are relatively short and fast flowing. They are the Volturno, Sangro and Bradano rivers. There are limestone caves and caverns at Castellana in Puglia.

Fig. 5 Satellite map of Mezzogiorno

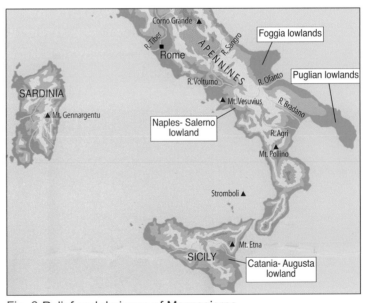

Fig. 6 Relief and drainage of Mezzogiorno

Fig. 7 A limestone cave in Castellana, Puglia

Fig. 8 A limestone plateau in Calabria

Soils

Like many peripheral regions, the Mezzogiorno has poor soils. The steep slopes of the Apennines make over half the land useless for agriculture.

The most fertile soils are found on the flanks of the volcanoes at Campania (Vesuvius) and Sicily (Mount Etna). The river valleys' soils contain deposits of alluvium on fertile floodplains. Excellent soils are found along the floodplains of the Volturno and Ofanto Rivers and along the Adriatic coast in the Foggia region where wheat and olives are grown.

The remainder of soils in the region are generally low quality and thin due to the fact that the parent rock of crystalline granite and limestone do not break down into fertile soil. They require irrigation and fertilisers.

Terra Rossa soils cover much of the landscape, especially in the far south. Terra Rossa soils form over weathered limestone and have a deep red colour. They are favoured by winegrowers. These soils are subject to soil erosion due to overgrazing and drought.

Fig. 9 Steep infertile slopes make farming difficult in the Mezzogiorno.

Human factors

The **physical** factors also interact with several **human** factors affecting the Mezzogiorno region. These two types of factors combine to influence the primary, secondary and tertiary activities that occur in the Mezzogiorno region.

Four main human factors affect the Mezzogiorno region. They are: (i) the historic system of land ownership, (ii) education and age of the workforce, (iii) transport and communications and (iv) government and EU policies. These human factors have created challenges to the development of the region. You will read about these in detail later in this chapter.

As with Ireland, funding and support schemes provided by the Italian government and the EU have all played a part in trying to overcome the problems faced by the Mezzogiorno region. Such was the level of poverty and decline in the Mezzogiorno that in 1950 the government set up the *Cassa Per Il Mezzogiorno* (South Italian Development Fund) in an effort to reduce the economic imbalance between north and south. Its aims were to stimulate the economic and social development of the region. It focused on agricultural, then industrial and infrastructural reform.

The EU allocates CAP, CFP and structural funds to the region. The Mezzogiorno has a GDP below 75% of the EU average. Therefore it is an EU Convergence region (see Chapter 15, page 303).

18.2 Economic activities and human processes in the Mezzogiorno

Primary activities in the Mezzogiorno

Agriculture

Like all peripheral regions, agricultural development in the Mezzogiorno faces several challenges. Despite the poor soils and mountainous terrain, agriculture is an important source of employment in the region.

Fig. 10 Agriculture is an important source of employment in the Mezzogiorno despite the poor relief.

Challenges facing the development of agriculture in the Mezzogiorno

1. Droughts affect the region in summer.
2. Underdeveloped water supplies.
3. Local markets with limited buying power due to widespread poverty in the region.
4. Underdeveloped transport network – the region is very isolated.
5. High transport costs due to long distances to EU markets.
6. Poorly-educated population.
7. Out-migration of young workers to the cities.
8. Underdeveloped farms due to ageing farmers unwilling to use new technology.
9. Unfair land ownership system.

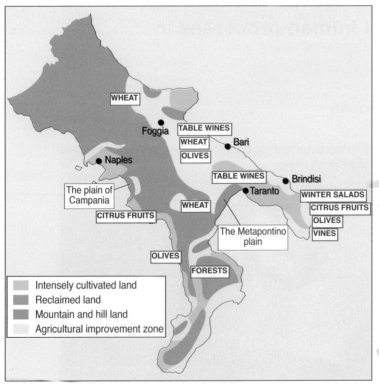

Fig. 11 Typical land use in the Mezzogiorno

Problems created by the land ownership system in the past

Absentee landlords owned vast estates known as *latifundia* and rented small plots of land called *minifundia* to tenant farmers. Landless labourers called *braccianti* worked the land. They were very poor.

The *latifundia* estates were underdeveloped as 75% of tenant farmers had no security on the land they farmed. Therefore tenants put little effort into improving soils or output as they might easily be evicted the following rental year. In some areas even fertile soils remained underdeveloped because of lack of interest. Therefore, the *latifundia* estates of the Mezzogiorno gave low yields yet took up huge areas of land (extensive farming). Sheep and goats were reared on these estates and low-quality wines were produced for local markets.

Seventy per cent of the *minifundia* were smaller than three hectares in size. Such small farms resulted in overcropped and overgrazed land. This meant that the soils were easily eroded and quickly became useless.

Solving the agricultural problems of the Mezzogiorno

1. The *Cassa* scheme broke up the *latifundia* and *minifundia* estates. This land was then redistributed to the former tenant farmers and to the *braccianti*. Farms averaged 5 to 50 hectares. These land ownership reforms increased the amount of land available for cultivation and helped the general development of the economy.

2. Investment in technology and mechanisation helped the economy to move away from subsistence farming to profitable commercial farming.

3. Co-operatives were set up to purchase produce in bulk for and from the farmers, raising their incomes.

4. Reclamation schemes took place at the marshes of the Metapontino area. Irrigation schemes were put in place using water from local rivers and wells. Improved transport due to the construction of the motorway known as the ***Autostrada del Sole*** now helps to quickly get the produce to market.

Fig. 12 Tenant farmers now own their land, increasing production.

5. Farmers were trained to farm their land more efficiently and to grow wheat and other high value **cash crops** such as peaches, strawberries and flowers. Productivity increased tenfold.

6. New villages and towns were built with important services.

Problems with the *Cassa* scheme: agriculture

1. Unfortunately, increased mechanisation has not provided many new jobs. There are still about 200,000 landless seasonally-employed day labourers/*braccianti*.

2. Some of the parcels of land are still too small (less than five hectares) to make economically viable farms.

3. In Sicily, the Mafia, which today is still influential, has hindered government efforts to implement reforms. Sicily continues to have extremely low per capita incomes and high unemployment levels. It still has many workers in the **hidden economy**.

4. Only 10% of the region was actually affected by land reform.

5. Overgrazing and drought are serious problems facing the area, as they lead to soil erosion, especially at times of flash flooding due to irregular rainstorms.

Modern farming in the Mezzogiorno

The agricultural reforms brought about by the *Cassa* scheme, EU Structural funds and the CAP have made farms much more productive. There has been a change from low-value crops to high-value produce such as vegetables and citrus fruits in the coastal lowlands. Incomes are higher than in the past.

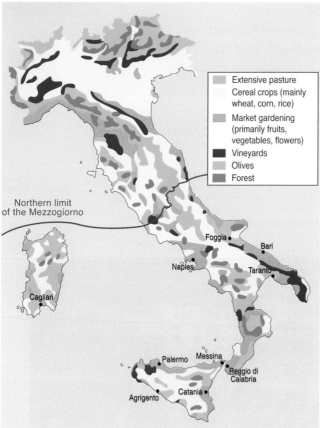

Legend:
- Extensive pasture
- Cereal crops (mainly wheat, corn, rice)
- Market gardening (primarily fruits, vegetables, flowers)
- Vineyards
- Olives
- Forest

Northern limit of the Mezzogiorno

Foggia
Bari
Naples
Taranto
Cagliari
Palermo · Messina
Reggio di Calabria
Agrigento · Catania

Fig. 13 Agricultural production in the Mezzogiorno

Fertilisers, reclamation and irrigation schemes have allowed farmland become more productive. There has been an increase in the irrigated cultivation of vegetables and salad crops, especially along the southern and eastern coasts. Wheat is also grown in the large reclaimed marsh area of the Metapontino in the Basilicata region.

Sheep and goats graze the higher mountains; vines are grown on lower slopes. Further south the aridity and poor soils mean farming is limited to olive growing, sheep-rearing and wine production (**viticulture**).

The Mediterranean climate and soil is perfect for growing olives. The olive tree is found only in the Mediterranean countries of Europe, Africa and the Middle East. It is a very drought-resistant tree but cannot tolerate frost or very wet conditions.

Olive production is increasing in Italy, making it the largest producer of olive oil in the world.

The Mediterranean climate provides warmth and sunshine, which promotes the early ripening of salad crops, olives, citrus fruits and vines. These are high-value crops sold throughout northern Europe. Several crop harvests are possible each season. Winter salads, vegetables and citrus fruits are grown in market gardens around the large industrial areas of Bari, Brindisi and Taranto and around Naples. The most intensive commercial farming occurs on the coastal lowlands.

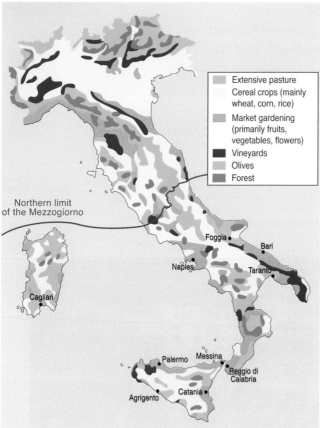

Fig. 14 Olive trees which grow well in the poor, thin soils of the Mezzogiorno

Forestry in the Mezzogiorno

The natural woodland of the region is mixed deciduous and evergreen hardwoods of cork oak, cypress, maritime pine and olive trees. These can tolerate the high temperatures and drought conditions. They also grow well in very poor, thin soils requiring few nutrients.

In the higher hills, beechwood, pine and silver fir trees grow. In Calabria chestnut trees are harvested.

Commercial forestry is not an important activity because of continuous deforestation. The climate does not allow the growth of dense stands of trees.

In areas where forests have been cleared, soil erosion has increased and all that grows is grass scrub called **maquis** and flowery plants known as **garrigue**.

370

The Metapontino region – A success story

This region is a coastal area beside the Ionian Sea. It has been transformed from a poor, backward, unproductive region to one of the most profitable agricultural areas in the Mezzogiorno.

- Before the *Cassa* scheme reforms, it produced wheat and olives. Its coastal plain was poorly-drained marsh infested by insects that carried malaria.

- Under the *Cassa* scheme, the marshes were drained, its rivers were harnessed for irrigation and land was redistributed amongst over 5,000 families. Farm sizes are on average six hectares.

- As a result, the region now produces high-value cash crops of vines, citrus fruits, flowers and salad crops. Transport links have been improved and farmers are now 10 times more productive than in the past.

Fig. 15 Map of the Metapontino region

Fishing

The Mediterranean is not as rich a fishing ground as the large open waters of the Atlantic coasts of Northern Spain.

The chief varieties fished are anchovy, tuna and sardines. Much of the catch is sold to the ever-growing tourist population in the resorts along the coast. Remaining fish is processed (fish meal), frozen or canned.

Most coastal towns have small fishing ports. The fishing industry is facing problems. The Mediterranean sea has a high salinity (saltiness) and is quite polluted which affects nutrient and oxygen levels and also limits the growth of plankton. It has a narrow continental shelf, hindering plankton growth. Increasing pollution is further damaging breeding grounds. The Adriatic coast of Italy suffers regular summer algae blooms due to the high concentration of nitrates from sewage in the water.

Fig. 16 A fishing town in the Mezzogiorno

Mineral and energy production in the Mezzogiorno

The Mezzogiorno region is limited in mineral wealth.

1. There is natural gas at Basilicata, Molise, Sicily and Calabria.
2. Oil, gas, sulfur and potash has been found near Siracusa in Sicily.
3. The permeable nature of the rock and the regular occurrence of summer drought has limited the region's potential for hydroelectric power.
4. The bulk of electricity produced in the Mezzogiorno is generated in thermal power stations using imported oil and local reserves of natural gas.
5. There are no coal deposits.

Secondary activities in the Mezzogiorno

Like many peripheral regions, wide-scale industrialisation never really occurred in the Mezzogiorno. It was bypassed by the industrial revolution due to physical and human factors.

Industry before 1950

Before 1950, the Mezzogiorno was unattractive for industry because it had:

1. An unskilled and uneducated workforce.
2. A poor local market with little money available for investment.
3. An underdeveloped agricultural sector.
4. A lack of resources.
5. A poor transport infrastructure due to the mountainous landscape.
6. A peripheral location – remote from large markets.
7. A high rate of emigration.

Fig. 17 Naples was selected as one of four industrial growth centres.

The *Cassa* scheme and industry

From 1965, the *Cassa* scheme promoted industry and tourism in the region. The scheme received funding of €2.3 billion between 1965 and 1970 to promote industrial location in the south by:

1. Providing finance to small and medium-sized industries; funding education and training schemes.
2. Giving grants and tax incentives to companies who relocated to the Mezzogiorno in an attempt to attract industry and others to decentralise operations from the north.
3. The selection of **growth centres** for investment for industrial development (see Fig. 19).
4. Offering cheaper land and greenfield sites for development and improving transport infrastructure.
5. Developing the natural gas deposits in Naples, Sicily and Calabria.

6. Enacting by-laws whereby 60% of all investment by public and semi-state enterprises has to take place in the region.

As you can see from Fig. 18 below, the industries that developed in these growth centres were the heavy industries of oil refining, petrochemicals and chemicals. These industries used local supplies of gas and imported oil. Steelworks and shipbuilding were established at coastal locations offering deep-water port facilities. Electronics and engineering companies chose to locate in areas with an educated workforce and a large market such as Naples.

Problems with *Cassa* scheme: industry

Despite all of these initiatives, the *Cassa* had limited success and the south still remains poor. The reasons are:

1. Most factories were capital-intensive, i.e. they provided little employment because machinery, not people, did most of the work. Some became known as 'cathedrals in the sun'.

2. Many factory workers were still involved in farming and took time off on a regular basis to undertake farm-work, lowering industrial productivity. Also, workers were not properly trained. As a result, many found the change to regular hours and factory work difficult to adjust to and absenteeism became a huge problem.

3. The larger industries failed to attract other industries to the region.

4. The creation of jobs in industry did not match the loss of jobs in agriculture.

5. Town planning and industrial developments were not integrated, i.e. new towns were built far away from industrial developments making it difficult for people to get to work.

6. There was an over-reliance on state investment rather than encouraging local initiative and self-reliance.

7. The privatisation of many former state-owned factories meant they are no longer required by law to locate in the Mezzogiorno and have moved north.

Industry today

The region continues to be economically disadvantaged compared to the north of Italy. The *Cassa* scheme tried to encourage social and economic development using a combination of grants, subsidies, loans and tax incentives designed to attract investment and jobs. The scheme created over three hundred thousand jobs in new industries but more than two million jobs were lost in agriculture.

The recent promotion of food processing factories has been more successful as they can link with local food production areas.

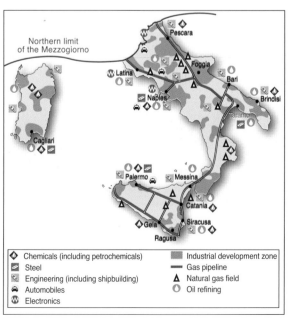

Fig. 18 Map of industrial centres

The four industrial centres selected by the *Cassa* for investment in the 1950s are still important growth centres today. These four centres were selected on the basis of their market, resources, energy supply, labour force, ports and infrastructure.

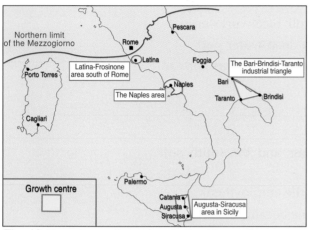

Fig. 19 Map of growth centres in the Mezzogiorno

1. **The Bari-Brindisi-Taranto industrial triangle**
   Steelworks, petrochemicals, electronics and engineering.

2. **The Naples area**
   Chemicals, oil refining, car manufacturing, shipbuilding.

3. **The Latina-Frosinone area south of Rome**
   Engineering, car manufacturing, oil refining, chemicals and steel.

4. **The Augusta-Siracusa area in Sicily**
   Oil refining, petrochemicals and engineering.

Many of Italy's engineering, steel and chemicals factories are run by state-owned companies, some of which are the largest in Europe. The government was in a position to decide where to invest and to promote the location of plants in the region. The most successful heavy industry is the state-owned steelmaker Finsider, which opened steelworks in Taranto in 1964. Taranto was chosen because it offered a deep-water port, good infrastructure, a local skilled workforce and proximity to an energy source. Most of the steel manufactured here leaves the Mezzogiorno region as not enough steel-using industries have been built here to use up this supply. EU structural funds have been used to address some problems. Between 1989 and 1993, more than €13 billion was invested in roads and education by the EU in the region.

Fig. 20 Capo Vaticano in Calabria

Tertiary activities in the Mezzogiorno

Tourism

Peripheral regions such as the Mezzogiorno are often dependent on tourism, based on the landscape and climate. The Mezzogiorno also has many historical and cultural attractions.

Tourism is growing but it is doing so at a slow pace and further investment in infrastructure and facilities is needed if the area is to compete with the north. Tourism is most successful along the coast but has yet had little impact inland.

Tourist attractions in the Mezzogiorno

1. The Mediterranean climate is hot, dry and sunny. Temperatures average 29°C in summer, attracting beach and city tourists. In winter, temperatures rarely fall below 11°C, although the mountain peaks are covered in snow, attracting skiers. This means that tourism can occur all year round, rather than only in summer.

2. The variety of unspoilt, natural and beautiful landscapes – such as the Bay of Naples, the Amalfi coast, sandy beaches and snow-peaked mountains, volcanoes such as Vesuvius and Stromboli – attract tourists throughout the year.

3. Tourists who like to visit ancient ruins can visit the historical cities of Pompeii and Naples. The art and architecture found in cities throughout the region is of great interest to tourists who enjoy visiting places of historical value.

4. The relaxed and family-oriented culture of Italians offers a child-friendly and stress-free holiday to tourists. Restaurants welcome children at all times.

5. The Adriatic coast of the Puglia region has a strong Greek and Roman influence, fine beaches and interesting historical sites.

6. Sicily is becoming increasingly popular as a tourist destination. It has been quite successful at promoting its history, beaches and festivals.

The *Cassa* scheme and tourism

The *Cassa* scheme recognised the many attractions of this invisible export. The Mezzogiorno has great potential as a tourist destination. Therefore, 15% of the *Cassa*'s funding was for tourism development.

The *Cassa* scheme developed more than 25 regions for tourism by providing grants to upgrade and build accommodation and provide facilities. It improved accessibility by building a motorway and an airport at Calabria. It also improved ferry connections to Sicily and Sardinia. Along with EU Structural funding these measures all helped to reduce the region's isolation.

Fig. 21 Ancient ruins in Pompeii, an important tourist attraction

The EU Structural funding for Italy has been concentrated on improving transport and communications infrastructure. Of the €12.3 billion to be invested under the 2007 - 2013 Italian National Development Plan, 85% of it is being allocated to the development of the Mezzogiorno region.

Transport and Communications

Several regions in the Mezzogiorno qualify for funding as EU convergence regions because their GDP is less than 75% of the EU average. These regions are Campania, Puglia, Calabria and Sicily. Transport and communications are key areas for improvement as these have been a human factor discouraging economic development in the region.

Most of the transport infrastructure in southern Italy was rebuilt after the destruction of the Second World War. However in the Mezzogiorno many important projects have failed to materialise, among them the subway system in Naples and more railways in the south to facilitate the movement of goods. The main transport problem is the mountainous landscape of narrow winding roads that are snow covered in winter or blocked by landslides triggered by heavy rain or earthquakes. The roads cannot carry the large trucks needed to carry goods in sufficient quantities to markets. Other problems include the need for costly bridges across valleys and tunnels through high mountains. The large distance from the wealthy, urban, northern Italian markets of Milan and Turin has led to long journey times and therefore high transport costs.

Under the *Vanoni* Plan (part of the *Cassa* Scheme) a massive investment in road infrastructure occurred. A major motorway project, the *Autostrada del Sole,* was constructed connecting Milan to Naples. At 754 km, it is the longest Italian autostrada and is considered the 'spinal cord' of the country's road network. It was designed to reduce transport times and costs for businesses and to encourage further economic development in the Mezzogiorno.

The Mezzogiorno ports of Naples, Taranto and Augusta are economically important export and import hubs for oil, gas and industrial goods. Italy is an important nation for container shipping in the Mediterranean.

More recent improvements involved the state-owned company Telecom Italia who provided telecommunications services in Italy until privatisation in the late 1990s. Telecom Italia is still the main internet and telecommunications service provider.

Fig. 22 Roads in the Mezzogiorno often require the construction of tunnels through mountains and bridges across valleys due to the region's relief.

Fig. 23 Port industry in Naples

The *Cassa* scheme and infrastructure development

Within the *Cassa* scheme, the **Vanoni Plan** was proposed. It aimed to encourage industrialists to invest in the Mezzogiorno. Therefore, between the 1960s and 1970s the *Cassa* and *Vanoni* plans invested in infrastructure to promote industrial development and tourism. They developed the *Autostrada del Sole*.

Human processes – People, language and religion

Italy has a population of 58 million. The Mezzogiorno has 40% of the land area but only 35% of the population. Twenty million people live in the region. Life expectancy is 76 years for men and 82 years for women.

It is a mainly Roman Catholic region with mature Protestant and Jewish communities. There is a growing Muslim community amongst the immigrant population.

The region is a melting pot of Greek, Roman and Arabic civilisations. Repeated settlement and conquests show their influences in food, architecture, culture and language. There are many dialects of Italian spoken. Recent immigration, especially from the countries of Serbia and Albania, has increased the number of ethnic groups, which are mainly Serbian-Italian.

Traditionally it has been an area of high birth rates and high emigration to North Italy, Switzerland, Germany and the USA. However, in recent years family size has declined due to the changing role of women in society, out-migration and the declining influence of the Catholic church.

The extended family unit is very important to Italians. It is still common for people to secure employment on a word-of-mouth basis or due to family connections.

Unfortunately, the region still faces a number of problems, including:

1. Illegal immigration and organised crime.
2. Corruption and financial scandals involving senior figures in the business and political world.
3. Out-migration.
4. An unemployment rate of over 20%.
5. Slow economic growth – the Mezzogiorno produces only 24% of Italian GDP.
6. Low incomes and low technical knowledge.
7. Increasing numbers of poor migrants into an economically depressed region.
8. Lower than average literacy rates.
9. A high dependency ratio (i.e. large numbers of children and elderly in the population).
10. An inadequate healthcare system.

Migration in Mezzogiorno

Mezzogiorno, unlike other peripheral regions, is an area of in-migration because of its location close to North Africa and the former Yugoslavia.

The main sources of this in-migration are Albania, Morocco, Romania, China and the Philippines. Together, these countries account for slightly more than 38% of residence permits granted.

Many immigrants have arrived from conflict zones in the independent states of Serbia and Croatia. This migration has not been welcomed by the Italian government. Some of these immigrants travel in dangerously overcrowded boats, many of which capsize in the choppy waters of the Adriatic. They are then rescued by the Italian coastguards. These immigrants are often deported.

Immigration has had an impact on the Adriatic Coast where thousands of immigrants land each year. For this reason, temporary and permanent shelters have been created.

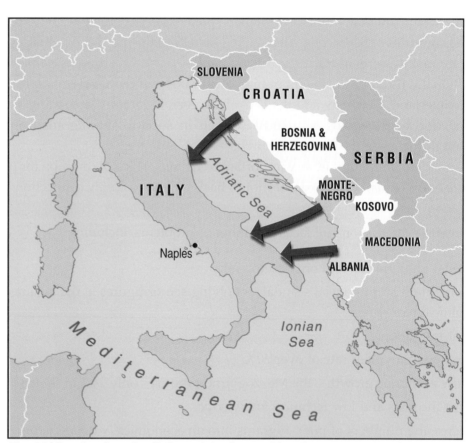

Fig. 24 Migration from the Balkan states is a problem for some regions in the Mezzogiorno.

Chapter Revision Questions

The Mezzogiorno

1. Using your atlas, draw a map of Italy. Locate and mark the following: two mountain ranges; two rivers; the neighbouring countries of Albania, Croatia, Serbia and Switzerland; the three regions of Italy. Focusing on the Mezzogiorno region, locate and mark six towns; three seas; Sicily, Sardinia and Corsica.

2. Using figure A, describe the main characteristics of a Mediterranean climate.

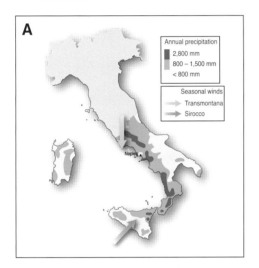

A

Annual precipitation
- 2,800 mm
- 800 – 1,500 mm
- < 800 mm

Seasonal winds
→ Transmontana
→ Sirocco

Naples

3. Look at the climograph below and then answer the following questions:
   (a) In the Mezzogiorno, which month is the wettest month?
   (b) What is the coldest month?
   (c) Calculate the annual range of temperature.

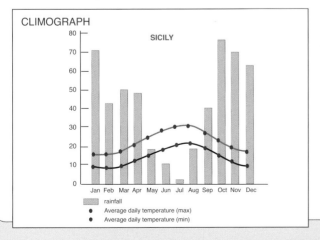

CLIMOGRAPH

SICILY

- rainfall
- Average daily temperature (max)
- Average daily temperature (min)

4. What factors make Mediterranean agriculture unique?

5. How do farmers in the Mezzogiorno deal with problems of drought and poor land?

6. Outline the advantages and disadvantages for the development of agriculture in the Mezzogiorno.

7. Explain the following terms: irrigation, *latifundia, Cassa Per Il Mezzogiorno.*

8. How has the *Cassa* scheme improved agriculture in the Mezzogiorno?

9. (i) Discuss the disadvantages of the Mezzogiorno for the location of industry.
   (ii) Describe efforts made by the *Cassa* to encourage industrial development in the region.

10. List the four regions selected as growth centres for development. Give two examples of industry established at each region. Explain why they set up in these regions.

11. Name and describe four advantages the Mezzogiorno has for the creation of a successful tourist industry.

12. Write a brief account of the role played by the *Cassa* to promote tourism.

13. Describe/outline the tourist attractions in the Mezzogiorno.

14. Explain the importance of the EU to the Mezzogiorno.

15. Describe the population characteristics of the Mezzogiorno.

16. Describe the cause and impact of immigration in the Mezzogiorno region.

OL Long Questions

17. **EUROPEAN REGIONS**
    With reference to any **one** European region, which you have studied, give and explain in detail **two** reasons why tourists might visit the region.

    LC Exam Paper

questions

18. **EUROPEAN REGIONS**

    Explain the importance of **one** of the primary industries listed below to the economy of **any** European region studied by you.
    - Agriculture
    - Forestry
    - Fishing
    - Mining/Energy

    LC Exam Paper

19. Describe the development of manufacturing industry in a European region (not in Ireland) which you have studied. Clearly state the name of the region in your answer.

20. Explain **two** advantages of tourism for the economy of a European region (not in Ireland) you have studied. Clearly state the name of the region in your answer.

21. Describe any **two** problems facing agriculture or manufacturing industry in a European region – not Ireland – of your choice.

HL Long Questions

22. **NON-IRISH EUROPEAN REGIONS**

    Examine the development of primary activities in **one** non-Irish European region of your choice.

    LC Exam Paper

23. Describe and explain any **two** factors that influence the development of secondary economic activities in a European region (not in Ireland) that you have studied.

24. Examine the factors that influence the development of one tertiary economic activity in a European region (not in Ireland) that you have studied.

25. Select a non-Irish European region and explain how (i) relief and (ii) climate have influenced the development of its agriculture.

    LC Sample Paper

26. Explain with reference to an example you have studied the characteristics of one peripheral/less developed region in Europe.

    LC Sample Paper

Chapter 19

The Dynamics of Regions (4)

– A European core and city region

At the end of this chapter you should be able to:

- Describe the Paris Basin as a core region.

- Name and describe the human and physical characteristics of the Paris Basin.

- Describe primary, secondary and tertiary activities in the Paris Basin.

- Describe the growth of the Paris city region.

- Explain how the growth of the Paris city region is being planned and controlled.

Contents

19.1   The Paris Basin – Physical and human characteristics, economic activities and human processes

19.2   The Paris city region

Questions

KEY THEME

The study of regions shows how economic, human and physical processes interact in a particular way. This can be demonstrated by examining two contrasting European regions. The boundaries and extent of city regions may change over time.

19.1 The Paris Basin
– physical and human characteristics, economic activities and human processes

Fig. 1 The Paris Basin
– location within France

A core economic region in Europe

The Paris Basin is a distinct core economic region because of its geology, soils, agricultural productivity, thriving economy and city of Paris. It has many natural and human advantages for settlement and industrial location (relief, climate, soils, accessibility, population). Over 21 million people live in the region.

The Paris Basin is low-lying and has a variety of fertile soils which have developed on the different rock types in the area. Each soil is associated with a particular type of agriculture, e.g. the clay soils of the Brie region support grasslands and dairy farming.

The Paris Basin is the largest manufacturing centre in France. The transport network of this region is well developed.

Paris is the capital city and centre of government and decision making in France.

The central part of the Paris Basin, the Île de France, contains 20% of the French population. The Paris Basin is a centre of in-migration and is culturally very mixed.

Physical factors/characteristics of the Paris Basin – relief, soils, drainage and climate

Relief and soils of the Paris Basin

The Paris Basin is a huge down-fold (**syncline**) in sedimentary rocks created over 400 million years ago. The rock layers have been folded so that in the east of the region the edges of the layers appear as ridges or scarps in the landscape. The biggest scarp is called the *Falaise de France*.

Each type of rock (clay, chalk, limestone, sand and gravel) has produced different soils which have influenced the type of farming across the basin. These different farming areas are known as *pays*.

In the centre of the basin, very fertile limon soil lies on the sands and gravels (see Chapter 14, page 268 – The North European Plain). This central region is extremely productive and is known as the **Île de France**. It is well known for its cereal production and is often called the Granary of France.

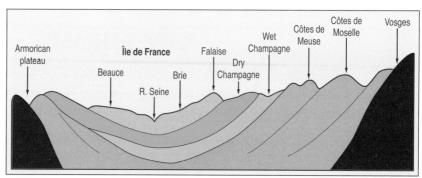

Fig. 2 Rock structure of the Paris Basin

Drainage

Three rivers flow across the region. The Seine and its tributaries (Yonne, Oise and Marne) flow north-west through Paris and enter the sea at Le Havre. The River Somme flows across the north of the Paris Basin and the River Loire flows west across the southern edge of the region.

Climate of the Paris Basin

The climate changes as you travel from west to east across the region.

In the west, the influence of the sea creates a **maritime** climate where summers are cool (16°C) and winters are mild (5°C), similar to Ireland's climate, with an average rainfall of 800 mm.

As the sea's influence does not reach the eastern part of the region, this area has a **continental** climate of hot summers (19°C) and cold winters (2°C). Rainfall is less than 700 mm with more rain in summer.

Between these two extremes (maritime and continental), there is a **transitional** type climate.

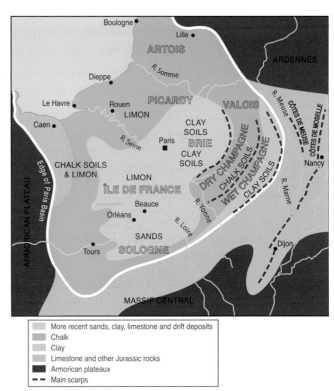

Fig. 3 Soils, rock types and drainage of the Paris Basin

Human factors/characteristics of the Paris Basin

The physical factors also interact with several human factors affecting the Paris Basin region. These two types of factors then combine to influence the primary, secondary and tertiary activities that occur in the Paris Basin region. Three main human factors affect the Paris Basin region. They are: population, transport infrastructure and government/EU policies.

Population characteristics of the Paris Basin region

The population of the Paris Basin region is over 21 million people. Of this about 10 million live in Paris city. As with all core economic regions, in-migration to the Paris Basin is common. The population is therefore culturally varied. This is because after the Second World War government schemes encouraged people to move to France to provide a labour force to rebuild the country. A large (1.3 million) immigrant population now lives in Paris. The immigrant population is composed of people from Spain, Portugal, China and Eastern Europe as well as former French colonies in north and west Africa. The majority of non nationals work in low-paid service industries and live in poorer high-rise buildings in the Parisian suburbs, e.g. La Courneuve. These poor suburbs lack many basic services and this has led to social unrest, violence and calls for stricter citizenship regulations. However the majority of people in the Paris city and Basin region are educated and wealthy. They provide both a labour force and a market for agricultural, industrial and service industries.

383

Transport infrastructure

Transport infrastructure is very well developed in the Paris Basin region. The city is the most important centre of the French motorway network. Paris has an extensive road network with over 2,000 km of roads. By road, Brussels can be reached in 3 hours, Frankfurt in 6 hours and Barcelona in 12 hours. The intercity rail network is efficient and fast. By train, London is now just two hours away, Brussels can be reached in just over one hour and Amsterdam in just over three hours. These connections make the Paris Basin an ideal location for industry and settlement.

Government / EU Policies

As with Ireland, funding and support schemes provided by the French government and the EU have all played a part in the development of the Paris Basin region and the country as a whole.

As the Paris Basin region is so densely populated, various policies were implemented to control the growth of the region and improve living and working conditions. The most important of these is the *Schema Directeur* of 1965 (see page 393). This was focused on the city of Paris and its immediate suburbs.

The EU allocates CAP and Structural funding which have added to the presence of excellent farmland making France the leading agricultural producer and exporter in Europe. France is a globally important core economic region generating the fifth largest GDP out of 144 countries in the world. Therefore, it receives less EU support than other EU countries. France is labelled as a Competitiveness and Employment region by the EU. France, and the Paris Basin in particular, has historically been an important producer of agricultural products.

Primary activities in the Paris Basin

Primary activities in the region have been influenced by physical and human factors, e.g. fertile soils, mild climate, low-lying relief, educated farmers and proximity to a rich urban market.

Agriculture

The fertile limon soil and the climate (maritime/continental) have allowed the production of wheat, barley and maize cereal crops throughout the region. Spring and early summer rainfall help crop growth and the long hours of summer sunshine are ideal for ripening crops. Close to the River Seine, alluvial soils also favour intensive commercial farming. The low-lying relief allowed the development of large (over 400 hectares), mechanised and highly productive farms.

The consumer market for farm produce is very big. Almost 21 million people live within the Paris Basin so farmers have easy access to a rich market, reducing their transportation costs.

Farm production in selected farming areas (*pays*) of the Paris Basin

In the Paris Basin a number of distinctive farming regions have developed based mainly on the soil rock types of the region. The relationship between soil and production is shown in the brief description of the *pays* below.

1. The Île de France

A low-lying, flat region covered with fertile limon soil. Most farms are very large (over 400 hectares) and produce wheat. Yields are the highest in France.

2. Beauce

This region is a limestone upland covered in limon soil. Farms here are large (e.g. 400 hectares) and mechanised. It is the main wheat-producing region. Sugar beet is also grown as a rotation crop.

3. Picardy and Artois (The Normandy region)

These two low-lying flat regions are also limon-covered and so specialise in cereal production such as barley and wheat. Sugar beet is also grown. On the coast, the climate is wetter due to the influence of the sea and soils become heavier. As a result, dairy farming is common.

4. Brie and Valois

In these two *pays*, clay soils occur. This soil produces good pasture land. Farmers here are dairy producers, famous for cheese (Brie cheese) and butter. Being so close to the urban area of Paris, they also supply fresh milk to the city.

Fig. 4 Cereal growing in the Paris Basin

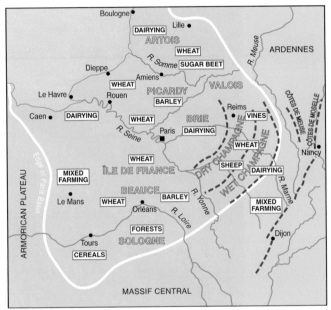

Fig. 5 Farming production in the *pays* of the Paris Basin

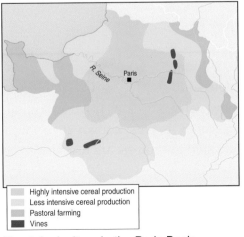

Fig. 6 Agriculture in the Paris Basin

5. The Champagne regions

These regions have clay-covered valleys between chalk ridges (**scarps**). The chalk ridges of the dry Champagne *pays* are infertile, well-drained soils but because they have a southerly aspect they are suitable for vines. It is here around the towns of Reims that the famous champagne wine is produced. These are the most northerly vineyards in Europe and as a result the wines from here have a unique taste. The production of wine is a specialist type of farming called **viticulture**.

Other scarp areas are less suited to vines; instead, they are used to rear sheep. Some farmers in less hilly areas improved their lands with fertilisers to produce cereals.

In the low-lying clay-covered wet Champagne *pays*, soils are better suited to pasture with dairying and beef cattle.

Fig. 7 The soils of the dry Champagne regions are suitable for vines.

6. Sologne

Here south of Paris, soils are infertile sands and gravels. Mixed farming is common. Low-value maize is grown as animal feed. The River Loire flows across this area and its valley is well known for vineyards and wine production. The region is well forested but forests are used for recreation rather than timber production.

Energy production in the Paris Basin

Energy consumption in the Paris Basin is high. Oil and gas are imported through the port of Le Havre where oil refining and petrochemical production form the basis of the economy.

Oil and natural gas

France has small oil reserves estimated at about 150 to 160 million barrels. They are located in the Paris Basin and in the Aquitaine region.

France is the third greatest oil-consuming country in Europe after Germany and Russia and tenth greatest in the world. It has to import 95% of its oil needs. The Paris Basin does not contain any gas reserves. Gas is brought to the Paris Basin by pipeline from gas wells in the Aquitaine Basin to the south and from the Netherlands.

Coal

Small reserves of coal existed in the north of the region, but in 2004 coal production was phased out completely. France now imports its coal needs.

Nuclear energy

France depends heavily on its nuclear-generating infrastructure for its electricity supply. Seventy-five per cent of French electricity is generated by nuclear power and its nuclear-generating capacity has increased by about ten per cent over the past decade. Ten of its thirty-seven power stations are located in and around the Paris Basin.

Secondary activities in the Paris Basin

Paris has more manufacturing industries than any other region in France. It is the economic centre of the country. The region is well served by air as it has two international airports.

The Paris Basin is attractive to industry for the following human and physical reasons:

1. Access/Communications

The River Seine runs through Paris for 13 km and its tributaries (e.g. Oise, Marne) provide a natural transport network across the region. Ports developed at Paris, Rouen and Le Havre enable raw materials and finished products to be transported easily. The low-lying relief enabled the development of the rail and road networks which are focused on Paris. The road network and TGV rail network is focused on Paris city making Paris very accessible and attractive to industry. This allows the manufacturing industry to easily distribute products and receive raw materials. The transportation network includes a metro and several airports as well as a direct rail link via the Channel Tunnel to London.

Fig. 8 The Eurostar travels to destinations in Britain, Germany, Holland, Belgium and Switzerland as well as destinations within France.

2. Population

The population of Paris city is over 10 million. The Paris Basin contains 21 million people which provides a skilled labour force. Many of these people are wealthy and provide a market for manufactured luxury goods. This attracts industry to the area.

3. Agricultural raw materials

There is a wide variety of agricultural products grown on the fertile soils, e.g. cereals, vines (wine), cattle (cheese, beef and milk), aromatic plants and seeds (lavendar). These provide raw materials for the food processing and cosmetics industry.

4. Government policy

The government has encouraged industrial development in the Paris Basin by designating eight **competitive clusters** in the region. These clusters bring industry, business and research together and aim to increase production in many new and existing industries. An example of one such cluster is **Cosmetic Valley**, a large area to the west of Paris. Covering six French *départements* in three regions, it includes 550 companies and six universities, accounting for 47,000 jobs and a turnover of €11 billion. Cosmetic Valley is a centre for specialist human resources in many businesses in the cosmetics industry from growing aromatic plants, creating and formulating products, manufacturing perfumes and cosmetics, control, testing and analysis laboratories, advertising and design and packaging.

Fig. 9 The Paris Basin is a major producer of cosmetics.

The factors listed on the previous page make Paris city a major industrial centre. It contains over 20% of the French workforce, and its factories produce a wide variety of goods.

Paris is known for such luxury products as expensive jewellery (Cartier), perfume (Yves Saint Laurent) and high-fashion (Chanel) clothing.

Car manufacturers such as Citroën have assembly plants in the city suburbs.

Fig. 10 Paris is famous for its high fashion industry.

The Central Business District (CBD) is in a section of the city, north of the river, where busy offices, small factories and fashionable shops are found. Specialist educational and academic printing and publishing activities are located close to the universities in the city, e.g. the world-famous Sorbonne university.

Heavy steel manufacturing (rail, steel and oil refining) is located further out from the city, along the river, close to the Canal St Denis. Food processing is a major industry in the region producing cheese (Brie), wine, bread and vegetables.

Tertiary activities in the Paris Basin

The Paris Basin is known for its tourism and transport services which are focused on the city of Paris. The city is easily accessible to all by air, road and rail links.

Tourism

Some 76 million people visit France each year. Of these the Paris Basin receives 45 million tourists annually. The city of Paris attracts nearly 30 million tourists annually and tourism accounts for just over 25% of employment in the city region. There is a wide variety of

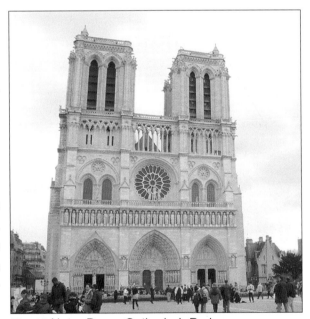

Fig. 11 Notre Dame Cathedral, Paris

natural and man-made tourist attractions in the Paris Basin. Tourists are attracted by the history, culture, scenery and fashion of the capital city – Paris – and its surrounding region. The scale of the tourism industry in the Paris Basin is immense.

More than half of all visitors to Paris (55%) are foreign. They are mainly from Britain, America, Germany, Italy and Japan. World economic recession has had an effect on lowering tourist numbers since 2009.

Fig. 12 **The glass pyramid at the entrance to the Louvre Museum**

Factors encouraging tourism in the Paris Basin:

1. It is easily accessible.

The city and region is easily accessible by air, rail and road. This accessibility encourages visitors to the region. It has 3 international airports (Charles de Gaulle, Orly and Paris Beauvais) and almost 400 different metro stations so travelling around the region is very easy. There is a high-speed land link to the UK via the Channel Tunnel as well as suburban and intercity rail services and the TGV. These transport methods make the city an important tourist destination for both domestic as well as overseas visitors.

2. There is a range of accommodation and tourist attractions.

Paris offers a wide range of accommodation catering for every category and age group of visitor, from the most luxurious to basic hotels, along with self-catering apartments, small guesthouses and hostels.

The attractions of the Paris Basin can be divided into those based in Paris city and those located in the surrounding Paris Basin region.

Fig. 13 **Disneyland Resort, Paris, is near Marne-la-Vallée – one of the 'new' towns.**

Attractions in Paris city

- The Disneyland Resort theme park is a short direct train journey from Paris city. It averages more than 12 million visitors each year. It is open all year round, offering a holiday for every age group.
- Paris city is known as the 'City of Light' due to its fame as a centre of education and ideas and its early adoption of street-lighting. It contains many famous and unusual buildings, museums, theatres and galleries, e.g. Notre Dame Cathedral, the Louvre museum, the Eiffel Tower, the Pompidou Centre and dance shows such as the Moulin Rouge. The Louvre attracts 5 million visitors each year and the Eiffel Tower attracts 5.5 million tourists.
- Paris is also one of the fashion capitals of the world. Many world famous clothing labels and perfume brands, e.g. Chanel, Christian Dior and Yves Saint Laurent, are manufactured in the region and sold in the exclusive fashion houses along the Boulevard Haussmann and the Champs Élysées.
- People also avail of the many guided tours on offer by boat along the Seine, by open-top bus or with walking tours in this very compact city.

Attractions in the Paris Basin region

- The medieval walled city of Caen and the castles of Orleans are popular attractions.

- The beaches of Normandy, which preserve the battle sites of World War II, attract many thousands of people who wish to remember relatives who died in the war and others who are interested in military history.

- Reims cathedral is known for its Gothic architecture and is the viticulture capital of the regions. Other vineyards in the Basin also attract many tourists.

- Versailles, a city outside Paris renowned for its royal chateau, is an important attraction for history, art and architecture enthusiasts. As with other attractions in this region it is linked by an excellent train route.

Fig. 14 Gothic architecture at Reims Cathedral

Communications and transport in the Paris Basin

Like all core economic regions Paris has an excellent **transport infrastructure.** The development of its transport network has been helped by the flat, low-lying or gently undulating landscape **(topography)** as well as the River Seine and its tributaries.

Paris has been building its transportation system for centuries and is continuously improving it.

Since the 1960s the transport network in the Paris Basin has been developed under a long-term master plan called the *Schéma Directeur.* Under this plan a large proportion of the growing Parisian population (over 1.5 million) was to be located in 5 new towns built about 25 km from the city. Providing transport infrastructure for this population affected the location and type of transport services that were built, e.g. rail, metro and road systems. As in Ireland the French transport network radiates out from its capital city. As a result the Paris Basin is highly accessible because it is a route focus.

Paris is a central hub of the national intercity rail network. Six major railway stations are connected to three networks: (i) The TGV serving four high-speed rail lines, (ii) the normal-speed Corail trains and (iii) the suburban rail lines (Transilien).

The most important transportation system in Paris is the **metro** with 400 stations connected by 214 km of rails.

Ninety per cent of the electrical energy used by metro, trains and tram transport is produced by nuclear and hydroelectric power plants so pollution levels in Paris are lower than the EU average.

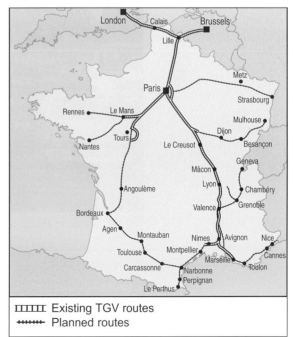

Fig. 15 TGV map of Paris and France

391

Paris is served by two major airports: Orly Airport, which is south of Paris, and the Paris-Charles de Gaulle Airport, near Roissy-en-France, which is one of the busiest in the world. It is the hub for the national airline, Air France. A third and much smaller airport, Beauvais Tillé Airport, located in the town of Beauvais, 70 km to the north of the city, is used by charter and low-cost airlines.

Paris is the focus of the French motorway network and is surrounded by three motorways: the Périphérique and two other motorways serving the inner and outer suburbs.

The city also has a bike-sharing system called Vélib. More than 20,000 public bicycles are available at 1,450 parking stations, and they can be rented for short and medium distances. As in Dublin this has proved to be very successful.

Due to the high population, traffic congestion is still a problem in the city. Reducing the number of cars is a priority. Bus lanes have been introduced but have not significantly reduced congestion as Parisians prefer to use their cars instead of the bus. However, introducing a congestion charge as has been done in London is not seen as a politically acceptable solution. The high-rise and compact international business quarter La Défense to the west of Paris has been successful in reducing congestion as it is completely pedestrianised and is well served by public transport.

Fig. 16 Traffic in Paris city centre

19.2 The Paris city region

The Paris city region

The sprawling city of Paris is home to 10 million people. Paris dominates all aspects of French economic and social life. It is a primate city. In this case, the next largest city is Marseilles. Paris is the centre of decision making, employment and cultural activities in France. Today, it contains 20% of the national workforce.

The growth of Paris has slowed the development of other towns and cities in the region. People and business prefer to be in or close to Paris.

As a result, urban planners have had to encourage the growth of the surrounding towns and control the growth of Paris. Dublin city and county planners are facing a similar challenge.

Reasons for the growth of Paris:

1. It is a bridging point across the River Seine.
2. It is in the centre of the fertile floodplain of the River Seine and limon-covered Paris Basin.
3. It is the focus of road and rail routes in France.
4. It is the capital city.
5. It is the focus of industrial development.
6. It has a long tradition in craftmaking and the textiles industry.
7. It is a centre of in-migration.

A policy to control the growth of Paris

The *Schéma Directeur*

In the late 1950s and early 1960s, Paris city suffered from overcrowding; traffic congestion; air, water, noise and visual pollution; inner-city decay and urban sprawl.

In 1965, city planners published a major plan called the *Schéma Directeur* to accommodate the expected population growth to 14 million by the twenty-first century.

Fig. 17 **Paris is a route focus**

Fig. 18 **La Défense - an important business centre in Paris**

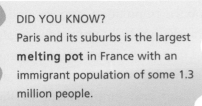
DID YOU KNOW?
Paris and its suburbs is the largest **melting pot** in France with an immigrant population of some 1.3 million people.

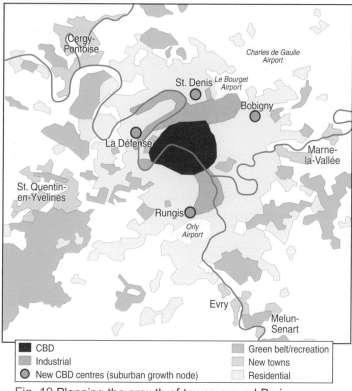

CBD
Industrial
New CBD centres (suburban growth node)
Green belt/recreation
New towns
Residential

Fig. 19 Planning the growth of towns around Paris

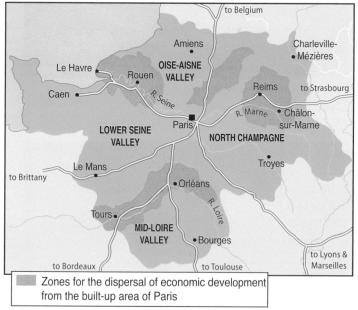

Zones for the dispersal of economic development from the built-up area of Paris

Fig. 20 Planning for the growth of Paris

Its aims are:

1. To control the rate of growth of the city.
2. To expand the metropolitan area to take in the entire Paris Basin, including cities which, although situated almost 200 km from Paris, are only an hour away by high-speed train.
3. To improve housing conditions in socially disadvantaged areas, reducing social unrest.
4. To improve and enlarge recreational space.
5. To improve the transport system.
6. To decentralise employment to the suburbs.

In order to realise these goals, the *Schéma Directeur* planners chose a policy that encouraged the growth of towns around Paris. As in Dublin, a new-town policy was implemented north and south of the River Seine. Five such new towns were built, which after a slow start grew quite quickly. The new towns include La Défense (business centre), the area around Roissy airport (*aéroville*), Marne-la-Vallée (near Disneyland Resort, Paris) and the Orsay-Saclay-Massy-Orly zone.

The most successful is St. Quentin-en-Yvelines, 30 km south-west of Paris with a population of more than 150,000 and the creation of 40,000 new jobs. The area around Disneyland Resort, Paris at Marne-la-Vallée has also succeeded in accommodating the decentralisation of Paris. Overall, industry, housing and trade have improved and are being carefully monitored to stop urban sprawl and environmental pollution in the Paris region and hinterland.

Since it was implemented the *Schéma* has been revised regularly to adapt to the changing needs of modern society. The most recent update is the *Schéma Directeur de la Region Ile-de-France* (SDRIF), which was adopted in 2008. It provides planning directives for the region up to 2030. This policy aims to control urban growth, population density and the use of space in the region. It recommends social, economic, zoning and transport improvements along with strict preservation laws on rural and natural environments. It looks at housing, infrastructure, community services, recreation and employment in the city and suburbs while carefully maintaining and preserving the international reputation of the Paris city region.

Chapter Revision Questions

The Paris Basin

1. Using your atlas draw a map of France. Locate and mark in the following: the Pyrenees; the French Alps; neighbouring countries of Belgium and Spain; the Rivers Seine, Loire, Rhone, Saône and Loire; the Paris Basin region; Paris, Lyons, Tours, Lille, Marseilles, La Harve and Calais.

2. Briefly describe the rock structure and soils of the Paris Basin.

3. Describe and account for the differences in climate across the Paris Basin.

4. Draw a sketch map of the Paris Basin. Mark in and label the different soils and farming regions/*pays*.

5. Pick any two farming areas in the Paris Basin and briefly describe the soil type, rock type and farm produce.

6. What forms of energy are used in the Paris Basin? Briefly discuss the source of these energy resources.

7. List three reasons why the Paris Basin is attractive to industry.

8. Name and describe three attractions the Paris region offers to tourists.

9. Explain in detail why Paris is a core economic region.

Paris city region

10. What factors have led to the growth of the Paris city region?

11. What is the *Schéma Directeur*? Why was it needed?

12. What are the aims of the *Schéma Directeur*?

13. Name three new towns built around the edge of Paris.

14. Discuss the operation of planning strategies to control urban growth in a city you have studied.

HL Long Questions

15. 'The boundaries of city regions have changed over time.'

    Discuss this statement with reference to one example you have studied.

    LC Exam Paper

16. Explain with reference to one example the causes and consequences of changes in the boundaries of a region over time.

    LC Sample Paper

The Paris Basin

OL Long Questions

17. **EUROPEAN REGIONS**

    With reference to any **one** European region, which you have studied, give and explain in detail **two** reasons why tourists might visit the region.

    LC Exam Paper

18. **EUROPEAN REGIONS**

    Explain the importance of **one** of the primary industries listed below to the economy of **any** European region studied by you.
    - Agriculture
    - Forestry
    - Fishing
    - Mining/Energy

    LC Exam Paper

HL Long Questions

19. Examine the growth of an urban area in a European region – not Ireland – of your choice.

20. **NON-IRISH EUROPEAN REGIONS**

    Examine the development of primary activities in **one** non-Irish European region of your choice.

    LC Exam Paper

21. Examine the factors that influence the development of **one** tertiary economic activity in a European region (not in Ireland) that you have studied.

22. Describe and explain any **two** factors that influence the development of secondary economic activities in a European region (not in Ireland) that you have studied.

23. Examine how the distribution of population, in a European region (not Ireland) that you have studied, has been influenced by the region's level of economic development.

24. Examine the factors that influence the development of **one** economic activity in a European region (not Ireland) that you have studied.

395

Chapter 20
Brazil –
A Non-European
Region

At the end of this chapter you should be able to:

- Describe the physical characteristics of Brazil.

- Describe the primary, secondary and tertiary activities of Brazil.

- Describe the differences between urban and rural Brazil.

- Describe Brazil's population referring to migration, colonialism and economic development.

- Give a brief account of different cultures within Brazil.

- Describe the reasons for, and consequences, of the deforestation of the tropical rainforest in Brazil.

Contents

20.1   Physical characteristics and economic activities

20.2   Population, migration and urbanisation in Brazil

20.3   Cultural regions in Brazil

20.4   Deforestation of the tropical rainforests in Brazil –
        a challenge for the future

        Questions

KEY THEME

The study of regions shows how economic, human and physical processes interact in a particular area.

20.1 Physical characteristics and economic activities

Background information

Brazil is famous for its football, its carnivals and its Amazonian rainforests, but there is much more to this enormous country. It is the fifth-largest country in the world after the Russian Federation, Canada, the USA and China. Brazil is a country of young people; almost two thirds of its people are under 30 years of age. They are mostly descended from migrants who came to Brazil from other parts of the world, especially Europe and Africa. Its population is about 193 million.

Brazil is a country of stark inequality. Its wealth is very unevenly distributed – 60% of its population live in poverty.

A United Nations Development Programme (UNDP) report stated that the richest 10% of Brazilians are 85 times wealthier than the poorest 10%.

The average income per capita in 2009 was €2,237 but this is not a true reflection of income as over 40 million Brazilians live on less than €1 per day.

South America was colonised by Portuguese and Spanish explorers. In 1494, the Treaty of Tordesillas divided the continent into Spanish-speaking and Portuguese-speaking areas. Brazil fell into the Portuguese-speaking zone. Therefore, the official language of Brazil is Portuguese. In the 1800s, many thousands of Europeans settled in Brazil.

Brazil is a republic. It has an elected president who is head of state and head of government.

Like the US, Brazil is divided into states. It has 26 states and one federal district where the capital city of Brasilia is situated. The central government is located in this city.

Each state has its own government. Within each state there are town councils that deal with decisions at local level.

Physical characteristics – relief, drainage, climate and soils

Relief

The most prominent geographical features of Brazil are the Brazilian Highlands (also known as the Brazilian Plateau) and the basin of the Amazon River.

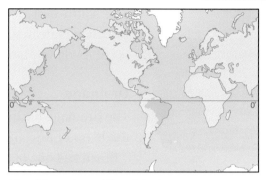

Fig. 1 Location of Brazil in the world

At its widest, Brazil is 4,319 km wide – almost the distance from London to New York.

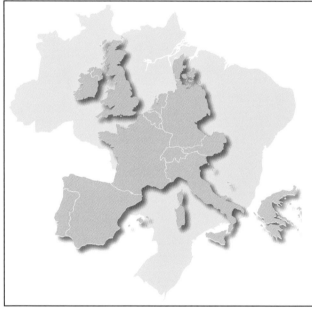

Fig. 2 Relative sizes of Brazil and Europe

Brazilian plateau/highlands
Central plains and lowlands
Guiana highlands

Fig. 3 Relief regions of Brazil

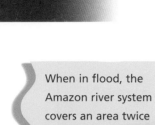

The south east of Brazil is mountainous (up to 3,000 m) and forms part of the Brazilian Plateau which makes up 60% of the country. The rest of the country is made up of lowland plains.

Drainage

The drainage basin of the Amazon occupies almost one third of Brazil. The basin is made up of lowlands, swamps, floodplains and rainforests.

Brazil has one of the largest river systems in the world. It has eight major drainage basins. The Amazon-Tocantins-Araguaia basins in the north drain over 56% of the country.

Other major rivers in Brazil are the Rio de la Plata and the São Francisco.

> When in flood, the Amazon river system covers an area twice the size of Ireland to a depth of 10 m.

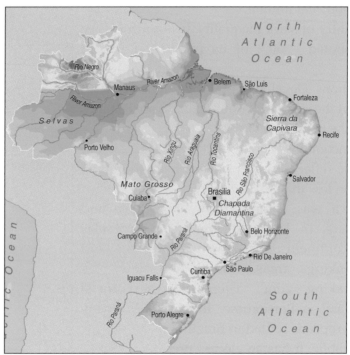

Fig. 4 Drainage of Brazil

Climate of Brazil

Brazil's climate is strongly influenced by its latitude, size and wide variation in relief. Brazil lies between 5°N and 32°S of the equator. Because it is such a large country, Brazil has five climatic zones that can be placed into three main groups: **equatorial**, **tropical** and **semi-arid**. Only the northern and western regions of Brazil are equatorial; 90% of the country experiences a tropical climate. Due to local variations in relief and complex wind patterns, the north-east of Brazil around Belem experiences a semi-arid climate. At the country's southern extreme, there have been frosts south of the Tropic of Capricorn during the winter (June – August). In some years there have been snowfalls on the mountainous areas of the Brazilian highlands in Paraná State.

The equatorial climate

This climate occurs in the lowland Amazon Basin region between 5°N and 5°S of the equator. The sun is high overhead all year round and this causes intense heating of the land. Daytime temperatures reach 32°C with night-time temperatures of 22°C. The intense heating of the land causes the air above it to heat up. As the moist hot air rises it cools and water vapour condenses to form **convectional rain**. This type of rain falls daily and leads to the high annual precipitation amounts of over 2, 000 mm. Rainfall amounts reach as high as 3,000 mm per year in parts of the western Amazon and close to Belém. The Amazon region is notoriously humid. Evaporation rates are high and humidity can reach 90%. There are no clear seasons in equatorial Brazil, just slight variations in the cloud cover with the summer (December – April) being cloudier and slightly wetter.

> The distance between the equator and the Tropic of Capricorn is about 3,000 km.

The tropical climate

Most of Brazil experiences a tropical climate with monthly average temperatures above 18°C. Because Brazil is such a large country the tropical climate shows variations in rainfall due to changes in latitude. Most of the centre-west of Brazil has 1,500 to 2,000 mm of rain per year with a pronounced dry season (May – November) while the south and most of the Atlantic coast as far as Salvador and Bahia have similar amounts of rainfall but without a distinct dry season.

The tropical climate is warm and sunny, but the influence of the Brazilian highlands causes temperatures to vary between 15°C to 30°C. Along the coastline south of Recife the mountains trigger **relief rain** from the south-east trade winds. Coastal cities such as Rio de Janeiro, Recife and Salvador have average temperatures ranging from 23°C to 27°C. These warm temperatures are moderated by the constant south-east trade winds.

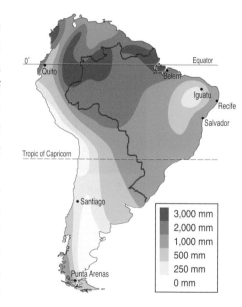

Fig. 5 Rainfall in Brazil

The semi-arid climate

The north-east is the driest part of the country. The semi-arid climate of this region is caused by a complex meeting of four different air masses in the area (known as the System of Disturbed Currents) which leads to irregular rains and **drought** in the state of Paraiba. This area has the lowest annual rainfall recorded in Brazil (278 mm per year). Rainfall is scarce and there are severe droughts occurring in cycles averaging seven years. The north-east region is also the hottest part of Brazil. Between May and November temperatures of more than 38°C have been recorded.

When rain does fall, the *caatinga,* a region of semi-desert vegetation used primarily for low-density ranching, turns green.

Soils

One important type of soil in Brazil is the **Terra Rossa** which occurs in the state of São Paulo. This soil is dark red and contains plenty of humus. It is an excellent soil in which to grow coffee trees. In the Amazon Basin, the most fertile **alluvial** soils occur where the rivers flood regularly and leave nutrient-rich alluvium over large stretches of flood plain. Under the tropical rainforest is the **latosol**. This soil is closely related to the forest vegetation. It becomes infertile **laterite** once deforestation occurs due to the leaching caused by heavy rainfall.

Fig. 6 Trees with smooth thin barks

Natural vegetation

Tropical rainforest is the main vegetation in Brazil covering over 60% of the country. Many of the trees have straight trunks that don't branch until a height of 30 m or more forming a thick shady canopy. The majority of the trees have smooth, thin bark because they do not need protection from water loss or freezing temperatures. It also makes it difficult for plant parasites to grip the trunks. Although the majority of the Amazon rainforest within Brazil is still well preserved, more than 90% of the Atlantic coast forest has been destroyed by human activity.

Tropical rainforest
Tropical semideciduous forest
Paraná pine forest
Palm forest
Thorny scrub
Savanna
Grassland
Mangrove and/or dune vegetation
Wetlands

Fig. 7 Natural vegetation

Savanna/*Cerrado* is grassland containing trees and shrubs. It is found in central Brazil on the plateau region. This region has a dry season (November - January) and plants adapt by having very thick bark to conserve water. The *cerrado* is a biologically rich land that is being threatened by soya and corn farming.

Thorny scrub/*Caatinga:* The *Caatinga* vegetation is stunted, thorny trees. This region is also known as the 'white forest' due to the pale grey appearance of the trees. It is found in north-east Brazil. The *Caatinga* region has extremely hot, almost desert conditions. Soil temperatures can reach 60°C. During the dry season (November - January) trees lose their leaves and their roots grow up through the soil surface to catch moisture before it evaporates in the dry conditions.

Primary activities in Brazil

Brazil has many resources. It is a major producer of agricultural, mineral and timber products. Its rank in the production and export of some primary products is shown in Fig. 8.

Agriculture

Agriculture and agribusiness is worth about 25% of Brazil's GDP; farmland occupies over 60 million hectares. In 2010, agriculture accounted for 36% of all exports. The EU buys roughly 42% of Brazil's agricultural exports of coffee, cattle, sugar cane, crops and wood.

Brazilian farmers are encouraged to use modern techniques and the government invests millions in research and development of new farming methods and crops. In some areas sophisticated crop rotation is now being used involving a six-year cycle of corn, eucalyptus, soya and pasture to preserve soil fertility and keep yields high. This also reduces farmers' dependence on any one crop.

1st	It is the world leader for the production and export of **coffee, beef, sugar** and **oranges.**
2nd	It is ranked second in the world for the production of **soya beans**.
3rd	It is ranked third in the world for the production of **poultry.**
6th	It is ranked sixth in the world for **pork** and **milk** production.

Fig. 8 Brazil and agriculture

Crop production

About 7% of the farm land in Brazil is arable.

Corn, soya and sugar cane are the main crops. In 2010 over 53 million tonnes of corn were grown. Brazil and Argentina account for half of the global production of **soya beans**. To improve production, Brazilian scientists have developed soya plants that can grow in the hot conditions of the savanna regions in the interior of Brazil. These areas were once difficult to farm because of the climate and acidic soils. Soya bean production soared once these resistant varieties were identified and developed. Soya is an important **cash crop** for Brazil. In 2010, more than 62 million tonnes of soya was produced on lands stretching across 22 million hectares, an area approximately the size of Britain. Soya farms are highly mechanised and employ only one person for every 400 acres.

The increase in soya bean production is partly due to the need for non-genetically modified soya in Europe and the demands for safe animal food by European farmers following BSE scares. However, soya bean production is linked to increased deforestation in the Amazon as land is cleared for soya plantations.

Brazil contains a large area (547 million hectares) of *cerrado* – the savanna grassland that is slowly being converted to the production of grain, oil seed crops and beef cattle.

The tropical climate over much of Brazil has limited wheat production to the southern states where temperatures are cooler. Because of this, Brazil imported over 10 million tonnes of wheat in 2010.

Sugar cane production employs over 900,000 people. Fifty per cent of the sugar cane is used to produce a biofuel called **ethanol** which is used as an alternative to petrol. Ninety per cent of the sugar cane is grown in south-central Brazil.

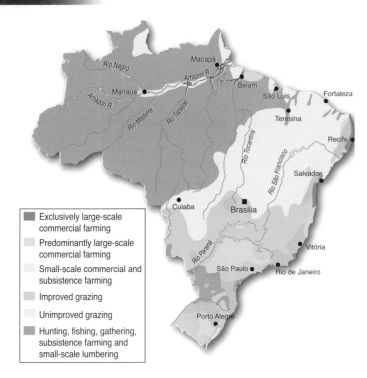

Exclusively large-scale commercial farming

Predominantly large-scale commercial farming

Small-scale commercial and subsistence farming

Improved grazing

Unimproved grazing

Hunting, fishing, gathering, subsistence farming and small-scale lumbering

Fig. 9 Agricultural land use in Brazil

Fig. 10 Soya bean transportation and storage in Brazil

Coffee production

Brazil is the world's largest and most powerful producer of coffee. It holds over 32% of the world market. Coffee production is economically and socially very important to the country. Per capita consumption of coffee is 4.2 kg per year. The coffee industry provides an income for more than 10 million people. Production in 2010 was worth over €9 billion to the economy. Production is controlled by several multinational companies, e.g. Nestle, Kraft and Douwe Egbert. It is a labour

Fig. 11 Coffee-producing areas of Brazil

intensive industry as the delicate coffee plants require constant attention and the drying process is only partly automated in many regions.

The major coffee-producing areas (see Fig. 11) are found along the south-east coast with Minas Gerais growing 46% of all Brazilian coffee. The state of Espirito Santo is the next largest producer, growing 25% of Brazilian coffee. A wide variety of coffee beans are grown with the Arabica bean the most common. Like the wine-producing regions of France each coffee-growing region in Brazil grows coffee beans with a distinctive flavour.

The influence of physical factors (soils, relief and climate) on the coffee industry in Brazil is very important as coffee plants require specific growing conditions. Brazil has all the conditions necessary for coffee plants to grow strongly.

Growing conditions required for coffee plants
1. A tropical climate with temperatures ranging from 15°C to 24°C.
2. Absence of frost.
3. Deep well-drained soils.
4. Humid conditions with plenty of rain (1,500 mm – 2,000 mm per year).
5. High altitude (over 700 m to reduce pest attack).

The rainfall, humidity and temperature conditions associated with the tropical climate encourage coffee growth. Coffee trees flower between September and November. Humidity is needed during this period to ensure coffee buds will develop properly. The buds turn into beans that growers will start harvesting in April. Any frost or dry conditions during the budding season can seriously damage the annual crop.

Large parts of Brazil have deep well-drained Terra Rossa soils and the Brazilian highlands provide the correct altitude for plants.

As previously mentioned, coffee plants need a tropical climate, well-drained soils and an altitude above 700 m. These requirements make a large part of the state of western Bahia also suitable for coffee production. Here the climate is ideal, the soils are moderately sandy and the altitude over most of the area is above 700 m. In western Bahia coffee growers are converting large areas of woody grassland (savanna/*cerrado*) into coffee plantations. To do this the *cerrado* vegetation is knocked down by pulling a heavy chain or cable between two tractors across the land. Woodcutters saw, remove and sell the larger wood to the soya bean processing mills in the area to use as fuel. The remaining brushwood is burned. The land is then ploughed, fertilised and planted with coffee trees. There are environmental concerns about the loss of unique plants and animals in this fragile ecosystem due to clearance for coffee growing.

Fig. 12 Drying coffee beans in the sun is slow and labour intensive.

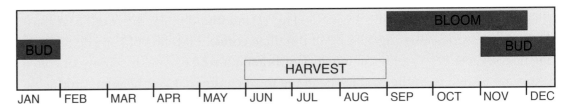
Fig. 13 Coffee crop calendar for most of south-central Brazil

Cattle production

The scale of cattle production is quite high compared to Ireland. One thousand hectares and six hundred cows are needed to make a reasonable living. Meadows and pastures occupy about 19% of the country. Clearing rainforest for beef production is controversial and has led to demands by environmentally-conscious consumers to have beef produced on land that has not been taken from rainforests.

SIX QUICK FACTS ON CATTLE PRODUCTION IN BRAZIL

1. Brazil has over 165 million cattle – almost one for each person in the country.
2. Over 35 million cattle are slaughtered each year.
3. Brazilians consume on average 38 kg of beef per person each year. Brazil is ranked third in beef consumption, behind Argentina and Australia.
4. Brazil has the world's largest commercial cattle herd.
5. Ten per cent of beef is exported and this figure is increasing.
6. Brazil is the world's largest exporter of beef.

Forestry

Forestry is an important economic activity in Brazil. If the rainforest of Brazil was a country it would be the size of the seventh largest country in the world. The main trees harvested are tropical hardwoods, e.g. teak, mahogany. These are high-value hardwoods where a single tree may be worth €15,000. Timber production contributes 3.5% to Brazil's GDP and provides 6 million direct and indirect jobs. It is estimated that the total area of planted and native forest is 4.7 million km².

Just under 2% of the total forest cover is man-made forest of mainly pine and eucalyptus trees. These forests are concentrated in the south of the country where they are used in the cellulose and paper industry.

In 2010 the value of exported timber from Brazil was €2 billion, with 30% of these exports going to EU member states. Other major markets include the USA and China. Within Brazil, the state of São Paulo is the largest consumer of timber products.

More than 85% of timber production from natural forests comes from the Amazon region, where over 3,000 logging companies are in operation. In Amazonia legal timber is produced from native forest areas or from managed forests. However, it is estimated that as much as 80% of the total timber production in the Amazon is from illegally cleared forest.

Recent reforms are aimed at improving this situation. New regulations on forest management have been driven by global concern over deforestation in the Amazon. However, it is difficult to enforce these reforms and much of the forest is still illegally burned and cleared by cattle ranchers and soya growers.

Mining

Brazil has a wide range of minerals such as diamonds, iron ore, copper, gold, oil, bauxite, zinc, tin, nickel, platinum and uranium. Many of these are exported in their raw state.

Brazil has 1.8% of world reserves of copper. The only producer of copper concentrate in Brazil is located in the state of Bahia, producing almost a quarter of a million tonnes of copper concentrate.

Scrap copper is also processed along with almost half a million tonnes of copper imported from Chile and Peru.

Copper is exported to Argentina (33%) and the United States (28%). This is worth over €84 million.

Domestic consumption of metallic copper is expected to increase as a result of investments being made in the energy, automobile and telecommunication sectors.

Fig. 14 Open-cast mining in Belo Horizonte

Oil

Two large oil fields have been discovered 250 km off the coast of Rio De Janerio. They are the Tupi field and the huge Sugar Loaf field. The Tupi field makes Brazil the tenth largest producer of oil in the world. The Sugar Loaf field is the fourth largest oil field in the world, equivalent to 40% of all oil ever discovered in Brazil. It is a deep water field and not yet in production. The country now has reserves of over 700 million barrels. These will reduce the country's reliance on imported crude oil and improve the country's balance of payments. For example if Brazil trades a barrel of oil at €86 per barrel it will add up to €3.4 trillion to its national wealth.

Secondary activities in Brazil

Brazil is a Newly Industrialised Country (**NIC**). This means that its economy is undergoing rapid industrialisation, increased foreign direct investment and increased global trade. Manufacturing is a growth industry in Brazil. The percentage employed in the manufacturing industry in Brazil is increasing by almost 3% per year, especially in the south-eastern state of São Paulo.

The main industrial products ranked by the value of sales are diesel oil, processed iron ore and cars. The south-east region produces over €384 billion worth of manufactured products each year, 60.7% of total sales. Other manufactured products include machinery, processed food, electronic equipment and textiles. Brazil is the world's fourth largest producer of commercial aircraft.

Modern manufacturing in Brazil is the result of human factors, mainly government policies, that have combined with its physical factors such as resources, soils and climate.

Human factors leading to the development of industry in Brazil

Government policy after the Second World War

Industrial development grew rapidly after the Second World War when shortages of imported goods forced Brazil to consider making its own. A huge industrial investment programme for self-sufficiency, the **Import Substitution Industrialisation scheme** (ISI), was established using World Bank loans. Many large multinational companies, e.g. Shell and Ford Motors, set up factories in the country.

Fig. 15 Port industry - a focus of investment

As well as being self-sufficient, the government also wanted to protect its manufacturers from outside competition. Tariffs and bans were placed on imported products. This made foreign goods too expensive to buy and there was little trade with other countries.

Five events have occurred since the 1970s that have opened up Brazil's economy to the world and greatly increased the numbers of countries with which it trades: (i) the oil crisis, (ii) the debt crisis, (iii) the formation of Mercosur, (iv) the Real Plan and (v) an International Monetary Fund (IMF) Rescue Package.

These events have had a major impact on manufacturing in Brazil. They have led to the strong position this NIC is in today.

(i) 1970s oil crisis

In the 1970s economic problems began to appear due to Brazil's dependence on imported oil. When the oil crisis of 1973 triggered a huge rise in worldwide oil prices, Brazil could not afford to pay for the oil it needed. In order to reduce oil imports a government scheme called the **National Ethanol Programme** was launched to replace cars using fossil fuels with cars that used ethanol (a **biofuel**) produced from sugar cane. Brazilian car manufacturers developed cars that could run on a mix of ethanol and petrol or on ethanol alone. This reduced petroleum imports.

(ii) 1980s – Brazilian debt crisis

In the 1980s the financial crisis continued with monthly inflation rates running at over 50%. Brazilian manufacturing collapsed. The government managed to bring the debt and economy under control using a series of **Structural Adjustment Programmes (SAPs)** introduced by the World Bank and IMF. SAPs encouraged the production and export of cash crops such as soya as a means of paying off Brazil's debt.

(iii) 1990s – Formation of Mercosur

In 1991 the Southern Common market, **Mercosur**, was establised. This allowed free trade between South American countries and provided a large market for Brazilian manufactured goods. Trade then began to increase with other South American countries.

(iv) The Real Plan

In 1994 the government implemented the **Real Plan** to reduce inflation and increase the value of the Brazilian currency. A new currency, the Real (pronounced ray-al), was introduced and was very successful. Brazil's economic position recovered and industrial production increased. Production of aircraft, cars, trucks, tractors, machinery, food processing, electrical and electronic equipment and textiles began to rise.

(v) 2000s – IMF Rescue Package

At the start of the twenty-first century economic problems reoccurred. Brazil received an **IMF** rescue package of €23 billion. Economic growth resumed and Brazil's central bank paid back this IMF loan in 2005, a year ahead of schedule. The most recent global financial crisis hit Brazil in September 2008 but Brazil only experienced six months of recession and was one of the first international markets to begin a recovery. The Brazilian economy grew by 5% in 2010. The unemployment rate in 2010 was 6.9% .

Fig. 16 São Paulo is an important business centre.

Location of industry in Brazil

The industrialised economic hub of Brazil is found along the south-east coast around the cities of Rio de Janeiro, São Paulo and Belo Horizonte. Many multinational companies have located their head offices in these cities. These cities contain a labour force, ports and raw materials and they provide a large market. The most successful manufacturing industries are cars, steel, petrochemicals, engineering and cement. Brazil is the world's third largest producer of commercial aircraft. Just over 40% of the country's population (79 million) is concentrated in the south-east of Brazil. The area is rich in minerals and its manufacturing industries are the most advanced in the country.

Physical factors affecting location of manufacturing in Brazil

Most manufacturing is located in the south-eastern states of Brazil because of a combination of physical factors listed below.

1. Raw materials such as limestone and iron ore are found nearby in the Minas Gerais region. In addition, most ironworks and steelworks are here.
2. Oil and gas fields have been discovered and exploited offshore from Rio de Janeiro.
3. The south-east coastline has many sheltered deep water harbours which are now used for the import and export of raw materials and finished goods by ship.
4. Brazil has huge supplies of cheap hydroelectric power (HEP), 90% of which is produced in the Amazon Basin. Nearly €69 billion has been spent on several hundred power projects, most under the **Advança Brazil** scheme. This has encouraged the location of energy intensive steel industries close to their raw materials in the south east.

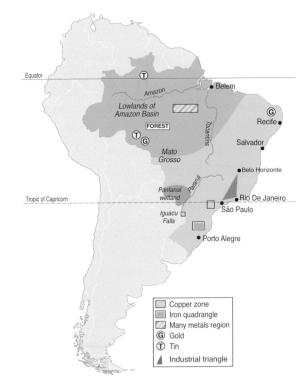

Fig. 17 The location of raw materials and natural resources in Brazil.

Car manufacturing in Brazil

- Car manufacturing is a growth industry in Brazil. In 2010 car sales increased by 10% and over three million new cars were sold. Brazil has the fifth largest car market in the world. There are 13 domestic Brazilian car manufacturers as well as North American multinational companies such as Ford Motors, Volkswagen, Fiat and General Motors to supply demand. The car manufacturing industry is located in the south-east of Brazil in the cities of São Paulo, Rio de Janeiro, Belo Horizonte, Curitiba and Porto Alegre.

- The Brazilian car manufacturing industry employs over 130,000 people. Brazilian car engineers are world leaders in the design of small cars. Wealthy business entrepreneurs see the car industry as a profitable opportunity.

- The majority of cars in Brazil run on **flex fuel** (E85), a combination of petrol and ethanol. The manufacture of electric cars is not a profitable business because (a) Brazil has its own oil reserves and (b) its sugar plantations which provide the raw material for ethanol have a strong political lobby. Diesel fuel is not commonly used in passenger cars in Brazil, although buses and trucks do rely on this fuel.

Fig. 18 Cars are important to Brazil's prosperity.

Advantages of Brazil for car manufacturers

- It has low levels of car ownership (1 car for every 6.5 people) compared to North America (1 car per 2 people). This means the potential new car sales market in this NIC is much larger than in other countries where car ownership is more common. This attracts foreign multinational companies.
- There is a pool of skilled and cheap labour.
- Local and regional governments supported the development of manufacturing plants by paying up to 50% of their set-up costs.
- The south-eastern states are close to the ports of Rio de Janeiro and Santos for exporting cars to other countries.
- There is plenty of electricity for the factories from gas, nuclear and hydroelectric power stations.
- There are many component factories in the cities that make parts like tyres, brake pads and material for car seats. This reduces production costs.
- As Brazil develops, its population is getting wealthier and more people have spare income that they can use to buy a car.

- The Brazilian government has encouraged car manufacturing by removing taxes on new cars. In a country where the cost of running a car is 37% higher than elsewhere in South America this measure has been successful in encouraging sales.

- Brazil's transportation infrastructure across its 26 states is one of the worst in the world. The Brazilian government intends to spend approximately €13.6 billion between 2010 and 2013 on improving the road infrastructure plus roughly the same amount on public transportation (rails, metro and bus). These factors will encourage continued growth in the manufacture of passenger cars and trucks.

- Such is the attraction of south-east Brazil for car manufacturing that General Motors is investing €1.7 billion in its Brazilian plants and Ford Motors is investing €2.75 billion between 2010 and 2015 creating 1,000 new jobs in the industry. Fiat has already invested €2.1 billion in its existing huge factory in Betim near Belo Horizonte. When finished it will be Fiat's largest global assembly plant.

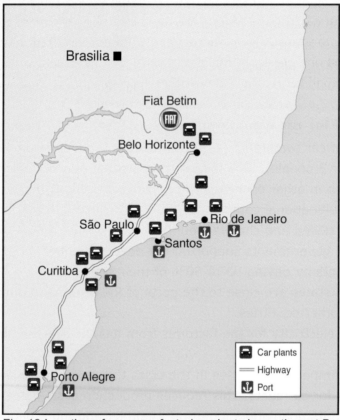

Fig. 19 Location of car manufacturing plants in south-east Brazil

Tertiary activities in Brazil

The services sector employs the majority of workers in Brazil. Service industries are a growth sector in Brazil due to improvements in tourism, transport, healthcare and education.

Transport in Brazil

The transport industry in Brazil is underdeveloped and the scale of improvements required is an economic burden on the country. The quality of transport facilities is uneven. Cities generally have better services than rural areas.

Physical factors such as the size of the country, extensive areas of forest and wetland and the isolation of urban areas from each other make the provision of an efficient transport network costly and difficult. Human factors such as government policy have led to improvements in infrastructure.

Road is the most commonly used method of transport followed by rail, waterways and air routes. Manufacturers and businesses are at a disadvantage due to high transport costs in Brazil. Port fees are twice as expensive in Brazil as elsewhere in South America and road haulage costs for soya are €21 per tonne compared to €10 per tonne in Argentina and €11 per tonne in the USA.

Even though successive Brazilian governments have prioritised roads over railways and waterways, little more than 10% of Brazil's road network is paved, and even these are poorly maintained. The exceptions are the main toll roads managed by private operators, e.g. the main São Paulo-Rio de Janeiro motorway. At present the government aims to invest one per cent of GDP in transport infrastructure. This is more than the amount that will be invested in health and education. The building and maintenance of roads is a quick way for the government to inject cash into the local economy and generate, even if temporarily, an increase in employment levels.

The **Trans Amazon Highway** is a major road project that aims to open up the Amazon Basin to development. Over 10,000 km of roads across the interior to neighbouring countries in the west are under construction.

The country's 30,000 km rail network has grown by 20% since it was privatised and upgraded in the late 1990s. But despite government efforts to get more freight on trains, railways remain underused and account for only 25% of total freight movement. Only the lines operated by iron ore exporters are used to their full capacity. Efficient rail routes are limited to a few well developed tourist routes. Most cities have metros and São Paulo has one of the most advanced public transport systems in the world. A high-speed rail connecting São Paulo and Rio de Janeiro is currently under development. The high-speed line is expected to be operational by 2014.

Brazil's great potential for river transport remains largely unexploited. Waterways currently account for only 13% of haulage traffic, even though Brazil has a 48,000 km network of navigable rivers.

Ports such as the one at Santos near São Paulo, which handles around one quarter of the country's foreign trade, have undergone some modernisation over the past 15 years. However, they remain congested and expensive, especially at harvest times when trucks laden with grain arrive for loading.

The country's main international airports are in Rio de Janeiro and São Paulo. These are also congested. This will be an important issue to be resolved before the flood of visitors pours in for the soccer World Cup in 2014 and Olympic Games in 2016. Belo Horizonte is the main international airport outside of Rio and São Paulo.

The government plans to improve transport services by privatising rail lines, modernising ports, introducing toll roads and decentralising road maintenance to local governments.

Tourism in Brazil

Tourism is a growth industry in Brazil. It is becoming an important part of the Brazilian economy by providing employment. More than eight million people are employed in tourism and two million of these are directly employed in the sector. Tourism income is worth €60 billion per year to the economy and tourism accounts for 7.1% of Brazilian economic activity.

Overall domestic tourists account for 11% of tourism-related spending in Brazil. Most domestic tourists are from São Paulo. They account for 27.8% of domestic tourism expenditure. This reflects the higher income levels of people in São Paulo which is an economic core region of Brazil.

Fig. 20 Tourist attractions in Brazil include the cable car at Pão de Açúcar, Rio de Janeiro and the Iguaçu Falls.

Tourism attractions in Brazil

Top visitor attractions:

- Rio de Janeiro has many iconic sights: the Pão de Açúcar (Sugar Loaf Mountain), with its cable car; the Corcovado, with its statue of Jesus Christ the Redeemer; Copacabana and Ipanema Beach with their beautiful people and mosaic sidewalks.
- Ecotourism is developed in the Amazon Valley cities such as Belém and Manaus, the Iguaçu Falls in the south and the wetlands of the Pantanal located in the western central region.
- Brazil is famous for its carnival, which usually takes place in February. The carnivals in Rio de Janeiro, Salvador and Olinda are the most famous.
- Rio de Janeiro's annual Samba Schools Parade attracts millions of domestic tourists every year.
- São Paulo is also a major city destination attracting 1.7 million foreign tourists throughout the year.

Despite being such a large country with so many attractions, international tourism to Brazil is underdeveloped. Just 6.5 million tourists visited Brazil in 2010. This is a tiny amount compared to Spain's 52 million tourists per year. Foreign tourists are economically important spending €2.2 billion a year in the country.

Reasons for the underdevelopment of Brazilian tourism

Crime: Brazil is seen as a dangerous destination due to the illegal drug business, kidnappings and crime – all of which has been widely covered by the international media.

Misleading advertising: During the 1970s and 1980s the Brazilian government's international tourism brochures showed scantily-clad women by the beach or dancing during carnival. This promoted illegal sex tourism and discouraged families and older travellers from visiting the country.

Lack of tourism infrastructure: The poor road and rail network combined with badly-trained workers in the catering industry has discouraged all but the hardiest tourists who don't mind tough conditions. They usually travel as cheaply as possible and do not generate much business while in the country.

Promoting tourism in Brazil

The Brazilian government has launched its *Plano Aquarela 2020* (**Plan Watercolour 2020**). This international campaign aims to double the number of foreign visitors in the next ten years. The plan promotes five tourism sectors: **sun and beach holidays; ecotourism; sports; culture and business**; and **event holidays**. The 2014 World Cup and the 2016 Olympic Games hosted by Rio de Janeiro will also result in a large increase in international visitors. Road and rail infrastructure is being improved under the Avança Brazil scheme and most workers at hotels and restaurants in the main tourist destinations are now well trained.

20.2 Population, migration and urbanisation in Brazil

Population characteristics

Brazil is the largest country in South America. It has a population of more than 193 million people and is the fifth most populous country in the world. Brazil's birth rate is 18.43 per 1,000 and its death rate is 6.35 per 1,000.

The population increased significantly between 1940 and 1970 as Brazil passed through Stage 2 and into Stage 3 of the **Population Cycle**. This population increase was due to a decline in the mortality rate because of better nutrition and healthcare. In the 1940s the annual population growth rate was 2.4%, rising to 3% in the 1950s. Since the 1970s population growth has decreased significantly. This was due to a drop in birth rates caused by improved wealth, healthcare and literacy as economic modernisation and urbanisation occurred. From 1960 to today, life expectancy throughout Brazil rose from 51 years to 72.6 years. In the past many people were lucky to live to 44 years. Changes in the shape of the population pyramids in Fig. 21 on page 414 show this effect. Today the population growth rate is only 1.2% per year.

ACTIVITY

Describe three changes in the shape of the population pyramids on page 414 between 1975 and 2050. State one reason for each of the changes you see.

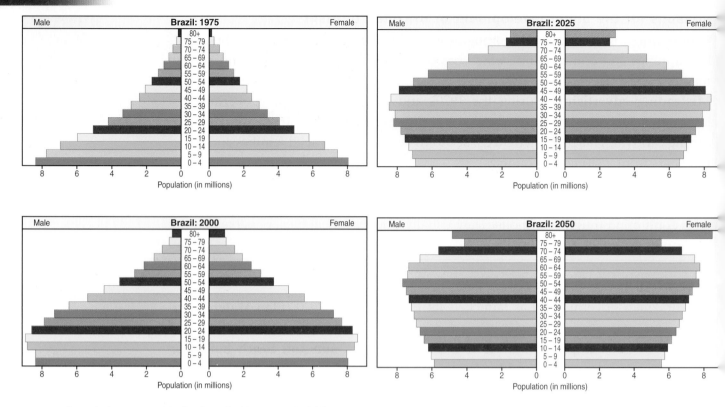

Fig. 21 Population pyramids for Brazil: 1975, 2000, 2025 and 2050

Population density and distribution

Brazil's average population density of 22.3 people per km² is quite low compared to that of many other countries. Patterns of internal migration have had a major impact on the distribution of the population. Over 133 million of the 193 million Brazilians live on or near the Atlantic coast of the south-eastern and north-eastern states, as these areas are cooler, accessible and more urbanised. The population is heavily concentrated in the south-eastern region (79.8 million) and north-eastern region (53.5 million). Two areas, the centre-west and the north regions that together make up 64.12% of the Brazilian territory, have a total of only 29.1 million people. These regions contain large areas of inhospitable *cerrado* and rainforest vegetation.

The interior region of Brazil (centre-west) has a man-made population centre in the new capital city of Brasilia. This carefully planned capital city was constructed in three years between 1957 and 1960. It was intended to be a gateway to the riches of the Brazilian interior. Many peasant workers were attracted to work there and lived in temporary camps about 30 km away on the

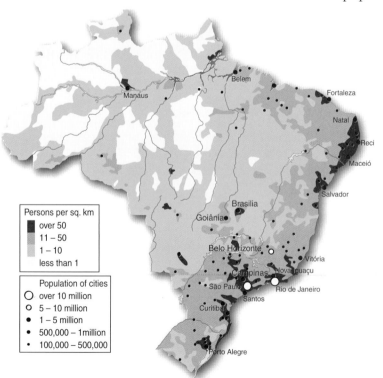

Fig. 22 Population density in Brazil

outskirts of the newly developing city. Upon completion of the new capital it was presumed these peasants would return to their home area but this never occurred. Many continued to live in the camps which quickly became *favelas* (shanty towns). The people in them are called the 'anti-Brasilias'. The wealthier people who moved to the new city, attracted by 100% salary raises and big apartments, find the heat, humidity and air-conditioned lifestyle uncomfortable during the working week and quickly leave the city each weekend and at holidays for the cooler conditions in their home cities along the coast.

Fig. 23 Brasilia was built to encourage development and settlement in the Amazon region.

The impact of international migration on Brazil

Brazil is a country of migrants. As much as 40% of its population has migrated at some point in their lives. International migration in the fifteenth century by Portuguese colonists has influenced Brazilian history, population, culture and economic development. The huge scale of rural to urban migration has also caused rapid urban growth and led to the existence of *favelas* in most major cities. Government sponsored urban–rural resettlement programmes have led to new settlements in the Brazilian interior.

Impact of migration due to colonialism

International migration by the Portuguese who first colonised Brazil led to economic growth in Brazil and the introduction of Europeans and Africans to the population.

Brazil was first colonised in the fifteenth century by Portuguese explorers and settlers who migrated there in search of wealth and a new life. Over the next 400 years these settlers established a plantation system of agriculture, producing sugar cane and coffee. They used imported slave labour. These slaves were forced migrants taken from west Africa to the north-east city of Salvador which was the largest slave port in the world at the time. African slave descendents now form an important part of Brazil's population and culture in the north-east region.

The coffee trade in particular caused rapid economic growth in the state of Minas Gerais and attracted many international migrants from Germany and Italy. European migrant plantation owners exported coffee, gold, sugar and timber using slave labour. These European migrants became very wealthy business people who then influenced the political system in the country. A social system of rich, powerful, colonial landowners/politicians and a poor powerless working society developed.

Tensions caused by this extremely unequal society eventually led to important social and economic changes in Brazil. Examples of such change include:

1. Declaring independence from Portugal in 1882 and becoming a constitutional monarchy.
2. The abolition of slavery in 1888.
3. The construction of a new capital city, Brasilia, in order to reduce the influence of the former colonial capital, Rio de Janeiro, and to develop the Amazon region.

The impact of internal migration in Brazil

The towns established by Portuguese settlers, e.g. Rio de Janeiro and São Paulo, are today rapidly growing mega-cities. These cities have grown due to four unique migration patterns within Brazil.

Migration from poor North East to richer South East

Organised migration from overpopulated urban areas to Amazonia

Rural to urban migration

Fig. 24 Internal migration in Brazil

1. Out-migration from north-east Brazil

North-east Brazil is one of the poorest regions in the country with 32% of all poor Brazilians concentrated in this one area. Belem is the main city and much of the region is dry *cerrado* – vegetation that is hard to cultivate. People in this region have migrated from the countryside to Belem but the majority of poor rural dwellers move to the richer south-eastern cities of Salvador, Rio and São Paulo. There they find unskilled work in manufacturing or services and live in *favela* settlements.

2. In-migration to south-east Brazil

The south-east of Brazil is an economic core region. Per capita GDP in the south-east is 300% greater than that of the north-east. There are many opportunities for skilled and unskilled workers. The movement of millions of rural and urban poor from all areas of Brazil to the cities of Rio and São Paulo has led to rapid urban growth and the development of *favelas*.

3. Rural to urban migration

Farmers are amongst the poorest people in Brazil. Almost 43% of the nation's destitute are found in the agricultural sector. Small farmers, especially those from the north-east, who scarcely make a living from the land regard moving to the cities as a way to escape their desperate poverty. As a result there is a continued migration of farmers from the land to the cities.

4. Urban to rural migration

For many decades the Brazilian government encouraged the settlement of the interior of Brazil, e.g. Brasilia. These government-sponsored settlement programmes encouraged hundreds of thousands of poor urban families to move from the city slums to farmland in central Brazil. In part this was to reduce the tension between rich and poor in the cities and clear away the *favelas*. Land was sold cheaply (a few

Euros per hectare) or even given away free. This urban to rural migration has had an impact on the population distribution in Brazil. In some regions, such as the southern state of Bahia, 28% of people in the region are there because of the government settlement programme. However, people soon found they had swapped one type of poverty for another as once the forest was cleared the latosol soil quickly became infertile and unproductive.

Urbanisation in Brazil

Almost 80% of Brazilians live in urban areas. The cities and towns are growing quickly for several reasons: People still have large families, life expectancy is rising (since 1960 life expectancy has risen steadily; today it is 69 years for men and 76 years for women) and the rural to urban migration patterns described earlier have all caused urban growth.

The gap between the rich and poor in Brazil is clearly seen in the cities. Many cities have squatter settlements known as *favelas*. These areas of irregular and poor-quality housing are often crowded onto hillsides and as a result, *favelas* suffer from frequent landslides during heavy rain. Most *favelas* are inaccessible to traffic due to their narrow streets. The explosion in *favela* growth dates from the 1940s when the government's industrialisation programme attracted hundreds of thousands of migrants into the cities.

In recent decades *favelas* have been troubled by drug-related crime and gang warfare. Police have little or no control in many *favelas*. The growth of *favelas* has led to government removal campaigns.

It is estimated that there are more than 3,500 *favelas* in Brazil. Most of these are found in three cities: Rio de Janeiro, São Paulo and Recife.

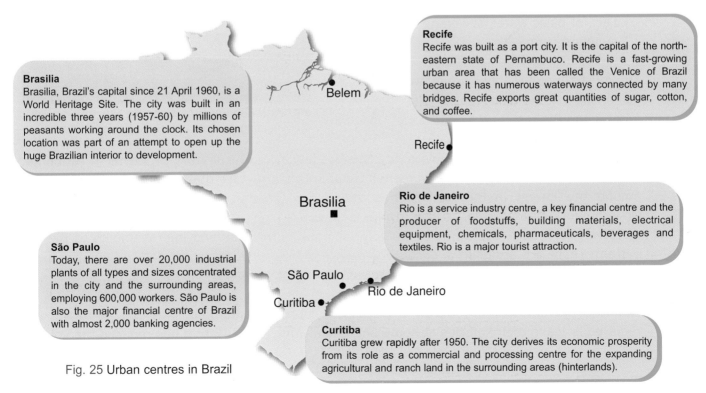

Recife
Recife was built as a port city. It is the capital of the north-eastern state of Pernambuco. Recife is a fast-growing urban area that has been called the Venice of Brazil because it has numerous waterways connected by many bridges. Recife exports great quantities of sugar, cotton, and coffee.

Brasilia
Brasilia, Brazil's capital since 21 April 1960, is a World Heritage Site. The city was built in an incredible three years (1957-60) by millions of peasants working around the clock. Its chosen location was part of an attempt to open up the huge Brazilian interior to development.

Rio de Janeiro
Rio is a service industry centre, a key financial centre and the producer of foodstuffs, building materials, electrical equipment, chemicals, pharmaceuticals, beverages and textiles. Rio is a major tourist attraction.

São Paulo
Today, there are over 20,000 industrial plants of all types and sizes concentrated in the city and the surrounding areas, employing 600,000 workers. São Paulo is also the major financial centre of Brazil with almost 2,000 banking agencies.

Curitiba
Curitiba grew rapidly after 1950. The city derives its economic prosperity from its role as a commercial and processing centre for the expanding agricultural and ranch land in the surrounding areas (hinterlands).

Fig. 25 Urban centres in Brazil

case study

Urban growth of São Paulo

São Paulo is the largest city in South America with a population of over 17 million. It is a densely populated (7,216 people per km²) **agglomeration** – a city made up of smaller urban centres. São Paulo is made up of 39 urban areas that have grown and merged to make one huge city. The city is over 80 km wide and 40 km long. Development of the city is occurring in ways into the city.

São Paulo is the business centre of South America. Its wealth was originally based on the coffee industry. It rapidly industrialised in the twentieth century and today it is also a global services centre. Its huge market is a magnet for multinational corporations. Economic growth has increased employment and wages.

People move to São Paulo's *favelas* to escape the poverty-stricken interior of the country or the drought-ridden north-east of Brazil where unreliable rains and government policies have left many people struggling to cope on poor land. These push factors encouraged people to move to São Paulo. Over 20% of people in São Paulo are from the north-east of Brazil. There are also jobs and better health and education services available in the city; these act as a pull factor attracting migrants. São Paulo is now the most ethnically diverse city in the country.

Because of rural to urban migration São Paulo has the greatest number of *favela* residents of any city in Brazil. The largest *favela* settlement in the city is Heliópolis.

Urban problems in São Paulo

- Traffic congestion
- Air and water pollution
- Growth of *favelas* and overcrowding
- Lack of formal housing
- Lack of basic water, sewerage and electricity supplies in *favelas*

Fig. 26 In São Paulo *favelas* exist side-by-side with the gleaming skyscrapers of the business district.

The most serious of these urban problems in São Paulo are traffic congestion, the growth of *favelas* and the resulting air and water pollution.

Traffic causes 90% of São Paulo's air pollution, leading to respiratory problems in residents. São Paulo's pollution levels are worsened by poor infrastructure design, petrol prices that are among the lowest in the world (encouraging car ownership) and old polluting vehicles. Government initiatives to reduce traffic and congestion in São Paulo include an orbital motorway to reduce city traffic by 20%, additional metro lines and improvements to the rail system. These are designed to encourage people to use public transport and to take cars away from the densely populated city centre areas.

The local government introduced a **pollution** control programme, whereby motorists are required to leave their vehicles at home one day a week. This system has reduced the volume

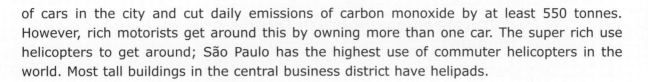

of cars in the city and cut daily emissions of carbon monoxide by at least 550 tonnes. However, rich motorists get around this by owning more than one car. The super rich use helicopters to get around; São Paulo has the highest use of commuter helicopters in the world. Most tall buildings in the central business district have helipads.

São Paulo has tackled the **favela** problem in two ways. Up until the 1990s the government response was complete neglect. When ignoring the problem did not resolve it, the local government evicted people, demolished the *favelas* and constructed buildings on the newly vacant land. Meanwhile, the displaced residents were given modest relocation payments and encouraged to move 'somewhere farther out', usually onto low-lying or poor quality public land. This approach moved the *favelas* further out of the city.

Since the 1990s the local government introduced a slum demolition-and-redevelopment programme nicknamed Cingapura (the Portuguese pronunciation of Singapore). Under Cingapura, the Municipality of São Paulo cleared out all the *favelas* built beside rivers, railway lines and highways. They then built footpaths and brightly painted multi-storey housing blocks, each with its own gated entryway. These apartments have running water, sewerage and electricity.

But these high-rises are unpopular compared with renovating the informally built homes in the *favelas*. So the local government now improves existing homes. The streets are paved and street lighting is installed. This combines an improved sense of community with better housing and social services.

Fig. 27 *Favelas* are notorious fire hazards - flames spread quickly due to cramped conditions and the use of poor building materials to construct the makeshift houses.

20.3 Cultural regions in Brazil

Cultural regions in Brazil (ethnic groups, language and religion)

Brazil is a racially mixed country but also a remarkably integrated society. Its population shows the results of large-scale immigrations and integrations. Any divisions between people tend to be socio-economic rather than racial.

Fig. 28 Brazil has a mix of population groups.

Ethnic groups

Most Brazilians descend from three main population groups:

1. The country's indigenous Indian people (**Amerindians**). Before colonisation there were an estimated six million Amerindians. Today only a few hundred thousand pure-blooded Amerindians remain.
2. People of white European descent (mostly Portuguese settlers) make up over half the population.
3. People of black African (former slaves) descent.

Since the arrival of the Portuguese in 1500, considerable intermarriage between these three groups has taken place. A sizable number of more recent immigrants are Japanese. Today therefore five major groups of people make up the population of Brazil.

1. Native Americans living mainly in the north-west border regions and remote parts of the Amazon Basin, e.g. the Yanomami.
2. Portuguese whose ancestors colonised Brazil in the 1500s. Found mostly in the south-eastern regions.
3. Black Africans, whose ancestors were brought over to Brazil as slaves, are concentrated in the north-east around Salvador.
4. European immigrants who came to Brazil in the 1800s and in the first half of the twentieth century from various parts of western, central and eastern Europe.
5. The Japanese who first came to Brazil from the early 1900s to the 1940s. Most live in São Paulo State or the south of the country. (In fact Brazil contains the largest number of people of Japanese ancestry outside of Japan.)

Ethnic origin	Percentage	
White	48.43%	(about 92 million)
Multiracial	43.80%	(about 83 million
Black	6.84%	(about 13 million)
Japanese	0.58%	(about 1.1 million)
Amerindian	0.28%	(about 536, 000)

Language and religion

An important unifying factor in Brazil is the Portuguese language which has been adopted by all Brazilians. It is the official and most widely spoken language in the country. However, Brazilian Portuguese has become very distinct from its European counterpart. It is strongly influenced by Amerindian and other immigrant languages. Spanish is also spoken in the border areas and in schools. Other languages include German, Italian, Japanese, English and Amerindian languages.

There are 163 different indigenous languages. In the east and north-east regions of Brazil, most native Indian languages have been lost due to prejudice and official policy. This is a similar situation to the fate of the Irish language during the Plantations. Today, according to the Brazilian constitution, teaching in indigenous Amerindian areas must be bilingual in order to maintain the cultural identity of the native peoples.

The presence of Roman Catholicism is another unifying factor. More than 73.8% of the population is Roman Catholic. In fact, Brazil has the largest Roman Catholic population in the world. There is also a significant Protestant minority and a number of African religions. In Salvador the African Candomblé religion is common reflecting the African origin of its inhabitants.

The Amerindian tribes

Sixty per cent of all Amerindian tribes are concentrated in the Amazon Basin. The experience of these Amazonian Indians shows the interaction between political, social and economic activities. They make up small communities that are the remains of once larger native (indigenous) populations. It is estimated that there are 206 indigenous tribes in Brazil. Although it was predicted during the 1960s that the native Amerindians of Brazil would disappear in the future, this has not happened. Even so, there are still very few Amerindians living in such a large area of land, a fact used against them by those who think that they are standing in the way of development.

Fig. 29 Amazonian river settlement.

Brazil is believed to have the largest number of un-contacted people in the world. Today the National Indian Foundation reports the existence of 67 different un-contacted tribes. Before colonisation by Portuguese settlers there were over six million Amerindians. Since then their numbers have decreased dramatically due to disease, slavery and massacre, invasion of their territory, deportation and government assimilation schemes.

Fig. 30 Amazonian Indians

The best known Amazonian Indians are the Yanomami. The Yanomami depend on the forest for their livelihood. They practice a method of farming called **shifting cultivation** which involves the use of **slash and burn** to clear a small area of the forest in which to live. They are quite nomadic, frequently moving to avoid areas that become overused. In the cleared areas they grow bananas, gather fruit, hunt animals and fish. Children stay close to their mother and most of the childrearing is done by women. The Yanomami men may have more than one wife but most unions are monogamous.

Recognition of their native lands is necessary for the survival of the Amazonian Indians but it does not protect them from continuous threat and conflict. Miners, loggers, mineral prospectors and land owners continue their legal and illegal onslaught into interior lands to exploit valuable rainforest resources ranging from wood to gold, copper to diamonds. They also clear forest for cattle ranches and soya bean and coffee plantations. In some regions of Paraná State the rate of forest clearance is over one hectare per second.

However, in the large areas they do occupy, the Amerindians have preserved an amazing richness in terms of biodiversity and knowledge that has an unknown market value. Brazilian indigenous people have made enormous contributions to the world's medicine with their knowledge. This knowledge is used for profit by pharmaceutical corporations – the global market for plant-based medicine is worth €18 billion. However, none of the tribes gain from this wealth. Many tribal medicine men or shaman are over the age of 70. As their numbers decline, their tribes and the world loses irreplaceable knowledge of medicinal plants.

20.4 Deforestation of the tropical rainforests in Brazil – a challenge for the future

Rainforests are disappearing at a rate of about 40 hectares per minute, day and night. Its clearance is having a major impact on the world and its people. Deforestation rates are closely linked to performance of the Brazilian economy. Rates increase during times of economic growth and slow down during economic recession.

ECONOMIC ACTIVITY	% DEFORESTATION
	%
Cattle ranches	60
Small-scale subsistence farming	33
Fires, mining, roads, dams, urbanisation	3
Logging	3
Other commercial agriculture	1

THE CAUSES OF DEFORESTATION

1. Overpopulation and poverty in Brazilian cities creates political difficulties. There is a drive to encourage people to leave the *favelas* and move to farms in the forest. In some cases, land is given to these people free of charge.

2. The government wants to open up the Brazilian rainforest to exploit its timber and mineral wealth so that it can sell them to high consumption rich nations. Forest is cleared to create access to these mineral reserves.

3. Beef producers require more land to herd massive numbers of cattle for the beef trade. Forest is cleared for ranching. Forest is also cleared for huge soya bean plantations.

4. Brazilian industry requires more power if it is to develop and maintain its industrial strength. Forest is drowned under huge reservoirs as rivers are dammed.

Licences are given to mining companies to clear forests and mine for metals such as iron ore and copper. Timber companies are given rights to remove forest and sell timber abroad. The Brazilian government receives some of the profits made by these companies. This money is used to pay interest on the national debt.

Roads are being built across the Amazon forest to create access for logging

Fig. 31 Areas of deforestation in Brazil, 2005

companies, mineral companies, ranches and hydroelectric power (HEP) stations. The longest road is the Trans-Amazonian Highway, a 5,300 km road, built across Brazil from east to west. Other major roads are the Belém-Brasília Highway and the Northern Perimeter Highway.

An unlimited water supply and ideal river conditions have led to the development of many HEP stations. Over 125 new HEP dams have been built in the Brazilian forest area. One example is the Tucuri Dam which caused over 2,500 km² of rainforest to be flooded. More than 8,000 people lost their homes and thousands of animals died.

Illegal timber production is also leading to deforestation. Fuelled by a demand for cheap supplies of plywood and tropical timber locally and abroad, illegal timber is estimated to account for 80% of all timber produced in the Brazilian Amazon.

The Brazilian government announced plans in 2000 for a scheme called *Avança Brasil* (**Advance Brazil**) which was scheduled to last from 2000 to 2008. This is a €30 billion plan to cover much of the Amazon rainforest with 10,000 km of highways, hydroelectric dams, power lines, mines, gas and oilfields, canals, ports, logging concessions and other industrial developments.

Scientists predict that these developments will lead to the damage or loss of between 33-42% of Brazil's remaining Amazon forest. However, the government is finding it difficult to raise the money for these projects.

Fig. 32 Mining is a cause of deforestation in Brazil.

IMPACT OF THE FOREST CLEARANCE ON PEOPLE AND SOILS IN BRAZIL

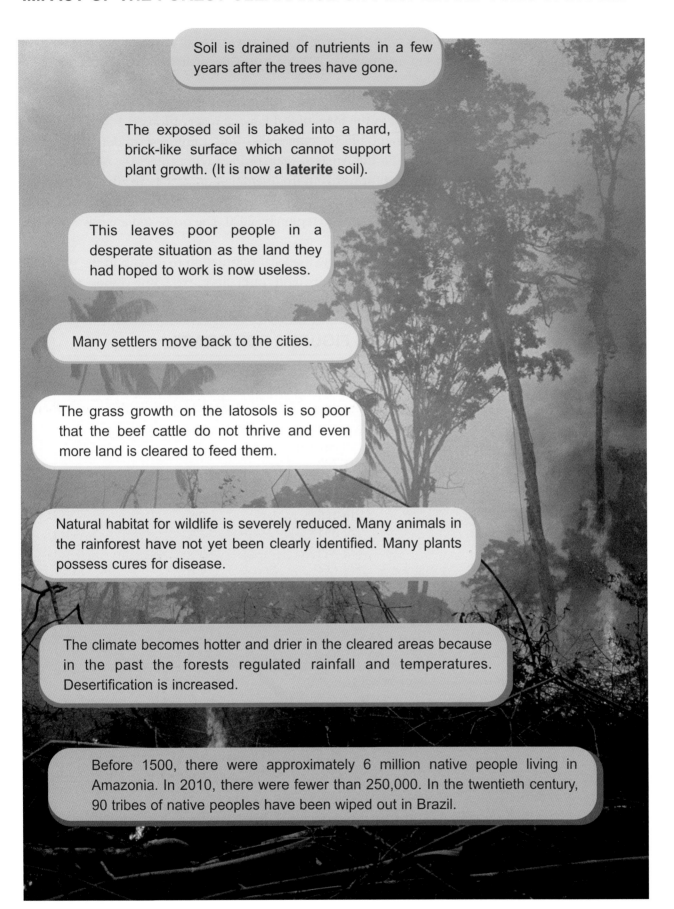

Soil is drained of nutrients in a few years after the trees have gone.

The exposed soil is baked into a hard, brick-like surface which cannot support plant growth. (It is now a **laterite** soil).

This leaves poor people in a desperate situation as the land they had hoped to work is now useless.

Many settlers move back to the cities.

The grass growth on the latosols is so poor that the beef cattle do not thrive and even more land is cleared to feed them.

Natural habitat for wildlife is severely reduced. Many animals in the rainforest have not yet been clearly identified. Many plants possess cures for disease.

The climate becomes hotter and drier in the cleared areas because in the past the forests regulated rainfall and temperatures. Desertification is increased.

Before 1500, there were approximately 6 million native people living in Amazonia. In 2010, there were fewer than 250,000. In the twentieth century, 90 tribes of native peoples have been wiped out in Brazil.

The challenge for the future –
Allow economic development and protect the forest

Brazil's rainforest is as big as Western Europe, covering 60% of the country's national territory. Experts say as much as 20% of it has been destroyed by development, logging and farming.

About 4% of the Amazon forest is protected in environmental reserves, and another 20% is protected in the form of indigenous reservations.

In 2004, the government placed over 2,000 km² rainforest under government protection. The reserves in the Amazon state of Para will protect the rainforest from logging, mining and other forms of environmental degradation. In 2010 the Brazilian government designated four new protected areas and pledged to reduce deforestation by 80% in the Amazon region by 2020. The protected areas will be used for ecotourism.

The reserves are designed to allow the local population to remain in the protected area, tapping rubber, picking fruits and nuts and extracting other renewable products from the forest.

DEFORESTATION FIGURES FOR BRAZIL

Year	Deforestation Sq km	Change %
1995	29,059	95%
1996	18,161	-38%
1997	13,227	-27%
1998	17,383	31%
1999	17,259	-1%
2000	18,226	6%
2001	18,165	0%
2002	21,651	17%
2003	25,396	19%
2004	27,772	9%
2005	19,014	-31%
2006	14,285	-49%
2007	11,651	-18%
2008	12,911	11%
2009	7,484	-42%

SKILLS EXERCISE

Using a suitable graph, represent the trend in deforestation in Brazil between 1998 and 2009.

Find up-to-date information on the rainforest in Brazil, log onto www.mongabay.com

While Brazil has some of the most strict environmental laws in the developing world, it struggles to enforce them. This is due to the size of the country, lack of money and pressure from business and some agricultural producers who regard environmental protection as a barrier to progress.

questions

Chapter Revision Questions

1. Using an atlas and maps from this textbook, draw an outline map of Brazil. On it mark the following: Brazil's neighbouring countries; the cities of Curitiba, Recife, Rio de Janeiro, Salvador, São Paulo, Brasilia and Belo Horizonte; the Brazilian highlands; the Amazon and Tocantins rivers, the states of Bahia and Minas Gerais; the equator and the Atlantic Ocean.

2. Name one lowland and **one** upland region in Brazil.

3. On an outline map of Brazil mark on and label the River Amazon, River Parana, River Tocantins and River São Francisco.

4. Describe the **three** main climatic zones of Brazil.

5. What effect does latitude, altitude and prevailing wind have on the climate of Brazil?

6. Name and describe **three** soils found in Brazil.

7. Describe **three** types of natural vegetation found in Brazil.

8. Describe agriculture in Brazil under the headings: Crops, Cattle and Forestry.

9. (i) What natural advantages does Brazil have for coffee production?
   (ii) Where are the main coffee producing regions?
   (iii) How important to the Brazilian economy is coffee production?

10. Describe mining and oil production in Brazil.

11. Brazil is an important manufacturing nation. Outline the development of manufacturing in Brazil since the Second World War.

12. Why is most manufacturing located in the south-east of Brazil?

13. Describe the factors affecting car manufacturing in Brazil.

14. Describe transport services in Brazil under the headings: Roads, Rail, River, Air and Port Services, Problems, Government influence.

15. Describe tourism in Brazil under the headings: Physical attractions, Human attractions, Disadvantages, Economic importance, Government influences.

16. What effect did colonialism have on the population of Brazil?

17. What effect has internal migration had on the population distribution of Brazil?

18. Describe **two** reasons for the growth of São Paulo.

19. Describe **two** problems caused by the growth of São Paulo and how they are being reduced.

20. What is the birth rate, death rate and life expectancy in Brazil?

21. What is the population density in Brazil and describe the distribution of population.

22. Name, locate and account for the presence of **three** different cultural groups in Brazil.

23. Why is the rainforest in Brazil under threat?

24. What factors have led to the high levels of deforestation in Brazil?

25. What is the impact of deforestation on people and soils in Brazil?

OL Long Questions

26. **NON-EUROPEAN REGIONS**

    With reference to **any** non-European, continental or sub-continental region you have studied: Describe **two** factors which have influenced its industrial development.

    LC Exam Paper

27. **NON-EUROPEAN REGIONS**

    Describe the influence which **either** climate **or** the physical landscape has on the development of tourism in any non-European continental or sub-continental region which you have studied.

    LC Exam Paper

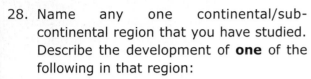

28. Name any one continental/sub-continental region that you have studied. Describe the development of **one** of the following in that region:

    Tourism

    Agriculture

29. Examine the importance of agriculture to any **one** non-European continental/sub-continental region which you have studied.

    Clearly state the name of the region in your answer.

HL Long Questions

30. Describe how any **two** of the following have influenced human activities in a continental / sub-continental region you have studied:
    – climate
    – soil
    – relief
    – drainage

    LC Exam Paper

31. Draw an outline map of a non-European/sub-continental region you have studied. Mark on and identify:
    – a major city
    – a named physical region
    – a named river
    – the location of a named resource

32. Examine **two** factors that have influenced primary activities in a non-European region you have studied.

33. Account for the development of **one** tertiary economic activity in any one continental / sub-continental region that you have studied.

34. Describe and explain the growth of one major urban area in a continental/sub-continental region that you have studied.

35. Describe and explain the importance of culture in defining regions in a continental/sub-continental region that you have studied.

36. Describe and explain any **two** factors that influence the development of manufacturing in a non-European continental / sub-continental region that you have studied.

Chapter 21

The Complexity of Regions

(a) The growth and impact of the European Union

(b) The interaction between the Republic of Ireland and Northern Ireland

At the end of this section you should be able to:

- Outline the key events in the growth of the European Union (EU).

- Name the current EU member states.

- Discuss the advantages and disadvantages of EU enlargement.

- Discuss the social, political and economic impact of EU expansion.

- Discuss how a nation's sovereignty might be affected by the proposed EU constitution.

- Discuss the economic, political and cultural links between the Republic of Ireland and Northern Ireland.

Contents

21.1   European Union development and expansion

Case Study: Poland, the EU and Ireland

21.2   The impact of the expansion of the EU – economic, social/cultural and political issues

Case Study: The Turkish application to join the EU

21.3   Economic, political and cultural interaction between the Republic of Ireland and Northern Ireland.

Questions

KEY THEME

The boundaries and the extent of regions may change over time. The study of regions illustrates the geographical complexity of the interaction between economic, cultural and physical processes.

429

21.1 European Union development and expansion

The Beginnings of the European Union

Phase 1: The Creation of the European Coal and Steel Community (ECSC), 1950-53

Fig. 1 The six members of the European Coal and Steel Community, 1951

The building of a united Europe was one of the greatest undertakings of the twentieth century. Its aim was to end the old hostilities that led to the two world wars and to create more prosperity through co-operation among all Europeans.

In 1950, the French Foreign Minister, Robert Schuman, announced his plan which was the first step towards the modern EU.

Schuman wanted to encourage social and economic co-operation among countries that produced coal and steel. In 1951, six countries signed a treaty creating the **ECSC – The European Coal and Steel Community**. It was the first common market uniting the coal and steel industries of Belgium, France, West Germany, Italy, Luxembourg and the Netherlands.

Phase 2: The Treaties of Rome and the development of the EEC, 1957–64

In 1957, the six members of the ECSC signed two agreements called the Treaties of Rome. These marked the beginning of the EU we know today.

What did the Treaties of Rome do?

1. They created the **European Economic Community (EEC)**. The EEC was also known as the **common market** because its first aim was to enable free trade between its members. People, goods and money were now able to move freely between the member states.

2. They also created the Treaty of the European Atomic Energy Community (EAEC), more commonly known as **Euratom**, which sought to develop and grow nuclear industries. It also aimed to set safety standards for nuclear fuels and waste.

The impact of the EEC

As a result of the success of the Treaties of Rome, other European countries looked at the economic growth and benefits of the EEC and considered applying for membership.

Ireland, the UK, Denmark and Norway applied for membership in 1961 and again in 1967, but France was opposed to enlarging the EEC at that time.

In 1962, the EEC introduced the **Common Agricultural Policy** or CAP. This gave member states joint control over food production and ensured fair prices. It created a single market for agriculture.

Phase 3: The European Community–The EC, 1965 –1986

In 1965, the three bodies of the ECSC, EEC and Euratom merged into a single institution called the **European Community (EC)**. The EC was no longer just an economic community. It now made decisions about other issues such as social policies and justice.

1. Members of the EC elected people to represent their country in the newly-created European Parliament.

2. Ministers from each government attended regular Council of Ministers' meetings.

3. The European Commission – made up of representatives appointed by the government of each member state – and the European Court of Justice were established.

During the 1960s, most EC countries experienced economic growth and wealth, often as a result of the trade agreements between the member states. In 1968, custom duties between the member states were abolished. This was a very important step towards creating a **single market**.

As part of the EC, each member state had to make changes to their national laws in order to develop common laws shared by all member states. These are known as **sovereignty** changes. A good example of this is the Common Agricultural Policy (CAP), where community law has largely replaced national law, e.g. policies concerning the raising of beef cattle are the same in each member state.

Fig. 2 The 12 members of the European Community in 1986

New members

In January 1973, Ireland, UK and Denmark eventually joined the EC. The most immediate impact in Ireland of membership was seen through the workings and benefits of the CAP.

Greece became a member of the EC in 1981. Spain and Portugal soon followed in 1986.

> Sovereignty is the right of a country to make laws for itself that are independent of any other organisation's laws, including the EU.

Economic advantages of joining the EC

The transfer of funds from the richer core of the community, such as Germany, to the poorer peripheries, such as Ireland, benefited farming in this country and in other member states.

In 1974, the EU Heads of Government agreed to set up the European Regional Development Fund (**ERDF**) to encourage economic growth through subsidies. These subsidies are called **Structural funds** and they provide important financial help to all regions of Europe.

In 1979, the European Monetary System (**EMS**) was introduced. The EMS guarded against problems caused by sharp shifts in the value of national currencies.

Phase 4: The Single European Act, 1987–1991

In 1987, the **Single European Act (SEA)** was signed by all members of the EC. The main aims of this Act were:

1. To ensure the smooth operation of a single market among EC member states.

2. To introduce reforms needed due to the increased membership of the EC (Ireland, the UK, Denmark, Greece, Spain and Portugal had all joined since the Treaties of Rome had been implemented).

The SEA also included a new policy of co-operation on research and the environment among member states. Importantly, the SEA also introduced some European laws that were superior to national law. This was the first time that the members of the EC had agreed to allow European law to override national law. However, it only applied to a small number of laws.

In 1987, Turkey applied for membership. Consideration of Turkey's application has been difficult and complex due to its size, large population, human rights record and relations between its secular and Islamic communities.

In 1989, the Berlin Wall collapsed and the system of communism throughout Central and Eastern Europe came to an end. The reunification of Germany took place in 1990. Many Central and Eastern European states became democracies and took steps to apply for EC membership.

Fig. 3 The 15 members of the European Union in 1995

Phase 5: The Maastricht Treaty and the creation of the EU, 1992–96

In 1992, the **Maastricht Treaty** was signed by all members of the EC in which targets for the following were put in place:

1. A single European currency.

2. A common foreign and security policy.

3. A policy of tackling unemployment.

4. A stronger social policy.

5. A common European citizenship.

The Maastricht Treaty came into effect in 1993 and the European Community was officially renamed the **European Union (EU)**. The Treaty was of great importance as it showed that all EU members were in favour of creating a stronger, more united Europe, sharing the same policies on foreign, social, economic and security issues. In 1995, Austria, Finland and Sweden joined.

Phase 6: The Amsterdam Treaty: Reformation of EU structures and creation of the Euro, 1997–2002

Due to the increasing number of countries applying to join the EU, another treaty, known as the **Amsterdam Treaty**, was required to enable EU institutions to cope

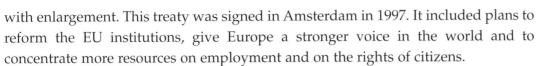

with enlargement. This treaty was signed in Amsterdam in 1997. It included plans to reform the EU institutions, give Europe a stronger voice in the world and to concentrate more resources on employment and on the rights of citizens.

In 1999, the **Euro** was created to replace the national currencies in 12 of the 15 member states. The Euro has been in use since 2002. The UK, Denmark and Sweden decided not to use the Euro. Instead, they chose to continue using their own national currencies.

Phase 7: The Nice Treaty and the Lisbon Treaty (2002–2009) and further enlargement of the EU

The Nice Treaty

This treaty came into operation in 2003. It contains directions on:

1. How many seats each country can have in the European Parliament (e.g. Germany as a bigger, wealthier and long-term member of the EU has more seats than Portugal which is a smaller, less wealthy and more recent member).

2. The weighting of votes (i.e. how many votes each country has – again, bigger countries have more votes than smaller countries).

3. Other issues concerning the Council of Ministers and the European Commission.

The Lisbon Treaty

On 1 December 2009 the Treaty of Lisbon came into operation. Under this treaty, decision making in the enlarged EU will become more efficient and the EU will become more involved with the social issues of its citizens. The Lisbon Treaty is concerned with three main areas:

1. A more democratic and transparent Europe

There will be much greater involvement by national parliaments in decision making in the EU. The treaty also gives a stronger voice to citizens.

2. A more efficient Europe

The Lisbon Treaty aims to provide effective and efficient decision-making, simplified working methods and voting rules.

3. A Europe of rights and values, freedom, solidarity and security

The Lisbon Treaty aims to create an EU which will look at the health of citizens in all member states. It also aims to improve the life of Europeans in such areas as freedom, security and justice, e.g. by combating terrorism and tackling crime.

Legend:
- EU
- Newest EU members
- Other candidate

Fig. 4 The 27 members of the European Union

SKILLS EXERCISE

Name the countries numbered 1–27 in Fig. 4

Reasons for the expansion of the EU

After the collapse of communism, there was a rush of applications from Central and Eastern European countries to join the EU. Various steps had to be taken to allow the EU to absorb the new applicants, e.g. the Amsterdam, Nice and Lisbon Treaties.

The issue of expansion caused much debate among EU members. Some strongly opposed the idea of admitting more countries, arguing that the cost of funding these poorer countries would be too high. Others were in favour of expansion, pointing out that increasing the prosperity of poorer states would ultimately benefit Europe as a whole by providing a larger market.

The EU is willing to welcome new members provided they fulfil the political criteria of:

1. Being a democracy.

2. Having a basic rule of law, i.e. a constitution.

3. Having strong respect for human rights, including respect for and protection of minorities.

4. Agreeing to an economic and monetary union with EU members.

During Ireland's presidency of the EU in January 2004, the EU became a community of 25 member states. The ten accession states who joined were: Malta, Latvia, Lithuania, Estonia, Cyprus, Slovenia, Slovakia, Poland, Hungary and the Czech Republic.

Bulgaria and Romania joined soon after in 2007. Before it can join, Turkey has to improve its human rights record and negotiate agreement with Greece over the island of Cyprus. Application for EU membership is in progress for a number of other European countries, e.g. Bosnia-Herzegovina.

> Find out more about the growth and history of the EU. Log onto:
> http://europa.eu/about-eu/eu-history/index_en.htm
> This site gives a brief history and a list of key events in each year.

TIMELINE SUMMARY OF THE DEVELOPMENT OF THE EU, 1950–2011

1951   The European Coal and Steel Community (ECSC) is established. Its members are Belgium, France, Italy, Luxembourg, West Germany and the Netherlands.

1957   The Treaties of Rome are signed by all members of the ECSC. The first treaty is an agreement to allow free trade between members of the ECSC and renames the ECSC as the European Economic Community (EEC). The second treaty is known as the Treaty of the European Atomic Energy Community (Euratom) and it aims to develop and grow nuclear industries in EEC member states.

1965   The EEC is renamed as the European Community (EC). The European Parliament, the European Commission, the European Court of Justice and the Council of Ministers are created.

1973	Ireland, the UK and Denmark join the EC.
1979	EMS established.
1981	Greece joins the EC.
1986	Spain and Portugal join the EC.
1987	The Single European Act (SEA) is passed.
1987	Turkey applies to join the EC.
1989	The Berlin Wall collapses and communism comes to an end.
1990	West Germany and East Germany reunify.
1992	The Maastricht Treaty is signed.
1993	The Maastricht Treaty comes into effect. The EC is renamed the European Union (EU).
1995	Austria, Finland and Sweden join the EU.
1997	The Amsterdam Treaty is signed, allowing the EU to reform its institutions in order to allow more countries to join.
1999	The Euro is created as the new single currency in all member states, except the UK, Denmark and Sweden.
2000	The European Parliament approves the enlargement of the EU, meaning that there is now no legal obstacle to allowing more members to join. The Nice Treaty is finally agreed upon after months of tricky negotiations between member states.
2002	Euro notes and coins replace national currencies in 12 EU states.
2003	The Nice Treaty officially comes into operation.
2004	Ten new members join the EU: Latvia, Lithuania, Cyprus, Malta, Estonia, Slovenia, Slovakia, Poland, Hungary and the Czech Republic. These ten countries became members of the EU on May 5, 2004, during Ireland's presidency of the EU, making a 25 member EU.
2007	Romania and Bulgaria join the EU.
2009	The Lisbon Treaty is signed into law.
2011	Estonia joins the Euro zone. Talks continue regarding membership for Croatia, Macedonia, Montenegro, Albania, Serbia, Bosnia-Herzegovina and Iceland. Membership for Turkey still has to meet accession conditions set out by the EU.

Poland, the EU and Ireland

FACTS ON POLAND
Population: 39 million
Area: 311,000 km²
Language: Polish
Currency: zloty
Average monthly salary: €571
Capital: Warsaw

Fig. 5 Map of Poland

- Poland is facing problems due to the large-scale emigration of its skilled workers. Up to two million Poles have left their country since the 2004 EU enlargement. The most popular destinations have been Ireland and the UK. Of these two million, the most numerous are young, dynamic, skilled and educated Poles. Normally they should easily find work in Poland but the attraction of higher wages and a more modern lifestyle available in other countries is hard to resist. Specialists of every type are leaving the country including teachers, IT specialists, doctors, nurses, plumbers, engineers and hairdressers.

- By 2010 more than 800,000 skilled Poles had left to work in other EU countries. This brain drain has led to skilled labour shortages in fast-growing cities such as Wroclaw. To combat this the government intends to make it easier for ethnic Poles living in neighbouring countries to come home and work in Poland.

- The Polish economy is growing. Exports of manufactured goods have increased on average by 20% a year since the country's entry to the EU. Despite this Polish companies face major difficulties finding new skilled employees even with a 15% unemployment rate.

- Poland is the bigget beneficiary of the 2007–2013 EU budget. It is receiving €30 billion to spend on transport infrastructure from Structural and Cohesion Funds. Spending this money efficiently is a challenge because (a) local government agencies across the country lack professionals to plan their investments and (b) construction companies lack workers to build the roads, railways and other facilities planned in the Polish National Development Plan for 2007–2013.

- From 2003 to 2010 the number of Poles living in Ireland grew from 4,000 to an estimated 150,000. The majority of them are under 35. Many are newly-qualified graduates unwilling to work for the low wages on offer back in Poland. (A recent OECD report found that Poles earn on average six times less than their western European counterparts.)

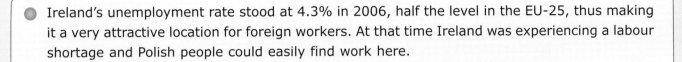

- Ireland's unemployment rate stood at 4.3% in 2006, half the level in the EU-25, thus making it a very attractive location for foreign workers. At that time Ireland was experiencing a labour shortage and Polish people could easily find work here.

- As some 420,000 extra workers were needed to maintain growth in pre-recession Ireland, the number of foreign workers coming here to work was high. Since the recession many of these workers have lost their jobs, especially in the construction and service industries.

- The remittances sent home by Polish workers is significant. In 2010 almost €800 million was sent back to Poland by Poles living and working in Ireland. This figure is expected to fall as Polish workers continue to return home due to the effects of the recession in Ireland.

- Because of Polish economic growth in recent years, Poland has become an attractive location for Irish business. In 2009 Irish industries invested €2.2 billion in their Polish operations.

COMPARING PAY DURING ECONOMIC BOOM YEARS

	Civil engineer €	Anaesthetist €	Builder €	Dentist €
Poland	35,000	35,000	10,000	31,000
Ireland	90,000	120,000	50,000	100,000

21.2 The impact of the expansion of the EU – economic, social/cultural and political issues

Economic impact of the expansion of the EU

As you have seen in Section 21.1, creating an EU of 27 member states took more than 40 years. Enlargement in 2004 and again in 2007 added 129.6 million people to the EU population. Careful management is now necessary to ensure all new members and applicants will add to, and achieve success in, the enlarged EU.

EU enlargement presents an unprecedented challenge for unity and **cohesion** (achieving the same level of development) between member states.

Economic disadvantages

1. The cost of enlargement of the EU

The initial cost of enlargement in 2004 was over €25 billion. Funding future reforms and modernisation will cost more money. A larger Europe will have to carefully deal with the costs/funds needed to support new members (e.g. CAP, Structural funds).

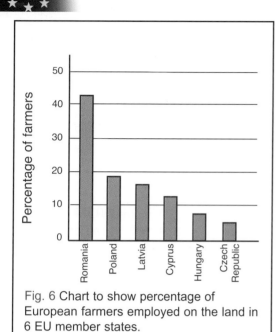

Fig. 6 Chart to show percentage of European farmers employed on the land in 6 EU member states.

2. Economic inequality

(a) Many new EU members are poorer than older member states. There is a great difference in per capita GDP between the richest 10% of the EU population and the poorest 10% of the EU population.

GDP IN SELECTED EU COUNTRIES		
GDP		% of EU average GDP
Romania	=	45%
Estonia	=	63%
Poland	=	61%
Hungary	=	63%
Cyprus	=	98%
Ireland	=	128%

(b) There is also a more difficult employment situation. It is estimated that over 3 million jobs will have to be created in the 12 member states who joined in 2004 and 2007 if their average level of employment is to be aligned with that of the rest of the EU.

(c) An enlarged EU now stretches into Eastern Europe. These countries are less developed technically, with poorer services and underdeveloped infrastructure systems. Production is inefficient due to the use of outdated machines by factories in declining heavy industrial areas. Up until 1990 these former Eastern Bloc countries were under centralised, communist government control.

Economic advantages

The new EU has excellent potential for economic growth.

The new member states in general have had a higher rate of economic growth than the older member states.

Enlargement has created a larger market (over 500 million people) for goods and services and provides for greater investment.

The migration of workers throughout the EU has seen many workers replace the **greying/ageing** labour force in some EU countries who do not have their own nationals to fill the jobs due to their declining populations, e.g. France and Germany.

Overall the benefits of economic integration are shown by higher growth rates, higher incomes and an improved standard of living. There will be opportunities for low-cost production and the raw material base will widen, attracting non-EU industries. Studies show that these benefits are felt by bigger countries before the smaller ones.

The average annual Bulgarian wage in 2010 was €1,759; in Romania it was €3,484. These two countries are the poorest in the EU. The average annual Irish wage in the private sector is €40,000.

The impact of EU enlargement on Ireland's economy and culture

The twenty-first century enlargement of the EU has had several economic and cultural impacts on Ireland.

Following the enlargement of the EU in May 2004, Ireland, Denmark, Sweden and the UK were the only four countries that allowed workers from the new member states (except Bulgaria and Romania) to move relatively freely across their national boundaries.

Economic impacts of expansion

It has opened up new opportunities for Irish businesses in terms of exporting goods, outsourcing labour and creating investment opportunities abroad.

Ireland's foreign-owned sector also benefited from the expansion of trade. Numerous foreign companies moved here, enticed by the low corporation tax rate. However, a number of countries, e.g. Latvia, have since followed Ireland's lead in offering such low rates of corporation tax. The workers in the more advanced new member states do not differ very much from Ireland in terms of their skill levels while their labour costs are much lower.

Immigrants to Ireland from the EU 10 (i.e. the 10 countries that became members of the EU in May 2004) have levels of education that are comparable to the native labour force in Ireland. However, they appear to earn considerably less than the native labour force and also to be in lower grade occupations. During its economic boom Ireland had a severe labour shortage. The arrival of more than 300,000 Polish and other eastern European nationals to Ireland over the last few years has meant the demands for labour could be easily met. They have had two positive impacts on the Irish economy in terms of GNP growth. Firstly, their taxes contribute to the economy when they buy goods and services while living here. Secondly, their presence means that wage rates have grown more slowly because of the availability of labour in the economy.

While Ireland has largely benefited from in-migration of people from the new member states, the scale of this migration had increased the price of renting and buying accommodation and increased congestion on transport and other infrastructure, e.g. translation services. Since economic recession and the collapse of the property market, these increases have been reversed. Rising unemployment has affected migrants more severely than Irish nationals, with migrants from the new EU member states being particularly badly hit.

Social impacts of expansion

Migration to Ireland by Eastern European nationals has had a lasting impact on the Irish workforce and wider society.

It has changed the composition of the Irish population by increasing its cultural diversity. In 2010 immigrants made up 4.5% of the Irish population.

Research published by Trinity College Dublin has found the standards required from Irish workers increased as a result of the presence of Eastern European migrants. As a result, Irish workers had to upgrade their skills and Ireland now has a more skilled and flexible labour force than ever before.

Migration has increased pressure on Irish workers to be multilingual. Irish workers still have a long way to go in terms of competing with other European workers as the majority

Fig. 7 Shops selling Polish food have opened in many cities and towns in Ireland.

of Irish people only speak one language. Polish people speak Polish and English, whereas most Irish people only speak English. Today everyone in Europe has English. Irish people are going to need another major language to compete with their European counterparts.

The arrival of Polish and Eastern European (EE) migrants has led to the emergence of new Polish/EE communities across the country and a visible presence in many schools, housing areas, shops and workplaces is clearly seen.

Irish society is much more aware of its capacity for racism and government campaigns against racism have been implemented.

Political impact of the expansion of the EU

The most important benefit of enlargement is the chance to create a peaceful society in a continent once known for political upheaval and conflict. Despite this an expanded EU has to face international problems and pressures. It has to deal with global challenges, e.g. economic recession, environmental pollution, terrorism and organised crime. There are fears expressed that the centre of power will shift from Western to Eastern Europe and that Atlantic and Mediterranean countries will become even more peripheral.

Talks continue to try to resolve the differences between the big and small EU member countries on policymaking, which will shape the EU of the future. The two sides are deeply split on issues involving the balance of power between the different EU institutions. The **Tiny Tyrants** (Ireland and other small countries) have banded together to fight any attempts by the larger countries to demand more power.

The proposed EU Constitution

Log onto:
http://news.bbc.co.uk/1/hi/europe/2950276.stm
This site gives a breakdown of what is proposed in the EU constitution and what the issues are.

The EU is working on a constitution. It will be the first time the Union has had one. All 27 member states must agree on the wording of its text before the constitution can be passed. This has meant several rounds of negotiations, and agreement has yet to be reached.

The constitution proposes a **bill of rights**, a **foreign minister** and a **single trade policy**. It even proposes a motto, '**United in Diversity**'. Once ratified, this constitution means that the EU will have greater international influence through its status as a single trade bloc.

At present there is great disagreement across Europe over the acceptance of this constitution. Ireland has postponed its referendum on the issue.

To find out more about the impact of the EU on Ireland log onto:
ec.europa.eu/ireland/ireland_in_the_eu/impact_of_membership_on_ireland/index_en.htn

The main proposals in the constitutional treaty are:

1. The EU will have a president. He or she will be chosen by the heads of national governments and be the main public face of the EU.

2. The President of the European Commission, the EU's administrative body, will have more authority and pick members of his/her team of commissioners from candidates in all EU countries. Each state will no longer be guaranteed the right to a seat on the European Commission.

3. The EU will have a foreign minister, whose job will be to represent the EU in issues of foreign affairs, security and defence. The divisions within Europe over the Iraq war and the Israeli/Lebanon conflict in 2006 suggest the role will be extremely difficult.

4. Common EU policies and standards will be extended into many new areas, e.g. external border controls, asylum policy and public health. National veto rights will be reduced. Some states want the EU in time to win authority over the most sensitive areas, such as taxation and defence. Other states are determined to block that idea.

5. The European Parliament will have much greater law-making powers, together with the Council of Ministers.

6. The parliament of each country will have a lesser role as more law-making responsibilities will shift to EU level. However, they will still be able to halt any unauthorised moves by EU bodies to take over certain areas of national sovereignty.

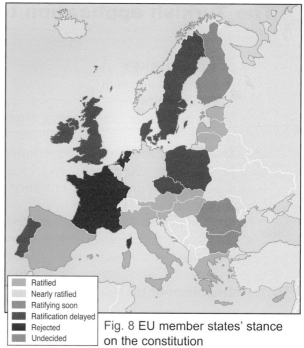

Ratified
Nearly ratified
Ratifying soon
Ratification delayed
Rejected
Undecided

Fig. 8 EU member states' stance on the constitution

Sovereignty and the EU constitution

The proposed EU constitution allows for a single foreign and security policy represented by an EU Foreign Minister. However, because of the difficulty in achieving a common voice, decisions on foreign policy will have to be unanimous. This means that when members disagree, as they did over the decision to invade Iraq in 2003 and will surely do so over any controversial issue in the future, foreign policy will effectively remain with individual national governments.

Individual governments will still have control over their financial decisions and their military.

The EU plans a new rapid-reaction military force, which could see military duty in places such as Macedonia where several member countries now have troops under the EU flag. However, the neutrality of several countries (e.g. Ireland) will affect the creation of a European Army.

There are areas in which the EU constitution would significantly expand the EU's powers, especially in the area of criminal law. The EU already has a dominant role in areas such as trade, monetary policy and farming.

Over the next 10 years the EU will face difficult decisions, major changes and tough challenges.

The Turkish application to join the EU

FACTS ON TURKEY
Population: 70.5 million
GDP: €547 billion
An officially secular state with a Muslim population.
Strong military influence in government.
Connects the European and Asian continents and controls the entrance to the Black Sea.
Turkey's move towards EU membership is hindered by complaints that human rights are not respected by the government and by its alleged mistreatment of the Kurdish people.

Fig. 9 Map of Turkey and bordering countries

The application by Turkey to join the EU has been under consideration since 1987. Its application for membership highlights three issues facing Europe in the twenty-first century. These can be summarised as:

1. Political issues at the European level.
2. Economic and social issues.
3. Geo-political issues (global political issues).

1. Political issues at the European level

The opposition of Austria to the opening of accession talks with Turkey revived memories that the Turks were stopped at the gates of Vienna from conquering Europe in 1683. This, like the Battle of the Boyne in Ireland, is an example of how historical political events can affect modern political decisions.

The French and Austrians have promised their people a vote on Turkish entry and at present there are clear majorities against Turkish membership in both countries. On the Turkish side, some nationalists are unhappy at being dictated to by the EU and would like to stop the accession process.

2. Economic and social issues

If it became a member, Turkey would be the biggest member state in terms of land area. It would be much poorer than other members and would require massive transfers of wealth from the west. The migration of poor Turks to wealthier EU states would be an unsustainable burden on those economies.

Turkey is a democracy but the army plays a much bigger role in political affairs than would be acceptable elsewhere in Western Europe. The current rule of law and respect for human rights and fundamental freedoms need to be improved.

3. Geo-political issues (global political issues)

- The Americans and the British are strongly in favour of Turkey's accession to the EU. As a member of NATO, Turkey was vital in the defeat of the Soviet Union in the Cold War and is equally important today in the war against Islamic extremism.

- The island of Cyprus has been unhappily divided between Greece and Turkey since the 1970s. Turkey refuses to recognise the Greek Cypriot goverment. This issue must be resolved before Turkey can progress to the next stage of its application for membership.

- Since the end of the First World War, Turkey has adopted the western alphabet, the western economic model and aspires to be a fully open democracy.

- Founders of the EU saw the Union as a way of ending the rivalries between Germany and France that led to two world wars in the twentieth century. The inclusion of Turkey in the EU could be a means of reducing the tensions between Christian and Islamic communities.

- Turkey borders some of the world's trouble **hot spots**, e.g. Iraq, Iran, Syria. Extending the border of the EU to those areas is opposed by many. At present discussions about Turkish membership have been postponed.

21.3 Economic, political and cultural interaction between the Republic of Ireland and Northern Ireland

Regions do not always have well-defined boundaries. Links between people who have something in common may reach across the political boundaries drawn by governments. These links may be sporting, political or business activities, common languages and/or religions.

An example of this is the complex relationship between the Republic of Ireland and Northern Ireland.

1. The Republic of Ireland and Northern Ireland

(a) Economic interaction

Trade

For many years trade between the Republic and Northern Ireland was restricted by customs and security posts at the border. This slowed down the movement of goods and people thus damaging the growth of trade between the two regions. Since 1973, barriers that restricted trade between the two regions have been reduced and/or removed.

Since the Good Friday Agreement in 1998, physical restrictions on the movement of people, goods and services between the two regions has eased. Border controls

have been removed and people can travel freely between North and South. This has had an important economic effect on the two regions. The value and volume of goods traded between the two countries increased.

The change in the economic interaction between Northern Ireland and the Republic of Ireland is shown in the table below. We depend on the North for many useful goods and services. In turn they are an important customer for produce from the Republic. Economic connections between the two are continually being strengthened.

Despite recession Ireland still has a trade surplus with Northern Ireland.

Over the past few years hundreds of thousands of shoppers from the Republic of Ireland have travelled across the border to shop in Northern Ireland. Many cash-strapped southern consumers found it impossible to ignore the difference in the price of goods between Northern Ireland and the Republic. The price difference was due to a favourable exchange rate, a lower VAT rate, a lower tax rate on alcohol and lower profit margins for Northern Ireland's retailers. A survey carried out by the TNS Worldpanel, which analyses the UK grocery sector, estimates that 3.5% of the Republic's retail market had migrated north (2010). Up to 25 % of goods bought in Newry were purchased in Euros. Cross-border shopping cost the Republic's economy over €810 million (2010). Southern retailers in border areas experienced closures and job losses as a result of cross border trade. However crossing the border may not be so worthwhile in future as less favourable exchange rates and increased tax rates in Northern Ireland make buying goods there less attractive for shoppers from the Republic.

> For the most recent statistics on trade between the Republic of Ireland and Northern Ireland log onto www.cso.ie and click on Databases – CSO Main Data Dissemination Service - Economy.

TRADE BETWEEN THE REPUBLIC OF IRELAND AND NORTHERN IRELAND 2005 – 2010

Year	Value of imports (billion Euro)	Value of exports (billion Euro)
2010	0.86	1.20
2009	0.94	1.28
2008	1.26	1.56
2007	1.35	1.74
2006	1.32	1.67
2005	1.27	1.57

> For up-to-date statistics on Irish tourism log onto www.failteireland.ie and click on Research & Statistics to get annual tourism facts.

Tourism

Tourism is another important economic activity that links the two regions.

In 2010, 10% of tourists arrived into Ireland via the North. The amount of money generated by Northern tourists is shown in the table on page 445.

SOURCES OF TOURISM REVENUE, 2005-2009 REP OF IRELAND					
Revenue = € million	2005	2006	2007	2008	2009
Britain	1,274.2	1,372.4	1,387.3	1,348.5	1,034.6
Northern Ireland	178.8	189.8	202.8	210.5	209.9
Mainland Europe	1,238.6	1,354.5	1,404.7	1,517.0	1,179.7
North America	738.2	815.1	823.3	667.7	621.1

Tourism Fact Card, Fáilte Ireland

(b) Political interaction

In the past the political relationship between the Republic of Ireland and Northern Ireland had been difficult. There were several reasons for this, such as Article 2 of the Irish constitution which claimed authority (**jurisdiction**) over the whole island of Ireland. Also, 30 years of religious (**sectarian**) conflict between Catholics and Protestants in the North prevented full political interaction between the Irish and British governments.

Since the **Good Friday Agreement** in 1998 there has been increased political co-operation between Northern Ireland and the Republic of Ireland. This was illustrated by the establishment of the **North-South Ministerial Council** (NSMC) in 1999. The NSMC comprises Ministers of the Northern Ireland Administration and the Irish Government working together. The Northern Ireland Assembly was established as part of the Good Friday Agreement in order to ensure that both communities – unionist and nationalist – participate in governing the region. It has authority to legislate on a wide range of areas and to elect the Northern Ireland Executive (cabinet). It sits at Parliament Buildings in Stormont in Belfast.

Fig. 10 The Waterfront Hall, Belfast is a product of the 'peace dividend'.

There are six North/South Bodies, which implement the policies decided by the NSMC on an all-Ireland basis.

The main functions of these organisations are as follows:

Waterways Ireland: Responsibility for specified navigable inland waterways.

Food Safety Promotion Board: The promotion of food safety awareness throughout the island.

Trade and Business Development Body (InterTradeIreland): The promotion of trade and business.

Special European Union Programmes Body: This manages and oversees various EU programmes aimed at developing North/South relations.

Foras na Gaeilge: This is responsible for the promotion of the Irish language and of Ulster-Scots culture.

Foyle, Carlingford and Irish Lights Commission: This is responsible for the management and development of Lough Foyle and Carlingford Lough, as well as the inland fisheries of the Foyle and Carlingford Areas.

Other areas for cooperation

Apart from the official bodies outlined above, political co-operation between the North and South covers several other socio-economic areas:

1. Common Agricultural Policy issues, Animal and Plant Health Policy and Research and Rural Development, e.g. co-operating over the control of Foot and Mouth disease.

2. In the case of tourism, it was agreed that a publicly-owned limited company (**Tourism Ireland Ltd**) would be established by Bord Fáilte Éireann and the Northern Ireland Tourist Board to promote the island of Ireland overseas as a tourist destination.

Find out more about the NSMC in general. Log onto:
http://www.northsouthministerialcouncil.org

(c) Social and cultural interaction

Cultural links between Northern Ireland and the Republic of Ireland are varied. Some organisations and events operate on an all–Ireland basis, e.g. the Fleadh Cheoil, the GAA, Comhaltas Ceoltóirí Éireann and the Scout Association of Ireland. Boxing and rugby clubs operate across the 32 counties and both sports have a mix of unionist and nationalist members.

However, there is a lack of interaction between nationalist and unionist groups within some sports. The GAA for example has traditionally had a strong nationalist membership. Until recently, members of the Northern Ireland security forces were excluded from membership of the GAA. In the spirit of the Good Friday Agreement, some of its rules were changed to remove the ban.

Education is another area where cultural interaction between the two groups has been minimal. This is due to the physical separation of loyalist and nationalist communities. As a result, most schools rarely have an even mix of religions and their location can lead to difficulties if children from a nationalist background attend a mainly loyalist school or vice versa. However, the number of integrated schools in Northern Ireland is beginning to increase.

Other organisations and events promote cooperation and links between the North and the South, e.g. The President's Award (Gaisce) for developing individual skills and taking part in community work and Carshare, a cross-border iniative developed by the Northern Ireland Department for Regional Development and the Republic's Department of Transport.

Interreg – An EU scheme to promote social, economic and cultural development between regions

At the European level a programme known as Interreg has been developed to foster co-operation between regions. The Republic and Northern Ireland have both benefited from participation in this scheme.

Since 2007, Interreg has been financed by the EU Cohesion Policy. More than €13 billion has been allocated to all border regions within the EU, including Ireland's border region.

Investment in local business development by Interreg helps to expand the level of trade between North and South. Developing local industry and investment in small and medium-sized enterprises (SMEs) provides new business opportunities and creates economic strength and growth. This helps to encourage local and Foreign Direct Investment in the border region. An example of this is a scheme known as the **Midas Project**, which is a two-year joint initiative between Dundalk Institute of Technology, the University of Ulster and Dream Ireland Ltd, Belfast.

The Midas Project supported the development of creative and digital media, particularly within games software, film and broadcast, design, animation and music technology. By 2009 companies involved in Midas had secured contracts with RTÉ, BBC and Microsoft.

Chapter Revision Questions

European development and expansion

1. Draw a map of Europe in your copybook. Colour code it using the list below according to the date these countries joined.

   Founding members: colour green
   1973 member(s):   colour yellow
   1981 member(s):   colour red
   1986 member(s):   colour blue
   1995 member(s):   colour purple
   2004 member(s):   colour brown
   2007 member(s):   colour pink

2. Look at pages 432–433 to find out what happened in each of the years listed below. Copy this timeline into your copybook and write your answer after each year. Four have been completed for you.

Year	Event in EU development
1951	
1957	
1962	
1965	
1968	Customs duties between member states lifted.
1973	
1974	
1979	
1987	Single European Act signed
1989	
1990	
1993	
1995	
1997	Amsterdam Treaty on reforming EU
1999	
2000	
2002	Euro coins in circulation
2004	
2007	
2009	
2011	

3. Discuss the impact of EU membership on Poland.

4. Discuss the impact of Poland's membership of the EU on Ireland.

5. Name and describe **two** economic challenges and **two** economic advantages to the enlargement of the EU.

6. What is the likely political impact of EU enlargement on member states? Use examples in your answer.

7. Describe the main points of the EU constitution.

8. What is the meaning of sovereignty?

9. How will an enlarged EU affect the sovereignty of individual countries?

10. Using sources of information other than your textbook, pick a country that has joined the EU since 2000. Write three points of information about it.

11. 'Turkey has many issues to address before becoming a member of the EU'. Discuss this statement.

12. How did the Good Friday Agreement improve social and economic relations between Northern Ireland and the Republic of Ireland?

13. Discuss the role of the North-South Ministerial Council. Use the headings:
    (a) North–South bodies.
    (b) Areas for cooperation.

14. Name three cultural links between Northern Ireland and the Republic of Ireland. Use your own knowledge where necessary.

15. Describe Interreg and how it helps to develop enterprise / business.

16. What is the economic impact of cross-border shopping on the Republic of Ireland?

OL Short Questions

17. Examine this map of Europe which shows FOUR different categories of countries in Western Europe.

EU
Newest EU members
Other candidate

Match the following countries with the correct categories:
(a) Existing member states
(b) New member states
(c) Applicant state
(d) Non-EU states

Countries	Category
Turkey	
Poland, Slovenia	
Norway, Switzerland	
Romania, Bulgaria	

HL Short Questions

Europe

18. Fill in the following table, which refers to the European Union [EU]:

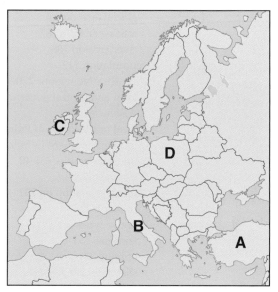

Description	Letter	Country
Not a member of the European Union		
One of the original six members of the EU		
Joined EU in 1973		
Joined EU in 2004		

OL Long Questions

19. In 2004 ten new countries joined the European Union.
    (i) Name and describe **one** positive effect this had on Ireland.
    (ii) Name and describe **one** problem which this has created for Ireland.

    (LC Exam Paper)

HL Long Questions

20. Describe and explain two impacts on Ireland of the enlargement of the European Union.

    (LC Exam Paper)

21. Examine the economic and/or cultural impact of expansion on any one member state of the EU.

    (LC Exam Paper)

Index

A

Ablation 142
Abrasion
    glacial erosion146
    marine erosion 167
    river erosion 108
Accumulation 142
Administrative regions 270-72
    local and central government
        agencies 270
    local government in France 272
    local government in Ireland 270-1
Aerial Photographs 231-40
    direction 233
    finding location on 232
    function 234
    house types 236
    land use 233
    oblique 231
    sketch of 239
    uses of 240
    vertical 231
Air compression 167
Alpine folding 56
Anticline 55
Anticylone 244
Arches 171
Arête 148
Armorican folding 56
Ash 41
Asthenosphere 2, 3
Asymmetric fold 55
Attrition
    marine erosion 167
    river erosion 108
Avalanches 201-2

B

Bank caving 109
Basal flow 143
Basalt 65
Batholiths 44, 64-5
Bays 170
Beaches 173
    bay head beach 173
    cusps 174
    nourishment 179
    storm beach 173
Bedding planes 65, 94
Bedload 109
Bergschrund 148
Block mountains 60
Blowholes 171

B (continued)

Border Midlands West region 309-331
    physical characteristics 310-11
    population 312-13
    primary activities 315-8
    secondary activities 318-20
    tertiary activities 321-24
Boulder clay 153
Boulder clay plains 153
Brazil 396-426
    Amazonian Indians 421
    colonialism 415-6
    cultural regions 420-22
    deforestation 423-25
    favelas 417
    migration 415-6
    physical characteristics 397-401
    population 413-15
    primary activities 401-06
    secondary activities 406-10
    tertiary activities 411-13
Breakwaters 180
Bull Island 181-3

C

Calderas 42
Caledonian folding 56
Canalization 127
Carbonation 85, 94
Caves 97, 171
Cavitation 109
Chalk 66
Cirque glacier 144
City/urban/nodal regions 353-59
    Dublin city region 355-57
Cliffs 169
Clints 95
Coal 66
Coastal processes 163-66
    Bull Island 181-3
    human interaction with 179-86
Coastal protection 179-8
    Courtown 184-6
Cold front 244
Cohesion funds 302-3
Common Agricultural Policy 304-5
Common Fisheries Policy 304-6
Competitiveness and employment region 303
Compressional waves 21
Concave slope 221
Conglomerates 67
Consequent streams 134
Conservative plate boundary 13
Constructive plate boundary 11

Continental drift 5
Continental–continental plate collision 9
Convection currents 3, 4
Convergence regions 303
Convergent plate boundary 9
Convex slope 221
Core 2
Corrasion 109
Corrie 148
Corrie glacier 144
Courtown 184-6
Crevasses 144
Crust 2
    continental 3
    oceanic 3
Crystallisation of salts 84
Cultural regions 273-83
    language region 273-9
    Gaeltacht regions in Ireland 273-76
    language regions in Belgium 277-9
    religion 280-83
    Islamic world 282-83

D

Decentralisation 328
Deltas 123-26
    bird's foot 125
    estuarine 125
    arcuate 125
Depression 244
Destructive plate boundary 9
Divergent plate boundary 9, 11
Dolerite 64
Dolines 96
Dome volcanoes 43
Doming 60
Drainage basin area 103
Drainage patterns 104-106
    dendritic 105
    radial 106
    trellis 106
Drift 147, 152
Drumlins 154
Dykes 45

E

European Union 429-41
    Amsterdam Treaty 430-1
    constitution 438-39
    enlargement 431-32, 435-39
    ECSC 428
    European Community 429
    Maastricht Treaty 430
    Nice Treaty 431
    Lisbon Treaty 431
    Single European Act 430
    sovereignty 429, 439
    Treaties of Rome 428
    Turkey's application 440-1
Earth, structure of 2
Earthquakes 19-33
    aftershocks 20
    depth of 20
    early warning system 28
    effects of 24
    global seismic network 21
    Haiti 29-31
    intensity 22
    magnitude 22
    prediction 32-33
    preventing earthquake damage 32-33
    SE Asian earthquake 25–7
    shock waves 20
    tremors 20
Elbow of capture 137
Endogenic forces 2
Epicentre 20
Erosion 88
Erratics 155
Eskers 156-8
Eustatic movement 132, 186-8
Even slope 221
Exfoliation 84
Exogenic forces 2
Extrusive igneous rock 65

F

Fault gouge 69
Fault scarp 58
Faulting 58
    types of fault 58-9
Fiords 151, 188
Firn 142
Fissure 38
Flood plains 121-2
Fluvioglacial deposition
    landforms 156
Focus 20
Folding 54
    types of 55
Freeze–thaw 83-4

G

Gabions 180
Geothermal energy 45, 75
    Iceland 75-7
Glacial
    abrasion 146
    deposition 147
    drift 147, 152
    erosion 146
    landforms 147-58
    plucking 146
    processes 145

transport 146
trough 150
Glaciated valley 150
Glaciation 141
   of Ireland 158-9
   Midlandian 159
   Munsterian 159
Glaciers 144
   ablation 142
   accumulation 142
   movement of 143
   types of 144
Gneiss 69
Gorges 116
Graben 60
Graded profile 111
Graded slope 221
Graphs 243-59
   bar 249-50
   choropleths 255
   climographs 253
   pie 248
   radar charts 253
   scatter plot 252
   trend 251
   triangle 251
   wind rose 254
Granite 64-5
Greater Dublin Area 333-59
   physical characteristics 334-5
   population 335
   primary activities 338-41
   secondary activities 341-4
   tertiary activities 344-50
   transport services 345-6
Grikes 95
Groynes 179-80

H

Hanging valleys 150-1
Headlands 168
High 244
Horsts 60
Hotspots 15
   Hawaiian Islands 16
Human influence on mass movement 204-7
Human interaction with coastal
   processes 179-86
Human interaction with river processes 127-32
Human interaction with the rock cycle 72-7
Hydration 86
Hydraulic action
   marine erosion 166
   river erosion 109

Hydrolysis 87
Hypabyssal rock 64

I

Igneous rock 64-5
   extrusive 65
   hypabyssal 64
   intermediate 64
   intrusive 64
   plutonic 64
   volcanic 64-5
Incised meanders 134
Inner core 2
Interlocking spurs 114-5
Intermediate rock 64
Intrusive igneous rock 64
Island arcs 10
Isostatic uplift 132, 186-7

K

Karst 93-8
   Burren, The 95
   surface landforms 94-5
   underground landforms 94-5
Knickpoints 133

L

Laccoliths 45
Lagoon 176, 182
Lahars 199-200
Landslides 200-3
Language regions 273-9
   decline of Irish language 275
   support for Irish language 276
Lava 39
   acidic 39
   basic 39
   plateaux 43-4
Levees 122
Limb 55
Limestone 66, 93-8
   surface landforms 94-5
   underground landforms 94-5
   karst landscapes 93-8
   pavement 95
Lithification 65-7
Lithosphere 2, 3
Littoral drift 167-8
Long profile 111
Longshore drift 167-8
Lopoliths 45
Love waves 21
Low 244

M

Magnetism 7
Mantle 2

Marble 69
Marine deposition
    landforms 173-8
    processes of 167
Marine erosion
    landforms 168-73
    processes of 166
Marine transport
    processes of 167
Mass movement 194-207
    classifying 196
    deforestation and 205-6
    Derrybrien bogflow 207
    factors affecting 195-6
    human influence on 204-7
    overcropping and 204-5
Meander scars 119
Meanders 117-8
    incised 134
Metamorphic rock 68-70
Metamorphism 68
    effects of 68
    thermal 68
    dynamic 69
    regional 69
Mezzogiorno 362-78
    Cassa Per Il Mezzogiorno 367
    migration 378
    physical characteristics 363-7
    population 377
    primary activities 367-72
    secondary activities 372-4
    tertiary activities 374-7
Mid–Atlantic Ridge 8
Midlandian glaciation 159
Misfit stream 137
Modified Mercalli scale 22-3
Mohorovicic discontinuity 2
Moraine 153-4
    englacial 154
    ground 154
    lateral 154
    medial 154
    recessional 154
    terminal 154
Mortlakes 119
Mountain building 56
Mudflows 198
Munster ridge and valley province 57
Munsterian glaciation 158-9

N

National Development Plan (NDP)
    325
National Spatial Strategy (NSS) 304–5,
    326, 359
Neve 142

Nivation 148
Normal fault 58
Nunataks 159

O

Occluded front 244
Oceanic–continental plate collision 9
Oceanic–oceanic plate collision 10
Onion weathering 84
Orogeny 56
OS Maps 210-40
    ancient settlement 226
    calculating area 222
    cross sections 222
    direction 215
    distance 218
    grid references 216-7
    height 220
    latitude and longitude 216
    legend 214
    National grid 216
    scale 211-2
    settlement patterns 226-28
    sketch of 239
    slope 221
Outer core 2
Outwash plains 156
Overfold 55
Overthrust fold 56
Oxbow lakes 119
Oxidation 86

P

P waves 20
Pacific Ring of Fire 9
Pangaea 5-6
Paris Basin 381-94
    physical characteristics 382-3
    population 383-4
    primary activities 384-7
    secondary activities 387-9
    tertiary activities 389-92
Passive margin 7
Paternoster lakes 152
Peneplains 136
Physical regions 264-69
    climate 264
    climate of Ireland 265
    geomorphic 268-9
    North European Plain 268-9
Piedmont glacier 144
Pillars 98
Plastic flow 143
Plate boundaries 9
    conservative/transform/transverse 13
    constructive/divergent 11-12

continental–continental plate
collision 11
destructive/convergent 9
oceanic–continental plate collision 9
oceanic–oceanic plate collision 10
passive margin 7
summary of 14
Plate tectonics 4
Plates 3
Plucking 146
Plumes 10
Plutonic rock 64
Point bar 118
Pumice 41
Pyramidal peak 148
Pyroclastic flow 40

Q

Quartzite 69

R

Raised beach 189
Raised cliff 190
Rayleigh waves 21
Regions 262-447
    complexity of 262-87
    concept of 263
    economic, political & cultural
    interaction of 435-45
    types of 263
Regolith 195
Rejuvenation 132-4
REPS 304
Reverse fault 58
Revetments 180
Rias 188
Ribbon lakes 150
Richter scale 22
Rift valleys 60
    African Rift Valley 61
Rivers 102-37
    capture 137
    cliff 118
    Clonmel 130-31
    confluence 103
    deposition 110
    depth 108
    drainage basin area 103
    drainage patterns 104-06
    energy 107
    erosion 108
    human interaction with 127-32
    landforms 111-26
    life cycle of 111
    load 107
    mature stage landforms 117-121
    old stage river landforms 122-26

processes of river deposition 110
processes of river erosion 108-9
processes of river transport 109-10
R. Rhine 127-8
rejuvenation 132-4
slope 107
terraces 133
Three Gorges Dam 129-30
transport 109
velocity 107-8
youthful stage landforms 112-17
Rock armour 180
Rock cycle 71
    human interaction with 72-7
    Tara mines 73-5
Rock falls 202-3
Rotational slip 143
Rotational slumps 200

S

S waves 20
Saltation 109-10
Sambre-Meuse Valley 299-301
San Andreas Fault 13
Sand spits 175
Sandstone 67
Satellite photographs 259
Schéma Directeur 393
Schist 69
Scree 83
Sea stacks 171
Sea walls 180
Sea–floor spreading 7-8
Sedimentary rock 65-7
    lithification 65
    organically formed 66
    inorganically formed 67
    chemically formed 67
Seismographs 21
Shale 67
Shear waves 20
Shield volcanoes 42
SIAL 3
Sills 45
SIMA 3
Simple fold 55
Sinkholes 96
Slumps 169, 200
Socio–economic regions 291-306
    core regions 292-3
    Drogheda 295-8
    peripheral/less developed regions
        293-4
    regions of industrial decline 294-5
Soil creep 197-8
Solifluction 198

Solution
    marine 167
    rivers 109
Stacks 171-3
Stalactites 98
Stalagmites 98
Stepped slope 221
Striae 146
Structural funds 302-4
Stumps 172
Subduction 9
Subsequent streams 137
Superimposition 135
Surf zone 168
Surface processes, summary of 88
Suspension 109
Swallow holes 96
Symmetric fold 55
Syncline 55

T

TACs 306
Talus 83
Tarn 148
Tear fault 59
Tectonic cycle 4
Tephra 38
Terracettes 197
Terranes 9
Tetrapods 180
Thrust fault 59
Tombolo 176-7
Traction 110
Transform fault 59
Transform plate boundary 13
Transport 21 328
Transverse plate boundary 13
Trenches 9
Truncated spurs 150
Tsunami 24
    Southeast Asian tsunami 24
    warning system 28
Turloughs 97

U

U–shaped valley 150-2
Urban boundaries 353-9
    growth of Dublin 355-7
    growth of Paris 393
    policy to control growth of Dublin 359
    policy to control growth of Paris 393

V

Valley glacier 144
Vent 38
Volcanic cones 42

Volcanic igneous rock 64-5
Volcanic landforms
    external/extrusive 42
    internal/intrusive 44
    plutonic 44
Volcanoes 37-52
    active 38
    distribution 38
    dome 43
    dormant 38
    effects of 45-6
    extinct 39
    lava plateaux 43-4
    Montserrat 51-52
    Mount St Helens 48-50
    prediction of 46-52
    products of 39-41
    shield 42
V–shaped valleys 112-4

W

Warm front 244
Waterfalls 116-7
Watershed 103
Wave refraction 166
Wave–built terrace 169
Wave–cut platform 168-9
Waves 164
    backwash 165
    constructive/spilling 165
    destructive/plunging 166
    fetch 164
    swash 165
Weather maps 244-7
Weathering 81-87
    mechanical 82-4
    chemical 85
    biological 87
Wegener, Alfred 5
Windgap 137